BIG BOOK OF
Beautiful
Beads

krause
IOLA, WISCONSIN

Table of *CONTENTS*

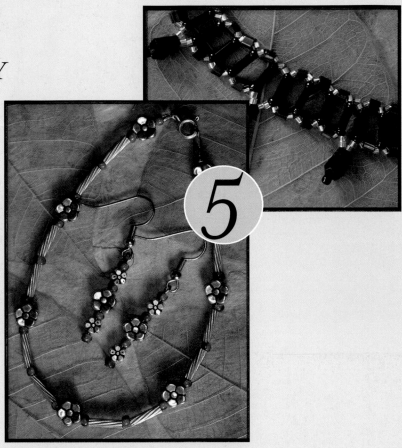

THE COMPLETE GUIDE TO
Beading
Techniques

258

FRENCH-BEADED FLOWERS:
New Millennium
Collection

416

Introduction

Beautiful beading is everywhere—on fine jewelry, exquisite handbags and fun and elegant home décor. If you like the art of beading, you will love this book with its over 500 pages of beautiful bead projects for people of all abilities. Make gorgeous beaded earrings and necklaces. Create beaded accessories for all occasions. Learn many terrific beading techniques and stitch a bag like a pro. Make beaded flowers that complement any home decor.

We've compiled four beading books into this amazing *Big Book of Beautiful Beads*. This book provides you with over 150 projects to satisfy your need to bead. In addition to the projects, you will find basic materials and techniques in the beginning of each section to help you get started. Make sure to look at the Table of Contents for a list of projects and the resource page at the end of each section for help finding materials. Whether you're beginning your first beading project or are looking for new inspirations, this book will get you on your way to beautiful beaded projects!

Quick & Easy

Beaded Jewelry

Elizabeth Gourley
Ellen Talbott

Dedication

This book is dedicated to our loving families: Mike, Amy, Greg, Alan, Walter, and George.

Acknowledgments

We would like to thank Amy Tincher-Durik for believing in our ideas and Christine Townsend for all her hard work and great editing. Thanks also to Donna Mummery, the designer of this book. We would like to thank our friend, Jane Davis, who, with all her creative energy, gives us the extra little push and motivation it takes to go ahead and get off the couch and write a book. And we can't forget to thank our families for being there for us.

Photographs by Ellen Talbott

Table of Contents

Chapter One 10

Chapter Two 23

Chapter Three 35

Chapter Four 59

Chapter Five 67

Chapter Six 114

Introduction:
Tools, Thread
and Wires,
Findings

To bead or not to bead—that is the question— but only if you've never beaded before. Once you start beading, you can't stop: You'll never entertain the *thought* of whether to bead or not—you'll just *bead*! That's how easily beading can become an enjoyable part of life.

Beads and making beaded adornment have been around for so long, from the beginning of mankind, that by now the need for beads and beading is instinctive—nearly (in our opinion) as basic as the need for food and shelter. We must warn you: A full-blown case of "bead addiction" can turn your world upside down … you may find (like we did) that since you must bead, the dust in your home accumulates and your golf clubs never see the light of day. You may end up spending every spare minute (and some minutes you perhaps shouldn't spare!) beading.

In order to help relieve this problem, we have written this book. The thirty projects can be quickly and easily finished, leaving us with more time for the rest of the things in our lives. Each sophisticated piece comes with instructions for a matching set. In just a few hours of work, you will have beautiful jewelry, from casual to evening wear, to show off—or give as gifts—to all your friends and family members … and still get that dusting done.

If you've never beaded before, this book will offer help to you, too. One look at the things you can do with a few beads and a small amount of effort, and the "to bead or not to bead" question will be quickly answered: To bead is the only way to be!

We've been beading for many years. Ellen started out collecting beadwork from her forays into the Southwest, picking up anything beaded by Native Americans. She also collects African beadwork. Finally, she decided to try beading for herself and hasn't stopped!

Liz was inspired to bead by her friend, Kari, who made beaded earrings. One day they went to the bead store together. Oh! So many beautiful beads and so little time! The ideas of what one could make with beads filled Liz's head to overflowing and all her spare time is spent buying beads, looking at beads and, of course, *beading*.

So it is our love of beads that led us to create this book in the hopes of sharing with others. Use this book as a resource guide: Make the projects, get inspired, and most of all have fun! Be creative! Feel free to change the colors of the projects or to use your favorite beads or findings in place of the ones used in this book.

If you have trouble finding supplies, we have provided a resource list at the back of the book.

Abbreviations Used in This Book
PNT – *Pass the needle through*
PNBT – *Pass the needle back through*
BT – *Back through*

TOOLS

The tools needed for making beaded jewelry are fairly basic and inexpensive. Jewelry makers' pliers and wire cutters are essential tools of the trade, along with beading needles, knotting tweezers, scissors, bead boards, and glue.

PLIERS

Round-Nose Pliers
These pliers have tapering cylindrical ends perfect for making loops in wire or on head pins and eye pins. They can be used to hold small findings and are also useful for closing the loops on bead tips.

Chain-Nose Pliers
These versatile pliers have tapered half-round ends. They are good for gripping, crimping, wire wrapping, opening and closing jump rings, and squeezing bead tips closed.

Flat-Nose Pliers
The flat-nose pliers have flat, straight ends that don't taper. The inside surface is smooth and won't make marks on the wire or findings. Use them to bend wire at angles, to open and close jump rings, and to squeeze bead tips closed.

These are the three basic "you must have" pliers. The following are more specialized pliers that you might like to have to make things a little easier.

Bent Chain-Nose Pliers
These pliers are like chain-nose pliers, except the ends are curved at about a thirty-degree angle. They are good for getting into hard-to-reach places, gripping, and wire wrapping.

Crimping Pliers
These pliers are used for only one thing, but they are very good at what they do. Crimping pliers have two indentions on their inside surfaces. The one closest to the handle is the crimper, which makes a dimple in the crimp bead. The indention closest to the tip of the

pliers is called the rounder and this finishes off the crimp by squeezing the crimp bead into a round shape.

Split-Ring Pliers

These pliers have thin, tapering ends. The tip of one of the ends is bent inward at a sharp angle. They are used to open split rings of all sizes for ease in attaching them to other split rings or other findings.

Loop-Closing Pliers

These pliers are useful for closing jump rings or chain links without marking the surface of the metal. The inside surfaces of the pliers are smooth and have slots for holding the links or the jump rings.

Wire-Looping or Coil Pliers

These pliers have one smooth flat end and one similar to round-nose pliers, only with three tiers along its length. This is used for making wire coils or wire loops that are consistent in size. You can make three different sizes with them.

Rosary Pliers

Rosary pliers are a combination round-nose pliers and side wire cutters.

WIRE CUTTERS

There are two basic kinds of wire cutters: The side cutter and the end, or flush cutter. The side cutter has blades on the inside surfaces of the jaws and is good for cutting wire or tiger tail. The flush cutter has the blades on the tips of the jaws and is good for cutting things flush, so no wire tail remains.

Specialized cutters, of the side-cutter variety, are also made for tiger tail and stretchy cord.

SCISSORS

Scissors are used to cut beading thread. We like to use embroidery scissors because their slender, sharp ends makes cutting the thread close to the bead easier. There is also a thread cutter that has no finger holes, has very sharp edges, and works well for snipping thread or cord.

KNOTTING TWEEZERS

Knotting tweezers are not only good for making knots, but also are handy to have about for picking up or holding small beads or findings. They have sharp precision tips and slender jaws.

Clockwise from the center: Knotting tweezers, embroidery scissors, crimp pliers, bent chain-nose pliers, flush wire cutters, side wire cutters, rosary pliers, round-nose pliers, chain-nose pliers and flat-nose pliers.

An assortment of beading needles.

NEEDLES

There are three basic kinds of beading needles: big-eye needles, twisted wire needles, and beading needles.

Beading Needles

Beading needles have sharp ends and are shaped like sewing needles, but they are much thinner, have smaller eyes and don't taper to the end. The eyes are small enough to fit through tiny bead holes. Beading needles come in several sizes based on their length and thickness. The lengths are approximately 1-1/4", 2", and 3". The 3" needles are used mostly for bead-loom work. The most popular thickness of beading needles are from #10s (thick) to #15s (very thin). In this book, we used primarily #11s and #12s. These two sizes fit well in size 11° seed beads.

Twisted Wire Beading Needles

These needles are useful for larger thread or cord that won't fit through the eye of a beading needle. They are made of a length of wire twisted back on itself, so they don't have a sharp point. The eye is a large loop that collapses as it goes through the bead. Twisted needles come in four sizes: light, light-medium, medium-heavy, and heavy.

Big-Eye Needles

Big-eye needles have one large eye that runs the length of the needle. Only the two ends of the needle are attached. These needles have sharp points. They are used for easy threading no matter how thin or thick the thread.

JEWELRY MAKERS' BEAD BOARDS

Bead Boards

Bead boards are used to design and measure your bead strands before you string them. They are made of wood, plastic, or flocked plastic. They usually have inch markings along the strand indentions and have space for one to five strands, depending on the size of the board.

Beading Trays

Beading trays are good for use with seed beads. You can keep the different color seed beads you might need for a project separated and the beads are spread out for ease in picking them up. Some come with lids for storage and travel.

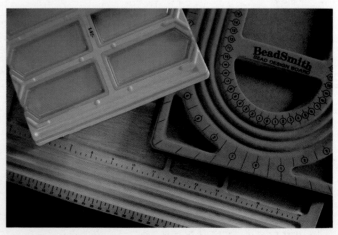

Bead boards and trays.

GLUE

Glue is an essential tool in making beaded jewelry, from securing knots to attaching beads to findings. You can find many bonding-cement type glues at craft or bead stores. The best glues will adhere almost any surfaces and, when dry, will be clear, flexible, and waterproof.

THREADS AND WIRES

There are many different materials used to string beads together. In fact, you can use virtually whatever fits through the beads you want to use. However, there are several common threads and wires used in the beading world today.

THREAD

Nylon Beading Thread or Nymo™

Nymo (nylon monofilament) looks like dental floss, and is great for using with seed beads and for making bead strands. It comes in black and white plus a variety of other colors. Thinnest is size 000, medium-thin is size 0 or A, size B is medium, D is medium-thick and sizes E, F, FF, and FFF are thickest, respectively.

Silamide

This is a type of twisted nylon thread that comes in sizes A or 0. This thread is not as stiff as Nymo. It is good for seed beads or bead strands.

Kevlar™

Kevlar is another seed bead thread that is very strong, since it is made from the same material as bulletproof vests. It comes in black or a yellowish off-white color.

Silk or Nylon Twisted Thread

This thread is used for knotting. It most often comes on cards, but you can get it on spools. The sizes on cards are numbered, the thinnest being 0 and the thickest being 16. Some brands use the alphabet sizing with 00 being thinnest, C and D being medium weight and FFF the thickest.

Stretchy Cord

Stretchy cord is elastic cord used most often for bracelets and other jewelry. It comes in several diameters. Pick the one that fits through your beads the best. The thin size can fit through seed bead holes. Thinnest is size .5mm and 2mm is the thickest. It comes in several colors, but the most popular is clear.

Stretchy Floss

There is also stretchy floss that looks similar to Nymo thread, but it is elastic. This type is harder to find and tends to fray, but is easier to knot than the stretchy cord.

Satin Cord

Satin cord is great for knotting or stringing a few larger beads. It comes in many colors and three main thicknesses: 1mm, 1.5mm and 2mm. Cotton or hemp cord is also made to be used with beads.

Leather or Imitation Leather Cord

Leather or imitation leather cord works great with large-holed beads. It comes in sizes from .5mm to 3mm.

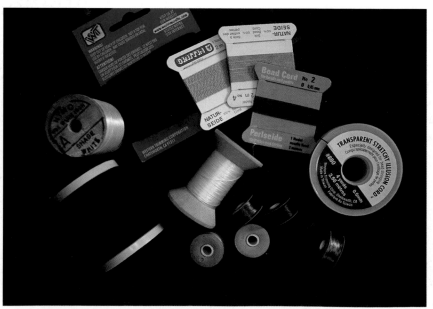

A variety of threads and cord.

Beading wire.

WIRE

Beading Wire or Tiger Tail

Beading wire is made of several thin wires twisted together and then covered with nylon. It comes in several sizes: .012 and .014 are thin, .018 and .019 are medium, .022 and .024 medium-thick, .026 thick. Tiger tail is good for stranding and for beads with sharp edges that might cut through other beading threads. Crimp beads are used with tiger tail.

Memory Wire

Memory wire is a stiff, pre-coiled wire that will return to its original shape after being pulled apart. It is made in three coil sizes: One to use for necklaces, one for bracelets and one small one that is ring sized. It usually comes in packages with twelve loops of wire that must be cut to one loop for necklaces or from one to four for bracelets and rings. Memory wire is too stiff for jewelry pliers, so you have to use regular pliers when making loops on the ends.

Wire for Jewelry Making

Wire comes in gold or silver tone metal, aluminum, or precious metal (gold-filled, 14k or 18k gold and sterling silver). Wire known as niobium comes in many different colors. Beading wire is sized by gauges with 8 gauge being thickest and 34 being thinnest.

Sizes 18-, 20-, 22-, 24-, 26-, and 28-gauge round wires are the most popular sizes for beadwork. Ultra thin size 34 is great for seed beads. Wire also comes in square, half-round, and triangle shapes. Their gauges are also numbered with the higher the number the smaller the diameter and the lower the number the bigger the diameter. These wires are good for wire wrapping.

FINDINGS

Findings are used to put beads, thread and/or wire together to make personal adornment. They are a very important part of jewelry making. Findings include, but are not limited to: clasps, bead tips or knot covers, head pins, eye pins, jump rings, split-rings, bullion or French wire, cord tips, crimp beads, bails or triangles, cones, bell caps, bead caps, spacer bars, barrette backs, earring wires and posts, pin backs, neckwires and chains.

These findings can be found in precious metal (14k or 18k gold, sterling silver), titanium, gold plated or silver plated, gold filled, surgical steel (ear wires and studs mostly), nickel-plated, brass, copper and gold tone or silver tone metal. You can even find jump rings, eye pins, head pins, and a few other findings in red, pink, blue, purple, green, and yellow.

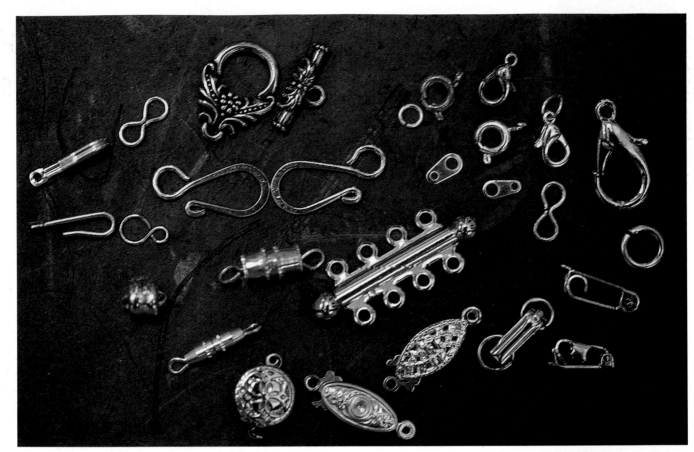

Clasps. Counterclockwise from 11:00 o'clock: Fancy toggle clasp, hook and eye clasps, barrel clasp, magnetic clasp, torpedo clasp, insert-style clasp, fishhook clasp, tube clasp, fold-over clasps, lobster clasps and spring ring clasps.

CLASPS

Clasps are used to hook necklace, bracelet or anklet ends together. There are many types of clasps, the most common ones being the spring ring, fishhook, lobster-claw, hook and eye, barrel, magnetic, fold-over, two-to-five-strand tube, bar and ring or toggle, and insert-style.

Spring Ring Clasp

Spring rings are circular in shape, and you need either a jump ring or a chain tab to complete the clasp. To open a spring ring, you press down on the push tab. It has a spring mechanism so that once the tab is released the clasp automatically closes.

Fishhook Clasp

Fishhook clasps are made with security in mind. One end of the clasp is shaped like a fishhook. The hook side is inserted into the other end of the clasp, over a little bar. Then the fishhook side is pushed until it snaps shut. Even if this clasp were to pop open, the fishhook would still be attached because of the little bar.

Lobster Claw Clasp

These clasps are similar to spring rings in that they have a push tab to open them, and they close automatically when the push tab is released. The other end of the clasp can be a jump ring or a chain tab.

Hook and Eye Clasp

Hook and eye clasps are very basic clasps comprised of a hook and a double ring end or a jump ring end. They are easy to use: Simply place the hook into the ring. Some hook and eye clasps are in an "S" shape.

Barrel Clasps

Barrel clasps look like little barrels when closed. They are screwed open and closed. Torpedo clasps are similar to barrel clasps, but they are thinner.

Magnetic Clasps

These clasps are simply two very small but powerful magnets set inside round clasps that have one smooth side and one side with a loop for connecting the jewelry strand. The two smooth sides are attracted to each other. Magnetic clasps are easy to open and close.

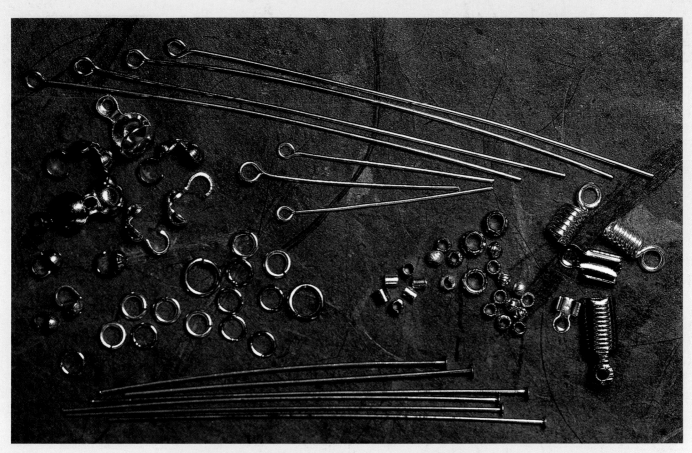

Findings. Counterclockwise from the top: Eye pins, bead tips, jump rings, head pins, tube crimps, crimp beads, cord tips, and cord coils.

Fold-Over Clasps

Fold-over clasps are the kind found on many watches or bracelets. The fold-over side goes into the bar side and folds over the bar and clips onto itself.

Tube or Slide Lock Clasps

Tube or slide lock bars are clasps that have from two-to-five loops on one side of both ends to attach separate strands. To close the clasp, one side slides up and over the other side.

Toggle Clasps or Bar and Ring Clasps

This clasp consists of a large ring and a bar. The bar is longer than the diameter of the ring. Slip the bar into the ring by holding the bar in a vertical position. Then let go of the bar and it will go back to its horizontal position and be secure on the other side of the ring.

Insert-Style Clasps

These clasps are usually fancy clasps that come in different shapes. Some are round, some are square, and some are the shapes of animals or hearts. The smaller end is inserted into the larger end and snapped closed. They are similar to a fishhook clasp without the little bar.

BEAD TIPS OR KNOT COVERS

Bead tips are used to hide knots at the ends of necklaces and bracelets and have a loop at one end to attach the clasp to. There are three kinds of bead tips: The standard, the side-clamp-on and the bottom-clamp-on style. The standard style consists of a little cup to hold the knot and a hole in the bottom for the thread to go through and a loop at the top to attach the clasp. The loop is closed with round-nose pliers. The side-clamp-on style has its hinge on the side and two little cups that, when squeezed together, go over the end knot. There is a circular loop on the top for attaching the clasp. The bottom-clamp-on style is sometimes called a clamshell. It also has two little cups that, when squeezed together, cover up the knot; however, its hinge is on the bottom and has a hole in it for the thread to go through. On the top of one of the little cups is a loop for attaching the clasp. Use round-nose pliers to close the loop around the

Findings. Counterclockwise from the upper right corner: Cones, fancy separators, bead caps, bails, cord caps and, in the middle, bell caps.

clasp. We prefer the bottom-clamp-on or clamshell type bead tip—it covers the knot completely and seems the most secure of the three.

JUMP RINGS & SPLIT RINGS

Jump rings are rings of wire that are round or oval, soldered or non-soldered. They are sized by the diameter and run from 2mm all the way up to 12mm. They are used for joining and/or attaching clasps, chains, eye pins, head pins, and wire loops. They join dangles to earrings or necklaces and combine beads with wire and/or chains. Split rings are rings of doubled wire and are used like jump rings. They come in a wide variety of sizes from 5mm to 28mm.

CRIMP BEADS

These beads are used instead of knots on beading wire such as tiger tail. They secure the ends and help make the loop used to attach clasps. They come in sizes 2mm, 3mm, and 4mm. Crimp beads can't be used with thread or cord, because when you crimp them tight, it might cut the thread or cord. You can also use crimp tubes in the same manner as crimp beads.

HEAD PINS AND EYE PINS

These findings are very important in beaded jewelry making. They are used to make dangles, earrings and bead links. Head pins are lengths of wire with a round pinhead on one end and eye pins are lengths of wire with a round loop at one end. They are measured by thickness and length. The thickness is measured in inches with .020" being the thinnest and .029" the thickest. The shortest length is 1/2" and the longest is 4" long. Some head pins have flattened paddle-type heads instead of round heads.

CORD TIPS

Cord tips are used with cord larger than 2mm. There are two kinds of cord tip. The cord crimp has a loop for attaching the clasp and flaps that are folded over the cord end and squeezed tight. It also has a sharp arrowhead-shaped piece of metal sticking out of the bottom middle of the tip; this grabs the cord and holds it tight. The other kind of cord tip is basically a cup with a loop on one end. The cord is glued into the cup.

CORD COILS

These are a form of cord crimp. A cord coil is a length of coiled wire that has a loop on one end for attaching the clasp. It is slipped onto the end of the cord and then the coil farthest from the looped end is crimped tight.

CONES

A cone is used in multi-strand jewelry to help hide the ends of all the strands. Cones have a wide mouth and a smaller hole on the other end.

CORD CAPS

Cord caps are similar to cones; they look like cups with holes on the bottom. They are used for multiple strand jewelry to hide the knots.

BEAD CAPS

A bead cap is a little metal cup with a hole in the bottom which is strung on next to a bead so it fits over the bead like a cap. You can have one bead cap per bead or two, one on each end of the bead.

BELL CAPS

Bell caps are used to make any object that doesn't have a hole in it into a bead by giving it a hole without drilling. They are caps with prongs and a loop on the top. Bend the prongs around the object and glue in place. Bell caps come in small sizes and large sizes with four or seven prongs. Use whatever size fits the object the best.

BULLION OR FRENCH WIRE

Bullion is made up of coils of thin wire, and is used to reinforce the section of beading cord or thread that is threaded through the clasp. It comes in long lengths that must be cut to size.

BAILS OR TRIANGLES

These findings are used to make pendants. Some kinds are glued to the bead or stone. Others have

prongs that fit into the hole of the pendant. Triangles are used when the hole of the pendant is too far down on the bead or the pendant is too thick to use a jump ring.

SPACER BARS

Spacer bars are used on multi-strand necklaces or bracelets. They are threaded on at intervals along the necklace or bracelet to keep the strands equidistant from each other. They come in several sizes with holes to accommodate from two to ten strands. They can be plain or fancy.

NECK WIRES

These are rigid rings of wire that fit around your neck. They come with a threaded-ball-screw clasp. Most neck wires are fairly thick, so you must use large-holed beads. They are usually 16" in diameter.

EAR WIRES

Ear wires are meant for pierced ears. Clips and screw-ons are for non-pierced ears. There are five main types of ear wires for pierced ears: Fishhook, kidney-shaped, lever-back, hoops, and posts or studs. They come in several wire weights from 24-gauge (lightest) to 20-gauge (heaviest). Fishhook ear wires are basically just that, hooks that fit into your ears. They have a small loop on the front end so you can add the beaded designs or dangles. A kidney ear wire is a wire bent into a kidney shape with a little hook bent into the bottom end of the wire that the top wire end fits into to close the earring. They also have a dip in the front

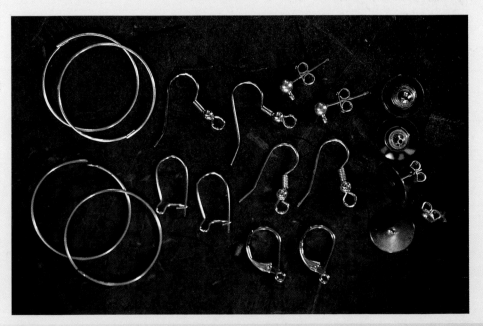

Ear wires. Counterclockwise from the upper left corner: Silver hoops, gold hoops, kidney wires, lever backs, flat pad studs, comfort clutch earring backs, drop studs, and fishhooks.

Findings. Counterclockwise from the upper left corner: Eyeglass chain findings, stickpins, barrette backs, and pin backs.

end of the wire to use to add the dangles, etc. A lever-back ear wire has a sophisticated hinge and a lever on the back of the ear wire that can be snapped open and closed. It also has a loop on the front for adding the beads. A hoop earring wire can be used as a plain earring or you can liven it up with beads. Post or stud ear wires come in two forms. The flat pad ear studs or drop ear studs. The flat pad ear studs have a flat metal surface on the front of the stud to use as a place to glue the beadwork. Drop ear studs have a small loop on the front to use to attach dangles, etc.

Pin Backs

These are used for making pins or broaches. They come with flat round, oval or rectangle fronts where you can glue almost anything to make into a pin. They also come with a rectangle front that has holes in it so you can glue or sew whatever you are using to make a pin. They come in various lengths from 3/4" to 2".

Barrette Backs

Barrette backs are very similar to pin backs. They are found in longer lengths than the pin backs and are used to hold hair.

Eyeglass Chain Findings

These findings are used to make eyeglass chains and have loops at either end, one loop to attach to the eyeglasses and one to attach to the beads.

Chain

Chains come in bulk or precut lengths in many link styles. Two basic link styles are the cable chain and the figaro chain. Each of these styles comes in fancy variations and different weights, from light chain (.4gms) to heavy chain (23gms).

Cable chain

Figaro chain

BEADS

Once upon a time, long, long ago, one of our ancient predecessors poked a hole in a bone or a seed or a stone, and lo! The beloved bead was born.

Anything with a hole through it can be considered a bead. Beads are made from many different things in many different shapes and sizes ... there are metal beads, novelty beads, pressed glass beads, lampwork beads, pearl beads, semi-precious stone and gemstone beads, crystal beads, faceted glass beads, wood beads, horn beads, bone beads, shell beads, seeds as beads, cloisonné beads, trade beads, ceramic beads, drop beads, seed beads, pony beads, Japanese tubular beads, white heart beads, bugle beads, druk beads, rondelles, cane glass beads, cat's eye fiber optic beads, miracle beads, hex beads, triangle beads, square beads, acrylic and plastic beads, polymer clay beads, and heishe beads—and there are many more types of beads.

Beads. Counterclockwise from the upper left corner: An assortment of seed beads, crystal beads, bugle beads, faceted glass beads, and cathedral beads.

Counterclockwise from the upper left corner: Stone beads, shell beads, wood beads, seeds as beads, metal beads, bone beads, and horn beads.

Beads. Counterclockwise from the upper left corner: Lampwork beads, druk beads, cat's eye beads, novelty beads, and pressed glass beads.

Chapter 2

Jewelry Standards and Techniques

JEWELRY STANDARDS

Standard Jewelry Lengths (including clasp)

Bracelet: 7" or 9"

Anklet: 10"

Choker: 14" or 16" depending on neck size; chokers fall just above the collarbone.

Princess: 18"

Matinee: 20"-24"

Opera: 28"-32"

Rope: 40"-45"

Dog Collar: Snug-to-the-neck necklace of three or more strands.

Bib: Necklace of three or more strands with each strand shorter than the one below it.

Lariat: A necklace, 48" or longer, the ends of which are not joined; it is either tied or wrapped around the neck.

Graduated Necklace: Necklace of any length with beads that gradually increase in size with the largest bead in the center and the smallest beads at the clasps.

Uniform Necklace: Necklace of any length that has beads of a uniform size.

BEADS PER INCH ON A STRAND

Use this chart to figure out approximately how many beads you'll need for a project. All numbers are approximate.

Seed Beads

Size 16° - 28 beads per inch

Size 11° - 18 beads per inch

Size 8° - 11.5 beads per inch

Size 5° - 7.5 beads per inch

Seed beads are measured with degree symbol numbers. Size 24° is the smallest seed bead, size 11° is the most popular at about .09" and size 5° is the largest at about .22". Sizes 24° through 16° are very tiny and haven't been manufactured since the late 1800s. Most other beads are measured using millimeters.

Round Beads

2mm – 13 beads per inch

4mm – 7 beads per inch

8mm – 3.25 beads per inch

10mm – 2.5 beads per inch

12mm – 2 beads per inch

TECHNIQUES

How to Attach a Clasp Using Thread

Attaching a clasp using beading thread is quite simple. Make sure to leave a fairly long tail on both ends of the piece. String one end of a clasp onto one end of the thread. Wrap thread around the clasp loop several times by passing thread through the loop several times, and pull tight. Tie a double-half hitch knot right below the clasp loop (fig. 1). Repeat one or two times. Then hide the tail through a few beads. For extra security, tie another overhand knot, if the bead holes are big enough to hide the knot (fig. 2). Cut off the excess thread. Place a dab of glue on the first knot to secure it. Let dry. Using the tail of thread on the other end of the piece, repeat the instructions.

clasp loop onto the wire, then pass the wire back through the crimp bead, pulling tight so that there is just a small loop between the crimp bead and the clasp loop (fig. 1). Crush the crimp bead, first with the crimping hole of the crimping pliers (fig. 2) and then finish it off by squeezing the dimpled crimp bead with the rounding hole of the pliers (fig. 3). When crimping, try to keep the wires separated so that one is caught on one side of the dimple and one on the other side. Cut the excess wire about 1/2" from the crimp bead. String your beads making sure the first few beads go over both strands of wire to hide the excess tail. When you finish stringing on the beads, string on one crimp bead, and then the other end of the clasp. Pass the wire back through the crimp bead

Figure 1

Figure 2

How to Attach a Clasp Using Crimp Beads and Tiger Tail

Attaching a clasp using crimp beads is one of the easiest ways of attaching a clasp. Attach one end of the clasp before you start stringing your beads. Here's how to do it: On the length of tiger tail or beading wire, string one crimp bead (make sure that if you are using thin beading wire you use a smaller crimp bead and if you are using thicker wire or more than one strand of wire use the larger diameter crimp bead). Slip the

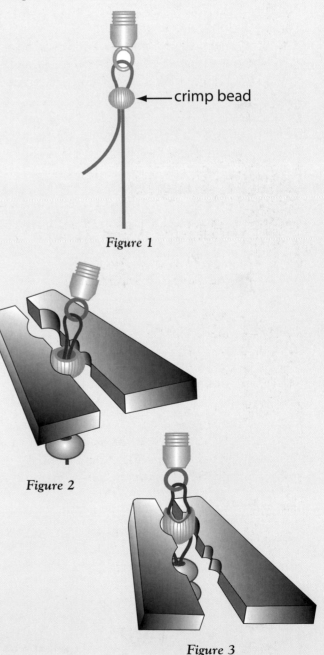

← crimp bead

Figure 1

Figure 2

Figure 3

and pull tight, making sure the beads are tight against the crimp bead and clasp end. Then squeeze the crimp bead with crimp pliers. Pass the tail end of the wire back through several beads then cut the excess.

How to Attach a Clasp Using Bead Tips (Bottom Clamp-On or Clamshell-Type Bead Tips)

There are several ways to attach a bead tip to the thread. If you are using thick thread or multiple threads, you can attach a bead tip by tying a knot. First string on a bead tip then tie an overhand knot or two as tightly into the bead tip as possible (fig. 1). If you have multiple threads, you may tie a square knot. Cut excess thread and place a drop of glue onto the knot. Then using pliers (flat-nose or chain-nose), squeeze the bead tip closed over the knot. When the beading thread is thin and the knot or knots would slip right out of the bead tip, you may use a seed bead to help hold the thread in the bead tip. First, string a clamshell bead tip onto the thread then string a seed bead. Size 11° seed beads work well. Pass the needle through the bead again then tie an overhand knot. Repeat one or two times. Make sure the bead is pulled tightly inside the two cups of the bead tip (fig. 2). Cut excess thread from the knot. Place a dab of glue over the bead and the knot and squeeze the bead tip cups shut over the knot and the bead using chain-

nose or flat-nose pliers. If you have two or more thin threads, you may tie the thread ends together over the bead using a square knot (fig. 3). To attach a clasp to the bead tip, slip the clasp onto the hook on the top of the bead tip (fig. 4). Close the bead tip hook using round-nose pliers and a turning motion (fig. 5). Repeat on the other end of the piece.

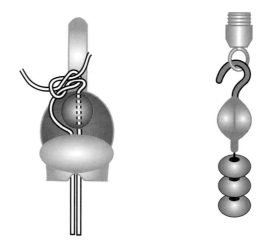

Figure 3   *Figure 4*

Figure 5

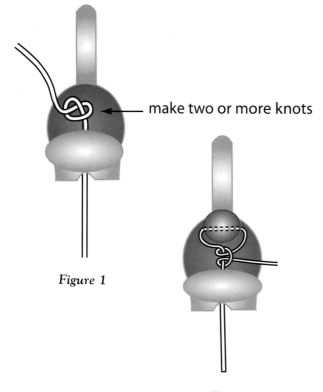

make two or more knots

Figure 1

Figure 2

How to Attach a Clasp Using Cones and Eye Pins

This technique is good for multiple strands. Make your strands and then, if you are using thread, tie the strands together with an overhand knot. Then tie the ends, with one or two double-half hitch knots, to the eye of an eye pin (fig. 1). Secure the knots with glue. Then slip the eye pin into a cone. The cone should cover the knots. Now make a loop in the end of the eye pin that sticks out of the cone. (See fig. 2. To make a loop, see "How to Use a Head Pin or Eye Pin" in this section.) While you are making the loop, attach a clasp to it. When using beading wire or tiger tail, use crimp beads to attach the tiger tail to the eye pin (figs. 3 and 4). You can use cord caps in the same manner as cones.

How to Attach a Clasp Using Cord Tips

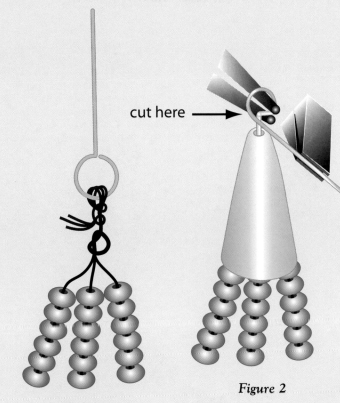

cut here →

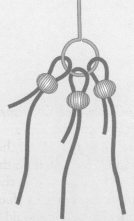

Figure 2

Figure 1

Figure 3   Figure 4

To use the crimp-style cord tips to end a piece of jewelry, simply place the cord end onto the middle section of the cord tip (fig. 1). Using chain-nose or flat-nose pliers, fold the cord tip flaps (one side over the other) over the cord and squeeze tight (fig. 2). To use the cup-style cord tip, place a drop of glue inside the tip and then insert the end of the cord into the tip (fig. 3). Let dry. Use a jump ring to attach the loop end of both kinds of tips to a clasp.

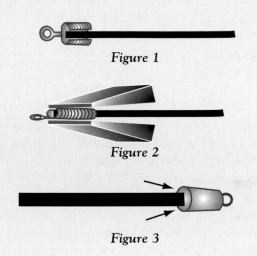

Figure 1

Figure 2

Figure 3

How to Use a Head Pin or Eye Pin

Head pins and eye pins are used mostly to make beaded dangles or earrings. Simply string on beads of your choice and then make a loop on the end of the wire. You can make a plain loop or a wrapped loop. There are two ways to make a plain loop on the end of a head pin or an eye pin. One way is to use flat-nose pliers to make a 90 degree bend in the wire close to the last bead. Cut the wire about 1/4" from the bend. Next, use round-nose pliers to grab the end of the wire and turn the pliers forming the wire into a loop (fig. 1). The other way to make a plain loop on the

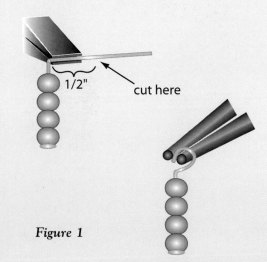

1/2"   cut here

Figure 1

end of a head pin or eye pin is to make a 90 degree bend with flat-nose pliers in the wire close to the last bead. Then grab the wire with round-nose pliers next to the bend and, by hand, wrap the wire around the top jaw of the round-nose pliers (fig. 2). Cut the excess wire and then close the loop with the pliers by squeezing the cut end even with the head pin or eye pin. You can also make a wrapped loop. Wrapped loops are more secure. To make a wrapped loop, you use the flat-nose pliers to make a 90 degree bend in the wire. Grab the wire with the round-nose pliers next to the bend. Then wrap the wire around the jaw of the round nose pliers by hand. Next, using chain-nose pliers or flat-nose pliers (keep holding the loop with the round nose pliers), coil the wire around the head pin or eye pin right under the bend in the wire (fig. 3). You may coil the wire around the eye pin or head pin two, three, or even four times depending on the look you want. When you are done coiling, clip off the excess wire, and then flatten the cut end with pliers.

You can make your own eye pins by making a small loop at one end of a length of wire.

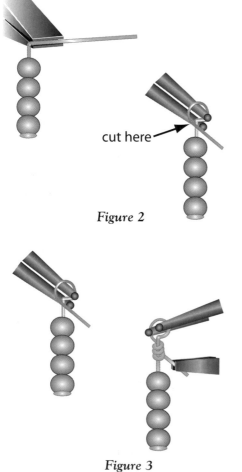

cut here

Figure 2

Figure 3

How to Make a Jump Ring and How to Open and Close a Jump Ring

To make your own jump rings, get a nail or knitting needle with the desired diameter and wrap your wire around the nail or needle several times. Remove the coil from the nail or needle and, with side-style wire cutters, cut the coil down the center (fig. 1).

To properly open a jump ring, use pliers to spread the ends sideways away from each other (fig. 2). Close a jump ring the same way.

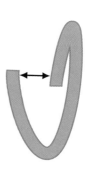

Figure 1   *Figure 2*

How to Tie Knots

The overhand knot is one of the most common knots. It is small, made with one thread (or many threads treated as one). Make a loop in the thread, bring one end of the thread through the loop, and pull tight (fig. 1).

Figure 1

The double-half hitch knot is used with a working thread and a stationary thread. Bring the working thread over and under the stationary thread, then under and over the stationary thread again and through the loop formed by the working thread (fig. 2). Pull tight.

Figure 2

The square knot is a very secure, widely used knot. It is used to tie two threads together. Bring the left-hand thread over and under the right-hand thread, then bring the right-hand thread over and under the left-hand thread (fig. 3). Pull tight.

Figure 3

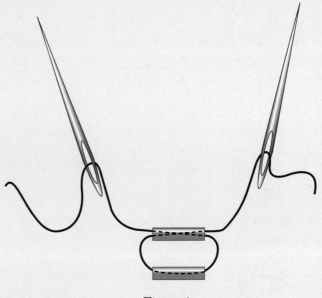

For knotting a bead strand, use overhand knots. To make the overhand knot as close to the beads as possible, put the loop of the knot on the middle of the bead, then hold the thread at the base of the bead with knotting tweezers, and pull the thread end tight with the other hand (fig. 4). It is very important to tie the knots as uniformly as possible and to make all the knots go in the same direction. Do not over-tighten the knots, as this tends to make the strand bunch up or buckle.

Figure 4

How to Tie a Stop Bead

A stop bead is used at the end and/or the beginning of a strand of beads to keep the beads from falling off the thread, and to keep the tension of the beadwork tight. You can make a stop bead by tying a square knot around a bead or you can simply *PNT* the bead twice. This way is not as secure as the square knot, but it is easier to remove (fig. 1).

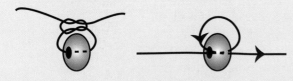

Figure 1

How to Make the Ladder Stitch

Start with a length of thread that has a needle threaded on both ends. String one bead and move it to the center of the thread. * String one bead on one of the needles and then pass the other needle through the bead in the opposite direction. Pull both needles at the same time until the bead is tight up against the first bead * (fig. 1). Repeat between asterisks until the desired length is reached.

Figure 1

How to Make the Chevron Chain

This stitch is fun and simple. You can easily change the look of the chain by using different beads: bugle beads or bi-cone beads, seed beads or druk beads. Change the color arrangement and the bead count—all these things affect the look you get, but the basic stitch remains the same. To make the chevron chain with seed beads, string on 10 seed beads, *PNBT* the first four beads strung on. This forms the first "stitch" (fig. 1). String on six seed beads then *PNT* the sev-

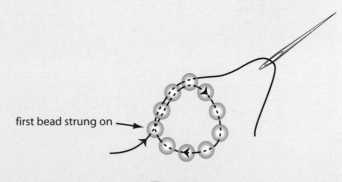

first bead strung on →

Figure 1

enth bead strung on the first stitch (fig. 2). This is the second "stitch." String six seed beads, *PNT* the fourth bead strung on the second stitch (fig. 3). This is the third "stitch." Repeat the third stitch until the desired length. To use bugle beads for the "Vs" on the chevron chain, string one seed bead, one bugle bead, one seed bead, one bugle bead, and three seed beads. Then *PNBT* the first seed bead, bugle bead, and second seed bead. This forms the first "stitch" (fig. 4). String three seed beads, one bugle bead, and *PNT* the third seed bead strung on the first "stitch." This forms the second "stitch" (fig. 5). String on three seed beads and one bugle bead, *PNT* the third seed bead strung on the second stitch. This is the third "stitch" (fig. 6). Repeat the third "stitch" until the desired length.

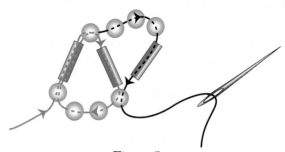

Figure 5

Figure 6

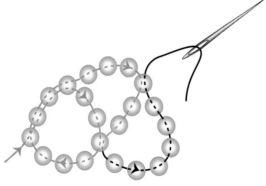

Figure 2

How to Make the Daisy Chain

The two kinds of daisy chain stitches used in this book are the single daisy and the attached daisy.

To make a single daisy chain stitch, string the desired amount of seed beads and then *PNBT* the first bead, forming a circle, the "petal beads." String one bead for the middle of the daisy (usually a different color or size than the "petal beads"). Then *PNT* the bead in the center of the bottom of the "petal beads." This forms the daisy. Several beads are strung on between the daisies (fig. 1).

Figure 3

Figure 4

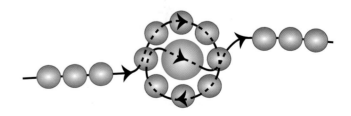

Figure 1

The attached daisy stitch starts out the same way as the single daisy stitch, but instead of stringing beads between the daisies, you attach the daisies to each other. There are two ways to do this. One way is to string on the desired amount of beads then *PNBT* the first bead forming a circle. Then string on the middle bead and *PNT* a bead on the bottom of the circle. * Next string on two beads, and *PNBT* the two bottom beads of the circle and then *BT* the two just strung on. These are the attachment beads (fig. 2). To make the next daisy, string on the same amount of beads as on the first daisy's circle minus two beads. *PNBT* one of the attachment beads, forming a circle, and then string on the middle bead and *PNT* one of the bottom beads of the circle (fig. 4). * Repeat between asterisks as many times as desired.

The other way to make attached daisies is to string the desired amount of beads and make a circle by *PNBT* the first bead strung on. String on the middle bead, *PNT* a bead from the bottom of the circle then *string on one bead, *PNT* adjacent bead on the circle, string on one bead and then *PNT* the first bead just strung on (fig. 3). String on the same amount of beads from first circle minus two beads. String on the middle bead and *PNT* bead from the bottom of the circle (fig. 4). * Repeat between asterisks as many times as desired.

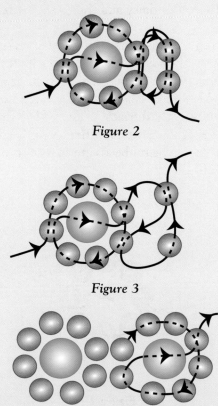

Figure 2

Figure 3

Figure 4

How to Make Vertical Netting

Vertical netting starts out with stringing a base strand. This is simply a strand of the desired beads in the desired length. The rows are vertical and two-sided, the downward side of the row and the upward side. Vertical netting works well with seed beads, but any kind of bead can be used. You can jazz it up with different-sized beads as connecting beads and/or add dangles to the ends. You can also change the number of beads used, so the "holes" of the netting will be smaller or larger. For ease in explaining this stitch, we used blue and green beads. After you make the base strand, *PNBT* some of the base strand beads until the thread is coming out where you want the vertical netting to start.

Row 1

(In this example, we used a one "hole" row.)
Downward side of the row—string one green bead, five blue beads, one green, five blues, one green, one blue. *PNBT* one green.

Upward side of the row—string five blues, one green, five blues. *PNT* the first green bead from the downward side of row and then *PNT* the next seven beads on base strand.

Row 2

Downward side of the row—string one green, five blues. *PNT* last green bead from the upward side of the previous row. String five blues, one green, and one blue. *PNBT* one green.

Upward side of the row—string five blues, one green, five blues. *PNT* the first green bead from downward side of the row and then *PNT* the next seven beads on base strand (fig. 1). Repeat Row 2 until the piece has reached the desired length. For longer rows just repeat the downward side of the row for as many numbers of "holes" you want, and do the same for the upward side.

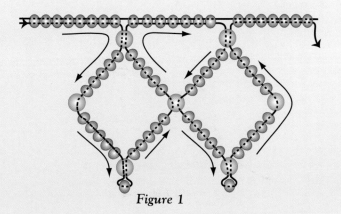

Figure 1

How to Make the Square Stitch
Row 1
String on as many beads as needed for the project.

Row 2 and all others
String two beads, then *PNT* (in the opposite direction of Row 2) second-to-last bead from Row 1 and then back through the second bead just strung on (fig. 1). String one bead, then *PNT* (in the opposite direction of Row 2) the third bead from Row 1, and then back through the bead just strung on. (fig. 2). Continue in this manner stringing on one bead at a time until the end of the row. Remember to make a two-bead stitch at the beginning of each row.

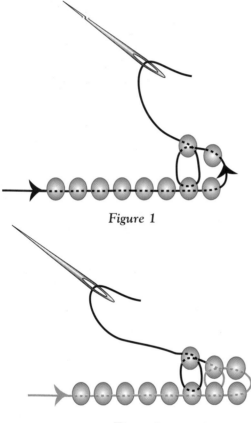

Figure 1

Figure 2

Decrease at the Beginning of the Row
To decrease at the beginning of the row, weave thread back through previous row until the thread comes out of the bead where you want the row to start (fig. 3).

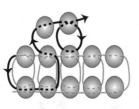

Figure 3

Decrease at the End of the Row
To decrease at the end of the row, simply stop adding beads at the place you want the row to end.

Increase by One Bead
To increase by one bead at the beginning of the row string on two beads, *PNBT* the last bead of previous row, then *PNBT* the second bead just strung on (fig. 4).

To increase by one at the end of the row on two consecutive rows, simply string on one bead and treat it as if it was square-stitched on that row. Then string on two more beads, then *PNBT* the first of the three beads just strung on. *BT* the third bead strung on, and then finish the row in the normal manner (fig. 5).

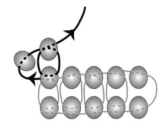

Figure 4

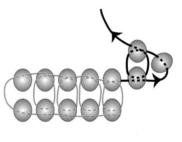

Figure 5

Increase at the Beginning of the Row
To increase at the beginning of the row, string on the desired number of beads, skip the last bead strung on and then *PNBT* the other beads strung on. When you get to the body of the work, start the row as normal (fig. 6).

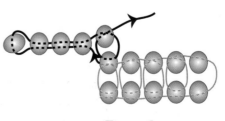

Figure 6

Increase at the End of the Row

To increase at the end of the row simply string on the amount of beads that you want to increase by and, on the next row, treat them as if they had been square stitched (fig. 7).

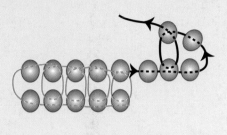

Figure 7

How to Make the Right Angle Weave Stitch
Row 1

String on four beads. *PNBT* the first three beads strung on. This forms the first stitch. * String on three beads and *PNT* the end bead of the first stitch and back through the first two beads strung on. This forms the second stitch (fig. 1). * Repeat between asterisks for the desired number of stitches. In each stitch the thread alternates directions.

Row 2

If you ended Row 1 with the thread coming out of the top of the end bead, then *PNBT* the top bead of last stitch from Row 1. String on three beads. *PNBT* top bead from Row 1 and then *PNBT* the first of the three beads strung on. This is the first stitch of Row 2. String on three beads. Then *PNT* (in the opposite direction from Row 2) the top bead of the next stitch from Row 1. Then *PNBT* the end bead of the previous stitch and both beads just strung on. This is the second stitch of Row 2. Then *PNT* the top bead of the stitch from Row 1 (fig. 2). String on two beads. *PNT* end bead of previous stitch, and the next top bead from Row 1 and through the first bead strung on. This is the third stitch of Row 2. Continue in this manner adding two beads for each stitch until desired length. As in Row 1, the thread will alternate directions in each stitch.

If you ended the Row 1 with the thread coming out of the bottom of the end bead, then for the second row you must *PNT* the other three beads of this last stitch. The thread is now coming out of the top bead from the last stitch with the needle facing in the same direction as the first row.

Now string on three beads and *PNBT* the top bead

then *BT* the three beads just strung on. This is the first stitch. Next *PNT* the top bead from the next stitch on previous row (fig. 3). String on two beads then *PNBT* the end bead from the stitch you just made and *BT* the top bead and the first bead you just strung on. This forms the second stitch. Now string on two beads, *PNT* the top bead from the next stitch from Row 1 (going in the opposite direction of Row 2). Then *PNT* the end bead from the previous stitch and *BT* the two beads just strung on. This is the third stitch. Repeat the second and third stitches until the desired length. The rest of the rows are a repeat of Row 2.

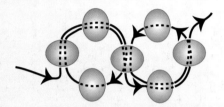

Figure 1

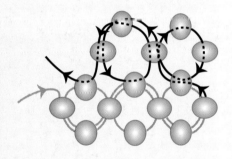

Figure 2

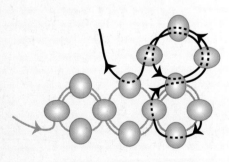

Figure 3

How to Make Even-Count Peyote Stitch and Even-Count Tubular Peyote Stitch

The flat peyote stitch used in this book is the even-count flat peyote. To make even-count flat peyote, you must first string on an even number of beads. These beads will make up the first two rows. For Row

3, string one bead then skip a bead and *PNT* the next bead (fig. 1). String a bead, skip a bead and *PNT* the next bead (fig. 2). Repeat until the end of the beads. For Row 4: On this row it will be easy to identify which beads are on each row. The beads from the last row will definitely be higher than the beads from the previous row. *String one bead *PNT* next stepped up bead.* Repeat between asterisks until the end of the row. Continue in this manner until the desired length.

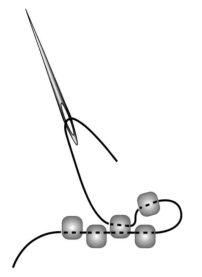

Figure 1

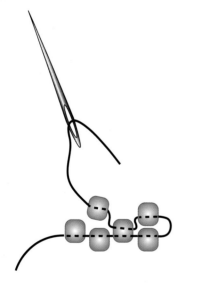

Figure 2

To do even-count tubular peyote stitch, string on an even number of beads. *PNBT* the first bead strung on forming a circle. These beads will form rounds one and two. Keep the circle tight by holding the tail of thread. You will have an odd number of beads for each round. (This is called Even-Count Tubular Peyote because you start with an even number of beads, but the beads-per-round end up being an odd number.)

Round 3: String one bead, skip a bead, from the bead circle, *PNT* the next bead from the bead circle (fig. 3). * String one bead, skip a bead, *PNT* next bead (fig. 4). * Repeat between asterisks until the end of the circle. *PNBT* first bead from this round, so that the needle is properly positioned for the next round. Pull tight.

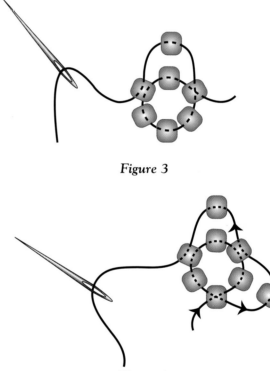

Figure 3

Figure 4

Round 4: On this round it will be easy to identify which beads are on each round. The beads will be definitely higher from Round 3 than the beads from Round 2. * String one bead, *PNT* the next stepped up bead. * Repeat between asterisks until the end of the round. Then *PNBT* the first bead of the round so that the needle is positioned properly for the next round. Pull tight. Continue in this manner until the piece is the desired length.

3

Bead
Stranding
Projects

The very first beading technique was the
bead strand. Small fossil sponges with natural
holes in them were found in England lying
together in graduated sizes—suggesting they were made
into a necklace some 50,000 years ago. Bead strands are
the most basic of beaded adornment. In this chapter, we
have included seven strand projects, one twisted-strand project,
and two braided-strand projects.

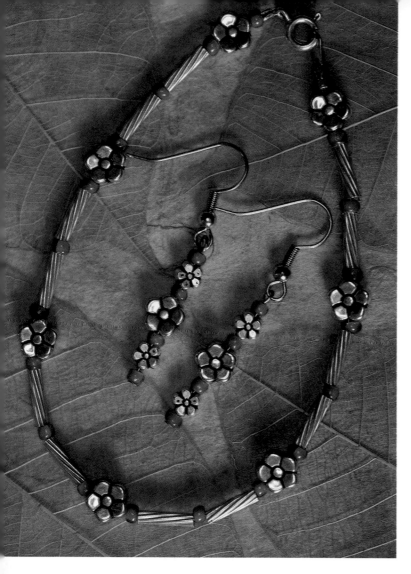

Metal Flower Anklet and Earrings

ANKLET

MATERIALS

14 twisted silver metal bugle beads 3/8" long
20 pink white-heart (or color you prefer) seed beads, size 8°
5 silver metal flower beads, 7mm (or whatever kind of metal bead that suites your fancy)
2 silver crimp beads, size 2mm (or size to fit your beading wire)
1 silver spring ring clasp
Beading wire size .018", 1-1/2 yards

TOOLS

Wire cutters
Crimp pliers

Figure 1

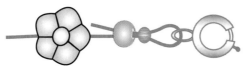

Figure 2

Figure 3

Step 1
Attaching One End of the Clasp
Using about 1 yard of beading wire, string one crimp bead, then one end of the clasp. Bring the wire back through the crimp bead. Pull tight (fig. 1). Squeeze crimp bead with crimp pliers. Cut off excess wire to about 1/2".

Step 2
Stringing the Beads
String on beads in this order (make sure the first few beads go over both strands of wire. See fig. 2):
* one pink, one flower, one pink, one bugle, one pink, one bugle. * Repeat between asterisks five times then string on one pink, one flower, one pink.

Step 3
Attaching the Other End of the Clasp
String on a crimp bead then a jump ring or tab whichever you are using for your clasp, then thread wire back through the crimp bead and pull tight making sure beads are tight up against crimp bead and tab. Squeeze crimp bead with crimp pliers. Cut excess wire to 1/2" and pass back through the beads to hide (fig. 3).

EARRINGS

MATERIALS

2 silver metal flower beads, 7mm
4 silver metal flower beads, 5mm
8 pink white-heart seed beads, size 8°
2 silver head pins
1 pair silver fishhook ear wires

TOOLS

Flat-nose pliers
Crimp pliers

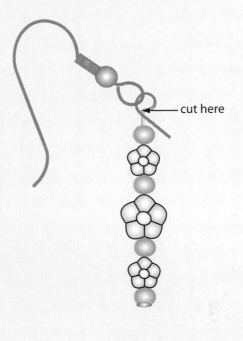

Step 1
Stringing the Beads onto a Head Pin

String beads onto head pin in this order: one pink, one small flower, one pink, one large flower, one pink, one small flower, one pink.

Step 2
Attaching the Earring Wires

Using flat-nose pliers, make a 90-degree bend in the wire close to the last bead (fig. 4). With round-nose pliers, grab the wire as close to the bend as possible and, with your free hand, turn the wire around the jaw of the pliers into a loop (fig. 5). Slip the earring wire onto the loop, cut the excess wire, and close the loop (fig. 6). Repeat Steps 1 and 2 for second earring.

Figure 6

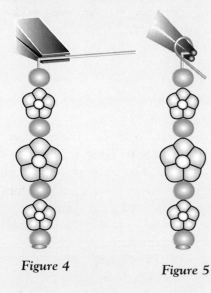

Figure 4   **Figure 5**

Using the same technique as the anklet, you can create different styles of jewelry by changing the beads, colors, and arrangements.

Lemon Necklace and Bracelet

Step 1
Attaching One End of the Clasp
Using about 1-1/2 yards of beading wire, string a crimp bead, then one end of the clasp. Bring the wire back through the crimp bead. Pull tight. Squeeze the crimp bead with the crimp pliers. Cut the excess wire to about 1" (fig. 1).

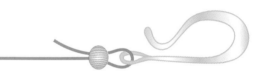

Figure 1

Step 2
Stringing the Beads
String *one druk, one yellow transparent, one purple triangle, one yellow transparent, one druk, one yellow transparent, one purple triangle, one yellow transparent, one druk, one yellow transparent, one purple triangle, one yellow transparent. String on one druk, and one lemon bead.* Make sure the first few beads go over both strands of wire to hide the excess. Repeat between the asterisks three times. Next string on one druk, one lemon, one druk and one lemon. For the other half of the necklace repeat between the asterisks three times then string on one druk, one transparent yellow, one triangle, one transparent yellow, one druk, one transparent yellow, one triangle, one transparent yellow, one druk, one transparent yellow, one triangle, one transparent yellow, one druk.

NECKLACE

MATERIALS

24 purple silver-lined triangle beads, size 6°
48 transparent yellow seed beads, size 8°
34 yellow druk beads, 4mm
9 glass lemon beads
2 gold crimp beads
1 gold hook and eye clasp
Beading wire, size .012, 1-1/2 yards

TOOLS

Crimp pliers

Step 3
Attaching the Other End of the Clasp
String on a crimp bead then the other end of the clasp. Thread the wire back through the crimp bead and pull tight, making sure beads are tight up against the crimp bead and the clasp. Squeeze the crimp bead with the crimp pliers. Cut the excess wire to about 1" and hide the end by passing the wire back through the beads.

BRACELET

MATERIALS

8 purple silver-lined triangle beads, size 6°
16 transparent yellow seed beads, size 8°
16 yellow druk beads, 4mm
7 yellow glass lemon beads
2 gold crimp beads
1 gold hook and eye clasp
Beading wire, size .012, 1 yard

TOOLS

Crimp pliers

Step 1
Attaching One End of the Clasp
Using 1 yard of beading wire, repeat Step 1 from the necklace instructions.

Step 2
Stringing the Beads
String *one druk, one transparent yellow, one triangle, one transparent yellow, one druk, one lemon bead.* Make sure the first few beads go over both strands of wire to hide the excess. Repeat between the asterisks six times. Then string on one druk, one transparent yellow, one triangle, one transparent yellow and one druk.

Step 3
Attaching the Other End of the Clasp
Repeat Step 3 from the necklace instructions.

Black and Silver Necklace and Earrings

Step 1
Attaching the Clasp

Cut a length of tiger tail 20" long. String on one crimp bead, and one end of the clasp. Then pass the tiger tail back through the crimp bead. This will form a loop with the clasp on it. Pull tiger tail end tight so the crimp bead is close to the clasp. Leave a short 1" tail (fig. 1). Squeeze the crimp bead with the crimp pliers.

Figure 1

NECKLACE

MATERIALS

10 small silver flat flower or spacer beads
4 metal accent beads
26 gray transparent silver-lined seed beads, size 10°
18 silver lined twist bugle beads, 15mm
4 black oval faceted beads, 7mm x 5mm
1 round faceted smoky gray crystal bead, 12mm
2 silver bead caps
2 crimp beads
Beading wire or tiger tail, size .018, 1 yard
1 torpedo clasp (skinny barrel clasp), 10mm

TOOLS

Crimp pliers
Wire cutters

Step 2
Stringing the Beads

String on one gray seed bead, * one bugle bead, and one gray seed bead. * Repeat between the asterisks five times. String on one metal accent bead, one gray seed bead, one bugle, one gray seed bead, one small spacer, one black oval faceted, one small spacer, one gray seed bead, one bugle, one gray seed bead, one small spacer, one black oval faceted, one small spacer, one gray seed bead, one bugle, one gray seed bead, one small spacer, one metal accent, one silver bead cap, one gray crystal (12mm), one silver bead cap, one metal accent, one small spacer, one gray seed bead, one bugle, one gray seed bead, one small spacer, one black oval faceted, one small spacer, one gray seed bead, one bugle, one gray seed bead, one small spacer, one black oval faceted, one small spacer, one gray seed bead, one bugle, one gray seed bead, one metal accent, one gray seed bead, * one bugle, one gray seed bead. * Repeat between the asterisks five times.

Step 3
Attaching the Clasp
Attach this clasp end the same way as you did the other end. Leave a 1" tail and pass it through the beads until the tail is hidden in beads.

EARRINGS

MATERIALS

2 metal accent beads
8 gray transparent silver-lined seed beads, size 10°
2 silver-lined twist bugle beads, 15mm
2 round faceted smoky gray crystal bead, 12mm
2 silver bead caps
2 silver head pins
2 silver fishhook ear wires

TOOLS

Flat-nose pliers
Round-nose pliers

Step 1
Making the Dangles
On a head pin, place one gray seed bead, one bead cap, one smoky gray crystal, one bead cap, one gray seed bead, one bugle, one gray seed bead, one metal accent, one gray seed bead.

Step 2
Attaching the Earring Wires
With flat-nose pliers, bend the head pin close to the beads in a 90-degree angle. Slip on an earring wire, then with a round-nose pliers make a loop, and cut off the excess wire. Repeat Steps 1 and 2 for the other earring.

Tooth Necklace and Earrings

NECKLACE

MATERIALS

3, 5 or 7 baby teeth (or gemstone chips to match the jasper)
1 strand of 4mm fossil beads natural color, 16" length (or 4mm fancy jasper)
1 gold barrel clasp or your favorite clasp
3, 5 or 7 bell caps, large and/or medium and/or small to fit teeth or gemstone chips
2 gold crimp beads
Beading wire, size .012, 1 yard

TOOLS

Crimp pliers
Bonding glue

Step 1
Attaching the Teeth (Gemstone Chips) to the Bell Caps
Insert one end of a tooth or chip into the bell cap and use the flat-nosed pliers to carefully adjust the legs of the bell cap to fit the shape of the tooth or chip. Depending on the size of the teeth or chips you have chosen, you will use either large, medium, or small bell caps. We used both small and medium bell caps on this necklace. Now remove the tooth or chip from the bell cap and drop a dab of bonding glue into the bell cap. Reinsert the tooth or chip, giving the bell cap legs a final adjustment (fig. 1). Set aside until glue dries. Repeat as many times as you have objects. Odd numbers seem to work the best. We used seven and three in these examples.

Figure 1

Have you ever wondered what to do with those baby teeth that the "tooth fairy" removes from under the pillow? Well, you need not wonder any longer. Make a keepsake necklace and matching earrings! If you have no children, puppies' or kittens' baby teeth will do just fine. And for those who find the thought of a tooth necklace offensive, you can use stone chips.

Step 2
Stringing the Beads

Using about one yard of beading wire, string one crimp bead then one end of the clasp. Bring the wire back through the crimp bead. Pull tight. Squeeze the crimp bead with crimp pliers. Cut off the excess wire to about 1/2". String on 36 fossil beads (or fancy jasper), making sure the first few beads go over both strands of wire. Then string on one molar-type tooth, four fossil beads, one incisor-type tooth, four fossil beads, one incisor-type tooth, four fossil beads, one puppy tooth. Now repeat backwards after the puppy tooth so that it is symmetrical. Then string on 36 fossil beads. Replace the teeth with gemstone chips if you prefer. Adjust the bead count and spacing, if you have fewer teeth to use. We didn't use jump rings on the bell caps of the teeth, but we did on the green gemstone necklace; it depends on the look you want. If you do want to use jump rings, attach a jump ring to each bell cap and string the beading wire through the jump ring.

Step 3
Attaching the Other End of the Clasp

String on a crimp bead then the other end of the clasp. Bring the wire back through the crimp bead and pull tight. Make sure beads are tight against the crimp bead and clasp. Squeeze the crimp bead with crimp pliers. Cut the excess wire to 1/2" and pass it back through the beads to hide.

TOOTH EARRINGS

MATERIALS

2 baby teeth (or gemstone chips)
2 bell caps
2 fishhook ear wires
2 jump rings

TOOLS

Crimping pliers
Bonding glue

Step 1
Attaching the Bell Caps

Attach a bell cap to each tooth or chip using the same instructions as the tooth necklace.

Step 2
Attaching the Ear Wire

Use a jump ring to attach the bell cap to the earring wire (fig. 2). Repeat Steps 1 and 2 for the other earring.

Figure 2

Using stones instead of teeth.

Pink Stretchy Bracelets and Earrings

BRACELET

MATERIALS

23 lantern-cut Swarovski crystals, 4mm
1 small tube of light pink seed beads, size 11°
White stretchy floss (fibrous elastic) or
  .5mm clear stretchy cord, 3 yards

TOOLS

Twisted wire bead needle
Bonding glue

Step 1
Stringing the Beads
Using about 1 yard of floss and the twisted beading needle, string 31 light pink beads, then one crystal. Repeat three times. Strand should measure 7". Make one more. Then for the third bracelet, string beads in the following pattern: 10 light pink, one crystal, three pink, one crystal, three pink, one crystal. Repeat four times.

Step 2
Tying Off the Stretchy Floss
When you are done stringing the beads, tie a square knot (right over left, then left over right) keeping the beads tightly together. Thread the tails into the beads on either side of the knot (fig. 1). Place a dab of glue on the knot and wiggle it so the glue also goes into the holes of the beads on either side to hold the tails in the beads. Let dry, then cut off excess floss. Repeat for each bracelet.

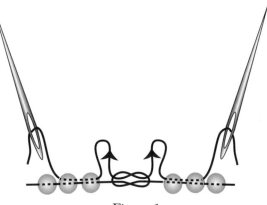

Figure 1

EARRINGS

MATERIALS

8 lantern cut Swarovski crystals, 4mm
62 light pink seed beads, size 11°
White beading thread, 2 yards
2 bead tips
2 lever back ear wires

TOOLS

Beading needle, size 12
Flat-nose pliers
Round-nose pliers
Bonding glue

square knot using both thread ends
(fig. 3). Place a drop of glue on the
knot and squeeze the bead tip closed
(using flat-nose pliers) over the knot
and the seed bead.

Step 1
Stringing the Beads and
Attaching a Bead Tip
Thread a beading needle with about 1 yard
of beading thread. String on one clamshell
bead tip, one crystal, 12 pink seed beads,
one crystal, three pink, one crystal, three
pink, one crystal, 12 pink. *PNBT* the first
crystal and bead tip forming a loop (fig. 2).
String on one pink seed bead and tie a

Figure 3

Step 2
Attaching the Ear Wire
Slip earring wire onto bead tip and using
round-nose pliers turn bead tip hook
closed around earring wire loop. Repeat
Steps 1 and 2 for second earring.

Figure 2

Grapes Necklace and Earrings

NECKLACE

MATERIALS

10 transparent green leaf beads, 7mm x 12mm
10 gms purple iris seed beads, size 11°
16 transparent lavender silver-lined triangle beads, size 5°
14 transparent green-lined topaz triangle beads, size 5°
4 transparent green cube beads, 5mm
1 transparent green round bead, 7mm
5 grape beads (or other novelty beads if you can't find grapes with the hole at the top)
1 gold lobster claw clasp
Nymo beading thread, black, size B, 4-1/2 yards
2 gold eye pins

TOOLS

Beading needle, size 11
Round-nose pliers
Flat-nose pliers
Wire cutters

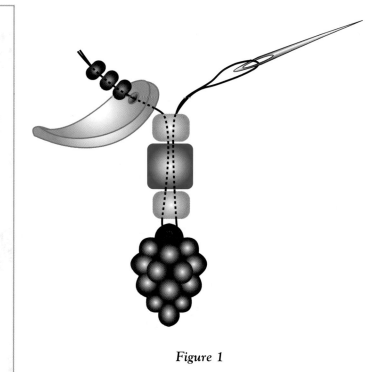

Figure 1

Step 1
Stringing the Beads
Using about 2 yards of doubled thread, tie a stop bead at the end of the thread leaving a 6" tail. String on 2-1/4" of purple iris seed beads, then * one green lined topaz triangle bead, one lavender triangle and one green lined triangle. Then string 7/8" of the purple iris seed beads. * Repeat between the asterisks two times.

Step 2
Making the Grape Dangle
* String on one leaf bead, one lavender triangle, one green cube bead, one lavender triangle, one grape bead, then *PNBT* one lavender triangle, one green cube bead, one lavender triangle (fig. 1). String on one leaf, and 10 purple iris seed beads. * Repeat between the asterisks one more time. Make the middle dangle the same as the other two, except instead of the green cube bead, string on the 7mm green round bead, and when done with the dangle, string on the 10 purple iris seed beads. Then repeat between the asterisks two more times. On the last repeat, instead of 10 purple iris beads, string on 7/8" of the purple iris beads. Repeat between the asterisks from Step 1 three times, but on the last repeat, instead of 7/8" of purple iris beads, string on 2-1/4" of purple iris beads. Set aside.

Step 3
Making the Eye Pin Clasp Ends of the Necklace

Put one green lined triangle bead onto an eye pin. Pass the long end of the eye pin wire into the clasp loop and make an eyelet on the end (fig. 2). Repeat for the other end of the clasp.

← cut here

Figure 2

Step 4
Attaching the Clasp Ends to the Necklace

Now, using the end of thread on the necklace, *PNT* one of the eyelets several times, pull tight and tie two knots. *PNBT* about 1/2" of the purple iris beads to hide the thread and cut off the excess (fig. 3). Remove stop bead from the other end of the necklace and repeat Step 4 using the other beaded eyelet.

Figure 3

EARRINGS

MATERIALS

18 purple iris seed beads, size 11°
4 transparent green lined topaz triangle beads, size 5°
2 transparent lavender triangle beads, size 5°
4 transparent green leaf beads
2 grape beads
2 gold fishhook ear wires
Nymo beading thread, size B, 2 yards

TOOLS

Beading needle, size 11

Step 1
Making the Grape Earrings
Use about 1 yard of doubled thread. String on a grape bead leaving about a 12" tail. String on one lavender triangle, one leaf bead, one green lined triangle, nine purple iris seed beads. *PNT* the loop of one of the earring wires (fig. 4). String on one lined green triangle bead, one leaf bead, then *PNBT* the lavender triangle, grape bead and *BT* the lavender triangle. Now *PNBT* all the beads, and then tie a square knot with the tail thread and the needle thread (fig. 5). Pass both the thread ends through several of the beads to hide and then cut off the excess. Repeat for second earring.

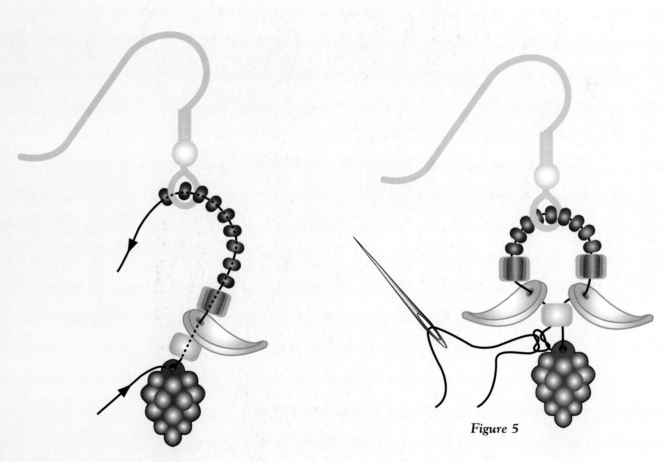

Figure 4

Figure 5

Three-Strand Flower Necklace and Earrings

NECKLACE

MATERIALS

23 transparent green leaf beads
8 dark pink flower beads with the hole in the middle
7 light amber flower beads
7 light pink flower beads
10 gms bronze silver-lined seed beads, size 11°
34 transparent amber seed beads, size 8°
68 matte light amber square beads, 3.5mm x 4mm
196 light yellow satin beads
1 gold lobster claw clasp
2 jump rings
2 three-strand separators
6 gold bead tips
Nymo beading thread, tan, size F, 12 yards

TOOLS

Round-nose pliers
Flat-nose pliers
Scissors
Beading needle, size 11

Step 1
Making the Strands
Strand 1
Thread a needle with doubled thread 2 yards long. Attach a bead tip to the end of the thread. (See Techniques, page 26.) * String on one square bead, one size 8° amber bead, one square bead, 15 bronze size 11° seed beads. * Repeat between asterisks 17 times then string on one square bead, one size 8° amber bead, one square bead. Attach bead tip to the end and set aside. The strand should measure 22-1/2" (excluding the bead tips).

Strand 2
Thread needle with doubled thread 2 yards long. Attach a bead tip to the end of the thread. String on 10 satin beads, one leaf bead, * four satin beads, one dark pink flower bead, one satin bead, and then PNBT the flower bead. (See fig. 1. When stringing on the flower bead, PNT the backside of the flower first and then BT the front of the bead.)

Figure 1

String on four satin beads, one leaf bead, four satin beads, one light pink flower bead, one satin bead, PNBT flower bead. String on four satin beads, one leaf bead, four satin beads, one light amber flower bead, one satin bead, PNBT flower bead. String on four satin beads, one leaf bead. * Repeat between asterisks six times then string on four satin beads, one dark pink flower bead, one satin bead, PNBT flower bead. String on four satin beads, one leaf bead, 10 satin beads. Attach a bead tip as close to the beads as possible. Strand should measure 20-1/4" excluding bead tips. When stringing this strand make sure you push the flower beads close to their neighboring beads, so that you won't get unsightly gaps in the bead strand.

Strand 3
Thread a needle with about 2 yards of doubled thread. Attach a bead tip at the end of the thread. String 10 bronze size 11° seed beads, * one square bead, one amber size 8° bead, one square bead, 15 bronze size 11° beads. * Repeat between the asterisks 13 times then string on one square bead, one amber size 8° bead, one square bead, and 10 bronze size 11° seed beads. Attach a bead tip as close to the beads as possible. The strand should measure 18-1/2" excluding the bead tip.

Step 4
Attaching the Strands to Separators and Clasps
Hold the two separators with the one-loop-edge on top and the three-loop-edge on the bottom, then you will attach Strand #1 to the right most loop on the right-hand-side separator and the left most loop on the left-hand-side separator, so Strand #1 becomes the bottom most strand. Attach Strand #2 to the middle loops and it becomes the middle strand. Attach Strand #3 to the remaining loops and it becomes the top strand. Now attach the clasp ends to the separators.

EARRINGS

MATERIALS
2 transparent green leaf beads
2 dark pink flower beads with the hole in the middle
2 light amber flower beads
2 light pink flower beads
6 bronze silver lined seed beads, size 11°
8 transparent amber seed beads, size 8°
16 matte light amber square beads, 3.5mm x 4mm
56 light yellow satin beads
1 pair gold drop ear studs
2 gold bead tips
Nymo beading thread, tan, size F, 2 yards

TOOLS
Round-nose pliers
Flat-nose pliers
Scissors
Beading needle, size 11

Step 1
Stringing the Beads
Thread needle with about 1 yard of thread and string on one square bead, one amber size 8° bead, one square bead, four satins. String on one dark pink flower bead, one satin bead and *PNBT* flower bead. (See fig. 1 from the necklace.) String on six satins, one square, one amber size 8°, one square, and one bronze seed bead. *PNBT* one square, one size 8°, one square, six satins, four satins (fig. 2). For next dangle, string on four satin, one leaf, one light amber flower, one satin, *PNBT* the flower bead. String on four satins, four squares, one size 8°, one square, one bronze. *PNBT* one square, one size 8°, one square, four satins, one leaf, four satins. For third dangle, string on four satins, one light pink flower, one satin, *PNBT* flower bead. String on six satins, one square, one size 8°, one square, one bronze. *PNBT* one square, one size 8°, one square, six satins, four satins and then *PNBT* the first square, one size 8° and one square bead strung on. String on bead tip with both thread ends and attach bead tip to thread and then attach drop ear stud to bead tip. Make two.

Figure 2

Seven-Strand Twist Necklace and Eyeglass Chain

NECKLACE

MATERIALS

2 large-holed turquoise beads, 10mm
1 hank of crystal gold-lined seed beads, size 10°
187 matte silver-lined transparent teal size seed beads, 6°
1/2 hank of opaque aqua seed beads, size 11°
2 silver eye pins
2 silver cones
2 silver jump rings
1 silver magnetic clasp
Nymo beading thread, black or blue, size F, 14 yards

TOOLS

Round-nose pliers
Flat-nose pliers
Beading needle, size 11
Bonding glue

Step 1
Stringing the Beads

Use 1-yard lengths of doubled thread. Make four crystal gold lined bead strands, 17" long, one matte teal size 6° bead strand, 17" long, and two aqua size 11° bead strands, 17" long. Place a stop bead at each end of the strands and leave about a 10" tail at the ends.

Step 2
Attaching the Cone and the Clasp End

Gather all the strands together and carefully remove the stop beads on one end of the strands. Tie all the strands together in a single overhand knot. Make the knot as close to the beads as possible. Slip a large-holed turquoise bead over all the strand ends and the overhand knot. Next, tie the strand ends to the eyelet of an eye pin using several knots. Place a dab of glue over the knots and clip the excess thread ends. Place one cone over the eye pin and make an eyelet on the end of the eye pin with the pliers. (See Techniques, page 26 for detailed instructions.) Attach a jump ring to the eyelet and one end of the clasp to the jump ring.

Step 3
Twisting the Strands

Gather the four strands of the crystal gold lined beads and twist together. Then take the remaining three strands and twist them around the crystal gold lined strands. Try to keep the aqua strands on opposite sides of the teal bead strand when twisting (fig. 1).

Step 4
Attaching the Other Cone and Clasp End

Carefully untie the stop beads from the ends of the strands, adjust the twists, if necessary, and make an overhand knot with all the strands. Make the knot as close to the beads as possible. Slip thread ends through a large-holed turquoise bead and cover the knot with it. Tie strands to an eyelet and attach a cone and the other end of the clasp as done in Step 2.

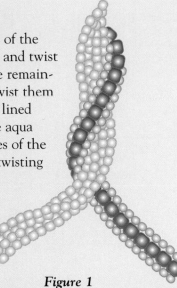

Figure 1

EYE GLASS CHAIN

MATERIALS

378 crystal gold-lined seed beads, size 10°
28 matte silver-lined transparent teal seed beads, size 6°
168 opaque aqua seed beads, size 11°
2 silver bead tips, clamshell style
2 silver jump rings
Nymo beading thread, black or blue, size F, 6 yards

TOOLS

Round-nose pliers
Flat-nose pliers
Bonding glue
Beading needle, size 11

Step 1
Attaching the Bead Tip and Stringing the Beads onto Two Threads

Thread two needles each with doubled thread, about 1-1/2 yards long. String a bead tip onto both needles and slip the bead tip down to the end of the threads

and tie two square knots in the bead tip. Cut off excess thread and place a drop of glue on the knots. Squeeze the bead tip closed over the knots with the flat-nose pliers. * Next, using both needles, string on three aqua beads, one teal bead, three aqua (fig. 2). String seven crystal gold-lined beads onto one needle, then do the same for the other needle (fig. 3). * Repeat between asterisks 26 more times, and to finish it off string three aqua, one teal, three aqua. Piece should measure 25".

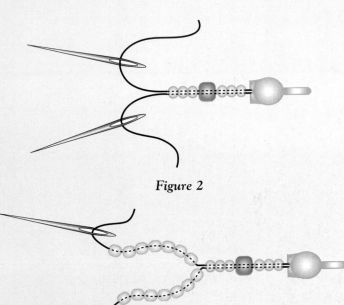

Figure 2

Figure 3

Step 2
Attaching the Other Bead Tip and Eyeglass Chain Findings

Attach a bead tip the same way as in Step 1, making sure you keep the bead tip close to the end beads. Slip the eyeglass chain finding onto the hook of the bead tip and turn the hook closed with the round-nose pliers. Do the same for the other end.

NECKLACE

MATERIALS

Light blue matte Japanese tubular beads
White iridescent seed beads, size 8°
Green iris bugle beads, 4mm
White Japanese tubular beads
1 oval faceted glass light blue and green bead,
    14mm x 10mm
2 crimp beads, 4mm
1 toggle clasp
Beading wire, size .018, 4 yards

TOOLS

Crimp pliers
Bonding glue
Masking tape

Three-Strand Braided Necklace and Headband

Step 1
Attaching One End of the Clasp
Cut three strands of beading wire, each 4 feet long. Slip a crimp bead on all three strands, then slip one end of the clasp onto all three strands. Pass all three strands back through crimp bead, forming a small loop. Squeeze crimp bead with crimp pliers.

Step 2
Stringing the Beads
String one of the strands with white size 8° beads, one with light blue tubular beads and the third one following this pattern: One white tubular, one green bugle, one white, one bugle. Make each strand about 10-1/2" long. Tie a stop bead on each end. Don't worry about the beading wire getting a few bends in it since this part of the wire will be hidden in the large faceted bead.

Step 3
Braiding the Strands
Attach the end with the clasp to a table or a flat surface using masking tape. Separate the strands and lay them flat. Braid them together: Take the strand on the right and bring it over the middle strand (fig. 1). Next, take the strand on the left and bring it over the newly-created middle strand (fig. 2). Repeat until the braid measures 7-1/2". When you get to the end you might have to remove some beads on one or two of the strands to even them up. All three should be the same length. Carefully remove stop beads, then hold the braid end tight in one hand, and string two white tubular beads onto all three strands. Push the white beads tight up against the braid, then string on the faceted glass bead and two more white tubular beads onto all strands.

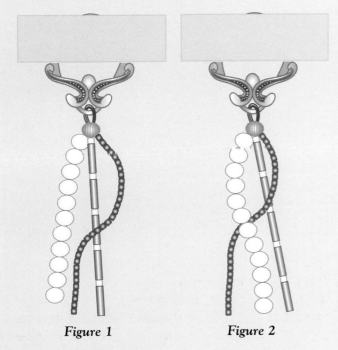

Figure 1   Figure 2

Step 4
Stringing the Beads on the Other Half of the Necklace
Remove the necklace from the table and string one of the strands with white size 8° seed beads, one with light blue tubular beads and one with this pattern: one green bugle, one white tubular, one bugle, one white. All strands should measure about 10-1/2". Tie a stop bead to each end.

Step 5
Braiding the Strands and Attaching the Other End of the Clasp
Braid the three strands together the same way you did in Step 3. When the braid measures 7-1/2" stop braid-

ing, remove any excess beads and the stop beads. String a crimp bead onto all three strands, then string on the other end of the clasp. Pass the three strands back through the crimp bead and pull tight so that the crimp bead is close to the braid, and the clasp loop is close to the crimp bead. Squeeze the crimp bead with crimp pliers and pass excess beading wire back through several beads then cut off the excess wire.

HEADBAND

MATERIALS
Light blue matte Japanese tubular beads
White iridescent seed beads, size 8°
Green iris bugle beads, 4mm
White Japanese tubular beads
1 large-holed green pony bead
1mm stretchy bead cord, 4 yards

TOOLS
Bonding glue
Masking tape

Step 1
Stringing the Beads
Cut three lengths of stretchy cord, about 4 feet each. Tie a stop bead on the ends of each strand. String one of the strands with light blue tubular beads, one strand with white size 8° beads, and on the other one follow the pattern: one bugle bead, one white tubular bead, one bugle, one white. The strands should measure 32". Push beads tight together and then tie a stop bead at each end.

Step 2
Braiding the Strands
Remove the stop beads from one side of the strands, then tie the three strands together using an overhand knot (fig. 3). Attach the ends that are tied together to a table or some other flat surface using masking tape. Separate the strands and lay them flat. Braid them together: Take the strand on the right and bring it over the middle strand (see fig. 1 from the necklace instructions). Next, take the strand on the left and bring it over the newly-

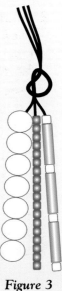

Figure 3

created middle strand (see fig. 2 from the necklace instructions). Repeat until braid measures about 21" or size to fit around your head. When you get to the end of the braid you may have to remove some beads on one or two of the strands to even them up. All three should be the same length. Carefully remove stop beads then tie the strands together using an overhand knot. Remove strands from the table.

Step 3
Tying the Ends Together
String the large green pony bead on one end of the braid and push it over the overhand knot then tie the two ends of the braid together using a square knot. Pull tight and cut off excess stretchy cord. Cover the knots with glue and slip the pony bead over the knots to hide them while the glue is still wet. Let dry.

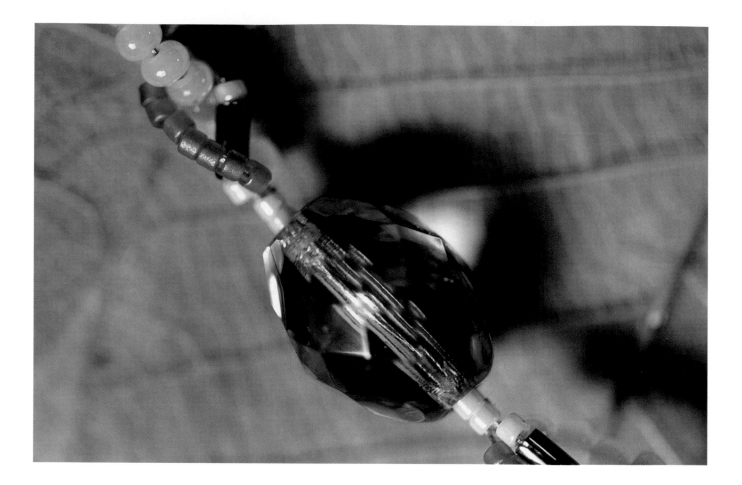

Seven-Strand Braided Bracelet and Barrette

BRACELET

MATERIALS

Gold lined seed beads, size 11°
Pink white heart seed beads, size 8°
Blue iris twist bugle beads, 1/4" long
Gold AB luster bugle beads, 1/4" long
Pink matte twist bugle beads, 1/4" long
Bronze triangle beads
Matte iris AB triangle beads
2 gold cones
2 gold clamshells
1 gold lobster claw clasp
2 gold jump rings
Nymo beading thread, black, size B, 7 yards

TOOLS

Beading needle, size 12, or whatever size fits your
      beads
Bonding glue
Masking tape

Step 1
Stranding the Beads
Thread the beading needle onto a one-yard length of
thread. Tie on a stop bead leaving at least a 6" tail.
Then string gold beads until strand measures 9". Set
aside. Repeat with all the other colors, so you have a
9" strand of each color. Pick up all seven strands and
tie them together in an overhand knot using the end
of the strands without the stop bead. Tie the knot as
close to the beads as possible.

Step 2
Braiding the Strands

Attach the knot to a table or other flat surface using masking tape. Lay all the strands flat. * Pick up the right-most strand and bring it over three strands then lay it down (fig. 1). Next, bring the left-most strand over three strands and lay it down (fig. 2). If you feel comfortable, you may hold all the strands in your hands while braiding. Keep the tension fairly tight. * Repeat between asterisks until you come to the end of the beads. The braid should measure 6". This measurement will vary depending on how tightly or loosely you braid. You might have to braid it over again if it is way too long or too short. Remove the stop beads making sure you hold the braid tight so it won't unravel. At this time also remove any excess beads, as the braiding process will make some of the strands longer than the others. Tie the strands into an overhand knot the same way you did at the other end of the braid. Make sure the knot is right up against the beads to hold the braid securely.

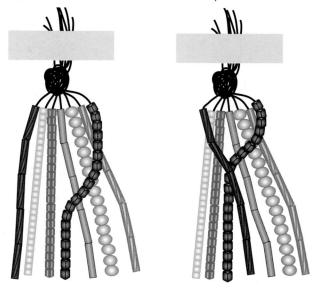

| Figure 1 | Figure 2 |

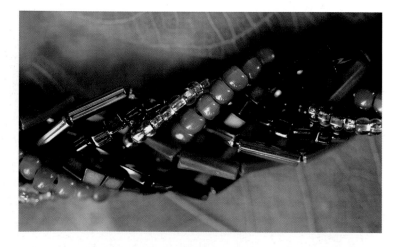

Step 3
Attaching the Cones and Clasp

Thread all seven strands through a gold cone and pull the strands tightly so that the knot and the end of the braid are hidden in the cone. Then thread all seven strands through a clamshell bead tip. Tie a square knot using three strands of the thread for one side and four strands for the other, making sure the knot is all the way inside the clamshell. Clip any excess thread and place a drop of bonding glue onto the knot. Using flat-nosed pliers, squeeze the clamshell shut over the knot. (If you prefer, you may attach the cones using the eye pin method, which is described in Techniques, page 26.) With a round-nose pliers, round off the hook at the end of the clamshell. Attach one end of the clasp with a jump ring. Repeat for the other side of the bracelet.

BARRETTE

MATERIALS

Gold-lined seed beads, size 11°
Pink-white heart seed bead, size 8°
Blue iris twist bugle beads, 1/4" long
Gold AB luster bugle beads, 1/4" long
Pink matte twist bugle beads, 1/4" long
Bronze triangle beads
Matte iris AB triangle beads
1 gold barrette back
Nymo beading thread, black, size B, 7 yards

TOOLS

Beading needle, size 12
Bonding glue

Step 1
Stranding the Beads

Repeat Step 1 of the bracelet instructions, except make the strands 4" long.

Step 2
Braiding the Strands

Repeat Step 2 of the bracelet instructions.

Step 3
Attaching the Braid to the Barrette Back

Cover the barrette back with glue. Tuck the end knots under the braid so they are not visible and lay the braid evenly onto the barrette back. Press and hold for a minute; let sit until dry.

4

Knotted Projects

The drape of a knotted necklace has a certain sophistication and grace. Knots add elegance to any necklace, but they don't just improve the looks of a necklace — they also serve a purpose. Knots between precious beads, such as pearls, keep them apart so they won't rub against each other and get scratched. If, heaven forbid, the necklace breaks, only one bead will fall to the ground instead of all of them scattering into every corner. Knots also come in handy when you want to highlight just one or a few beads.

Knotted Pumpkin Bead Choker and Bracelet

String one metal accent bead, one orange melon bead, and one metal accent bead. Tie another overhand knot, making sure it is up tight against the beads. This is the first bead grouping (fig. 2). Start another overhand knot about 2" away from the last knot so that the cord between the knots will measure 1-3/4" after you make the knot. String one metal, one orange, and one metal bead. Tie another overhand knot. (All bead groupings will have approximately 1-3/4" of cord between the knots.) The middle bead grouping is next. Use one metal, one oval wooden bead, and one metal bead. Now do two more orange bead groupings, for a total of five bead groupings; two orange groupings on both sides of the middle wooden bead grouping.

Figure 1

Figure 2

CHOKER

MATERIALS

10 metal accent beads
4 orange melon glass beads, 8mm x 10mm
1 oval painted wooden bead, 15mm x 23mm
2 crimp style cord tips, size to fit your cord
2 silver jump rings
1 silver lobster claw clasp, 15mm
Black satin cord, 2mm (or 1mm if bead holes are
    smaller), 1 yard

TOOLS

Flat-nose or chain-nose pliers

Step 1
Knotting the Beads Onto the Cord
Cut a 1-yard length of cord. Tie an overhand knot about 4" from one end of the cord (fig. 1). Pull snug.

Step 2
Adding the Clasp

Cut the end of the cord 1-3/4" away from the knot on the end bead group. Slip cord tip onto the end of the cord. The end of the cord should be exactly even with the neck of the cord tip (fig. 3). Squeeze the cord tip around the cord with pliers, by folding one flap down flat and then folding the other flap on top of the first one. Then add the lobster claw clasp to the cord tip with a jump ring. Repeat for the other side of the choker. Finished choker measures 16" without the clasp.

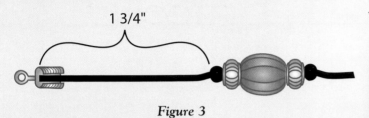

Figure 3

BRACELET

MATERIALS

6 metal accent beads
2 orange melon glass beads, 8mm x 10mm
1 round painted wooden bead, 16mm
2 crimp style cord tips, size to fit cord
2 silver jump rings
1 silver lobster claw clasp, 10mm
Black satin cord, 2mm (or 1 mm if bead holes are smaller), 1 yard

TOOLS

Flat-nose or chain-nose pliers

Step 1
Knotting the Beads onto the Cord

The bracelet is made the same way as the choker, except it has only three bead groupings: one orange bead group, one round wooden bead group, and one orange bead group. There is a 1" length of cord between the bead groups.

Step 2
Attaching the Cord Tips and Clasp

Repeat Step 2 of choker instructions, except have a 1" length of cord between the bead groups and the clasp ends. The finished bracelet measures 7-1/2" without the clasp.

Change the look of a knotted necklace by using stretchy cord and glass faceted beads.

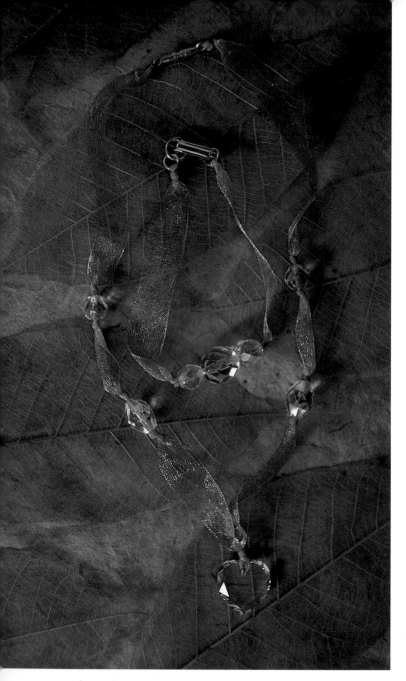

Blue Ribbon Crystal Heart Choker and Bracelet

Step 1
Attaching the Clasp

When using ribbon, cut the end to facilitate bead stringing (fig. 1). Thread the needle with the thin end. String on one side of the clasp and pull it beyond the cut part of the ribbon all the way down the ribbon to the other end, and tie an overhand knot. Bring the knot up close to the clasp before tightening. Trim off the short end of the ribbon to the knot (fig. 2).

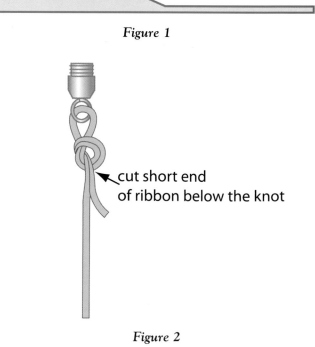

Figure 1

cut short end
of ribbon below the knot

Figure 2

CHOKER

MATERIALS

1 crystal heart pendant bead
2 oval faceted crystal beads, 12mm x 9mm
2 round faceted crystal beads, 8mm
1 gold triangle to fit the heart bead
1 gold torpedo clasp
Light blue gossamer ribbon, 1/2" wide, 1 yard

TOOLS

Twisted beading needle
Embroidery scissors
Chain-nose pliers

Step 2
Preparing the Heart for Stringing
Open the triangle and fit the open end into the hole in the heart. Carefully squeeze the triangle shut with the pliers.

Step 3
Stringing the Beads
String on one round bead (8mm), one oval bead (12mm x 9mm), the crystal heart, one oval bead (12mm x 9mm), and one round bead (8mm). Make an overhand knot 3" from the clasp. Slide the 8mm bead up to the knot and make another overhand knot, bringing the knot as close to the bead as possible. (See Techniques, page 28, for knot tying instructions.) Make another knot 1" away from the last knot. Slide the oval bead up to the knot and make another knot close to the bead. Slide the heart 2-1/4" away from the knot. Make an overhand knot using both sides of the ribbon, as in Step 1, fig. 2, only do not cut off the ribbon and have the triangle and the heart caught in the loop made by the knot. This will make the heart dangle. Make a knot 2" away from the heart knot. Knot and space the last two beads and clasp to match the first side of the choker.

Bracelet

MATERIALS

1 round faceted crystal bead, 12mm
2 round faceted crystal beads, 8mm
1 gold fold-over clasp
Light blue gossamer ribbon, 1/2" wide, 1 yard

TOOLS

Twisted beading needle
Embroidery scissors

Step 1
Attaching the Clasp
Repeat Step 1 from the choker instructions.

Step 2
Stringing the Beads
String on one of each of the following: an 8mm bead, a 12mm bead, and another 8mm bead. Tie an overhand knot 2-3/4" away from clasp knot. Slide all three beads up against the knot and then tie another overhand knot as close to the beads as possible.

Step 3
Attaching the Other Side of the Clasp
String on other side of the clasp and tie it 2-3/4" away from the last bead knot. Cut off the excess ribbon.

Use smaller ribbon and smaller beads for a different look.

Knotted Pearl Necklace and Anklet

Necklace

MATERIALS

1 card Griffen Perlseide No. 4 silk bead thread with needle
1 string, 16", of freshwater pearl beads, 4mm
2 bow beads or beads of your choice
1 gold spring ring clasp
2 gold bead tips

TOOLS

Knotting tweezers
Flat-nose pliers
Bonding glue

Step 1

Attaching the Bead Tip

Remove the thread from the card and tie two overhand knots, one right on top of the other at the end of the thread. Cut off the excess thread close to the knots. String on a bead tip, sliding it up to the knots. Apply a drop of glue to the knots, and close the bead tip over the knots with the pliers.

Step 2

Tying the Knots

Tie an overhand knot on the other side of the bead tip. (If this is your first time knotting, practice tying knots as close to a bead as possible before you begin the actual necklace. Note: It is very important to tie the knots as uniformly as possible and to make all the knots go in the same direction. Do not over-tighten the knots, as this tends to make the strand bunch up or buckle.) String on several pearls, and slide one up to the knot next to the bead tip. Tie an overhand knot as close to the pearl as possible. When you are tying an overhand knot, have the loop of the knot rest in the middle of the bead and hold the thread with the tweezers right under the bead (fig. 1). Pull the thread tight.

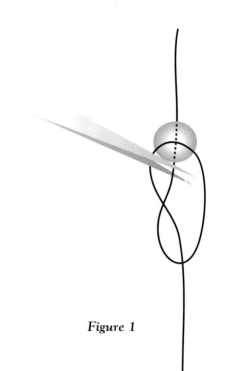

Figure 1

Slide another pearl up to the new knot, and make another overhand knot on the other side of that pearl. Repeat the knot-bead-knot pattern until the piece measures 7". String on a bow bead from the top of the bead (fig. 2). Make a knot on the bottom of the bow. Continue adding more pearls and knotting for another 8". String on the other bow bead from the bottom of the bead so the bows are going in opposite directions. Make a knot. String on and knot more pearls for another 7". String on the other bead tip, pushing it close to the last knot and make two overhand knots inside the bead tip. Cut off the excess thread. Place a drop of glue on the knots in the bead tip, and close the bead tip over the knots with the pliers.

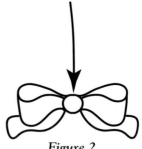

Figure 2

Step 3
Attaching the Clasp

Attach the clasp ends to the bead tips using the instructions from the Techniques section (page 25).

ANKLET

MATERIALS

Griffen Perlseide No. 4 silk bead thread
61 freshwater pearl beads, 4mm
2 bow beads or beads of your choice
2 pearl-like glass seed beads, size 8°
2 gold bead tips
1 gold spring-ring clasp

TOOLS

Knotting tweezers
Flat-nose pliers
Bonding glue

Step 1
Attaching the Bead Tip

Using the silk thread left over from the necklace, attach a bead tip to the end of the thread the same way as in Step 1 of the necklace.

Step 2
Tying the Knots

String on pearls and knot just like in Step 2 of the necklace until piece measures 2-1/2".

Step 3
Making the Dangle

String on a pearl-like seed bead (a seed bead was used here instead of a pearl because the pearls' holes are not big enough for the thread to pass through twice) then string on a bow bead from the top of the bead, and one pearl. *PNBT* the bow bead and the seed bead (fig. 3). Pull thread tight and tie an overhand knot next to the seed bead. There should be two knots above the seed bead: One on the thread going into the bead, and one on the thread as it comes out of the bead. String on pearls and knot just like in Step 2 for 4-1/2". Repeat the instructions for making the dangle, then string on pearls and knot for another 2-1/2".

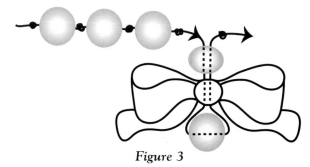

Figure 3

Step 4
Attaching the Bead Tip and the Clasp

String on a bead tip and tie two overhand knots one on top of the other inside the bead tip. Cut off excess thread. Place a drop of glue on the knots in the bead tip and close bead tip over the knots with the pliers. Attach clasp ends to the bead tips following instructions from the technique section.

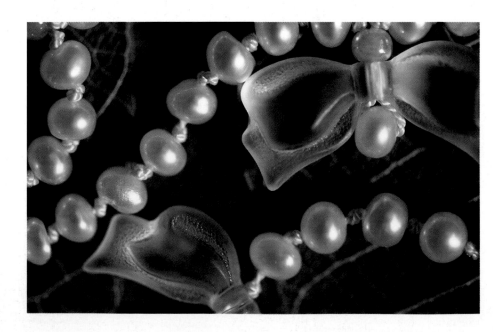

Bead

Weaving

Projects

There are many techniques for weaving beads into glass fabric that can be used to make stunning jewelry. We have included seven bead-weaving techniques in this book — ladder stitch; chevron and daisy chain; horizontal and vertical netting; peyote stitch, flat and tubular; square stitch; and the right angle weave.

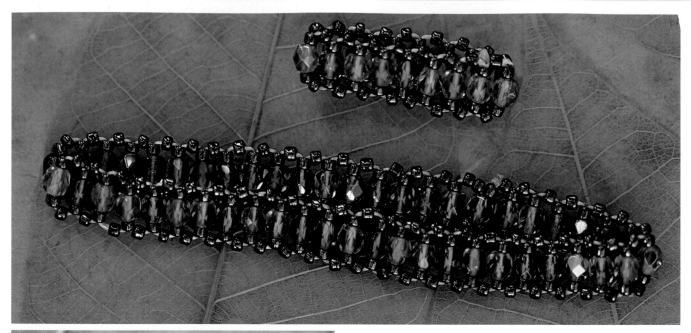

Green Ladder Stitch Bracelet and Ring

BRACELET

MATERIALS

49 faceted Czech fire polished beads in aqua, emerald and peridot, 4mm
Stretchy bead floss, 2 yards
196 hematite Japanese seed beads, size 11° (or any metal color)

TOOLS

2 twisted wire needles

Step 1
Ladder Stitch
Thread a twisted wire needle onto each end of a six-foot length of stretchy bead floss. String on two seed beads, one Czech 4mm bead, and then two more seed beads. Position beads so that they are in the middle of the floss. * Using the left needle, string one seed bead, one Czech bead, and one seed bead. (See fig. 1. We used the three colors of 4mm beads randomly.) Thread the right needle through these three beads going in the opposite direction of the thread already through the beads (fig. 2). Pull both threads tight until all beads fit snugly together. String one seed bead on right needle and one seed bead on left needle. (fig. 3). Push beads down until they touch the other beads. * Repeat between asterisks until bracelet measures 7" or the length to fit your wrist.

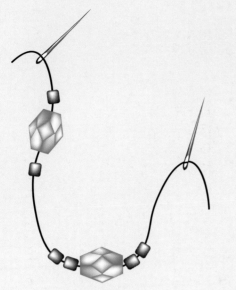

Figure 1

Figure 2

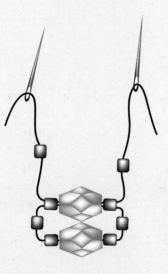

Figure 3

Step 2
Connecting the Ends Together
Bring the ends of bracelet together and insert needles (going in opposite directions) through the two seed beads and the one Czech 4mm bead on the end (the very first beads strung on). Pull both threads tight (fig. 4). To tie the thread ends together, pass the right needle through two seed beads, one Czech 4mm bead and two more seed beads, so that the two thread ends are right next to each other (see red thread on fig. 4). Tie a square knot. Secure knot with glue, slip thread ends into the beads next to the knot, making sure the glue goes into the holes also. Cut off any excess thread and let dry.

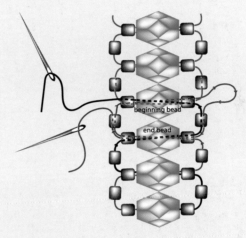

Figure 4

RING

MATERIALS
17 Czech faceted fire polished beads, aqua, emerald, and peridot, 4mm
Stretchy bead floss, 1 yard
68 Japanese seed beads, hematite or any metal color, size 11°

TOOLS
2 twisted wire needles

Step 1
Making the Ring
Repeat Steps 1 and 2 from the bracelet, except make it 2-1/4" long (or length to fit around your finger).

Purple and Black Ladder Stitch Necklace and Earrings

NECKLACE

MATERIALS

91 purple luster hex beads, size 8°
193 silver-lined gold-cut Japanese tubular beads
91 iridescent dark purple seed beads, size 11°
50 black hex bugle beads, 5mm
3 iridescent black faceted teardrop beads, 8mm
1 bronze heart
2 gold bead tips
1 gold barrel clasp
Nymo beading thread, black, size F, 3 yards

TOOLS

2 beading needles, size 12

Step 1
Making the Ladder Stitch Base
of the Necklace

Thread needles on each end of a 6-foot length of beading thread. Using one needle, string on one gold, one purple hex, one gold, one dark purple size 11°, one black bugle bead, one dark purple size 11°, one gold, one purple hex, one gold. Move these beads to the middle of the thread. String on one dark purple size 11°, one black bugle, one dark purple size 11°. Then pass the other needle through the beads in the opposite direction (fig. 1). * Using one of the nee-

Figure 1

dles, string on one gold, one purple hex, one gold. Now use the other needle to string on one gold, one purple hex, one gold. Push these beads down against the other beads. String on one dark purple size 11°, one black bugle bead, one dark purple size 11°. Then pass the other needle through the beads in the opposite direction. * Repeat between the asterisks 16 times or until the piece measures 3-1/2".

Step 2
Creating the First Dangle
With one of the needles, string on two gold beads, 1 faceted teardrop, then one dark purple size 11°, *PNBT* teardrop bead and string on two gold beads (fig. 2). On the other needle, string on two gold beads. Now string on one dark purple size 11°, one black bugle, one dark purple size 11°. Then pass the other needle through the beads in the opposite direction. Repeat between asterisks from Step 1, three times.

Figure 2

Step 3
Creating the Middle Dangle
Using the same needle as the first dangle from Step 2, string on two gold beads, one bugle, one purple hex, one bronze heart, one gold bead, one teardrop, one dark purple size 11°. *PNBT* teardrop, gold bead, heart, purple hex, black bugle, then string on two gold beads (fig. 3). Using the other needle, string on two gold beads. Now string on one dark purple size 11°, one black bugle, one dark purple size 11°. Then pass

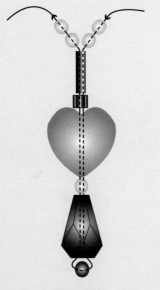

Figure 3

the other needle through the beads in the opposite direction. Repeat between asterisks from Step 1 three times.

Step 4
Creating the Third Dangle
Using the same needle as from Steps 2 and 3, create the third dangle by repeating Step 2.

Step 5
Ladder Stitch Base of the Necklace
String on one dark purple size 11°, one black bugle, one dark purple size 11°. Repeat Step 1, between the asterisks, 16 times or until the piece measures 3-1/2".

Step 6
Making One End of the Necklace
String on one gold, one bugle, one dark purple size 11°, one bugle, one gold. Do this on both needles separately. Now thread both needles through * one purple hex bead, one gold bead. * Repeat between asterisks for 1", adjusting length if necessary to fit your neck. Remember to make only half of the adjustment now and the other half on the other end of the necklace.

Step 7
Attaching the Clasp
Attach the bead tip as close to the beads as possible and attach clasp to the bead tip. See Techniques, page 25, for instructions on how to attach bead tip and clasp.

Step 8
Making the Other End of the Necklace
Thread about 3 feet of thread with two needles. Pass one needle through the dark purple size 11°, black bugle and dark purple size 11° at the beginning of the necklace. Center the beads in the middle of the thread and repeat Step 6.

Step 9
Attaching the Other End of the Clasp
Repeat Step 7.

EARRINGS

MATERIALS

2 purple luster hex beads, size 8°
4 silver-lined gold-cut Japanese tubular beads
2 black hex bugle beads, 5mm
2 black iridescent faceted teardrop beads, 8mm
2 iridescent dark purple seed beads, size 11°
2 bronze heart beads
2 gold head pins
2 gold kidney ear wires

TOOLS

Flat-nose pliers
Round-nose pliers

Step 1
Making the Dangles

Put one dark purple size 11° seed bead, one teardrop, one gold, one heart, one purple hex, one bugle, and one gold bead onto a head pin.

Step 2
Attaching the Ear wires

Bend the end of the wire at a 90-degree angle close to the last bead with the flat-nose pliers (fig. 4). Using round nose pliers hold the wire just above the bend and wrap the wire around pliers making a small loop. (fig. 5). Before closing the loop, slip on the earring wire. Cut wire with wire cutters and close the loop with the flat-nose pliers. Repeat Steps 1 and 2 for other earring.

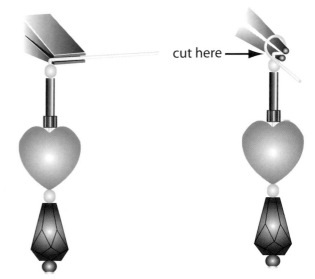

cut here →

Figure 4   **Figure 5**

Chevron Chain

Blue and Green Chevron Necklace

NECKLACE

MATERIALS

49 light green wonder beads, 4mm
294 metallic green seed beads, size 11°
53 matte cobalt blue seed beads, size 6°
44 blue transparent bi-cone beads, 10mm x 6mm
2 silver clamshell bead tips
1 silver round insert-style clasp
Nymo beading thread, white or light blue, size F, 3 yards

TOOLS

2 beading needles, size 11
Round-nose pliers
Flat-nose pliers

Step 1
Making the Chevron Chain
Necklace Base

Thread needle with 2 yards of thread. Leave a 12" tail. String on one wonder bead, one blue bi-cone, one wonder bead, one blue bi-cone, one wonder bead, three metallic beads, one cobalt bead, three metallic beads, and then *PNBT* the first wonder bead strung on, one blue bi-cone, and the next wonder bead. This is the first "stitch" (fig. 1). String three metallic beads, one cobalt, three metallics, one wonder bead, one blue bi-cone. Next *PNT* the third wonder bead strung on from first "stitch." This makes the second "stitch" (fig. 2). String on three metallics, one cobalt, three metallics, one wonder bead, one blue bi-cone. *PNT* wonder bead strung on in the second stitch.

This makes the third "stitch" (fig. 3). Repeat the third "stitch" 40 times, or until piece measures 10-1/2", keeping thread tension tight throughout. Make sure you end with a chevron (both ends look alike with the "V" going up). Tie an overhand knot and weave thread end back through the beads until secure and cut off excess. Do the same thing to the thread tail at the beginning of the necklace.

on the other end of the thread. String on three metallic, one cobalt, three metallic, and one wonder bead, to one of the thread ends and three metallic, one cobalt, three metallic and one wonder bead to the other (fig. 5). Now using both needles at the same time so that both threads go through the beads, string on one cobalt, three metallic, one cobalt, three metallics, one cobalt (fig. 6). Attach a bead tip. Now attach one end of the clasp to the bead tip. Repeat on the other end of the necklace.

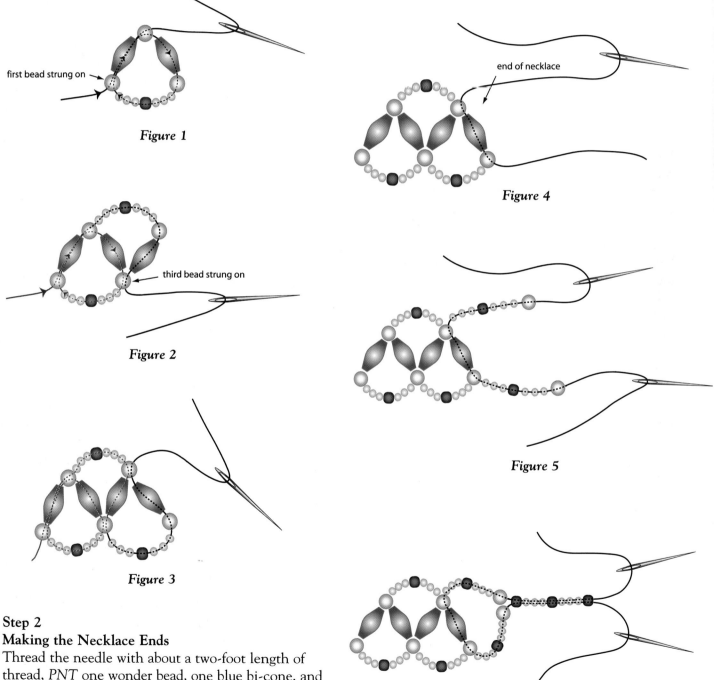

first bead strung on →

Figure 1

third bead strung on →

Figure 2

Figure 3

end of necklace

Figure 4

Figure 5

Figure 6

Step 2
Making the Necklace Ends
Thread the needle with about a two-foot length of thread, *PNT* one wonder bead, one blue bi-cone, and one wonder bead at one end of the necklace. Move the thread through the beads so that they are in the center of the thread (fig. 4). Thread another needle

EARRINGS

MATERIALS

8 light green wonder beads, 4mm
36 metallic green seed beads, size 11°
4 matte cobalt blue seed beads, size 6°
4 blue transparent bi-cone beads, 10mm x 6mm
1 pair of silver fishhook ear wires
Nymo beading thread, white or light blue, size F, 2
    yards

TOOLS

Beading needle, size 11
Round-nose pliers
Flat-nose pliers

Step 1
Stringing the Beads

Thread a needle with a length of thread about one yard long. String on six metallic beads, one wonder bead, one blue bi-cone, one wonder bead, three metallics, one cobalt, three metallics, one wonder bead, one blue bi-cone, one wonder bead, three metallics, one cobalt, and three metallics. Make sure the beads are in the middle of the thread. *PNBT* the second wonder bead strung on, the first blue bi-cone strung on, and the first wonder bead strung on (fig. 7).

Figure 7

Step 2
Attaching the Ear Wire

PNT the loop on the bottom of the ear wire and *PNBT* the first six metallic beads strung on (fig. 8). *PNBT* beads until thread comes out where the thread went in and make a square knot using both thread ends (fig. 9). Hide the knot in a bead and pass the thread ends through several beads, then cut off the excess.

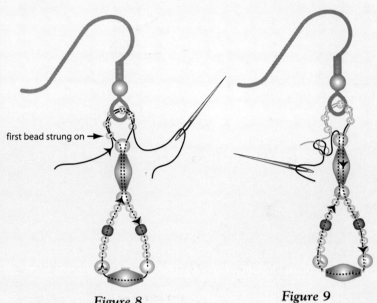

first bead strung on ➞

Figure 8   **Figure 9**

Using bugle beads in the chevron chain creates a different look.

Purple Chevron Choker and Earrings

CHOKER

MATERIALS

280 lavender seed beads, size 11°
150 silver gray Japanese tubular beads
68 clear AB-finish twist bugle beads, 4mm
3 clear glass faceted teardrop beads, 10mm x 7mm
3 clear glass lantern cut beads, 5mm
1 silver fish hook clasp
2 silver bead tips
White Nymo beading thread, size F, 4-1/2 yards

TOOLS

2 size 12 beading needles
Round nose pliers
Flat nose pliers

Step 1
Chevron Stitch Body of the Choker
Using about 3 yards of thread, string on one silver bead, one bugle, one silver, one bugle, one silver, two lavenders, one silver, and two lavenders. *PNBT* first silver, bugle, and silver beads strung on. Pull tight (fig. 1). This makes the first "stitch." Next string on two lavenders, one silver, two lavenders, one silver, one bugle, then *PNT* the third silver bead strong on the first "stitch." Pull tight (fig. 2). This makes the second "stitch." For "stitch" three, string on two lavender, one silver, two lavender, one silver, one bugle. PNT the second silver bead strung on the second "stitch" (fig. 3). Repeat "stitch" three 18 more times for a total of 21 stitches. The next "stitch" is the first dangle stitch. To make the stitch, string on two lavender, one silver, one lavender, one teardrop, one silver, one lantern cut, and one silver. *PNBT* the

lantern cut, one silver, one teardrop, one lavender, and one silver. Then string on two lavender, one silver and one bugle. *PNT* the second silver bead strung on from the stitch before (fig. 4). Repeat stitch three 7 times and then you are ready for the middle dangle stitch. String two lavender, one silver, two lavender, one silver, two lavender, one silver, one teardrop, one lavender, one lantern cut, one lavender. *PNBT* the lantern cut, one lavender, one teardrop, one silver, two lavender, one silver, two lavender, and one silver. String on two lavender, one silver, one bugle. *PNT* the second silver bead from the previous stitch. Repeat stitch three 7 times, then repeat the first dangle stitch to make the third dangle. Now finish the chevron body of the choker by repeating stitch three 21 times. Weave in the thread tails on both sides by going *BT* the beads until secure.

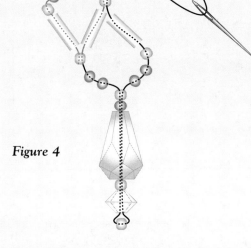

Figure 4

Step 2
Making the Ends of the Choker
Using about 2 feet of thread, *PNT* one silver, one bugle, and one silver bead from the last chevron stitch on the body of the choker. Move the thread through the beads until the beads are in the center of the thread. Thread another needle on the other end of the thread. On the end of the thread coming out of the top edge of the choker string two lavender beads. On the other end of the thread, string two lavender, one silver, two lavender beads (fig. 5). Now string the following beads onto both needles: *one silver, one bugle, one silver, two lavender, one silver, two lavender; * repeat between the asterisks two times then string on one silver, one bugle, and one silver. Attach a bead tip and then attach one end of the clasp to the bead tip (see technique section). Repeat Step 2 for the other end of the choker.

first bead strung on →

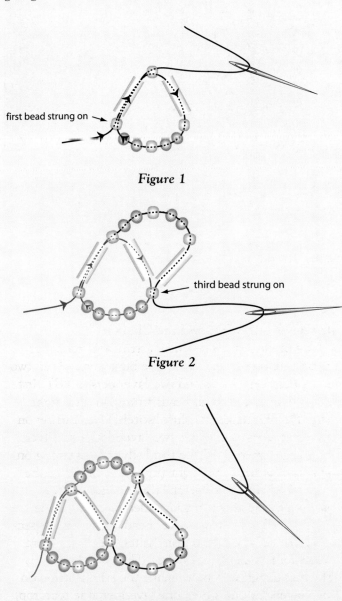

Figure 1

third bead strung on →

Figure 2

Figure 3

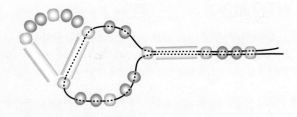

Figure 5

EARRINGS

Step 1
Making the Dangle
On a headpin, place the beads in this order: one lantern cut, one lavender, one teardrop, one lavender, one silver, one bugle, one silver and one lavender.

Step 2
Attaching the Earring Wires
Using flat-nose pliers, make a 90-degree bend in the wire close to the last bead. Cut the wire about 1/4" away from the bend, then with round-nose pliers grab the end of the wire and turn the pliers forming the wire into a loop. Attach the earring wire to the dangle using a jump ring. Repeat Steps 1 and 2 for the second earring.

Daisy Chain

Topaz and Lavender Daisy Chain Necklace and Bracelet

NECKLACE

MATERIALS

56 topaz round faceted glass beads, 5mm
1 topaz round faceted glass bead, 7mm
10 gms gold luster amethyst Japanese tubular beads
2 gold bead tips
1 gold barrel clasp
Nymo beading thread, white, size F, 6 yards

TOOLS

Beading needle, size 11
Round-nose pliers
Flat-nose pliers

Step 1
Making the Daisy Chain
Using about 6 yards of thread, string 12 amethyst beads leaving an 8" tail. Make a circle by *PNBT* the first bead strung on (fig. 1). String on one topaz bead (5mm), *PNT* the sixth bead from the first bead strung on (fig. 2). * String on one amethyst, *PNT* adjacent bead on circle, string on one amethyst bead. *PNT* the first bead just strung on (fig. 3). String on 10 amethyst beads, *PNT* the second bead strung on from the two amethysts strung on just before these 10 (fig. 4). String on one topaz bead (5mm), *PNT* the sixth bead strung on.* Repeat between asterisks 25 times.

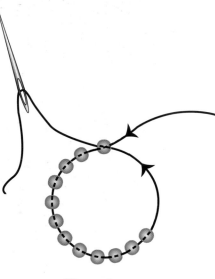

Figure 1

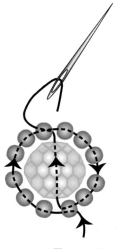

Figure 2

Figure 3

Figure 4

Step 2
Making the Dangle

PNBT the next three beads of the circle so that the needle is coming out of the bottom of the daisy (fig. 5). Make three more daisies; then make a daisy using the 7mm topaz bead and 15 amethyst beads instead of 10. When you are done with the big daisy, *PNBT* the beads of the daisies of the dangle so that the thread is coming out on the opposite side of the top daisy (fig. 6).

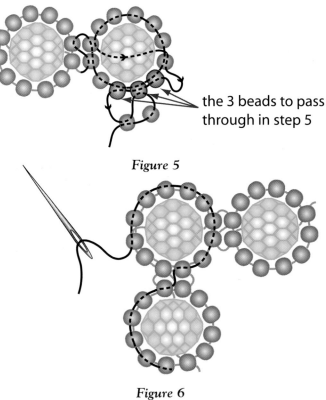

the 3 beads to pass through in step 5

Figure 5

Figure 6

Step 3
Making Second Half of the Necklace
Continue in the daisy chain making 26 more daisies for the other side of the necklace.

Step 4
Attaching the Clasp
Attach bead tips to each end of the necklace and then attach the clasp ends to the bead tips. (See Techniques, page 26.)

BRACELET

MATERIALS

23 topaz round faceted glass beads, 5mm
276 gold luster amethyst Japanese tubular beads
2 gold bead tips
1 gold barrel clasp
Nymo beading thread, white, size F, 4 yards

TOOLS

Beading needle, size 11
Round-nose pliers
Flat-nose pliers

Step 1
Making the Daisy Chain
Make the bracelet the same way as the necklace, but omitting the dangle. This bracelet has 23 daisies.

Step 2
Attaching the Bead Tips and Clasp
Attach the bead tips to the ends of the bracelet and then attach the clasp ends to the bead tips. (See Techniques, page 26.)

Black and Turquoise Triangle Daisy Chain Necklace and Earrings

NECKLACE

> ### MATERIALS
>
> *1 tube of green iridescent Japanese seed beads*
> *180 black seed beads, size 11°*
> *13 turquoise druk beads, 4mm*
> *31 black AB finish druk beads, 4mm*
> *2 silver clamshell bead tips*
> *1 silver lobster claw clasp*
> *Silamide beading thread, black, size A, 3-1/2 yards*
>
> ### TOOLS
>
> *Beading needle, size 12*

Step 1
Attaching One Side of the Clasp
Use about 3-1/2 yards of thread and attach one end of the clasp using a clamshell bead tip. (See Techniques, page 26.)

Step 2
Making the Daisies
*String two black seed beads, then to start the single daisy stitch, string 12 black seed beads. *PNBT* the first bead of the 12, forming a circle. String one turquoise druk bead then *PNT* the sixth bead from the first bead of the circle. Then string two black seed beads, two green seed beads (fig. 1). Next, make the attached daisy stitches. To do this, string 11 green seed beads. *PNBT* the first bead of the 11, then string one black druk bead. *PNT* the fifth bead from the first bead of the circle. String two green seed beads. *PNBT* the fifth and sixth bead of circle, then back through the two beads just strung on (fig. 2). String nine green seed beads. *PNBT* the first bead of the two beads. String one black druk then *PNT* the fifth bead from the first bead of the circle. Pull tight (fig. 3).

Repeat this stitch one more time for a total of three black druk-attached daisy stitches. Then, string on two green beads. * Repeat between the asterisks two more times. String two black seed beads then make one black seed bead turquoise druk daisy. String two black seed beads, two green seed beads. Then make two attached green seed bead black druk daisies, one attached black seed bead and turquoise druk daisy. Then make two more attached green seed bead black druk daisies. String two green seed beads and two black seed beads. Make one more black seed bead turquoise druk daisy. Then, string two black seed beads and two green seed beads.

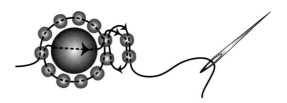

Figure 1

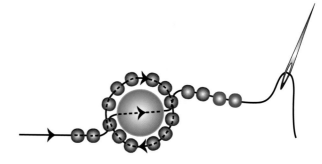

Figure 2

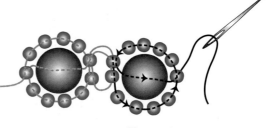

Figure 3

Step 3
Making the Daisy Triangle

Make three attached green seed bead black druk daisies. These will be the top of the triangle. When you finish the third daisy, *PNBT* the beads of the daisy, so that the needle is coming out of the bead next to the two-bead attachment (fig. 4). String two green seed beads. *PNBT* the two beads next to the attachment beads from the third daisy, then *PNBT* the two beads just strung on. String nine green seed beads. *PNT* the first bead of the two-bead attachment. String one black druk bead then *PNBT* the sixth bead of the 11 beads around the druk, and the seventh through the tenth, as well. Then *PNT* seventh and eighth bead from the middle daisy of the top of the triangle then *PNBT* the ninth and tenth bead of the daisy stitch you just made. *PNBT* the eleventh, first, second, third, fourth, fifth, sixth, seventh and eighth beads (fig. 5). String two green seed beads; *PNBT* the seventh and eighth beads, then *PNBT* the two beads just strung on. String nine green seed beads then *PNT* the first bead of the two beads strung on. String one black druk, then *PNT* the sixth bead of beads around druk, and also through the seventh and eighth. *PNT* the seventh and eighth beads of top left hand side daisy, then back through the seventh and eighth beads of the daisy you just made. Then back through the ninth and tenth of the daisy you just made. Then *PNT* beads nine and ten from middle top daisy. Then back through the ninth, tenth, eleventh, first, second and third of the daisy you just made (fig. 6). String two black seed beads, then *PNBT* the second, and third green seed beads. Then back through the two black seed beads. String 10 black seed beads. *PNBT* the first bead of the two attachment black seed beads. String one turquoise druk bead. *PNT* the sixth bead of the seed beads around druk, then *BT* to fifth, fourth, third and second. Next, *PNT* the sixth and fifth beads of middle row right hand side daisy, then *BT* the third and second beads of daisy you just made. Then *PNBT* the sixth, fifth, fourth, third, second, first, and eleventh of middle row right-hand-side daisy. Then through the tenth, ninth, eighth, seventh, and sixth beads of the third top daisy (fig. 7). Now you are done with the triangle.

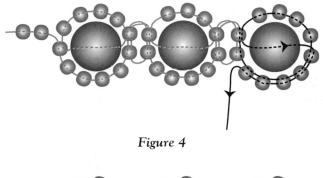

Figure 4

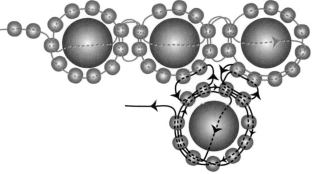

Figure 5

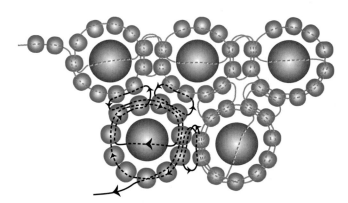

Figure 6

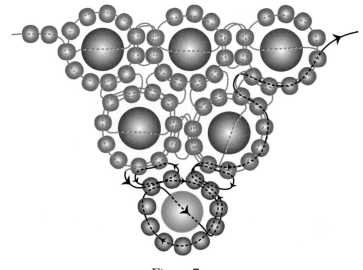

Figure 7

Step 4
Making the Other Half of the Necklace

This side is symmetrical to the other side. Work the same pattern of daisy stitches *backwards*.

Step 5
Attaching the Other Side of the Clasp

String one clamshell bead tip, one seed bead. Tie two or three overhand knots around bead making sure necklace beads are close to bead tip and seed bead is inside clamshell. Cut the excess thread and place a dab of glue over knots. Squeeze clamshell closed and slip other end of clasp over hook of bead tip and turn closed with round nose pliers.

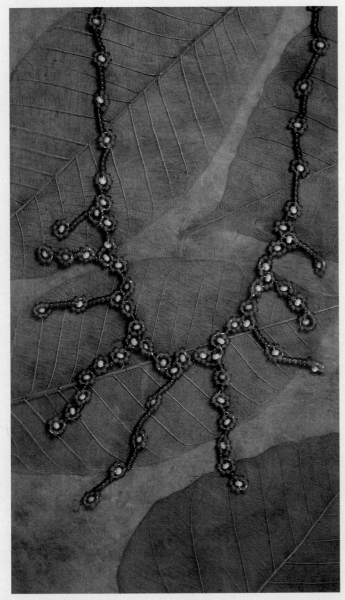

Using size 11° seed beads for the middle of the daisy creates a petite flower.

EARRINGS

MATERIALS

34 black seed beads, size 11°
48 green iridescent Japanese seed beads
Silamide beading thread, black, size A, 2 yards
1 pair of fishhook ear wires

TOOLS

Beading needle, size 12

Step 1
Making the Daisies

String two green seed beads then make two green seed bead black druk attached daisies and one black seed bead turquoise druk attached daisy. *PNBT* three daisies and two seed beads on the top (fig. 8).

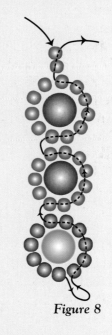

Figure 8

Step 2
Attaching the Ear wire

String five black seed beads. *PNT* the loop of the ear wire, then through the two green seed beads on top of the earring. Pull tight. *PNT* all the seed beads around the first black druk bead and back through the five black seed beads in the ear wire loop. Repeat several times. Cut off any excess thread. Repeat Steps 1 and 2 for the other earring.

Horizontal and Vertical Netting

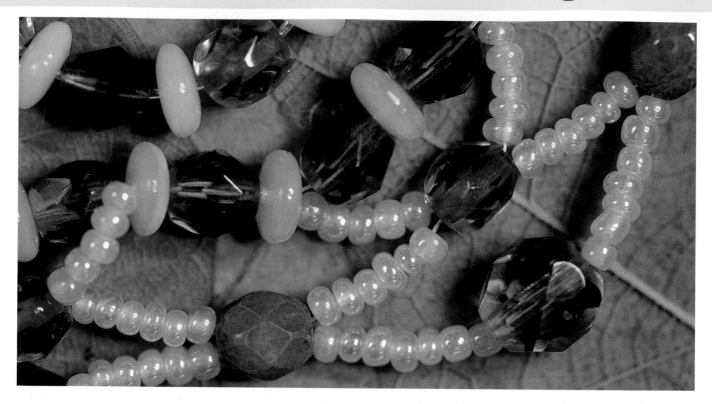

Blue, White, and Purple Netted Choker and Earrings

This choker is made using a horizontal netting technique.

CHOKER

MATERIALS

39 milky white rondelles, 7mm
40 transparent turquoise faceted glass beads, 6mm
9 purple-lined turquoise faceted glass beads, 6mm
8 opaque lavender faceted glass beads, 7mm
4 capri blue lantern-cut faceted glass beads, 6mm
2 light blue lantern-cut faceted glass beads, 5mm
1 transparent turquoise faceted glass bead, 8mm
5 gms pearl white seed beads, size 10°

2 silver clamshell bead tips
1 silver toggle clasp
Nymo beading thread, white, size F, 6 yards

TOOLS

Beading needle, size 11
Embroidery scissors
Round-nose pliers
Flat-nose pliers
Bonding glue

Step 1
Row One

Use about 4 feet of thread and tie a stop bead to the end of the thread with a square knot (fig. 1). String on one transparent turquoise bead (6mm), one rondelle, one transparent turquoise bead (6mm), one rondelle, keeping this pattern for 14-1/2". Tie on another stop bead as close to the beads as possible. Take the needle off of the thread.

Figure 1

Step 2
Row Two

Thread a new, 2-yard length of thread onto the needle. Tie a stop bead. *PNT* the first 14 beads from Row 1. * String on five white seed beads, one purple-lined turquoise bead, 5 white seed beads. Skip the next turquoise bead, rondelle and one other turquoise bead from Row 1, then *PNT* one rondelle, one turquoise, one rondelle from Row 1 (fig. 2). * Repeat between asterisks eight times. On the last repeat, instead of *PNT* the one rondelle, one turquoise, one rondelle, *PNT* the last 14 beads of the first row. Tie on a stop bead.

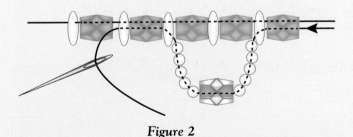

Figure 2

Step 3
Row Three

Using a new 4-foot length of thread, *PNT* the first 14 beads from Row 1 and the five white seed beads and one purple-lined turquoise bead from Row 2. String on six white seed beads, one lavender bead, and six white seed beads. *PNT* purple-lined turquoise bead from Row 2. Repeat between the asterisks seven

times. On last repeat, *PNT* purple-lined bead and five white seed beads from Row 2 and the last 14 beads from Row 1.

Step 4
Row Four

Thread a new 4-foot length of thread. Tie a stop bead. *PNT* the first 14 beads from Row 1, through five white seed beads and one purple-lined bead from Row 2, and six white seed beads and one lavender bead from Row 3. * String on six white seed beads, one light blue bead, six white seed beads. *PNT* one lavender bead from Row 3. * Repeat between asterisks two times except instead of one light blue bead, string on one capri blue bead each time. String seven white seed beads, one turquoise bead (8mm), and seven white seed beads. *PNT* the lavender bead from Row 3. Finish the row to match the first half of the row with two capri blue beads and one light blue bead. *PNT* the lavender bead, six white seed beads from Row 3, one purple-lined bead and five white seed beads from Row 2 and remaining 14 beads from Row 1. Tighten all strings.

Step 5
Attaching the Clasp

Remove all stop beads from one side of the choker. Using all strands string on a bead tip. Tie an overhand knot in the bead tip and while tightening the knot push the bead tip as close to the beads as possible. Cut off excess thread and place a drop of glue on the knot and squeeze the bead tip closed with the flat-nose pliers. Using round-nose pliers, close the bead tip hook over the loop on one end of the clasp. Repeat on other side of the choker.

EARRINGS

three white seed beads. With pliers, bend up the end of the hoop so it will fit into the loop of the hoop (fig. 3). Repeat for other earring.

MATERIALS

8 milky white rondelles, 7mm
2 purple-lined turquoise faceted glass beads, 6mm
4 capri blue lantern cut faceted glass beads, 6mm
4 light blue lantern cut faceted glass beads, 5mm
12 pearl white seed beads, size 10°
1 pair silver hoop ear wires

TOOLS

Flat-nose pliers

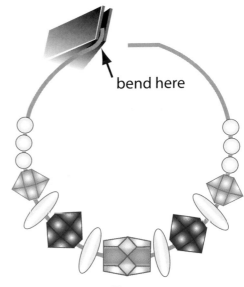

bend here

Figure 3

Step 1
Stringing the Beads
Onto one hoop earring wire, place three white seed beads, one light blue bead, one rondelle, one capri blue, one rondelle, one purple-lined bead, one rondelle, one capri blue, one rondelle, one light blue,

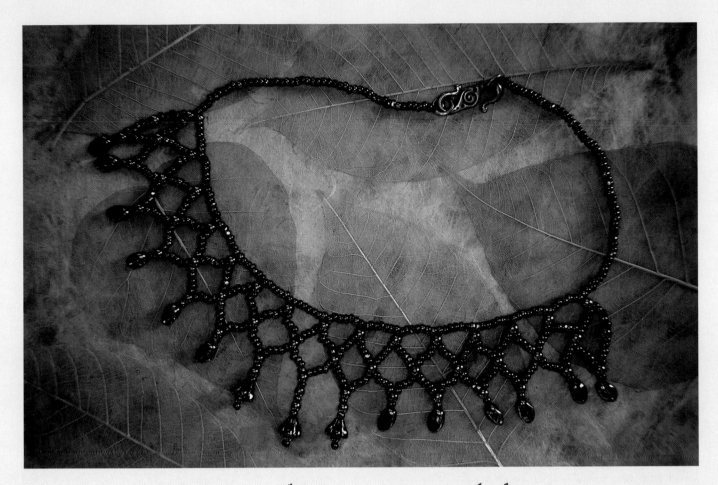

Vertical Net Necklace and Headband

Don't let the length of these instructions fool you. This project is quick and easy. Vertical netting is a simple technique.

NECKLACE

MATERIALS

1 copper "S" hook and eye clasp
2 strands, 18″, charlotte blue iris beads, size 8°
3 blue iris floret beads
12 teardrop (glass) copper iris beads, 8mm x 6mm
50 druk (glass) copper iris beads, 4mm
Nymo beading thread, black, size F, 4 yards

TOOLS

Beading needle, size 12

Step 1
Making the Base Strand

Using about 4 yards of thread, tie a charlotte stop bead leaving a 12" tail, then string on 191 charlottes, for a total of 192 beads. The base strand should measure about 15" and, with a 1" clasp, the finished necklace should measure about 16". Now attach one end of the clasp by wrapping the thread around the clasp loop about six times. Pull tight so that the beads are tight against the clasp and tie a double-half hitch knot. *PNBT* 47 charlottes and now you are ready to begin Row 1.

Step 2
Row 1
Downward side:
String one druk, five charlottes, one druk, five charlottes, one druk, one charlotte, and one teardrop. *PNBT* one charlotte and one druk.

Upward side:
String five charlottes, one druk, five charlottes. *PNT* the first druk bead from downward side of row and then *PNT* the next seven charlottes on the base strand (fig. 1).

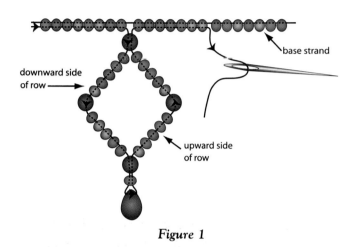

Figure 1

Step 3
Row 2
Downward side:
String one druk, five charlottes. *PNT* the druk bead from upward side of previous row, string five charlottes, one druk, one charlotte, one teardrop. *PNBT* one charlotte, one druk.

Upward side:
String five charlottes, one druk, five charlottes. *PNT* the first druk bead from downward side of the row and then *PNT* the next seven charlottes on the base strand (fig. 2).

Figure 2

Step 4
Rows 3-6
Same as Row 2.

Step 5
Row 7
Same as Row 2—except at the end of the downward side of the row, instead of stringing on a teardrop, string one druk, one charlotte, one floret, one druk, one charlotte. *PNBT* one druk, one floret, one charlotte and one druk (fig. 3). Finish the row same as Row 2.

Figure 3

Step 6
Row 8
Same as Row 7 (except for the dangle beads). String one druk, one charlotte, one druk, one charlotte, one druk, one charlotte, one floret, one druk, one charlotte. *PNBT* one druk, one floret, one charlotte, one druk, one charlotte, one druk, one charlotte, one druk (fig. 4). Now finish the row the same as Row 7.

Figure 4

Step 7
Row 9
Same as Row 7.

Step 8
Rows 10-15
Same as Row 2. At the end of Row 15, instead of passing the needle through seven charlottes on the base strand, tie a small knot and weave thread end into beadwork until secure. Cut off the excess thread.

Step 9
Attach Other End of the Clasp
Thread needle onto tail of thread at the end of the piece. String on the clasp end. Wrap thread about six times around the loop, and pull tight so beads are against the clasp. Tie a double-half hitch knot. Weave the excess thread through beads until secure and cut off any remaining thread.

HEADBAND

MATERIALS

4 strands, 18", of blue iris charlotte seed beads,
   size 8°
67 druk (glass) copper iris beads, 4mm
5 blue iris floret beads
12 teardrop (glass) copper iris beads, 8mm x 6mm
1 plastic tortoise shell headband
Nymo beading thread, black, size F, 4-1/2 yards

TOOLS

Beading needle, size 12

Step 1
Making the Base Strand
Use about 4-1/2 yards of black thread. String one size 8° charlotte stop bead, then string on 191 charlottes for a base strand with a total of 192 charlotte beads. Now make one end bead dangle by stringing one copper druk bead, one charlotte, one floret, one druk, and one charlotte. *PNBT* one druk, one floret, one charlotte, one druk, and 47 charlottes. Now you are ready to begin Row 1.

Step 2
Row 1
Downward side:
String one druk bead, five charlottes, one druk, five charlottes, one druk, one charlotte, and one copper teardrop. *PNBT* one charlotte and one druk.

Upward side:
String five charlottes, one druk, five charlottes. *PNT* the first druk bead from the downward side of row, and then *PNT* the next seven charlottes on the base strand.

Step 3
Row 2
Downward side:
String 1 druk, five charlottes. *PNT* last druk bead from upward side of previous row. String five charlottes, one druk, one charlotte, one teardrop. *PNBT* one charlotte and one druk.

Upward side:
String five charlottes, one druk, five charlottes. *PNT* the first druk bead from downward side of the row and then *PNT* the next seven beads on the base strand.

Step 4
Rows 3 and 4
Repeat Row 2.

Step 5
Row 5
Downward side:
String one druk, five charlottes. *PNT* the druk bead from the upward side of the previous row. String five charlottes, one druk, five charlottes, one druk, five charlottes, one druk, one charlotte, one teardrop. *PNBT* one charlotte, one druk.

Upward side:
String five charlottes, one druk, five charlottes. *PNT* the second druk bead strung on the downward side of the row. String five charlottes, one druk, five charlottes. *PNT* first druk from the downward side of the row. *PNT* the next seven beads of the base strand (fig. 5).

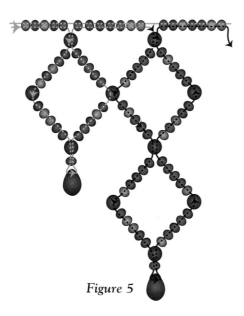

Figure 5

Step 6
Row 6
Downward side:
String one druk, five charlottes. *PNT* the druk bead from upward side of previous row (second one strung on upward portion of row). String five charlottes, one druk, one charlotte, one teardrop. *PNBT* one charlotte and one druk.

Upward side:
String five charlottes, one druk, five charlottes. *PNT* corresponding druk from the downward side of the row. String five charlottes, one druk, five charlottes. *PNT* the first druk strung on from the downward side of the row. *PNT* the next seven beads of the base

strand (fig. 6).

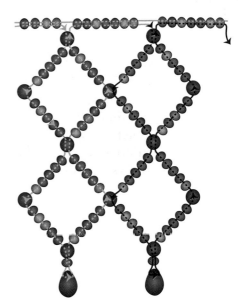

Figure 6

Step 7
Row 7
Row 7 is the same as Row 6 except at the end of the downward side of the row, where instead of stringing on a teardrop, string one floret, one druk, one charlotte, then *PNBT* one druk, one floret, one charlotte and one druk (fig. 7). Finish the row the same as Row 6.

Figure 7

Step 8
Row 8
Row 8 is the same as Row 7 except for the dangle beads. String one druk, one charlotte, one druk, one charlotte, one druk, one charlotte, one floret, one druk, one charlotte. *PNBT* one druk, one floret, one charlotte, one druk, one charlotte, one druk, one charlotte, one druk. Now finish the row the same as Row 7.

Step 9
Row 9
Same as Row 7.

Step 10
Rows 10 and 11
Same as Row 6.

Step 11
Rows 12, 13, 14, 15
Same as Row 2.

Step 12
Making the End Dangle
At the end of Row 15, *PNT* the 47 charlottes on the end of the base strand. Now string one druk, one charlotte, one floret, one druk, and one charlotte. *PNBT* one druk, one floret, one charlotte, one druk and 97 base strand charlottes, so the needle is coming out of the middle of the base strand.

Step 13
Attaching the Bead Netting to the Headband
Find the center of the plastic headband and place the base strand along the top of headband, matching centers. Wrap thread around headband between teeth and *PNT* three beads from base strand. Wrap thread around the headband between the next teeth and then through next three beads of base strand. Repeat until you reach the last tooth on the headband. *PNBT* the base strand beads until you reach the center of the headband. Attach the other side of the netting to the headband in the same manner.

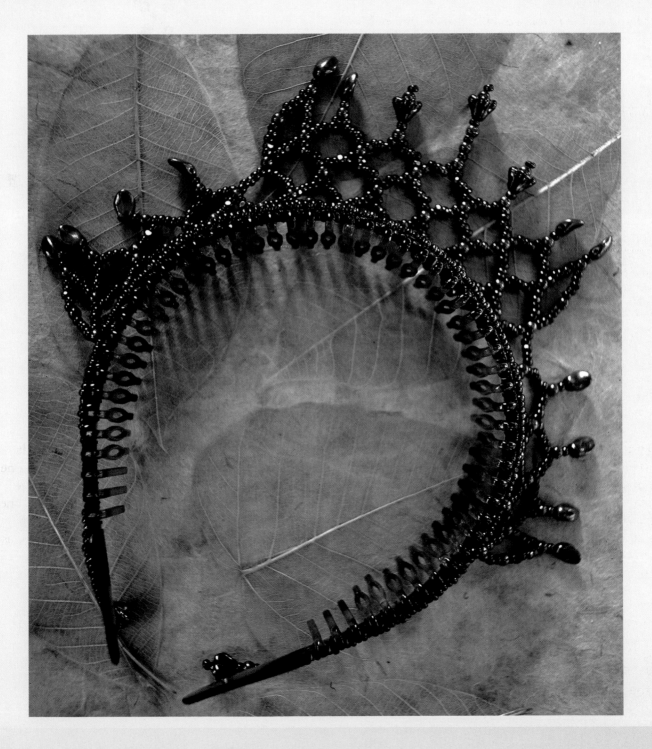

Peyote Stitch Bracelet and Barrette

BRACELET

MATERIALS

5 gms gold-cut silver-lined Japanese tubular beads
5 gms ruby semi-matte silver-lined Japanese tubular beads
5 squash-colored Japanese tubular beads
5 medium green Japanese tubular beads
5 sapphire Japanese tubular beads
6 opaque rose Japanese tubular beads
Nymo beading thread, red, size F, 2 yards
1 gold spring ring clasp

TOOLS

Beading needle, size 12
Embroidery scissors

Step 1
Peyote Stitch

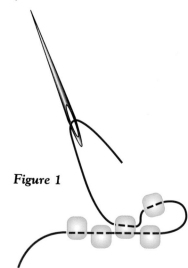

Figure 1

Thread the needle with 6 feet of thread. Leaving a 6" tail, string on five gold beads. *PNBT* the third bead strung on. (fig. 1.) String one gold bead, *PNBT* the first bead strung on. This makes the first two rows. (Follow the design chart for the colors of beads used. Read the chart from bottom to top, working right to left then on the next row left to right.)

For Row 3, string one bead *PNT* last bead from the previous row, string one bead then *PNT* the first bead from the previous row. Each row has two beads in it. Continue in this manner, repeating the design chart when necessary until the piece measures 6-3/4", ending with a pink bead and a red parallelogram. Finish off with two rows of gold beads so that each end of the bracelet is the same.

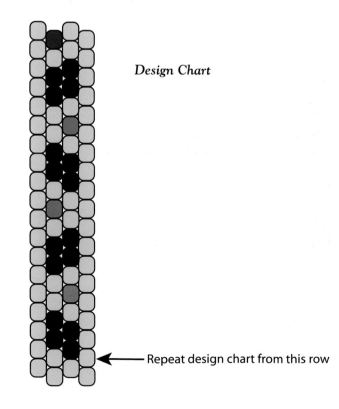

Design Chart

← Repeat design chart from this row

Step 2
Attaching the Clasp

With the remaining thread string on six gold beads and one end of the clasp. *PNBT* the beads of the last two rows of the peyote then back through the six gold beads, pulling tightly. Do this two or three more times, then tie a knot and weave the thread end through the beads until secure. Cut off the excess thread. (fig. 2.) Using the 6" tail of thread from the beginning of the bracelet, repeat Step 2.

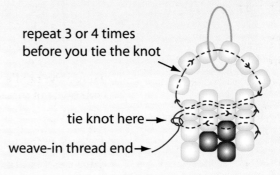

repeat 3 or 4 times
before you tie the knot

tie knot here →

weave-in thread end →

Figure 2

BARRETTE

Step 1
Peyote Stitch
Make another strip of peyote stitches as you did in Step 1 of the bracelet, only make this strip 2-1/2" long.

Step 2
Making the Fringe
PNBT the second bead down and *PT* four beads and come out through the third bead down on the opposite side. Now string on four gold beads, *PNT* the sixth bead from the top and through four beads to the third bead of the other side. (fig. 3.) Repeat until there are three or four rows left. Weave in the thread ends until secure. Cut off the excess thread.

Step 3
Gluing On the Peyote Strip
Place glue on the peyote strip and then put it onto the barrette finding, folding the ends of the peyote strip over the edges of the barrette. Let dry. If you want two barrettes, repeat Steps 1-3.

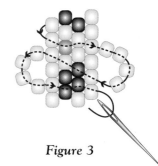

Figure 3

Tubular Peyote Sunset Bracelet and Earrings

BRACELET

MATERIALS

5 gm yellow seed beads, size 11°
5 gm yellow-orange seed beads, size 11°
5 gm orange seed beads, size 11°
5 gm red-orange seed beads, size 11°
5 gm red seed beads, size 11°
5 gm dark red seed beads, size 11°
2 red accent beads
1 gold spring ring clasp
Silamide beading thread, size A, 3 yards

TOOLS

Beading needle, size 12

Step 1
Tubular Peyote
Using about 3 yards of beading thread, string six yellow beads. Leave a 12" tail to use to attach the clasp later. PNBT the first yellow bead strung on forming a circle. These six beads will form Rounds 1 and 2 (fig. 1). Keep the circle tight by holding the tail of thread.

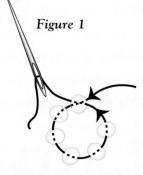

Figure 1

You will have three beads for each round. (This is called even-count tubular peyote because you start with an even number of beads, but the beads-per-round ends up being an odd number.)

Round 3

String one yellow bead, skip a bead from the bead circle, *PNT* the next bead from the bead circle (fig. 2). String one yellow bead, skip a bead, *PNT* next bead (fig. 3). String one yellow bead, skip a bead, *PNT* next bead. *PNBT* the first bead from this round, so that the needle is properly positioned for the next round. Pull tight.

Round 4

After this round, it will be easy to identify which three beads are on each round. Three of the beads will be definitely higher than the three from the previous row.* String one yellow bead. *PNT* the next stepped-up bead. * Repeat between asterisks two times. Then, *PNBT* the first bead of the Round so that the needle is positioned properly for the next round. Pull tight. Do 3/4" of tubular peyote with the yellow beads, then change to yellow-orange beads for 1/2", orange for 1/2", red-orange for 1/2", red for 1/2", dark red for 1/2", red for 1/2", red-orange for 1/2", orange for 1/2", yellow-orange for 1/2", and yellow for 3/4". (13 rounds equal about 1/2" and 17 rounds equal about 3/4".)

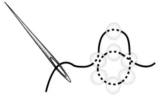

Figure 2

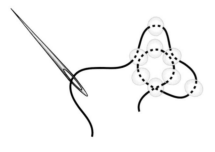

Figure 3

Step 2
Attaching the Clasp

When you are done with the last yellow round of the tubular peyote, string one red accent bead. Then string thread through the loop of the clasp. *PNBT* the red bead then through one of the yellow beads from the last row of the bracelet. Pull tight. *PNBT* red bead, loop of clasp, *BT* red bead then through the next yellow bead from the last row of the bracelet.

Pull tight. Repeat several more times using a different yellow bead from the last row each time. Now *PNBT* the peyote stitches until thread is secure and cut off the excess thread. Repeat for the other end of the bracelet.

EARRINGS

MATERIALS

5 gm yellow seed beads, size 11°
5 gm yellow-orange seed beads, size 11°
5 gm orange seed beads, size 11°
5 gm red-orange seed beads, size 11°
5 gm red seed beads, size 11°
5 gm dark red seed beads, size 11°
2 red accent beads
1 pair gold fishhook ear wires
Silamide beading thread, size A, 3 yards

TOOLS

Beading needle, size 12

Step 1
Tubular Peyote

Repeat Step 1 of the bracelet except change colors as follows: seven rounds of yellow beads, five rounds yellow-orange, five rounds orange, five rounds red-orange, five rounds red, five rounds dark red, five rounds red, five rounds red-orange, five rounds orange, five rounds yellow-orange, seven rounds yellow.

Step 2
Attaching the Ear Wires

String one red accent bead then string six dark red beads. *PNT* ear wire loop then *PNBT* red accent bead and pull tight. *PNT* one of the yellow beads from the last row. *PNBT* red accent bead and all six dark red beads holding on the ear wire. *PNBT* the red accent bead. Then *PNT* next yellow bead from the last row. Repeat one more time. Now weave thread through yellow beads until secure and cut off excess thread. Next you thread the needle onto the tail on the other end of the tubular peyote. *PNT* red accent bead, all six red beads, back through red accent bead, through one yellow bead from Row 1. Pull tight. Repeat two more times then weave tail into yellow beads until secure and clip off any excess. Repeat Steps 1 and 2 for the other earring.

Changing bead color and adding dangles can enhance the tubular peyote bracelet.

Technique **Square Stitch**

Square Stitch Scarab Choker and Belt

Make two squares of scarab square stitch, one 1" x 1-5/8" and one 1-1/2" x 1-5/8" and you can create two totally different projects: a lovely choker necklace and a belt buckle cover for your web belt.

CHOKER

MATERIALS

3 transparent light blue seed beads, size 5°
2 dark green round beads, 7mm
10 black Japanese tubular beads, 1.5mm
82 silver-lined gold-cut Japanese tubular beads,
*   1.5mm*
86 pink luster light olive Japanese tubular beads,
*   1.5mm*
88 metallic teal iris Japanese tubular beads, 1.5mm
209 opaque light blue Japanese tubular beads,
*   1.5mm*
1 silver neck wire
Nymo beading thread, black, size F, 4 yards

TOOLS

Beading needle, size 11 or 12

Step 1
Square Stitch
Using about 4 yards of thread, string on 19 light blue Japanese tubular beads. This is the first row.
For all other rows, string two light blue tubular beads, then *PNT* (in the opposite direction of Row 2) second-to-last bead from Row 1 and then back through the second bead just strung on (fig. 1). String one light blue Japanese tubular bead. *PNT* (in the opposite direction of Row 2) third bead from Row 1, and then back through the bead just strung on. Continue in this manner, stringing on one bead at a time, until the end of the row. Remember to make a two-bead stitch at the beginning of each row. Use the design

chart and continue in the square stitch until finished. Read the chart from left to right and right to left, up from the bottom of the chart to the top.

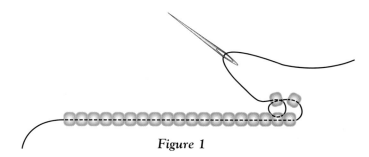

Figure 1

Step 2
Attaching Scarab to the Neck Wire
Pick three light blue size 5° seed beads by making sure the hole is large enough to fit onto the neck wire with room to spare for thread. If you have excess thread left over at the end of the design chart, use it to sew on the beads; if not, get new thread securing end of thread in the beads already worked. Sew the beads onto the square stitched scarab by following fig. 2. Wrap the thread through the beads two or three times. Secure the thread end into the already worked beads and cut off excess. Unscrew the ball at the end of the neck wire. Put on one dark green round bead, the three light blue beads sewn onto the scarab and then one more dark green bead. Slide the beads to the center of the neck wire and screw the ball back on.

last row →   weave-in thread end

Figure 2

black

metallic teal iris

opaque light blue

pink luster light olive

silver lined gold cut

Design Chart for Scarab Choker

Design Chart for Belt

black
metallic teal iris
opaque light blue
pink luster light olive
silver lined gold cut

BELT

MATERIALS

10 black Japanese tubular beads, 1.5mm
82 silver-lined gold-cut Japanese tubular beads, 1.5mm
86 pink luster light olive Japanese tubular beads, 1.5mm
88 metallic teal iris Japanese tubular beads, 1.5mm
309 opaque light blue Japanese tubular beads, 1.5mm
1 brown webbed belt and metal buckle
Nymo beading thread, black, size F, 4-1/2 yards

TOOLS

Beading needle, size 11 or 12
Bonding glue

Step 1
Square Stitch

String on 23 light blue Japanese tubular beads for the first row. Then, following the Scarab Belt design chart, work in the square stitch (same as Step 1 on the choker).

Step 2
Gluing the Square Stitch Scarab to the Belt Buckle

Using the bonding glue, glue the beads to the top of the metal belt buckle. Let dry.

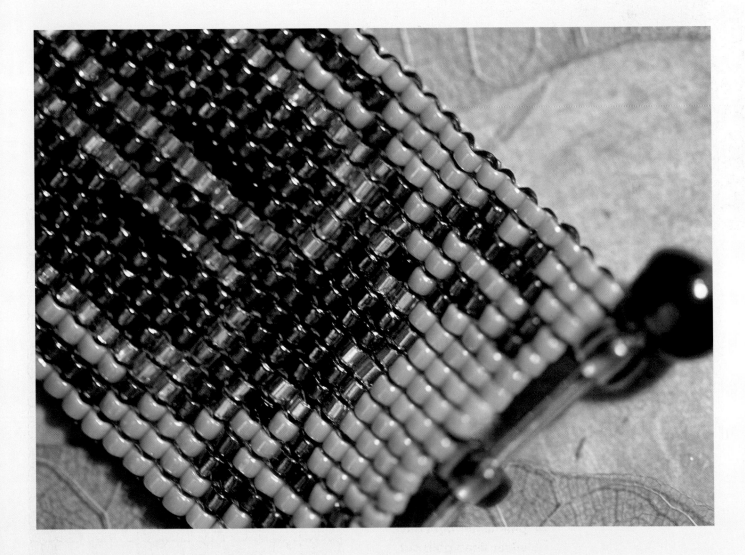

Square Stitch Flower Broach and Earrings

The broach and the earrings are made in exactly the same manner, except that the middle bead on the broach is larger than the middle bead of the earrings. And, of course, the earring flowers are glued to ear studs, and the broach flower is glued to a pin back.

BROACH AND EARRINGS

MATERIALS

90 white iridescent seed beads, size 11°
210 pearly lavender seed beads, size 11°
150 rose lilac seed beads, size 11°
90 bluish-purple seed beads, size 11°
9 kelly green translucent seed beads, size 11°
3 gold seed beads, size 11°
9 green leaf-shaped beads
1 yellow faceted glass bead, 4mm
2 yellow faceted glass beads, 3mm
1 small gold bar pin

1 pair of gold flat pad ear studs
1 pair of comfort clutch earring backs
Green felt
Nymo beading thread, white, size B (or the size to fit bead holes), 30 yards

TOOLS

Beading needle, size 12
Bonding glue

Step 1
Making the Petals for the Earrings and the Broach
Thread the needle on about 2 yards of thread. Using the square stitch (see Techniques, page 32, How to Make Square Stitch) and the design chart (Row 1 being on the bottom of the chart and Row 6 on top), make a petal. Increase on both ends of Rows 2 and 3, and decrease on both ends of Rows 5 and 6. Repeat four times for a total of five petals. Leave one yard-long thread end on one of the petals. Weave all the other thread ends into the petals. Each flower has five petals. This project needs three flowers so make ten more petals for the two earrings. Set aside.

that they overlap and form them into a tight circle (fig. 2). Then, holding them carefully in order, sew the petals in place by passing the needle between the beads (not through the beads) and catch the threads. Keep sewing the petals, one on top of the other, until they are fairly secure. Then pass the needle up through a bead in the middle of the petals and string on one yellow faceted bead (4mm for the broach and 3mm for the earrings) then string on one gold seed bead and *PNBT* the yellow faceted bead and back down through the bead in the middle of the petals and out the back of the flower.

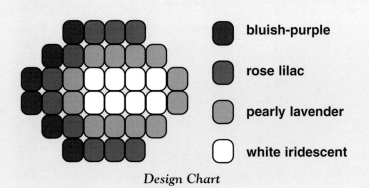

■	**bluish-purple**
■	**rose lilac**
■	**pearly lavender**
□	**white iridescent**

Design Chart

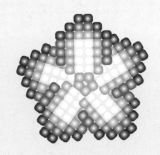

Figure 2

Step 3
Sewing On the Leaves
String on a leaf bead, one green seed bead, then *PNBT* the leaf bead. Attach to the backside of one of the petals by *PNT* one of the beads of the petal, making sure the leaf bead shows through two of the petals (fig. 3). It doesn't have to be too secure, because when you glue the flower to the felt the leaves will be held in place by the glue. Repeat two more times.

Step 2
Sewing the Petals Together
Use the 1 yard-long thread end to sew the petals together. Take five petals and sew them loosely together into a circle by passing needle through the bottom lavender beads of each petal. (See fig. 1.) It will be floppy, but that is okay. Arrange the petals so

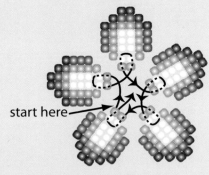

start here →

Figure 1

Figure 3

105

Step 4
Glue Flower to Felt

Cut a small circle of green felt about 5/8" diameter for the earrings and about 1" in diameter for the broach. Put glue on back of flower and glue it to the felt circle. Make sure you arrange the petals and leaves the way you want them to look. Let dry. Then glue the flower and the felt to the bar pin back or the flat pad earring stud (fig. 4). Let dry. On these earrings you must use the earring backs with the large plastic circle around them, because the earrings are heavy and will droop if the backs are the small kind.

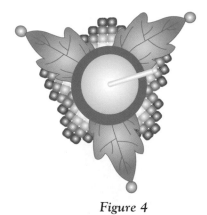

Figure 4

Crystal Right Angle Weave
Pink and Purple Bracelet
and Earrings

Bracelet

MATERIALS

24 pink Swarovski crystals, 6mm
75 purple Swarovski crystals, 3mm
2 silver clamshell bead tips
1 silver lobster claw clasp
Nymo beading thread, black or purple, size F,
3 yards
2 seed beads, size 11°

TOOLS

Beading needle, size 12
Flat-nose pliers
Round-nose pliers
Bonding glue

Step 1
Right Angle Weave

Use about 3 yards of thread. String on four purple crystals, leaving a thread tail about 12" long to be used later for attaching the clasp. *PNBT* the first three crystals strung on, forming a circle (fig. 1). This

Figure 1

circle forms the first purple "stitch." * String three purple crystals and *PNBT* the end crystal of the previous stitch and back through the first two crystals strung on (fig. 2). *Repeat between the asterisks one time, then * string one pink, one purple, one pink. This forms the pink-purple stitch. *PNBT* end bead of previous stitch and back through the first and second

Figure 2

beads strung on (fig. 3). * Repeat between asterisks one time. This forms the "flower." Repeat the three purple stitches, two pink-purple stitches pattern five more times for a total of six "flowers." Add three more purple stitches to the end.

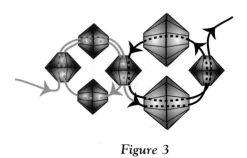

Figure 3

Step 2
Attaching the Clasp

Thread the needle through the clamshell bead tip and string on one seed bead. Pull the bead tight into the bead tip and tie several knots around the seed bead. Place a drop of glue over the knots and bead, and squeeze the clamshell bead tip closed with pliers. Slip clasp loop onto bead tip hook and close hook with round-nose pliers. Repeat Step 2 on the other end of the bracelet.

Earrings

MATERIALS

8 pink Swarovski crystals, 6mm
24 purple Swarovski crystals, 3mm
2 silver clamshell bead tips
1 pair silver lever-back ear wires
2 seed beads, size 11°
Beading thread of your choice, black or purple, size F, 2 yards

TOOLS

Beading needle, size 12
Flat-nose pliers
Round-nose pliers
Bonding glue

Step 1
Right Angle Weave

Use about 1 yard of thread leaving a 6" tail and make three purple stitches and two pink-purple stitches. Next *PNBT* the stitches so that the thread is coming out of the same bead as the thread tail (fig. 4).

Step 2
Attaching the Earring Wire

String both thread ends through a clamshell bead tip and one of the ends through a seed bead. Tie a square knot around the seed bead and pull tight, making sure that the knot and seed bead are snugly in the bead tip (fig. 4). Place a drop of glue on the knot and seed bead. Using flat-nose pliers, squeeze clamshell shut. Slip the ear wire loop onto the bead tip hook and close with round-nose pliers. Repeat Steps 1 and 2 for the other earring.

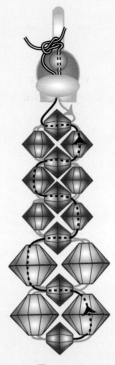

Figure 4

Blue and Roses
Right Angle Weave
Dog Collar and Ring

DOG COLLAR

Step 1
Row 1
Use about 3 yards of thread and leave a 12" tail.
String on four light blue druk beads. *PNBT* the first
three beads strung on. This forms the first stitch.
String on three more blue druk beads and *PNT* the
end bead of the first stitch and back through the first
two beads strung on. This forms the second stitch
(fig. 1). Make eight more stitches using blue druk

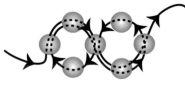

Figure 1

beads. Then make one stitch stringing on in this order: one green druk and two blue. For the next stitch, string on two blue and one green. * Make six more all-blue bead stitches, then one green, two blue, and then one stitch of two blue and one green. * Repeat between asterisks two times, then make 10 all-blue bead stitches.

Step 2
Row 2
PNT the top bead of last stitch from Row 1. String on three blue beads. *PNBT* top bead from Row 1 and then *PNBT* the first of the three beads strung on. This is the first stitch of Row 2. String on two blue beads. *PNT* top bead of the next stitch from Row 1. Then *PNBT* the end bead of the previous stitch and both beads just strung on. This is the second stitch of Row 2. Then *PNT* the top bead of the stitch from Row 1 and string on two blue beads. *PNT* end bead of previous stitch, next top bead from Row 1 and through the first bead strung on. This is the third stitch of Row 2 (fig. 2). Make seven more all-blue bead stitches. * For the next stitch, string one pink bead and one green bead. Then for the next stitch, string one green bead and one blue bead. Next make six all-blue bead stitches. * Repeat between asterisks three times, then make four more all-blue bead stitches.

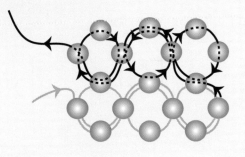

Figure 2

Step 3
Row 3
Using right angle weave stitch, make 46 all blue stitches.

Step 4
Making the Loop End of the Clasp
Pass the thread through the end beads until the thread comes out of the end bead of the middle row. String on 12 blue beads and *PNBT* the first bead of the 12, forming a loop (fig. 3). Weave thread back through some of the stitches until secure and then cut off the excess thread.

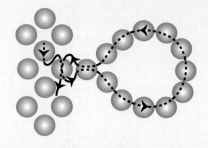

Figure 3

Step 5
Making the Bead End of the Clasp
Using the 12" tail of thread from the beginning of the first row, *PNT* the end beads until the thread comes out of the end bead of the middle row. String on two blue beads, one pink bead, the 10mm round glass luster bead with a rose, and one pink bead. *PNBT* the luster bead, one pink bead, and two blue beads. Weave thread through several stitches until secure and cut off the excess thread.

Step 6
Attaching the Center Dangle Bead
Using about 18" of thread, secure one end into choker by weaving it through several stitches until it comes out of the twenty-third end bead, next to the middle of the choker. String on one pink, the 18mm x 13mm luster bead, and one pink. *PNBT* the luster bead and the first pink bead. *PNT* the twenty-fourth end bead next to the middle of the choker and then weave in thread until secure and cut off excess thread.

RING

MATERIALS

28 light blue druk beads, 4mm
1 pink druk bead, 4mm
4 light green druk beads, 4mm
Nymo beading thread, size F, 1 yard

TOOLS

Beading needle, size 11

Step 1
Right Angle Weave Stitch

Using about 1 yard of thread, make four all-blue bead right-angle weave stitches. Make the next stitch using one green, one pink, one green. Then for the next stitch, string one green, one blue, one green. Make four more all-blue bead stitches.

Step 2
Making the Connecting Stitch

String one blue bead; *PNT* the end bead of the first stitch made. String one more blue bead, then *PNT* the end bead of the last stitch made, forming a circle (fig. 4). Weave end of thread back through stitches until secure. Cut off the excess.

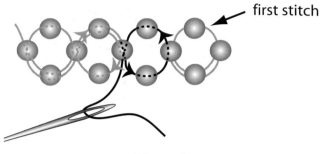

first stitch

Figure 4

Wirework Projects

This chapter skims the surface of all the things you can make with a little wire and beads. The basic techniques are few, but the possibilities are endless! The chapter has projects using memory wire, jump rings, head pins, eye pins, and chain.

Memory Wire
Choker and Ring

CHOKER

MATERIALS

1 loop of necklace memory wire, 14-1/2" long
6 gold AB bugle beads, 1/4"
12 white star beads, 5mm
4 light iris transparent teardrop beads, 5mm x 9mm
1 lantern-cut Swarovski crystal bead, 10mm
48 gold-lined seed beads, size 11°
72 light iris transparent triangle beads
2 crimp beads
2 gold clamshell bead tips

TOOLS

Crimp pliers
Flat-nose pliers
Flush style wire cutters

It is customary to end memory wire with a loop; however memory wire is very thick and it will bend most jewelers' round-nose pliers, so regular strength round-nose pliers must be used. We wanted to try something different, so we used a crimp bead and a bead tip to end the memory wire. You may use whichever technique you feel most comfortable with.

Step 1
Attaching the Crimp Bead and Bead Tip
to the Memory Wire
Slip bead tip, then a crimp bead onto one end of the memory wire. Crimp the crimp bead, using the crimp pliers, onto the very end of the memory wire. Use wire cutters to trim off any excess wire sticking out of crimp bead. Now slip the bead tip up to and over the crimp bead to hide it. Squeeze bead tip closed over crimp bead. Wiggle hook end of the bead tip back and forth until it breaks off.

Step 2
Stringing the Beads
String beads onto the memory wire in this order: one gold seed bead, three triangle beads, one gold, one star bead, one gold, three triangles, one gold, one bugle bead, one gold, three triangles, one gold, one star, one gold, three triangles, one gold, one bugle, one gold, three triangles, one gold, one star, one gold, three triangles, one gold, one bugle, one gold, three triangle, one gold, one star, one gold, three triangles, one gold, one teardrop, one gold, three triangles, one gold, one star, one gold, three triangles, one gold, one teardrop, one gold, three triangles, one gold, one star, one gold, three triangles, one gold, one purple crystal. Repeat this pattern backwards for the other side of the choker. Finish the end with a crimp bead and a clamshell bead tip, repeating Step 1.

RING

MATERIALS

1 loop of ring memory wire, about 3-5/8" long
2 gold clamshell bead tips
2 crimp beads
4 white star beads
15 light iris transparent triangle beads
10 gold-lined seed beads, size 11°

TOOLS

Crimp pliers
Flat-nose pliers

Step 1
Attaching the Crimp Bead and the Bead Tip

Attach a crimp bead and bead tip to one end of the ring memory wire the same way as described in Step 1 of choker instructions.

Step 2
Stringing the Beads

String the beads onto the memory wire in this order: one gold seed bead, three triangle beads, one gold, one star, one gold, three triangles, one gold, one star, one gold, three triangles, one gold, one star, one gold, three triangles, one gold, one star, one gold, three triangles, one gold. Attach a crimp bead and bead tip to the end of the wire.

Wirework Rosebud Bracelet and Anklet

BRACELET

MATERIALS

11 transparent pink triangle beads, size 6°
22 transparent green seed beads, size 10°
12 jump rings (handmade or store bought; for hand
    made, see Techniques, page 28)
26-gauge silver wire, about 18″
1 silver hook-and-eye clasp

TOOLS

Round-nose pliers
Flat-nose pliers
Wire cutters

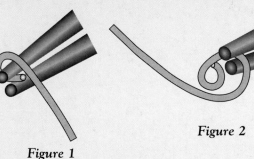

Figure 1

Figure 2

Figure 3

Step 1
Making the Wire and Bead Rosebuds

Cut a length of wire 1-1/2″ long. With round-nose
pliers grab one end of the wire, placing the wire about
1/8″ beyond the end of the pliers' nose and, using
your other hand, wrap the wire around the jaw of the
pliers forming a loop (fig. 1). Release the pliers from
the loop you just made and grab the wire just above
the loop and wrap the wire around the jaw of the pliers, moving the pliers up the wire as needed to form a
curve. Have the wire touch the loop after the curve
has been formed (fig. 2). Slip one green bead, one
pink bead and one green bead onto the wire end.
Make another loop and curve on the straight end of
the wire in the opposite direction of the first loop and
curve (fig. 3). Make 11 rosebuds (or enough to fit
your wrist).

Step 2
Attaching the Rosebuds Together
Using jump rings, attach the rosebuds together. See Techniques, page 28, on how to open and close a jump ring (fig. 4).

Figure 4

Step 3
Attaching the Clasp
Use jump rings to attach the clasp to the ends of the bracelet.

Use amber beads, the wrapped loop technique, and jump rings to create this lovely bracelet.

ANKLET

MATERIALS

15 transparent pink triangle beads, size 6°

30 transparent green seed beads, size 10°

16 jump rings (handmade or store bought; for handmade, see Techniques, page 28)

20-gauge silver wire, about 24″

1 silver barrel clasp

TOOLS

Round-nose pliers

Flat-nose pliers

Wire cutters

Step 1
Making the Wire and Bead Rosebuds
Make the rosebuds the same way as the rosebuds in the bracelet. Make 15 rosebuds (or enough to fit your ankle). You could also make more to create a choker or necklace.

Step 2
Attaching the Rosebuds Together
Use jump rings to attach the rosebuds together.

Step 3
Attaching the Clasp
Instructions for attaching the anklet clasp are the same as the bracelet instructions.

Rhinestone Necklace and Earrings

NECKLACE

MATERIALS

2 two-ring rhinestone florets
5 three-ring rhinestone florets
5 clear glass faceted teardrop beads,
    9mm x 7mm
12" fancy gold cable chain (six 1" lengths
    and two 2" lengths)
5 gold head pins
1 gold hook and eye clasp
21 gold jump rings

TOOLS

Round nose pliers
Flat nose pliers
Wire cutters

Step 1
Cutting the Chain
Using the wire cutters, cut the chain into six 1"
lengths and two 2" lengths. Set aside.

Step 2
Making the Dangles
Place a teardrop bead on a head pin. With the flat
nose pliers, make a 90-degree angle in the wire close
to the bead. Cut the wire 1/4" from the bend. With
the round nose pliers, grab the end of the wire and,
with a turning motion, bend the end of the wire into
a loop. Repeat with the other four teardrop beads for
a total of five dangles.

Step 3
Attaching the Dangles to the Florets
Attach each dangle to a 3-ring floret using a jump
ring (fig. 1).

Figure 1

Step 4
Putting the Necklace Together

Attach one end of the clasp to one of the 2" chains using a jump ring. Attach the other end of the chain to a 2-ring floret, also using a jump ring (fig. 2). Use a jump ring to attach a 1" length of chain to the other ring of the 2-ring floret. *To the other end of the 1" chain attach (using a jump ring) a 3-ring floret with the dangle at the bottom (fig. 3). Make sure the florets are facing up. On the remaining open ring of the floret, attach another 1" chain using a jump ring.* Repeat between the asterisks four times. Now attach the remaining 2-ring floret to the 1" chain using a jump ring. Then attach the remaining 2" chain to the end of the 2-ring floret. And finally, using a jump ring, attach the other end of the clasp to the chain.

Figure 2

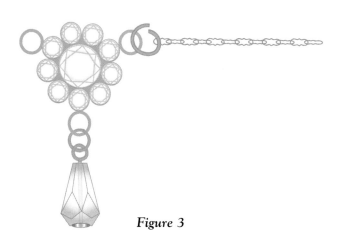

Figure 3

EARRINGS

MATERIALS

2 gold lever-back earring wires
2 two-ring rhinestone florets
2 gold head pins
2 gold jump rings
2 clear glass faceted teardrop beads, 9mm x 7mm

TOOLS

Flat-nose pliers
Round-nose pliers

Step 1
Making the Dangle

Place a teardrop bead on a head pin. Make a loop in the top of the head pin wire. See the technique section for detailed instructions. Attach the teardrop dangle onto one end of the 2-ring floret using a jump ring (fig. 4).

Figure 4

Step 2
Attaching the Earring Wire

Open the loop on the lever-back earring wire using the flat-nose pliers. Slip the loop into the ring on the floret opposite the teardrop bead. Close the loop with the pliers. Repeat Steps 1 and 2 for the other earring.

Carnelian Daisy and Chain Necklace and Earrings

This beautiful necklace was designed by Amy Gourley. She was inspired by jewelry worn in the Victorian age.

NECKLACE

MATERIALS

26-gauge gold wire, 7 feet
Figaro gold chain, 5 yards
1 gold fishhook clasp
2 fancy separator bars
15 gold jump rings
14 carnelian beads, 6mm
7 carnelian beads, 8mm
1 red glass drop bead, 1"

TOOLS

Side-style wire cutters
Chain-nose pliers
Round-nose pliers

Step 1
Making the Three Carnelian Daisies
First make the two small daisies. Use about 24" of the 26-gauge wire for each daisy. String six carnelian beads (6mm) onto the wire. Move the beads to the center of the wire. String the wire back through the first bead strung on forming a circle (fig. 1). String on one carnelian bead (6mm) and pass the wire through the fourth bead of the bead circle (this is a daisy chain stitch; see fig. 2).

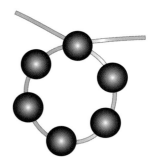

Figure 1

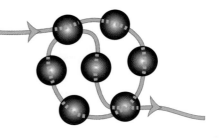

Figure 2

Make a wrapped loop (see Techniques, page 27, on how to make a wrapped loop) on each of the wire ends as close to the beads as possible (fig. 3).

Figure 3

Now make the large daisy. Use about 36" of 26 gauge wire. Repeat the directions for the small daisies only use the 8mm carnelian beads. Make only one wrapped loop and on the other end of the wire just wrap it twice around the circle wire between the two beads. Cut excess wire. Use a jump ring to attach the drop bead to the wrapped loop. Now attach a jump ring between beads two and three, and one between beads four and five (fig. 4).

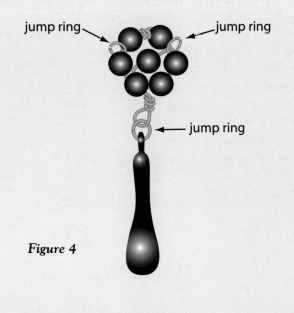

Figure 4

Step 2
Cutting the Chain and Attaching the Daisies
Cut four lengths of chain 3-1/4" long, four lengths of chain 3-1/2" long and four lengths of chain 4" long. Attach the chains with the short ones on top, medium ones in the middle and the long ones on the bottom. Use jump rings to attach the chain to all four of the wrapped loops on the small daisies and use the two jump rings already attached to the large daisy to attach the chains to the large daisy (fig. 5). Attach the end lengths of chain to the separator bars with jump rings (fig. 6). Make sure you keep the chains in the right order so they don't twist.
Step 3

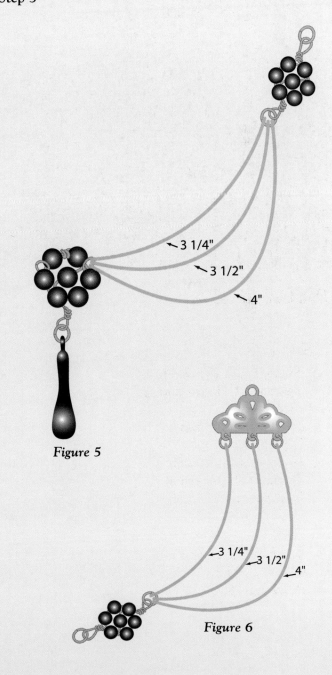

Figure 5

Figure 6

Attaching the Clasp

Use jump rings to attach the clasp to the separator bars.

EARRINGS

MATERIALS

26-gauge gold wire, 14"
2 gold jump rings
2 red glass drop beads, 1"
2 carnelian beads, 8mm
2 gold fishhook ear wires

TOOLS

Round-nose pliers
Side style wire cutters

Step 1
Making the Dangle

Cut a 7" length of 26-gauge wire. String on one carnelian bead (8mm) and move the bead to the middle of the wire. Make a wrapped wire loop on each end as close to the bead as possible (fig. 7). Attach a red drop bead to one of the wrapped wire loops using a jump ring.

Figure 7

Step 2
Attaching the Ear Wire

Using round-nose pliers, open the loop on the end of the ear wire. Slip the wrapped loop that doesn't have the drop bead on it into the loop of the earring wire and close the loop with the round-nose pliers. Repeat Steps 1 and 2 for the other earring.

Red Glass Beads and Wire Necklace and Earrings

NECKLACE

MATERIALS

2 red faceted teardrop beads (with the hole running down through them), 7mm x 5mm

1 smooth red glass teardrop bead, 13mm x 8mm

24 round faceted glass beads in various shades of red to orange, 5mm

34 round faceted glass beads in various shades of red to orange, 4mm

52 round faceted glass beads in various shades of red to orange, 3mm

7 gold head pins, .025″

18 gold eye pins (you might want to get extras just in case), .021″

2 gold jump rings

1 lobster claw clasp

1 length of 24-gauge gold wire, 2″

TOOLS

Round-nose pliers

Flat-nose pliers

Wire cutters

Step 1
Making the Beaded Crescents

Use darker beads for the middle of the necklace and then use lighter and lighter beads as you get toward the back of the necklace. Place one of each of the following, in the sequence given, onto an eye pin: 3mm bead, 4mm bead, 5mm bead, 4mm bead, 3mm bead. Bend the end of the wire at a 90-degree angle using the flat-nose pliers as close to the beads as possible.

With the round-nose pliers, grab the wire as close to the bend as possible and wrap the wire around the jaw of the pliers to form a loop the same size as the eye pin loop. (The round-nose pliers are tapered, so find a place on the pliers that is the same circumference as the eyelet on the eye pin and make the loops at this same spot every time—or you could use coil pliers.) Slide another eye pin into the loop you just made and cut the excess wire from the loop and close the loop with pliers (fig. 1). Using your fingers, bend the eye pin with the beads on it into a crescent

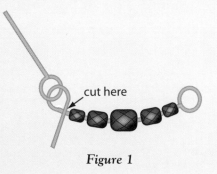

cut here

Figure 1

shape. Continue in this manner until you have eight beaded crescent shaped eye pins. Don't close the loop of the last crescent; set aside. Now make one more chain of eight beaded crescent shaped eye pins. Remember to leave the loop open on the last crescent.

Step 2
Making the Dangles
To make the center dangle place the 13mm smooth teardrop, and one round 15mm bead onto a head pin and then form a loop and close it. (See Techniques, page 27.) Set aside and then make the two side dangles. Place a 7mm faceted teardrop bead and three round 3mm beads on a head pin, form a loop, but leave it open. Make one more. Set aside. There are four more dangles: Two with one 5mm bead and two 3mm beads on a head pin and two dangles with one 5mm bead and one 3mm bead on a head pin. Make the loops on these four, but don't close them. Set aside.

Step 3
Making the Center Double Crescent
To make the center double crescent, attach an eye pin to the open eyelet end of one of the eight crescent chains. Also on this eye pin, attach one of the four bead faceted teardrop side dangles. Close the loops and make sure the dangle is attached under the crescent (fig. 2). At the straight end of the eye pin

attach a length of 24-gauge wire about 2" long by twisting the 24-gauge wire twice around the eye pin. Clip any excess wire (fig. 3). On the eye pin, place three 3mm beads, one 5mm bead, the center dangle with the smooth teardrop bead, one 5mm bead, and three 3mm beads. Form the beaded eye pin into a crescent, being careful not to let the beads slip off the end of the eye pin. Take the 24-gauge wire and put on one 3mm bead, one 4mm bead, one 5mm bead, one 4mm bead, and one 3mm bead. Now wrap the end of the 24-gauge wire twice around the eye pin just above the beads. Cut the excess 24-gauge wire and in the eye pin make a loop right above the wrapped 24-gauge wire. Close the loop. Now slip the open loop of the other four bead faceted teardrop dangle into the eye pin loop just made, and then slip the open loop of the other eight crescent chain onto the eye pin loop just made and close the loops.

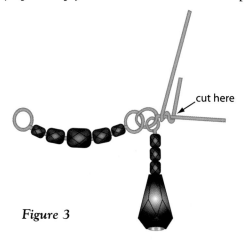

Figure 3

Step 4
Adding the Four Small Side Dangles
Attach the three bead dangles on the crescents on either side of the center double crescent. Attach the two bead dangles on the crescents on either side of the three bead dangles (fig. 4).

Figure 2

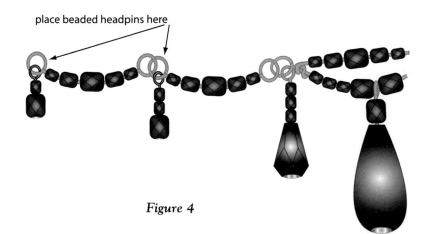

Figure 4

Step 5
Attaching the Clasp

Put jump rings on each end of the necklace and attach the lobster claw clasp to the jump rings.

EARRINGS

MATERIALS

6 red faceted teardrop beads (with the hole running down through it), 7mm x 5mm

28 round faceted glass beads in various shades of red to orange, 3mm

6 gold head pins, .025"

2 gold hoop earring wires

TOOLS

Round-nose pliers

Flat-nose pliers

Wire cutters

Step 1
Making the Dangles

Place one teardrop bead and one 3mm bead onto a head pin. Form a loop on the head pin as close to the beads as possible, cut excess wire, and close the loop with pliers. Make two. For the middle dangle, place one teardrop bead and two 3mm beads onto a head pin and form a loop, cut excess wire and close the loop.

Step 2
Stringing the Beads

Onto one of the hoop earring wires, string three 3mm beads, one two-bead dangle, two 3mm beads, one three-bead dangle, two 3mm beads, one two-bead dangle and three 3mm beads. Bend the end of the hoop up at a 90-degree angle so it will fit into the hole on the other end of the hoop. Repeat for the other earring.

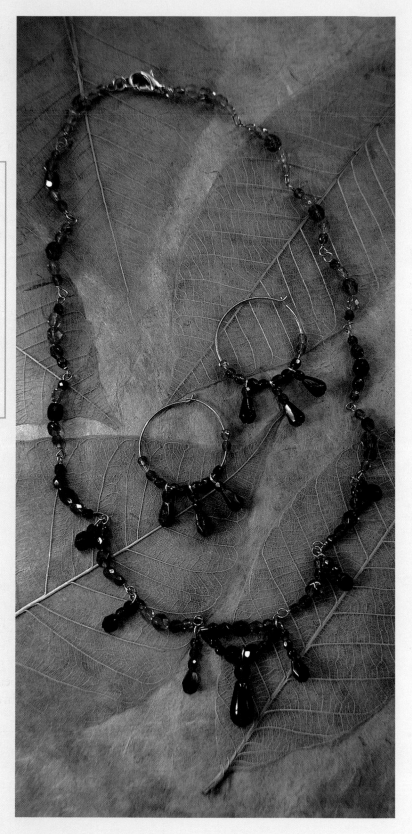

Jump Ring Netted
Necklace and Bracelet

This necklace is composed of 53 beaded eye pins connected by jump rings.

NECKLACE

MATERIALS

53 matte metallic olive green seed beads, size 6°
106 dark metallic with bronze finish seed beads, size 10°
5 black metallic luster finished faceted teardrop beads, 7mm x 5mm
42 gold jump rings, 5mm
53 gold eye pins
5 gold head pins
1 gold lobster claw clasp

TOOLS

Round-nose pliers
Flat-nose pliers
Chain-nose pliers
Wire cutters

Step 1
Making the Beaded Eye Pins
Slip one size 10° seed bead, one size 6° seed bead and one size 10° seed bead onto an eye pin. Using the flat-nose pliers, bend the straight wire above the beads at a 90-degree angle. Next, make a loop as follows: With the round-nose pliers, hold the wire as close to the bend as possible and, with your fingers or the chain-nose pliers, bend the wire around the top jaw of the pliers, pulling tight (fig. 1). Make sure the loop is the same size as the eyelet on the other side. Cut the excess wire and close the loop with round-nose pliers. (Determine where on the round-nose pliers it is the same diameter as the eyelet on the eye pin, and wrap the wire around the same spot every time you make a loop.) Make 53.

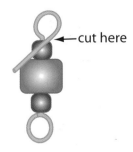

← cut here

Figure 1

Step 2
Constructing the Main Chain of the Necklace

Open a jump ring (see Techniques, page 28, for how to open and close a jump ring), and slip the loops from two beaded eye pins onto the jump ring. Close the jump ring. Now open another jump ring and slip it onto the other loop of one of the attached beaded eye pins. Pick up another beaded eye pin and slip one of its loops onto this jump ring also. Close the jump ring (fig. 2). Continue adding a beaded eye pin to the chain until you have eleven attached beaded eye pins. To one end of the chain attach a jump ring and two beaded eye pins. Close the jump ring. Allow the first beaded eye pin to dangle and the other eye pin will be used for the main chain. Attach a jump ring with three beaded eye pins to the empty loop of the eye pin that isn't dangling (the main chain one). Close the jump ring. Allow the first two beaded eye pins to dangle and use the third one as the main chain (fig. 3). * Attach a jump ring with three beaded eye pins to the empty loop of the main chain eye pin. Allow two beaded eye pins to dangle and use the third one as the main chain eye pin.* Repeat between asterisks four more times. Next add two beaded eye pins to a jump ring and the jump ring to the main chain eye pin. Allow one eye pin to dangle like the one at the beginning and use the other one as the main chain. To this main chain eye pin attach, with jump rings, 11 more beaded eye pins. The main chain is now finished.

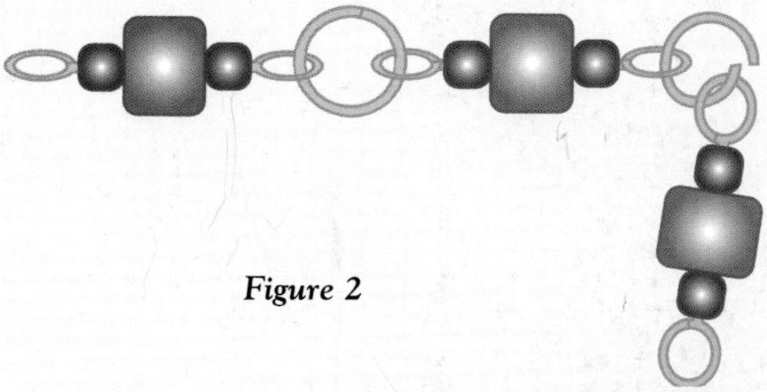

Figure 2

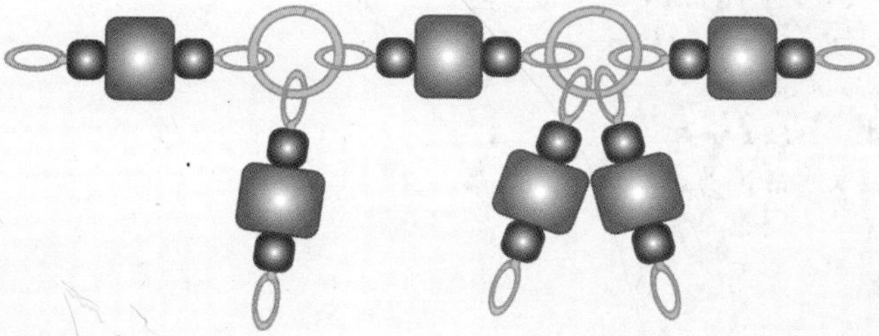

Figure 3

Step 3
Making the Five Teardrop Dangles

Put a teardrop bead onto a head pin and make a loop at the end as close to the top of the bead as possible. Make five and set aside.

Step 4
Row Two

Open a jump ring and place one of the teardrop dangles onto it. Connect the first two dangling beaded eye pins on the main chain with the jump ring with the teardrop dangle on it. Close the jump ring. Open another jump ring and slip a beaded eye pin onto it. Connect the next two dangling beaded eye pins with this jump ring (fig. 4). * Open another jump ring and slip two beaded eye pins onto it and then use this jump ring to connect the next two eye pins dangling from the main chain. Close the jump ring.* Repeat between asterisks twice. Then open another jump ring and slip on one beaded eye pin; use this jump ring to attach the next two beaded eye pins dangling from the main chain. Close the jump ring. Open another jump ring and slip one of the teardrop dangles onto it and use this jump ring to connect the last two beaded eye pins dangling from the main chain. Close the jump ring.

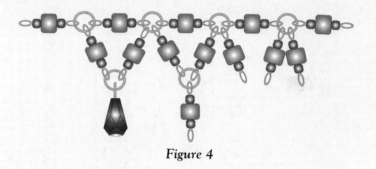

Figure 4

Step 5
Row Three

Open a jump ring and slip one of the teardrop dangles onto it, then use this jump ring to connect the first two dangling beaded eye pins from Row 2. Close the jump ring. * Open another jump ring and slip on one beaded eye pin, and use this jump ring to connect the next two dangling beaded eye pins from Row 2. Close the jump ring. * Repeat between asterisks once. To connect the last two beaded eye pins dangling from Row 3, use a jump ring with a teardrop dangle on it.

Step 6
Row Four
Open a jump ring and slip on the last teardrop dangle. Use this jump ring to connect the two dangling beaded eye pins from Row 3. Close the jump ring.

Step 7
Attaching the Clasp
Attach the clasp ends to each end of the necklace using jump rings.

BRACELET

MATERIALS
14 matte metallic olive green seed beads, size 6°
28 metallic dark with bronze tinge seed beads, size 10°
5 black metallic luster finished faceted teardrop beads, 7mm x 5mm
15 gold jump rings, 5mm
14 gold eye pins
5 gold head pins
1 gold lobster claw clasp

TOOLS
Round-nose pliers
Flat-nose pliers
Chain-nose pliers
Wire cutters

Step 1
Making the Beaded Eye Pins and the Five Teardrop Dangles
Make 14 beaded eye pins the same way as in Step 1 of the necklace. Make five teardrop dangles the same way as in Step 3 of the necklace.

Step 2
Making a Beaded Eye Pin Chain
Using jump rings, make a chain with three beaded eye pins.

Step 3
Constructing the Bracelet
* Put a teardrop dangle and a beaded eye pin onto a jump ring. Connect this jump ring to the three beaded eye pin chain. Let the teardrop dangle, then on the beaded eye pin attach another eye pin with a jump ring * (fig. 5). Repeat between the asterisks four times then add one more beaded eye pin.

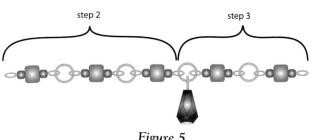

Figure 5

Step 4
Attaching the Clasp
Attach the clasp ends to each end of the bracelet using jump rings.

Resource List

Fire Mountain Gems
#1 Fire Mountain Wy., Dept. F036
Grants Pass, OR 97526-2373
(800) 423-2319 INFO
(800) 355-2137 ORDER
(800) 292-3473 FAX

www.firemountaingems.com

General Bead
317 National City Blvd.
National City, CA 91950
(619) 336-0100
(800) 572-1302 FAX

www.genbead.com

Creative Castle
2321 Michael Dr.
Newbury Park, CA 91320
(805) 499-1377

www.creativecastle.com

Kandra's Beads
570 Higuera St., Ste #125
San Luis Obispo, CA 93401
(800) 454-7079

www.kandrasbeads.com

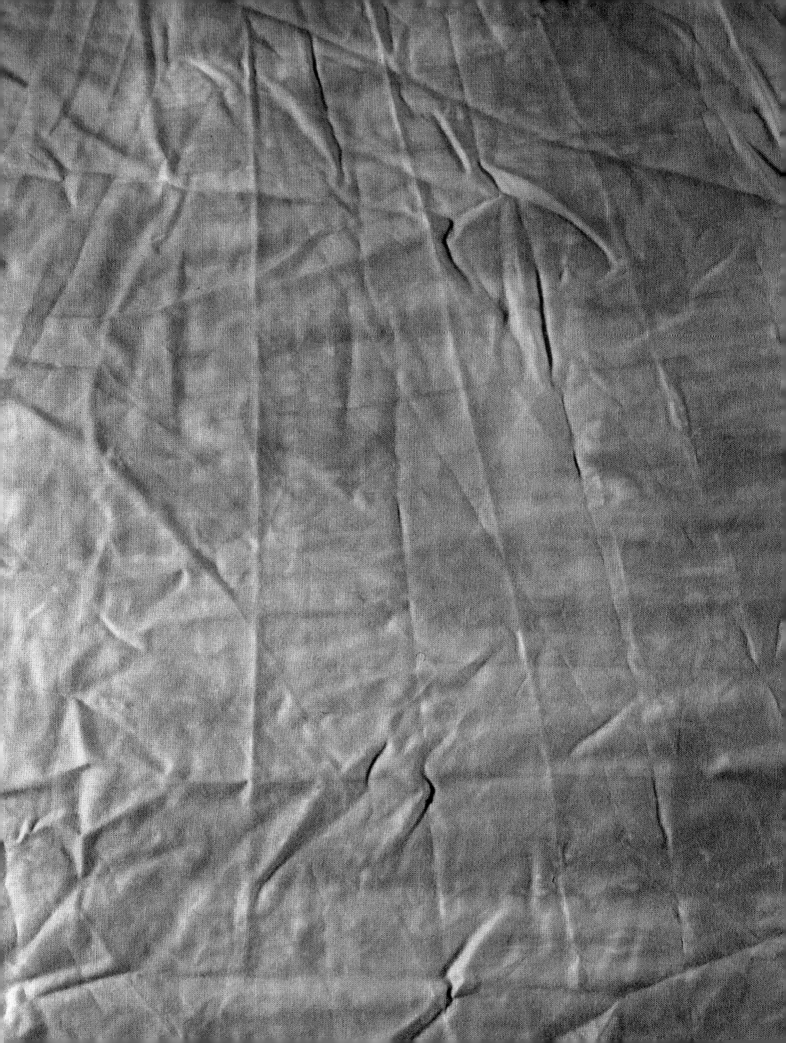

BEADED
Adornment

JEANETTE SHANIGAN

Acknowledgments

Many thanks to my beading students both past and present for being such willing "guinea pigs." Thank you to the Theiners for allowing me to teach at Frontier Imports. To Marcia for her extra help in chasing down just the right beads. Special thanks to my family -- Gordon, Donnavon and Shawn -- for their continued support and tolerance of my "bead habit"!

Like most beadwork artists, I have many books about beadwork. The books listed below, no doubt, influenced my techniques:

Blakelock, Virginia,
   Those Bad, Bad Beads
DeLong, Deon,
   Techniques of Beading Earrings
Schunzel, Veon,
   Creative Beaded Earrings
Starr, Sadie,
   Beading with Seed Beads, Gem Stones and Cabochons
Taylor, Carol,
   Creative Bead Jewelry
Wells, Carol Wilcox,
   Creative Bead Weaving
Williams, Gini,
   Beadz

I recommend these books for additional information and inspiration.

INTRODUCTION

I have intended for this book to be for the beginner *and* the experienced bead artist. Six of the most common beadwork techniques are clarified and illustrated. Each technique explanation precedes three to six projects. The projects vary in difficulty and complexity, the first project in each section being the easiest.

Like all beadwork artists, I have developed my own preferences, prejudices and idiosyncrasies. For example, I do not wax my thread; I am an ardent fan of Japanese beads, especially Delicas/antiques, I refuse to use plastic beads -- too tacky.

I firmly believe that if I intend to spend hours completing a piece, I ought to use materials that will enhance my labors. Who knows? Maybe I am creating a family heirloom or a great work of art! Although I have some personal opinions, I don't profess to have the definitive answers on the art of beadwork. Instead, I encourage you to find your own revelations through trial and error.

Beginners often seem disappointed with the caliber of their beadwork. This is always a surprise to me. Every other skill requires hours, even years of practice to achieve competency. Why shouldn't beadwork? It may be necessary to make several versions of the same project before the bead artist feels it is "perfect." Actually, Native Americans have the right idea with their spirit bead concept. The spirit bead is an *intentional* mistake in the beadwork to remind humankind that mere humans cannot expect to achieve perfection. So, don't focus on the mistakes; look at the skills attained and practice, practice, practice.

Finally, many of the illustrated examples appear very loose. Meaning, there is too much thread showing between the beads and stitches. This was necessary to show the movement of the needle and thread. Pull the beadwork tight while working, with little or no thread visible. Note: The abbreviation "N&T" means "needle and thread."

CONTENTS

PEYOTE STITCH TECHNIQUES - 216

SPLIT-LOOM TECHNIQUES - 234

GALLERY OF BEADWORK BY ALASKAN ARTISTS - 248

PART ONE
MATERIALS

JOHN JAMES

Beading
Aiguilles à Perles
Aufreihnadeln

Article No.
L4320

Size
No   10

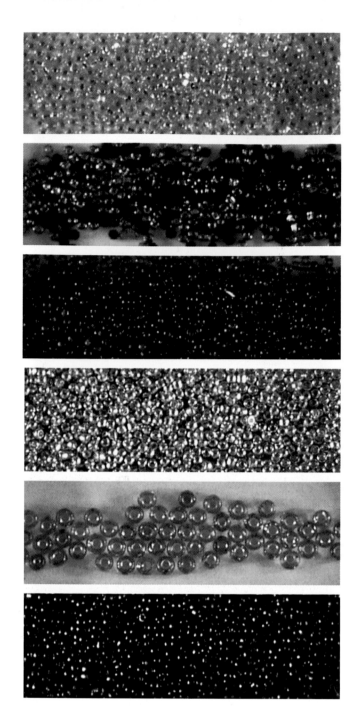

MATERIALS

Certain materials are essential to the beadworking process. This section describes materials necessary for general beadwork, as well as those required for the projects in this book. Note that there is a list of specific, required materials at the beginning of each project.

BEADS

Beads come in a variety of shapes, sizes, colors and finishes. Beads may be made of glass, gemstones, metals, wood, shells, bone, clay or porcelain. The possibilities are endless. Regardless of the type of bead, a good rule of thumb is to purchase the best quality bead that you can afford. High quality beads will be more uniform in size, the holes will be larger and consistent in size and any surface finishes will be more durable. The classification of beads used in this book are: seed beads and accent beads.

SEED BEADS

I recommend Japanese or Czech seed beads for these projects. If given a choice between the two, choose the Japanese seed beads. The holes tend to be larger and sometimes that's a necessity, rather than a luxury. It is also important to consider surface finishes and glass types when selecting seed beads. Some beads tend to recede (transparent, matte), while others stand out (opaque, silver-lined, gilt-lined, iridescent, metallic) visually in the design. Achieve the best results by using bold and subtle beads. When selecting beads, consider both the accentuated design areas and colors. Color is another aspect to consider when selecting seed beads. Frankly, some people have a natural knack for selecting colors, while others could use a thorough course in color theory. Often the colors in the cabochon or accent beads can be an invaluable guide. Those selling their beadwork may want to consider Americans' favorite colors: blue, red, green, white, pink and purple. Sometimes, dare to be radical in your color selections; the results may be surprising!

ACCENT BEADS

A variety of beads, including Austrian Swarovski crystals, Czech glass, gemstone, Peruvian ceramic, wooden and mother-of-pearl, are to accent the beadwork. As with seed beads, consider quality, color and composition when selecting accent beads. Some patience and perseverance may also be necessary. Finding just the right accent bead is equivalent to finding just the right accessories for a new outfit. It takes time.

NEEDLES

I recommend English beading needles in sizes 10, 12 and 13. Provided that you use good quality beads, these needles should work for all projects. Use a larger size 10 needle when sewing through leather or UltraSuede. I suggest long 12's for loom beading.

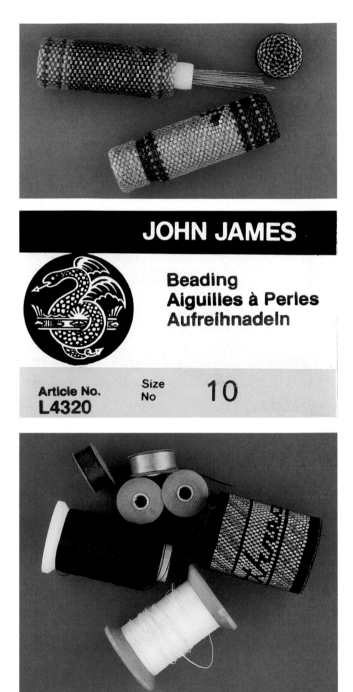

JOHN JAMES

Beading
Aiguilles à Perles
Aufreihnadeln

Article No. **L4320**   Size No   **10**

THREAD

I recommend Nymo™ thread in sizes **B** and **D**. Some people advocate Kevlar™ thread, but watch out; it can cut itself. Buy the largest quantity of thread available. Thread wound on bobbins tends to knot, twist and tangle more than thread wound on cones. When threading the needle, begin threading with the first end off the cone, then cut to the appropriate length. A good length for beginners is 4-6 feet. To avoid adding thread and/or dealing with knots, experienced beadworkers may want to use more in some situations.

WAX

"Knot gremlins" are a reality in beadwork! People use a variety of techniques to avoid those undesired, dreaded knots that mysteriously appear. Some people use beeswax or candle wax to wax the thread. Others prefer to become adept at removing knots and use nothing, which eliminates wax residue. Still others take the middle road and use a thread conditioner, such as Thread Heaven™. Some people even press thread with an iron. Only trial and error will determine a personal knot solution.

FELT vs. INTERFACING

Felt is available in a wide range of colors and I suggest using it with the back stitch. Some people prefer interfacing (pellon), but it is only available in black and white. A good compromise is fusible interfacing ironed to felt.

SUEDE LEATHER vs. ULTRASUEDE™

I suggest a lightweight leather, but UltraSuede also works. Although leather is a bit more stiff, both seem equally difficult to sew, but using a size 10 needle helps.

CLEAR NAIL POLISH

Any inexpensive brand will do. I use nail polish to set knots, strengthen frayed thread and stiffen beadwork. Because it contains acetone, nail polish can affect surface finishes on beads. Always check for colorfastness before using polish!

GLUE

I recommend Bond 527™ for several reasons: it is clear, thus colors will not become distorted. Bond 527 is very effective on a wide variety of materials (i.e., glass, leather, stone, etc.). Finally, a stiff bond is formed (when a generous amount is used). This bond eliminates the necessity to use a piece of plastic between the beadwork and the leather backing (as some suggest). Always allow sufficient drying time.

HINTS FOR USING PORCUPINE QUILLS

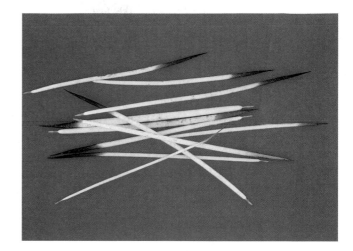

Porcupine quills add an interesting, natural touch to beadwork. However, quills do require special handling. My nieces and nephews, who live in Bush Alaska, often harvest quills from live animals for me. They use the towel trick, so as not to harm the animals. This trick is done by gently flicking a towel at a porcupine. A friend once harvested an entire road kill by stuffing it in a plastic bag, which in turn went in her freezer. Sometime later, she discovered that quills poke holes in plastic bags and the rather skunky smell had permeated her entire freezer. Dealing with frozen or fresh road kills is nasty! The moral -- don't be greedy; use the towel trick to harvest a few quills, and leave the rest for other scavengers!

ACQUISITION

Purchase porcupine quills at most bead/craft stores. "Harvest" quill from live animals or road kills. Painlessly accomplish this by gently flicking a bath towel at the animal. The quills will cling to the towel on contact. Discard any badly discolored or broken quills.

CLEANING

Natural quills are covered with animal dander and dirt and require washing before use. Soak the quills in a mixture of warm water and dishwashing detergent. Rinse well in warm water and dry on paper towels.

CUTTING

While the quills are still damp and flexible, cut off both sharp ends. Be careful! Trim ends away from your face and body. You might do the actual trimming inside a *clear* plastic bag or directly over the trash receptacle. Quills embedded in skin are painful and may cause infection.

STORAGE

Store quills in an airtight container. Keep container out of strong, direct light or sunlight.

USE

Cut the quills to the desired lengths. Use size 13 needles and **B** thread. Simply push the needle through the pithy center of the quill.

DYEING

Use a whole package, of commercial Rit-dye,™ to one or two quarts of water. Depending on desired color intensity, simmer quills for 15-30 minutes. Rinse quills in cold water.

FRAGILITY

Quills are extremely fragile and require TLC. To prevent splitting, coat the ends of the quills with clear nail polish. It helps to preserve the quills by applying a light coating of clear nail polish over their entire length. I do not recommend quills for an item that will endure a great amount of wear and tear, such as a belt buckle.

EQUIPMENT

Possessing the right tools will contribute to the pleasure in beadworking. It's handy to store these items in a "toolbox" (cookie tin, plastic container, tackle box). When people ask me where I store my equipment and beads, I laugh and say "a bedroom." I do also have a large tackle box with three removable, compartmented utility boxes that I take on trips to shows, classes, etc. Since I store my beads in the same utility boxes, it's easy to interchange them. Actually, the storage system seems to be an indicator of the level of addiction! Beginners often use something handy, such as cookie tins. The moderately hooked will spend money on a storage system, i.e., a tackle box. The true addicts take over the spare bedroom and label it a studio and/or begin lobbying for an addition to the house.

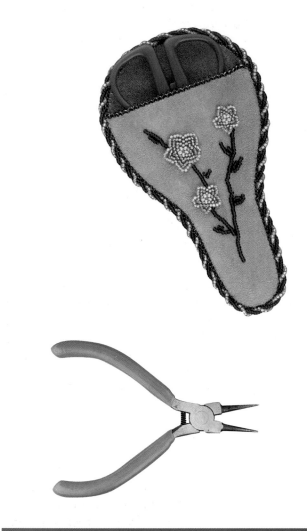

SCISSORS

A good, sharp pair of scissors is essential. Almost any scissors will cut thread, but leather and felt require a sharp pair.

NAIL CLIPPERS

These are ideal for trimming thread or soft flex wire close to the beadwork.

PLIERS

A pair of needle-nose pliers is a necessity. If you live in an all-male household, purchase the daintiest, most delicate, pink-handled pliers available. Otherwise, pliers will "turn up" missing or greasy! As the budget allows, purchase round-nose pliers, crimping pliers and wire cutters, which are useful additions to a toolbox.

BEAD TRAYS

During the beadworking process, a "bead palette" will be essential. Some people make piles of beads on a piece of leather. Others use ceramic watercolor palettes. Still others recycle metal lids from jars, or plastic lids from potato chip, nut or yogurt containers. Another option is a plastic six-compartment tray, with lids and pouring spouts, designed especially for beads. Whatever your preference, check the depth of the container. If it is too deep, it will be difficult to pluck beads from the tray.

COLORED MARKERS

These are useful for coloring obvious threads, or designs and patterns.

RULER

Accurate measurements are a must. Usually a six-inch ruler is sufficient.

POST-IT-NOTES

These are superb for marking places on patterns. It is a good idea to note the individual bead colors on the post-it-note. For example, you will determine color **A** at a glance.

LOOM

Purchase or make a loom to create the loom beading. This loom can be easily constructed and will work nicely for the necklaces in this book.

One 25" x 7" x 3/4" board (base)
Two 4" x 7" x 3/4" boards (sides)
Eight wood screws (1 1/2-inch long)
Two medium nails (1 1/2-inch long)
Two 6-inch springs
Four wood screws (1/2-inch long)

Pound each nail into the exact center of the sides. The nail should protrude about 1 inch. Fasten the sides to the base with the longer wood screws. Attach the springs to the top of the sides with the shorter wood screws. If desired, sand the edges a bit.

WORK AREA

The location where a bead artist chooses to work is a matter of personal preference. Some artists prefer to work at the kitchen table. Others work in the living room and enjoy "quality time" with family members. Some artists enjoy a workroom or a studio. Some even bead in bed, and later tell hilarious stories of spouses waking up with stray beads embedded in cheeks, etc.! Regardless of the site, a few amenities will make the work area more productive.

LIGHTING

Adequate lighting is reasonably the most important consideration. Most desirable is a combination of natural and artificial light. Tired, strained eyes quickly turn beadwork into drudgery!

BEAD STORAGE

There are several possibilities for bead storage: fishing tackle boxes, embroidery floss organizers or cookie tins. Store beads in small, individual plastic bags within the larger containers. If purchasing beads on hanks, always remember to immediately retie the strings at the top. It's also nice to have a cabinet just for storing bead paraphernalia.

MAGNIFYING GLASS

Some people, especially beginners, discover that a magnifying glass is a necessity for threading beading needles or working with tiny, tiny beads. Others discover that the difficulty is not caused by the size of the beads and needles, but that a trip to the eye doctor has been too long procrastinated! Beadworking is definitely not an art in which there is room to be vain about wearing corrective lenses!

HAND VACUUM

Kids spill 'em, pets spill 'em, spouses spill 'em, even bead artists spill beads. A hand-held vacuum is a good way to retrieve the beads quickly and easily.

LAP TRAY

Look for the type with a pillow attached to the tray. These are remarkably stable and make beadworking possible during long vehicle trips or while commuting.

PART TWO
BACK STITCH
TECHNIQUES

BACK STITCH TECHNIQUES

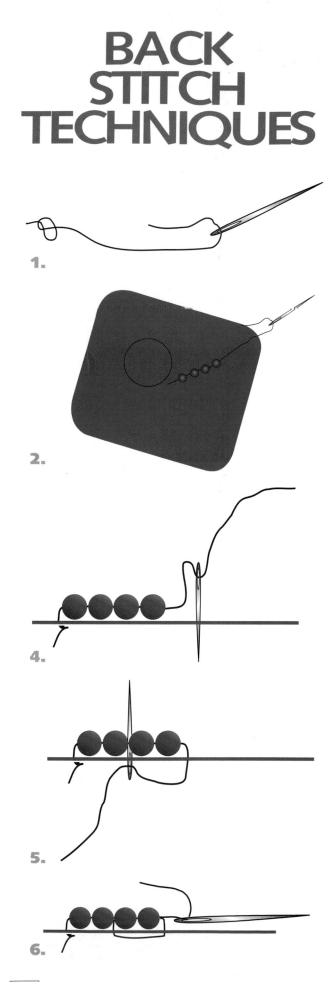

1.

2.

4.

5.

6.

Of all the beadworking stitches in this book, back stitch is most like hand-sewing or embroidery. It is often referred to as bead embroidery. The beads are initially sewn to some kind of fabric (felt, pellon or ultra-suede), then the beadwork is backed with leather or ultra-suede to hide the threads of the back stitching.

1. Thread the needle (size 12 or 13) with a single strand of **B** thread. Tie a knot in the end.

2. Bring the N&T from the back of the felt to the front, about half the width of the bead diameter from the cabochon or the last row of beads.

3. String four beads and push the beads down next to the point where the thread exits the felt.

4. Pass the N&T back through the felt. There should be NO thread showing between the beads.

5. Push the N&T back through the felt to the front between the second and third beads.

6. Pass the N&T through the third and fourth beads.

7. Repeat instruction numbers 3-6 until completing the entire row. Note that at the end it may be necessary to string fewer than four beads.

8. After completing a row, pass the N&T through all beads in the row. Give a slight tug to even or "round out" the row. I reference this step as "encircle" in the project directions.

9. Bring the N&T to the back of the felt. Repeat instruction numbers 2-8 to do another row.

10. After completing all the rows, bring the N&T to the back of the felt and tie a knot. Trim.

ADDING NEW THREAD

Simply bring the old thread to the back of the felt and knot. Tie a knot in the end of the new thread and push the N&T from the back to the front of the felt. If adding thread in the middle of a row, bring the N&T up through the last two beads in the row, then pass the N&T through the two beads. Continue with the back stitch.

TROUBLE-SHOOTING

1. Beadwork is bumpy -- Give beads plenty of room between the cabochons and the rows -- don't crowd them. Note step 2.

2. Thread shows between the beads -- The four beads need to be snug against each other before passing the N&T to the back of the felt. The needle also needs to be flush against the fourth bead. Note step 3.

3. Cabochon/concho falls off -- Use a generous amount of glue and dry on a flat surface 8-12 hours before handling.

TWISTED-EDGE CABOCHON SET

This is a striking, yet simple way to "frame" a particularly beautiful or interesting cabochon

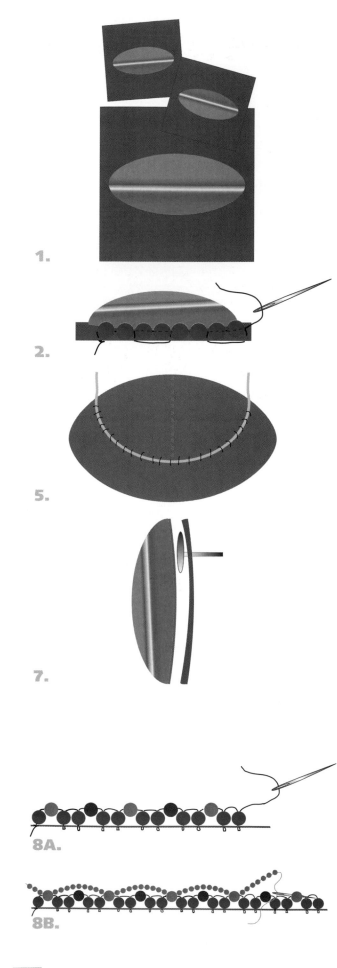

1.

2.

5.

7.

8A.

8B.

ONE 25 x 30MM CABOCHON
TWO 10 x 15MM CABOCHONS
SEED BEADS, SIZE 11, 2 COLORS
40 6MM CZECH GLASS BEADS
EIGHT 4MM CZECH GLASS BEADS
ONE 6 x 6-INCH FELT SQUARE
NYMO THREAD: B & D
NEEDLES: 10 & 12
TIGER TAIL OR SOFT FLEX WIRE, .015
LEATHER SCRAP
BOND 527 GLUE
NECKLACE CLASP
TWO EAR POSTS

1. Cut three pieces of felt: one 4x4-inch piece and two 2x2-inch pieces.

Glue the cabochons onto the center of each piece of felt and allow to dry thoroughly.

2. Use a size 12 needle and a single, knotted strand of **B** thread.

Work four rows of back stitch around the large cabochon.

Do the first two rows in color A and the second two rows in color B. Be sure to "encircle" each row; that is, pass the N&T through the entire row again.

3. Leaving a 1/16-inch edge, carefully cut out each cabochon.

4. Cut ovals out of leather, the same size as each of the cabochons.

5. Cut a 24-inch piece of tiger tail. Place and position the tiger tail on the back of the large cabochon and baste it into place. Be sure that each end is the same length and that each side of the tiger tail is equal distance from the center point.

6. Use a generous amount of Bond 527 and glue the large leather oval to the back of the large cabochon.

Dry thoroughly.

7. Sandwiching an ear post in between, glue each small cabochon to a leather oval.

Allow to dry.

8. Do the edge beading around each cabochon. Note that the twisted edge is a 3-step process, as illustrated. Use a single, knotted strand of **D** thread and a size 10 needle.

a. (3-1-2-1-2--2)

b. Make loops (7-9 beads) between the color **B** extended (point) beads.

Make loops (7-9 beads) between the color A extended (point) beads.

c. Pass the N&T from the color A point bead THROUGH the color B loop into the next color A bead point.

Tie off, clip thread and hide knot.

9. String beads on each piece of tiger tail:

one color **A**

three color **B**

one color **A**

three color **B**

one color **A**

one 4mm

one color **B**

one 6mm

one **B**

one 6mm

one **B**

one 6mm

one **B**

one 6mm

one **B**

one 6mm

one **B**

one 4mm.

Repeat pattern again.

String:

one **A**

three **B**

one **A**

three **B**

one **A.**

Ten 6mm and alternate with one **B**.

String a crimp bead and pass the tiger tail through the necklace clasp. Pass back through the crimp bead and several beads. Be sure that wire is not showing between the beads. Close the crimp bead with crimping pliers and trim off the excess tiger tail. Repeat for the other side.

8C.

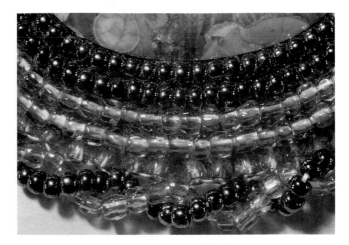

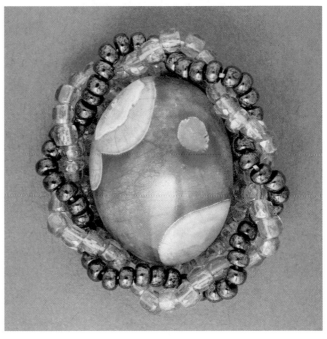

ANTIQUE-LOOK CABOCHON SET

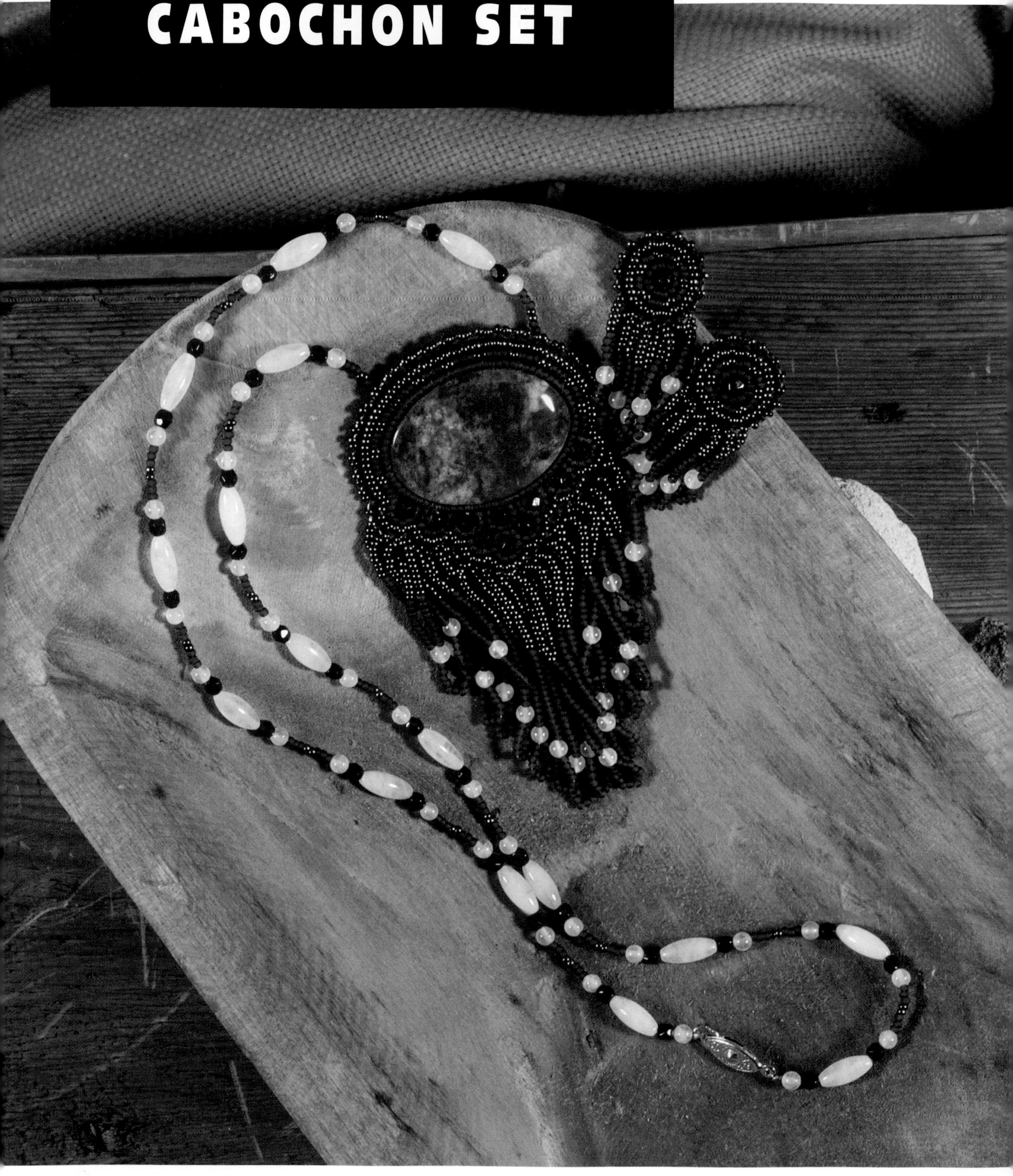

MATERIALS

BEADING NEEDLES: 10 & 12
NYMO THREAD: B & D
ONE 30 x 40MM OVAL CABOCHON
SEED BEADS, SIZE 11, TWO COLORS
44 4MM FACETED CZECH GLASS BEADS
61 4MM GEMSTONE BEADS
16 12MM OVAL GEMSTONE BEADS
ONE FELT SQUARE, 6 x 6-INCH
ONE YARD TIGER TAIL OR SOFT FLEX WIRE
TWO CRIMPING BEADS
ONE NECKLACE CLASP
TWO EAR POSTS
LEATHER SCRAP
BOND 527 GLUE

1. Cut three pieces of felt: one 4 x 4-inch piece and two 2 x 2-inch pieces.

2. Glue the cabochon in the center of the 4 x 4-inch felt square. Use a generous amount of glue and allow it to dry overnight on a flat surface.

3. Using a single, knotted strand of **B** thread and a size 12 needle, outline the cabochon with back stitch. Use seed beads, color **A**. When finishing this row and ALL subsequent rows, "encircle" the row. That is, pass the N&T once again through the entire row. This will even out the circle and reinforce the beadwork.

4. Measure the cabochon lengthwise and mark the center point on the felt. Sew a 4mm glass bead on this point next to the row of back stitching. Use back stitch to outline the glass bead on the three remaining sides with eight color **A** beads.

5. Continue adding and outlining beads in this manner on one side of the center 4mm bead. Complete four. Encircle all back stitching (as described in step 3). Add, outline and encircle three 4mm beads on the other side of the center bead.

6. Sew a 4mm glass bead below the center bead on the right. Outline it with six to seven color **A** seed beads. Repeat for the left side below the center 4mm bead. Encircle.

7. Sew a 4mm glass bead below the center bead between the two added in step 6. Outline the glass bead with five to six color **A** beads. Encircle.

8. Starting at one edge of the outlined 4mm glass beads, do back stitching to the other edge.
Pattern: three color **A**, two color **B**. Repeat.

9. Outline the entire edge with a row of color **B** back stitching.

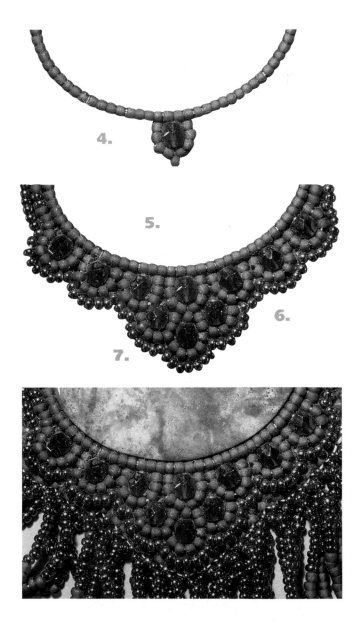

4.

5.

6.

7.

11.

12.

13.

10. Leaving a 1/16-inch edge, carefully cut out the beadwork.

11. Center the tiger tail (soft flex wire) on the back of the beadwork and baste it in place. Be sure the ends are equal distance from the center point. Glue a piece of leather to the back of the beadwork. Dry thoroughly on a flat surface. Trim away excess leather.

12. Using **D** thread and a size 10 needle, do edge beading around the beadwork. Start the edge beading approximately where the dangles will begin. If possible, use a LONG piece of thread. Complete the edge beading AND dangles without adding more thread. If desired, do the 4-3-2 edge around the top portion of the beadwork and the 3-2-1 edge around the bottom where the dangles will be located.

13. Dangles -- Bring the needle out through the desired point of the edge beading.
String:
> eight color **B**
> eight color **A**
> 4mm gemstone (or glass)
> 13 color **A** beads.

Pass the N&T through the 4mm bead and string eight color **A** and eight color **B** beads.

Pass the N&T through the next point on the edge beading. Continue adding dangles until completing 19-20.

Note that each dangles increases (or decreases) by one color **B** and one color **A**. Tie off, trim thread and hide knot between felt/leather layers.

14. String each end of the tiger tail by repeating this pattern --
> three color **A**
> two color **B**
> three color **A**
> one 4mm gemstone
> one 4mm glass
> one 1" oval gemstone
> one 4mm glass
> one 4mm gemstone.

Each side should be 12-13 inches in length.

15. String a crimping bead. Thread the tiger tail through the necklace clasp, back through the crimping bead and through two-four beads. Pull the wire tight and close the crimping bead with crimping pliers. Trim off excess wire. Repeat for the other side.

1. Sew a 4mm glass bead in the center of one 2 x 2-inch felt square.

2. Use the back stitch to outline the 4mm glass bead with three rows.

Row #1 = color **A**

Row #2 = two color **A** two color **B**

Row #3 = color **B**

3. Leaving a 1/16-inch edge, carefully cut out the beadwork. Cut a piece of leather the same size as the beadwork.

4. Placing an ear post in between, glue the beaded piece to the leather. Allow to dry.

5. Using **D** thread and a size 10 needle, do edge beading around the piece.

Start the edge beading where the dangles will begin.

6. Add dangles as in step13 above.

String:

five color **B**

five color **A**

4mm gemstone

seven color **A.**

Pass the N&T through the gemstone and string five color **A** and five color **B**.

Note that each dangle increases (or decreases) by one color B and one color A.

There should be five dangles.

7. Repeat for the other earring.

1.

4.

CONCHO MEDALLION SET

PART I: MEDALLIONS

LARGE MEDALLION

1. Using a glue gun, glue a large concho to a 4-inch felt square. Use Bond 527 glue to attach metal buttons to the felt.

2. Using **B** thread, do two rows of back stitch around the concho. Be careful to begin the second row with the placement of the single color **B** bead (centered above any two color **B** beads in row one). The intent of row 2 is to form color **B** points; if necessary, adjust the number of color **A** beads between the single color **B** beads.

First row: three color **A**, two color **B** (repeat)
Second row: one color **B**, five color **A** (repeat)

3. Sew a 6mm gemstone bead next to the second row of beads.

Outline it on the three exposed sides with ten to twelve color **A** beads.

Continue sewing gemstone beads and back stitch with seed beads until completing 12 sets.

4. Sew a color **B** crystal between each gemstone bead set.

5. Cut out the medallion. Cut close to the edge, but be careful not to cut the threads.

2A.

2B.

3B.

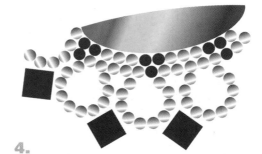

4.

159

6. Use a glue gun (or Bond 527) to glue each concho to a 3-inch felt square.

7. Back stitch a row around the concho: three color **A**, two color **B** (repeat).

8. Sew a 4mm gemstone bead next to the row of beads. Outline the three exposed sides with eight to nine color **A** beads. Continue and complete 12 sets.

9. Sew a color **B** bead between each gemstone bead set.

10. Carefully cut out the medallions.

Part II:
Dangles and Stringing

11. Cut two 30-inch pieces of tiger tail (soft flex).

12. Position the tiger tail on the back of the large medallion and attach it by basting through the felt across the tiger tail. Be sure that each side of the tiger tail is equal distance from the center point. Use Bond 527 to glue a piece of leather to the back of the medallion. Dry thoroughly on a flat surface. Trim the leather.

13. Using **D** thread and a size 10 needle, do edge beading with color **A** beads around the medallion. Start the edge beading approximately where the dangles will begin.

(3-2-2-1)

14. Bring the needle out through a point of the edge beading, string:

> three color **A**
> one color **C**
> three color **B**
> one color **C**
> one crystal
> one cylinder (bugle)
> one crystal
> one color **C**
> five color **A**
> one 6mm
> five color **A**.

Pass the needle through the:

> color **C**
> crystal
> cylinder
> crystal.

Then string:

> one color **C**
> three color **B**
> one color **C**
> three color **A**.

Pull the dangle tight and pass the needle through the next edge beading point. Continue adding until completing 13-14 dangles.

Increase (or decrease) each dangle by one color **A** and one color **B** bead.

15. String about 1 1/2 inches of beads on each piece of tiger tail. Duplicate the dangle pattern or create a new one.

16. Position the small medallions across the tiger tail and baste through the felt across the tiger tail.

17. Glue leather to the back of the small medallions. Dry thoroughly on a flat surface. Trim the leather.

18. Do edge beading around the small medallions.

19. String beads (to the desired length) on each piece of tiger tail. String a crimping bead. Thread the tiger tail through the necklace clasp, back through the crimping bead and through several beads. Pull the tiger tail tight, so there's no space between the beads. Close the crimping bead with crimping pliers and trim off the excess tiger tail. Continue until completing all four pieces.

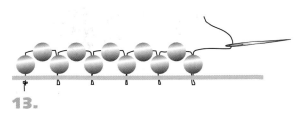

13.

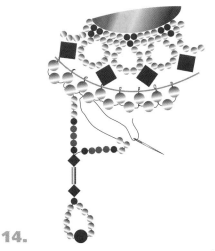

14.

PART III: MATCHING EARRINGS

Use the 5/8-inch conchos and the 3mm beads to make matching earrings. Use the small medallion pattern. Sandwich earring posts between the leather backing and the felt and glue with Bond 527 glue. Do edge beading around each medallion and add dangles, if desired.

"WOVEN" QUILL SET

MATERIALS

THREAD: NYMO B AND D
NEEDLES: 13 AND 10
80 8MM RICE BEADS
SEED BEADS, 2-CUTS, SIZE 11, ONE COLOR
EIGHT PORCUPINE QUILLS, 1 1/2-INCH LONG
6 X 6-INCH FELT SQUARE
LEATHER SCRAP
NECKLACE CLASP
TIGER TAIL OR SOFT FLEX WIRE, 1 YARD
TWO CRIMPING BEADS
TWO EAR POSTS
BOND 527 GLUE

PART I: NECKLACE

1. Clean and cut the quills. Cut the dark tips into 1/2-inch pieces. Use the remainder to cut 16 pieces that are each 5/8-inch in length. Note the hints for using quills in chapter one.

2. Cut the felt into a 4 x 4-inch piece and two 2 x 2-inch pieces.

3. Using a single, knotted strand of **B** thread and a 13 needle, sew a rice bead to the center of the large piece of felt.

4. Do three rows of back stitch around the rice bead. Be sure to "encircle" each row when finishing.

5. Sew eight pieces of the plain quill around the beadwork as indicated.

6. Sew down the remaining eight plain pieces of quill.

7. Sew on the dark-tipped quills.

8. Work three rows of back stitch around the quills.

9. If desired, sew a single bead to the felt between each set of quills.

10. Leaving a 1/16-inch edge, carefully cut out the beadwork.

11. Use the beadwork as a pattern to cut a piece of leather.

12. Fold the tiger tail in half. Smear the back of the leather with a generous amount of glue. Position the tiger tail in the center of the back. Top with the beadwork. Allow to dry on a flat surface.

13. Using **D** thread and a 10 needle, do 3-2-2-1 edge beading around the entire necklace pendant. Remember to start the edge beading about where the dangles will begin.

3.

4.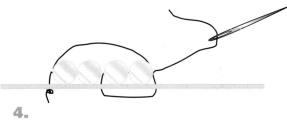

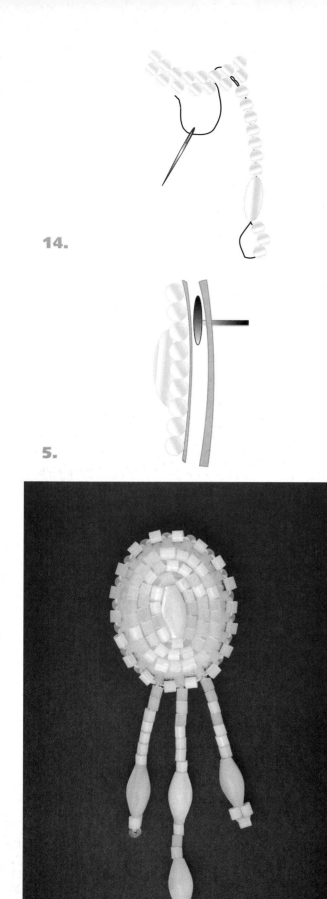

14.

5.

14. String the dangles, noting that these do NOT hang from the point beads of the edging.

String:

     seven beads

     one rice

     three beads.

Pass the N&T through the rice bead, the seven beads, as well as through the back side of the edge bead.

Pass the N&T down through the next edge bead and string another dangle. Note that each dangle increases (or decreases) by three beads and a rice bead. There should be nine dangles.

15. Tie off, trim the thread, and hide the knot.

16. String each side of the tiger tail with 22 sets of three beads and one rice bead. String a crimping bead and the necklace clasp. Pass the tiger tail back through the crimping bead and several other beads. Pull it tight and close the crimping bead. Trim the excess wire. Repeat for the other side.

PART II: EARRINGS

1. Sew a rice bead to the center of each of the 2 x 2-inch pieces of felt.

2. Do three rows of back stitch around the rice bead.

3. Leaving a 1/16-inch edge, carefully cut out the beadwork.

4. Cut a leather backing the same size as the beadwork.

5. Sandwich earring posts between the leather backing and the beadwork and glue with a generous amount of Bond 527. Dry.

6. Do edge beading around the earrings and add dangles as in instruction numbers 13-15 above. Do three OR five dangles, as desired.

BUTTERFLY CABOCHON SET

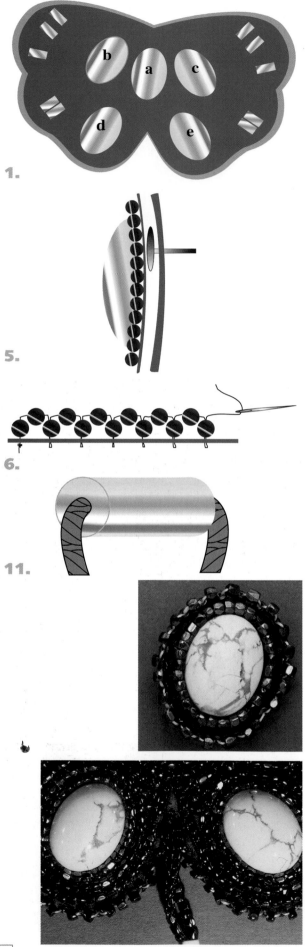

1.

5.

6.

11.

1. Cut three pieces of felt: one 4x4-inch piece and two 2x2-inch pieces.

Trace the butterfly template on the larger piece of felt.

Glue the middle cabochon (a) onto the felt as indicated.

Glue a cabochon onto each of the smaller pieces of felt. Allow to dry.

2. Use the back stitch to outline each of the cabochons. As you finish each cabochon, be sure to "encircle" the row; that is, pass the N&T through the entire row again.

3. Glue cabochons **b** & **c** onto the larger felt piece. Allow to dry.

4. Meanwhile, leaving a 1/16-inch edge, carefully cut out around each earring cabochon.

Cut two more ovals out of leather the same size as the beaded piece.

5. Sandwiching an ear post in between, glue each beaded piece to a leather oval. Dry.

6. Do 3-2-2-1 edge beading around each earring.

7. Continue with the butterfly and outline cabochons b & c with two rows of back stitching. "Encircle."

8. Glue on cabochons **d** & **e**. Allow to dry.

9. Outline cabs **d** & **e** with two rows of back stitch.

10. Use the back stitch to outline the entire butterfly shape.

11. Attach the cylinders and outline with back stitching.

12. Fill in the remaining exposed felt with back stitch. DON'T CROWD IT! Good back stitch should be flat, not bumpy.

13. Leaving a 1/16-inch edge, carefully cut out the butterfly.

14. Fold the tiger tail (soft flex) in half. Center the wire on the back of the butterfly and baste into place.

15. Glue the butterfly to a piece of leather. Dry thoroughly on a flat surface.

16. Cut out the butterfly. Starting at the lower center, use **D** thread and a size 10 needle and do 3-2-2-1 edge beading around the entire butterfly.

17. Work the dangle off two center beads of the edge beading.

String:

> 12 2-cuts
>
> one cylinder
>
> one 2-cut
>
> 6mm
>
> one 2-cut
>
> 6mm
>
> three 2-cuts.

Pass the N&T through the 6mm and the cylinder.

String 12 2-cuts and pass the N&T through the edge beading.

Take a stitch in the leather to secure, then knot and trim thread.

18. String each side of the tiger tail with 6mm, cylinders, and 2-cuts (pattern = 2-cut, 6mm, 2-cut, 6mm, 2-cut, cylinder, 2-cut) until you reach the desired length.

19. String a crimping bead. Pass the tiger tail through the hole on one end of the clasp and back through the crimping bead and at least one 6mm bead. Pull tightly, then use crimping pliers to close the crimp bead. Trim any excess wire.

*Enlarge the butterfly template, page 166, #1, by 50%, or decrease the photo, page 165, by 50%.

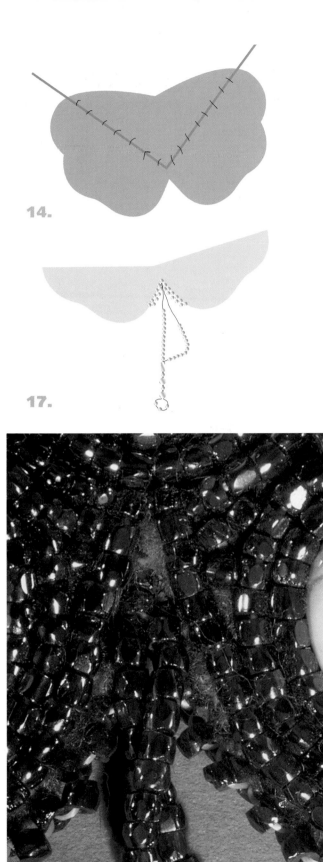

14.

17.

PART THREE
NETTING
TECHNIQUES

NETTING TECHNIQUES

Netting is a technique that results in a lacy, open weave. Netting can be done from top-to-bottom or from side-to-side and/or vertically or horizontally. The shape of the mesh and consequently, the beadwork can be changed by varying the number, size and type of beads used.

1. Begin by stringing the indicated number of beads or making a bead chain. This functions as the base row and part or all of the netting will be anchored off of this row.

2. Next, string the indicated number of beads and pass the N&T through the designated anchor bead in the base row.

3. Continue HORIZONTAL netting in this manner row-by-row until reaching the desired length. At the beginning of each new row, it will be necessary to pass the N&T through a certain number of beads to get to the first designated anchor bead.

4. Begin VERTICAL netting by stringing the entire bead length of the piece. A designated set of beads function as turn-beads. String more beads to these and anchor at various points on this row of turn beads. Finally, anchor the string to the base row.

1 & 2.

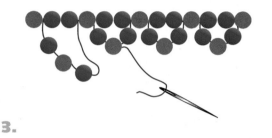

3.

ADDING NEW THREAD

Use the end of the old thread and the end of the new thread and tie a square knot as close as possible to the last bead on the old thread. Put a very small dab of clear nail polish on the knot. Put a needle on each end and work the tails into the beadwork for a half-inch or so. NEVER cut the threads at the knot! Clip off loose ends.

TROUBLE-SHOOTING

1. Thread shows in the netting -- Not enough beads were strung OR the work was not pulled tight after each bead addition.

2. Bigger holes in the mesh -- Too many beads were added or anchor beads were skipped. OR, the N&T was NOT passed through the designated number of beads to get into position to start a new row.

3. The pattern is off -- Use a post-it-note or ruler to mark each row in the pattern AND/OR remember the beginning of each new row shifts by one mesh.

NETTED CHOKER SET

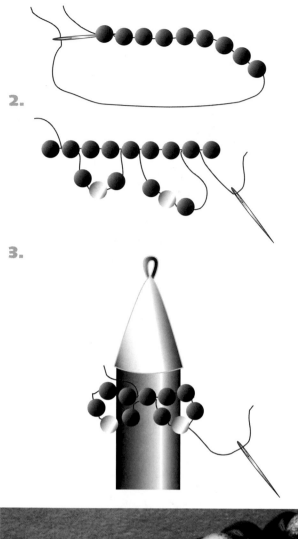

2.

3.

MATERIALS

THREAD: NYMO D
NEEDLES: 12
CORD, 5/32 IN DIAMETER, 17 INCHES LONG
SEED BEADS, SIZE 11, TWO COLORS
FOUR ROUND, FLAT SILVER BEADS, 3/4-INCH
    DIAMETER
ONE ROUND, FLAT SILVER BEAD, 1-INCH
    DIAMETER
EIGHT 4MM CZECH GLASS BEADS
TWO 6MM CZECH GLASS BEADS
FOUR HEAD PINS
TWO BELL CAPS
ONE BARREL CLASP
TWO EAR WIRES

A   **B**

PART I: CHOKER

1. Put a piece of cellophane tape on each end of the cord to prevent fraying. Cut the head off a head pin, push the pin halfway through the cord (1/4-inch from end) and twist one end of the pin around the cord several times. Push a bell cap over the other end of the head pin. Use round-nose pliers to form a loop in the head pin. Repeat for the other end of the cord.

2. Using a single, unknotted strand of thread, string nine color **A** beads.

Leaving a 6-inch tail, pass the N&T through the nine beads to form a circle.

Place the circle of beads around the cord next to a bell cap.

Tie a square knot and pass the N&T through the nearest bead.

3. String one **A**, one **B**, and one **A** bead, skip two beads and pass the N&T through the third bead.

Continue stringing one **A**-one **B**-one **A**.

Pass the N&T through every third bead until completing three loops.

Pass the N&T through the first TWO beads of the first loop.

4. Cover the entire cord with netting using this pattern:

      nine rows of **A-B-A**
      four rows of **A-A-A**

Repeat 14 times and end with nine rows of **A-B-A.**

5. Do one row of **A-A-A** netting.

Place two **A** between each center bead.

Stitch through the cord and back into the beads a couple of times to secure the beadwork.

Tie off in the beadwork and trim the thread.

6. Put a needle on the loose tail at the other end, stitch through the cord and back into the beads. Tie off.

7. Determine the location for the large-bead dangles.

Using a knotted strand of thread, sew through the cord to the location for the first dangle.

Pass the N&T through a bead, then string:

> three **A**
> one **B**
> three **A**
> Czech
> silver
> Czech
> three **A**.

Pass the N&T through the Czech, silver, and Czech.

String 3A, 1B, and 3A and pass the N&T through another bead on the choker.

Repeat for the other two dangles.

8. Tie off the thread in the beadwork and trim.

9. Attach a barrel clasp to the head pin loops.

PART II: EARRINGS

1. String a 4mm Czech, Flat silver, and a 4mm Czech bead on a head pin.

Trim the length, if necessary, then use round-nose pliers to make a loop in the head pin.

2. Attach ear wires.

NETTED BEZEL CABOCHON SET

PART I: NECKLACE

1. Use a single, unknotted strand of thread to string 64 seed beads.

Leaving a 4-inch tail, pass the N&T through the 64 beads to form a circle.

Tie a square knot and bring the N&T out the nearest bead.

2. String seven beads, skip three beads, and pass the N&T through the 4th bead of the bead circle.

Continue stringing seven beads and passing the N&T through every fourth bead until 16 points have been formed.

3. Bring the N&T out the CENTER (fourth) bead of the nearest point.

String five beads.

Pass the N&T through the CENTER (fourth) bead of the NEXT point.

Repeat 15 more times.

4. Bring the N&T out the center (third) bead of the nearest five-bead point.

Strings three beads and pass the N&T through the center bead of the next point.

Repeat 15 more times. Work this row loosely; there will be thread showing.

5. Center the cabochon on the beadwork and pull the thread to gather the beads around the cabochon. Reinforce the last netted row by passing the N&T through all the beads again. At this stage little or no thread should be showing in the last row.

6. Weave the thread to the knot, tie another square knot, dab with polish and trim.

7. Firmly press the back side of the cabochon into a leather scrap. Use the indentation marks as a pattern to cut an oval the size of the UNBEADED part of the back of the cabochon.

8. Push the tiger tail through the netting across the back of the cabochon. Position in center.

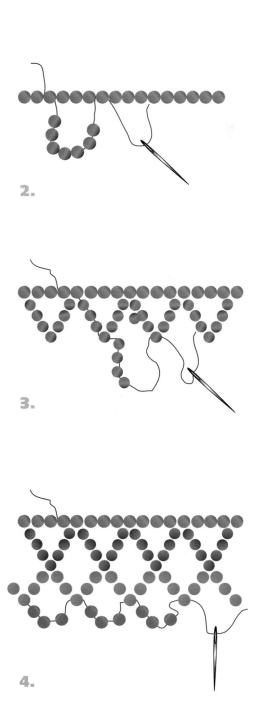

2.

3.

4.

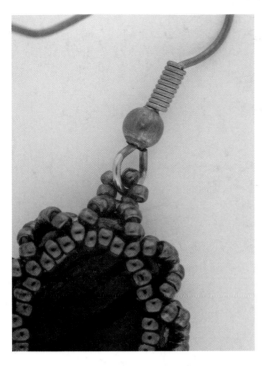

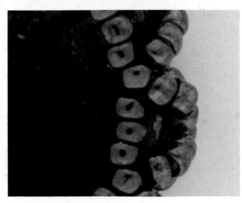

9. On one side of the tiger tail string one seed bead and one 6mm bead. Repeat this step 27 more times.

String a crimping bead and the necklace clasp.

Pass the tiger tail back through the crimping bead and a 6mm bead. Pull it tightly and close the crimping bead with crimping pliers.

Trim the excess tiger tail.

10. Repeat step 9 for the other side.

11. To hide the exposed tiger tail, glue the leather oval on the back of the cabochon.

PART II: EARRINGS

1. Make a circle of 36 beads as described in step 1.

2. Do three netted rows as described in steps 2, 3 and 4, except there will be nine points.

3. Center the cabochon in the beadwork. Be sure to center one of the points with the top of the cabochon. Continue as in step 5.

4. Weave the N&T to the single bead that connects the seven-bead and the five-bead points at the top of the cabochon.

String five beads and pass the N&T through the opposite side of the bead to form an ear wire loop.

Reinforce.

5. Weave the N&T to the knot and tie another knob. Dab with polish and trim.

6. Attach an ear wire.

7. Repeat for the other earring.

NETTED BEZEL "Y" NECKLACE AND EARRINGS

MATERIALS

NYMO™ THREAD, D
NEEDLES: SIZE 12 OR 10
THREE CABOCHONS, 15 x 20MM AND/OR
    20 x 25MM
DELICA™ BEADS: ONE COLOR (METALLICS
    CREATE A NICE CHAIN)
21 ACCENT BEADS: METALLIC, STONE,
    CRYSTAL, ETC.
TWO BEAD TIPS
ONE BARREL CLASP
TWO EAR WIRES
NOTE THAT THE NUMBERS IN PARENTHESES
    REFER TO THE LARGER CABOCHONS.

PART I: NECKLACE

1. Use a single, unknotted strand of thread.

String 32 (40) Delica beads.

Leave a six-inch tail, pass the N&T through the 32 (40) beads to form a circle.

Tie a square knot and pull the N&T out the nearest bead.

2. String five to seven beads, skip three beads and pass the N & T through the fourth bead of the circle.

Continue to string five to seven beads.

Pass the N & T through every fourth bead until eight (ten) points have been formed.

3. Bring the N & T out the **center** bead of the nearest point.

String five beads.

Pass the N & T through the **center** bead of the **next** point.

Repeat seven (nine) more times.

4. Bring the N & T out the center bead of the nearest five-bead point.

String three beads and pass the N & T through the center bead of the next point.

Repeat seven (nine) more times.

Note: Work this row loosely, thread will show.

5. enter the cabochon on the beadwork.

Pull the thread to gather the beads around the cabochon.

Reinforce the last netted row by passing the N&T through all the beads again.

Note: At this point, there should be no thread showing in the last row.

6. Weave the N&T to the centered hanger bead.
    String:
        ten Delicas
        three accent beads

2.
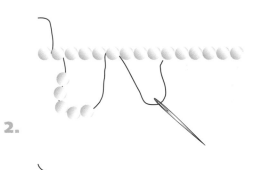

3.
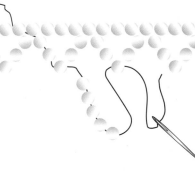

4.

ten Delicas
three accent beads
30 Delicas
three accent beads
150 Delicas
bead tip and one Delica.

7. Pass the N&T back through the bead tip and pull the strung beads taut.

Pass the N&T back through **all** the strung beads **and** through the centered bead on the cabochon.

8. String ten Delica beads and pass the N&T through the three accent beads.

9. String:

ten Delicas
three accent beads
30 Delicas
three accent beads
150 Delicas
bead tip and one Delica.

10. Pass the N&T back through the bead tip, through all the strung beads **and** the centered bead on the cabochon.

11. Weave the N&T to the loose tail and tie a square knot. Dab the knot with nail polish. Allow polish to dry and trim.

12. Attach the barrel clasp.

PART II: EARRINGS

1. Make a circle of 32 (40) beads as described in step 1 above.

2. Do three netted rows as described in steps 2, 3 and 4 above.

3. Center the cabochon in the beadwork.

Center one of the points with the top of the cabochon.

Continue as in step 5 above.

4. Weave the N&T to the single bead that connects the seven-bead and the five-bead points at the top of the cabochon.

String:

ten Delicas
three accent beads
six Delicas.

5. Reinforce the six Delicas by passing the N&T back through the six Delicas.

Note: Make sure this top loop is taut.

6. Pass the N&T through the three accent beads and string ten Delicas.

7. Pass the N&T through the center bead.

Weave to the loose tail and tie off.

Dab with nail polish, allow polish to dry and trim.

8. Repeat for a second earring.

9. Attach ear wires.

LEATHER AMULET BAG WITH NETTED BEZEL AND EARRINGS

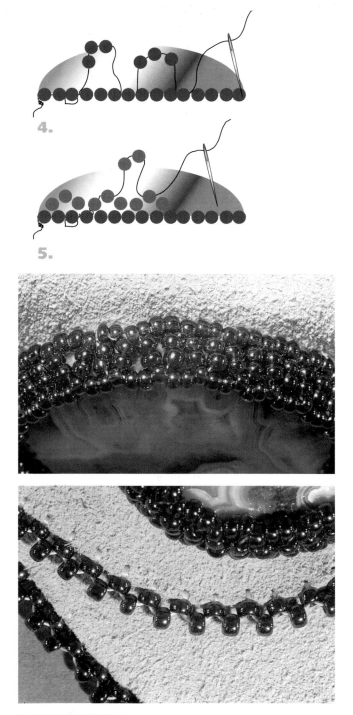

4.

5.

Part I: Amulet Bag

1. Trace the pattern on the leather scrap. Cut out the pattern pieces. See page 191 for pattern template.

2. Position the cabochon on the amulet bag flap. Lightly glue the cabochon in place.

3. Use a single strand of knotted **B** thread.

4. Work one row of back stitch around the cabochon. There should be 84 beads in this row (or another multiple of three).

"Encircle" the row.

5. Bring the N&T through any bead in the back stitch row.

String three beads and pass the N&T through the third bead.

Continue stringing three beads and passing through every third bead until there are 28 points (or the multiple divided by three).

6. Bring the N&T through the nearest center bead of a point.

String two beads and pass the N&T through the next point.

Continue placing beads between all points. It may be necessary to place only one bead between the points of the four corners. This will depend on the height of the cabochon.

7. Reinforce the two-bead row. Weave the N&T to the back-stitch row, go through the leather and tie off.

8. Form the bag by positioning the small piece of leather over the larger. Begin edge beading at the **X** and use the 3-2-1 edge to stitch the two pieces together. This also creates the decorative edge.

9. Count the number of spaces between beads, on the edge from the **X**, to the same point on the other side. This will determine the number of dangles.

10. String the dangles between the points on the edge.

String:

> 24 beads
>
> one 4mm
>
> 11 beads.

Pass the N&T through the 4mm and string 24 beads.

Pass the N&T through the next edge point.

Note: Each dangle will increase (or decrease) by two beads. Options: String mini-donut on with the 11 beads. If desired, string the three accent dangles after all the others have been strung.

Space evenly from the center and tie off.

11. Punch four holes in the leather for the necklace chain: two marks are on the pattern and two will be located next to the edge beading.

Thread one end of the soft flex wire down through the hole near the edge, then up through the next hole.

String beads (length to the next hole).

Pass the wire down through the third hole and up through the last hole near the edge.

12. String beads on the soft flex wire (pattern = your choice).

String a crimping bead and the necklace clasp.

Pass the wire back through the crimping bead and, if possible, a couple of other beads. Close the crimping bead with crimping pliers.

Repeat for the other side.

13. *Optional: Glue an oval and small pieces of leather over the back stitching and the wire on the back side of the flap. Note: This is for reinforcement and aesthetic purposes.*

PART II: EARRINGS

1. Use a single, unknotted strand of **D** thread, string six seed beads. Leave a 4-inch tail.

To form a loop, pass the N&T through all six beads.

2. String:

> 4mm glass
>
> 4mm stone
>
> oval stone
>
> 4mm stone
>
> 6mm glass
>
> 4mm stone
>
> 11 seed and one mini-donut.

3. Pass the N & T through the large beads and the six-bead loop.

4. Use the loose tail and the N & T to tie off.

Dab knot with nail polish, allow to dry and trim.

5. Repeat for the other earring.

6. Attach ear wires.

FEATHERS GALORE STRIPED AMULET BAG AND EARRINGS

MATERIALS

Nymo™ thread, D
Needle: size 12
Seed beads, size 11: two colors
Accent beads: 4mm Czech glass
    (fifty color **A**, 125 color **B**); seven large
    porcelain, glass or stone;
    twenty-one 6mm metal
20 metal feathers
Two head pins
Two ear wires

Part I: Amulet Bag

1. Use a single, unknotted strand of thread.
String 60 color **A** beads.
Use a square knot and tie the beads in a circle.
Pass the N&T through the first two beads.
Put the circle of beads around a paper roll.

2. Pick up three **A** beads, skip two beads and pass the N&T through the fifth bead (from the knot) in the circle.

3. Pick up three more **A** beads and pass the N&T through the eighth bead. Continue adding three beads in this manner until finishing the entire row.

At the end of the row pass the N&T through the **second bead** again, **and** through the **first two beads** of the first loop.

4. Pick up three **A** bead and pass the N&T through the center bead of the next loop. Continue adding sets of three beads until finishing the entire row.

At the end of the row, remember to pass the N&T through the first two beads of the first loop.

5. Follow the above row pattern.
Continue adding rows to complete the bag:
    one more row color **A**
    one row **A-B-A**
    two rows **B**
    five rows **A**
    one row **A-B-A**
    two rows **B**
    five rows **A.**

6. To close the bottom of the bag, align the center beads of each loop and stitch together.

7. **Create 19 dangles:** The N&T should come out the last center bead.
    String:
        eight **A**
        two **B**
        one **A**
        two **B**

A Czech glass
B Czech glass
A Czech glass
five B
feather
five B.

Pass the N&T back through the three Czech glass.
String:

two B
one A
two B
eight A.

Pass the N&T through the next center bead on the bottom of the bag. Continue adding each dangle in this manner. *Note: Each dangle increases (or decreases) by two A beads.*

8. **Create the closure flap**: Weave the N&T to the top row of the bag.

Pass the N&T through beads in the top row until the N&T is exiting the eleventh bead from the side.
String:

eight A
B Czech glass
metal
B Czech glass
large accent *(continued on next page)*

6.

B Czech glass
five **B**
feather
five **B**.

Pass the N&T back through all the large beads, then string eight **A** beads.

Pass the N&T through beads #15 and 14 on the top row.

String eight **A** and again pass the N&T through all the large beads, through the feather loop and back through the large beads.

String eight **A** and pass the N&T through bead #12 on the top row.

9. **String the neck chain:** Weave the N&T to the top side of the bag.

String this sequence of large beads:

Czech glass
large accent
Czech glass
metal
Czech glass
metal
Czech glass
metal
Czech glass
metal
Czech glass
metal
Czech glass
metal
Czech glass,
metal
Czech glass
large accent
Czech glass.

Czech glass = four **B-A-B-A**-four **B**
large accent = accent-**B**-metal-**B**-accent
metal = metal-**B**-metal-**B**-metal

10. Pass the N&T through the **A** bead at the other side of the bag.

To reinforce, pass the N&T through all beads in the neck chain.

11. Weave the thread into the bag and tie off.

PART II: EARRINGS

1. String:
B Czech glass
large accent
B Czech glass
metal.

B Czech glass on a head pin.
Use round-nose pliers to make a loop in the head pin.

2. Repeat for the other earring.

3. Attach ear wires.

BUGLE COLLAR SET

MATERIALS

THREAD: NYMO D
NEEDLES: 12
SEED BEADS, ONE COLOR, SIZE 11
140 12MM BUGLE BEADS
200 4MM FACETED CZECH GLASS BEADS
ONE BARREL CLASP
TWO EAR WIRES

PART I: CHAIN

1. String:

> six beads
> half of the barrel clasp
> six beads
> one 4mm bead.

Leaving a 4-inch tail of thread, pass the N&T through all the beads to form a circle.

Use the loose tail and the N&T to tie a square knot.

2. Pass the N&T through the 4mm bead.

3. String:

> four beads
> one 4mm bead
> four beads.

4. Pass the N&T through the 4mm bead in the first circle, then through four beads and the 4mm bead in the second circle.

5. Repeat steps 3 and 4 until 61 circles have been done.

6. String six beads, half of the barrel clasp, and six beads.

Pass the N&T through the 4mm bead of the 61st circle. Then pass the N&T through the next ten beads on the 62nd circle.

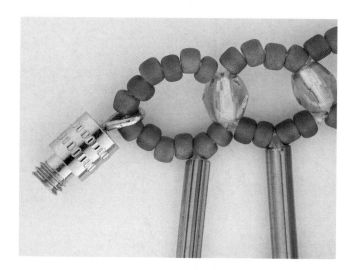

PART II: BUGLE NETTING

7. String:

> one bugle
> four beads
> one 4mm
> eight beads
> one bugle
> one 4mm
> three beads.

Pass the N&T through the 4mm and the bugle. String eight beads, one 4mm, and four beads and pass the N&T through the bugle bead.

8. Pass the N&T through the next four seed beads on the chain.

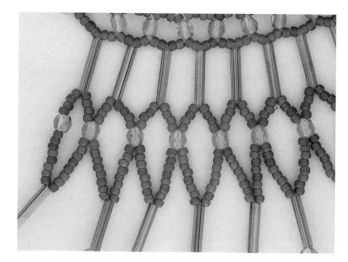

9. String one bugle and four beads.

Pass the N&T through the 4mm bead.

String eight beads, one bugle, one 4mm, and three beads.

Pass the N&T through the 4mm and the bugle.

String eight beads, one 4mm, and four beads.

Pass the N&T through the bugle bead.

10. Repeat steps 8 and 9 until netting is complete on the entire chain. Pull the beadwork tight after each addition of beads.

11. Tie off, dab clear nail polish on knots, and weave the loose ends into the beadwork.

PART III: EARRINGS
(USE THE NETTING AND THE BRICK STITCH)

1. Leaving a 4-inch tail and using an unknotted, single strand of thread, do a row of Commanche ladder with bugle beads, five bugles wide. Reinforce the row by passing the N&T back through the bugles to the first bugle.

2. String:

four beads

one 4mm

eight beads

one bugle

one 4mm

three beads.

Pass the N&T through the 4mm and the bugle.

String:

eight beads

one 4mm

four beads.

Pass the N&T through the second bugle of the bugle row.

3. Weave the N&T so it's coming out the bottom of the fourth bugle of the bugle row.

(This is easiest by simply looping through the threads at the top of the bugle row.)

String four beads and pass the N&T through the 4mm bead.

String:

eight beads

one bugle

one 4mm

three beads.

Pass the N&T through the 4mm and the bugle.

String eight beads, one 4mm, and four beads.

Pass the N&T through the fifth bugle of the bugle row.

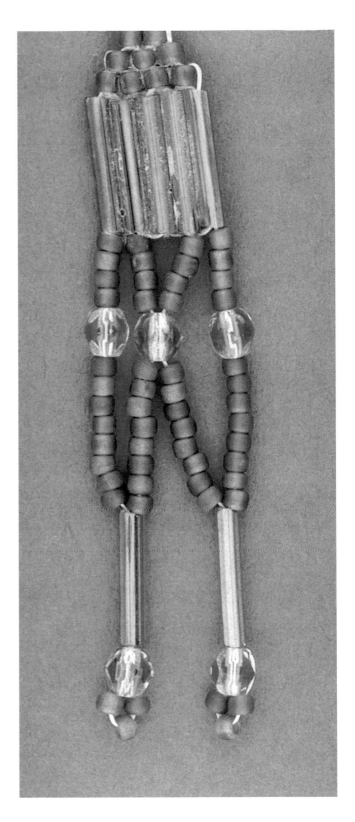

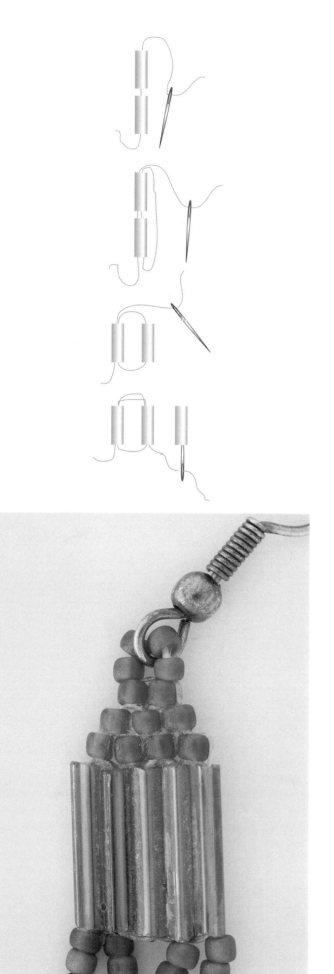

4. Be sure the netting is pulled tight, then do three rows of brick stitch.

5. To form the ear wire loop, string four beads and pass the N&T through the two top beads of the brick stitching. Reinforce by going through the loop again.

6. Weave the N&T down to the loose end and tie off.

7. Dab clear nail polish on the knot and trim.

8. Coat the BACK of the bugle row with clear nail polish to stiffen it.

9. Attach ear wires.

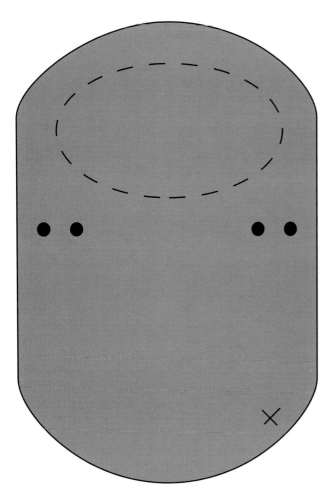

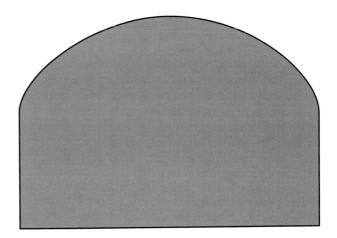

Leather Amulet Bag Template
Instructions on page 180

PART FOUR

BRICK STITCH
AND
EDGE BEADING
TECHNIQUES

BRICK STITCH AND EDGE BEADING TECHNIQUES

BRICK STITCH

Due to the popularity of the triangular earrings, brick stitch is probably the most well known of the beadworking stitches. The technique produces a flexible, versatile 'bead' fabric, which upon close inspection resembles a tiny brick wall. This technique is also referred to as Commanche weave.

1. Create the start row. This is usually the widest part of the piece. The start row is most commonly done with bugle beads or one or more seed beads:

bugle base   **single-bead base**   **double-bead base**   **triple-bead base**

This stitch is also referred to as a Commanche ladder.
a. Use a single, unknotted strand of thread.
b. Pick up two beads and pull the beads to the end of the thread leaving a 4-inch tail.
c. Pass the N&T through the first bead. Holding the tail, pull the needle until the two beads are side-by-side.
d. Pass the N&T down through the second bead.
f. Pick up another bead and pass the N&T down through the second bead.
g. Pass the N&T up through the third bead.
h. Continue adding beads in this manner until the desired length is reached.
i. Reinforce the ladder by weaving back and forth through the ladder to the first bead.

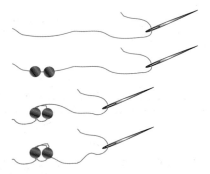

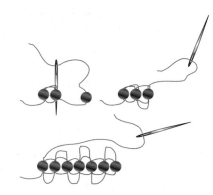

2. Do brick stitch utilizing one or both sides of the start row/Comanche ladder.
   a. Pick up one bead and pass the N&T under the first loop of thread on the start row.
   b. Bring the N&T through (bottom to top) the bead.
   c. Continue adding beads in this manner until you have used all loops of thread on the start row.

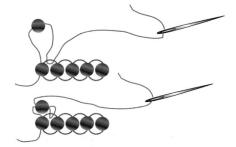

Note: brick stitch rows naturally decrease by one bead each row, thus forming a triangle.

3. To increase the number of beads in a brick stitch row, pick up two beads at the beginning of the row.

Pass the N&T under the first loop of thread and then through the SECOND picked up bead. Continue as usual across the row. At the end of the row, utilize the last loop of thread to add an additional bead.

ADDING NEW THREAD

There are two ways to add new thread. First, simply weave the old end into the beadwork, then weave in a new thread, being sure it is coming out the appropriate bead to continue brick stitching. Secondly, complete step 2a above, tie (square knot) on new thread using the old end and the new end, and do step 2b. The knot will be hidden in the bead. Weave in loose tails a bit and trim threads.

TROUBLE-SHOOTING

1. Start row is uneven -- Keep beads pulled snug together and do step 1i to snug up the beads
2. Beads sit at an angle on the start row -- Step 2b was not done
3. Threads show at the end of every other row (This is normal for traditional brick stitch).-- This is

useful in that increase beads can be attached using the end threads. Use markers to color the threads the same color as the end beads. Note: there is a weaving technique, much like increasing at the beginning of a row, that helps avoid end threads; I don't often use it because it causes the beads to sit at an odd angle.

4. **The beadwork curls** -- The tension is too loose or too tight OR the thread is too fine for the bead holes. Help avoid this by coating the back with clear nail polish and dry overnight.

EDGE BEADING

Just as the name implies, edge beading is used to finish off the edge of a piece of beadwork, especially if the beadwork is done on some kind of fabric. It may surprise some people to find edge beading lumped in with the brick stitch. Some of my students realized before I did, that simple edge beading is like brick stitch, except that the edge of the beadwork serves as the start row/Commanche ladder.

Years ago I created a kind of shorthand to help me (and eventually my students) remember how many beads to add each time. Here's an example: (3-2-2-1). The first number (3) indicates how many beads to pick up to start the edge beading. The middle numbers (2-2) indicate how many beads to add repeatedly around the beadwork. If the middle numbers are not identical, a unique pattern is being done. The last number (1) indicates how many beads are needed to finish off the beadwork. Although many of the projects suggest the simple 3-2-2-1 edge, there are many other possibilities. I have included some of those in this section. Feel free to make substitutions!

1. Always use **D** thread and a 10 or 12 needle for edge beading. The thicker thread fills the holes of the beads and the edge "stands up" better. Use a single, knotted strand of thread.

2. Push the N&T from the back side of the leather to the front side. This will hide the knot between the felt and leather layers. Take a tiny stitch through the leather and felt to the front edge of the beadwork. The needle should be flush against the last row of beads. If dangles will be added off the edge beading, always start the edge beading about where one of the outer dangles will begin.

3. String the indicated number of beads to start the edge, take a stitch through the edge (back to front), and pass the N&T through the last strung bead. Give a slight tug on the thread. Always take an adequate "bite" out of the fabric edge. The needle should be flush against the last bead row while

taking the stitch. Be careful not to catch any threads that hold the last bead row to the fabric.

4. Continue as in step 3, except pick up the number of beads as indicated by the middle numbers of the shorthand.

5. At the end, pick up beads as indicated by the last shorthand number.

Pass the N&T down through (top to bottom) the VERY FIRST bead in the edge, then through the felt/leather layers.

Pass the N&T back through the FIRST bead (bottom to top).

6. Weave into the beadwork and tie off OR add dangles. Push knot between felt/ leather layers to hide.

I do NOT recommend that a new thread be added. Start with enough to do the entire edge and even the dangles, if applicable.

1. **The first stitch is limp compared to the others.** -- It should be so, that is, until the last bead(s) is added.

2. **The spacing between the high points of the edge is uneven.** -- Practice, practice, practice. After awhile, even spacing comes naturally!

3. **The edge beading does not sit on the edge.** -- Same problem as with the brick stitch, note step 2b of brick stitch.

4. **The edge beading is loose.** -- Always give a little tug after each addition of beads.

MORE SUGGESTIONS FOR EDGE BEADING

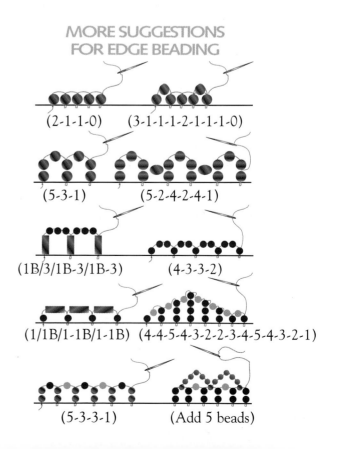

(2-1-1-0)   (3-1-1-1-2-1-1-1-0)

(5-3-1)   (5-2-4-2-4-1)

(1B/3/1B-3/1B-3)   (4-3-3-2)

(1/1B/1-1B/1-1B)   (4-4-5-4-3-2-2-3-4-5-4-3-2-1)

(5-3-3-1)   (Add 5 beads)

WILDFLOWER SET

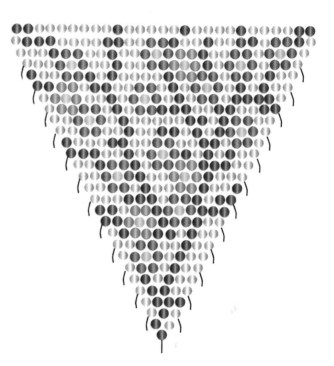

MATERIALS

BEADING NEEDLE: 12
THREAD: NYMO B
SEED BEADS, SIZE 11, 5 COLORS
43 4MM AUSTRIAN CRYSTALS
TWO EAR WIRES
CLEAR NAIL POLISH

PART I: NECKLACE

1. Start row: Leaving a 3-inch tail and using an unknotted, single strand of thread, start with a double-bead row, as illustrated below. Be sure to follow the color pattern.

2. Brick stitch single-bead rows, as illustrated. Follow the color pattern.

3. Be sure the thread is coming out the single center point bead in order to create the first dangle. String:

> 13 color **A**
> one color **C**
> one color **E**
> one color **C**
> 4mm bead
> three color **A.**

Pass the N&T through the 4mm bead, the remaining beads, and through the center point bead.

4. Weave the N&T to the next dangle point and make another dangle. Note that each dangle decreases in length by one color **A** bead. Be sure to note the locations of each dangle and continue making dangles up one side of the pendant.

5. Weave the N&T so it is coming out the outermost bead at the top of the triangle. String:

> two color **B**
> two color **C**
> two color **B** beads.

Pass the N&T through the second-to-last set in the double-bead row. Then pass the N&T through the outermost set and through the two **B** and the two **C** beads.

6. String six color **C** beads. Pass the N&Tthrough one color **C** bead, as illustrated.

7. String one color **D** bead and pass the N&T through color **C** bead #6 toward bead #7.

8. String:

> two color **B**
> two color **C**
> two color **B** beads.

Pass the N&T through color **C** beads #5 and #6 and through the two color **B** and color **C** beads, as illustrated.

9. Repeat steps 6, 7, and 8 until the flower chain is about 25 inches long. If desired, do four color **C** flowers to every one color **E** flower. Be sure to keep the beads in the chain pulled tight.

10. Attach the flower chain to the top of the other side of the pendant by stringing two color **B** beads, then passing the N&T through the appropriate double-bead set at the top edge. String two color **B** beads and pass the N&T through the other double-bead set.

Be sure the chain is NOT TWISTED!

11. Weave the N&T to the first dangle point and add dangles down the side. Note that the dangle length will increase by one color **A** bead.

12. Weave loose ends into the beadwork to secure and trim threads.

13. If desired, coat the back of the pendant with clear nail polish and allow to dry thoroughly on a flat surface. Be sure to check for colorfastness.

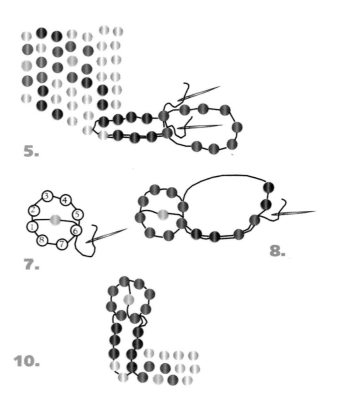

5.

7.

8.

10.

PART II: EARRINGS

1. Start row: double-bead row. Follow the color pattern.

2. Brick stitch single bead rows, as illustrated.

3. Make dangles up one side.

4. Weave the N&T to the fifth set of beads in the double-bead row.

String five color **A** beads, pass the N&T through the seventh double-bead set. Weave back through the fifth, the five beads and the seventh double-bead set to reinforce.

5. Make dangles down the other side.

6. Weave in loose ends and trim thread. Coat the back with clear nail polish, if desired.

7. Attach ear wires.

DONUT SET

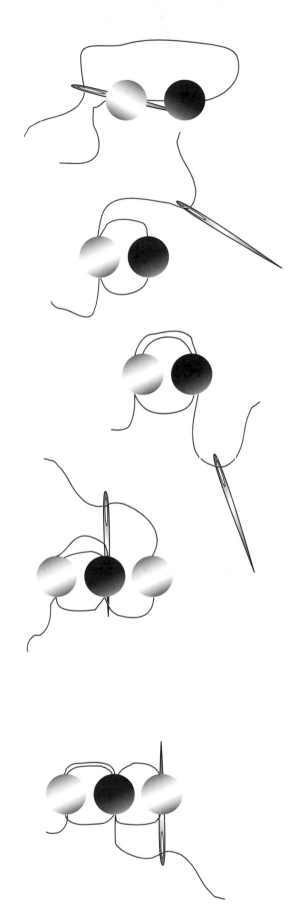

1. Use a single, unknotted strand of thread and string one **A** and one **B** Delica beads. Leaving a 3-inch tail, bring the N&T through the one **A** bead.

2. Pull the N&T until the two beads are side-by-side. Be sure to hold the thread tail!

3. Bring the N&T through the second (one **B**) bead.

4. String another 1A bead and pass the N&T through the second (one **B**) bead again.

5. Bring the N&T back through the third (one **A**) bead.

6. Continue adding beads in this manner until the entire start row is finished. Be sure to follow the pattern.

7. Reinforce the start row by passing the N&T back and forth through all the beads.

8. Pick up one **A** bead and pass the N&T under the first loop of thread on the start row.

9. Bring the N&T through the bead just picked up.

10. Pick up a one **B** bead, pass the N&T under the next loop of thread, and through the one **B** bead.

11. Continue adding beads in this manner, row by row, until the top row consists of just three beads. Each row will decrease by one bead.

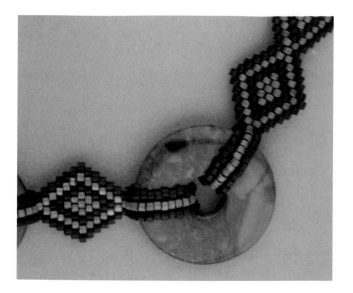

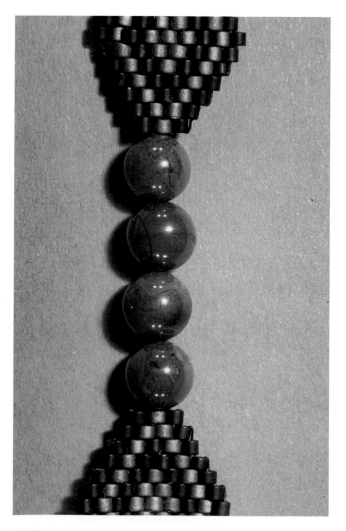

12. String 24 **A** beads, pass the N&T through the donut hole, and back through the first **A** bead.

Weave the N&T to the **B** bead, string 24 **B** beads, go through the donut hole, and back through the **B** bead. Repeat this step for the remaining **A** bead.

13. Weave the N&T back to the first bead of the start row. Turn the beadwork upside down and continue the brick stitch (instruction numbers 8-11). Be sure to follow the pattern.

14. Repeat step 12 to attach the beadwork to a second donut. Weave thread into the beadwork and trim.

15. Repeat instructions numbered 1-12 and attach the beadwork to the opposite side of the first donut.

16. Repeat step 13 and attach the beadwork (step 12) to the third donut.

17. Repeat instructions number 1-12 and attach the beadwork to the opposite side of the third donut.

18. Repeat step 13.

19. Increase EACH OF THE NEXT SIX ROWS: pick up 1A and 1B bead at the beginning of the row and pass the N&T under the first loop of thread and then through the 1B bead.

20. Continue brick stitching across the row as usual.

21. At the end of the row, stitch two beads utilizing the last loop of thread.

22. Do six rows of regular brick stitch. Be sure to follow the pattern.

23. Weave the N&T so it's coming out the center **B** bead. Remove the needle from the thread.

24. Repeat instruction numbers 17-23, but attach to the opposite side of the second donut.

25. Repeat instruction numbers 1-11, 13, 19-22 and make TWO pieces of beadwork. Weave thread into beadwork and trim.

26. Put the needle back on the donut thread and string three to six 6mm beads.

Weave the N&T through one of the beadwork pieces. The thread should exit the center **B** bead.

String eighteen to twenty one 6mm beads.

String one bead tip and a small bead.

Pass the N&T back through the hole in the bead tip and through the 6mm beads. Be sure it is tight and there is no thread showing between the beads. Weave the N&T through the beadwork again and pass the N&T through the 6mm beads again.

Weave the N&T into the beadwork attached to a donut and exit through the center B bead.

27. Repeat step 26 one or more times to reinforce.

28. Repeat steps 26-27 or the other side of the necklace.

29. Close the bead tips and attach the barrel clasp.

EARRINGS

1. Repeat steps 1-11, EXCEPT that the top row should consist of two **A** beads.

2. String six **A** beads and pass the N&T through the other **A** bead in the top row. Reinforce this loop.

3. Repeat step 13.

4. Make the dangles: string 6A beads, 6mm bead, and 3B beads.

Pass the N&T through the 6mm bead and the six **A** beads.

Pull the dangle taut and weave to the center **B** bead to make the next dangle. Each dangle increases in length by six Delica beads.

5. Weave the thread into the beadwork and trim.

6. Repeat the above steps For the second earring.

7. Attach earring wires.

8. If desired, coat the back of the beadwork with clear nail polish. This will stiffen it and secure the thread ends. Test for colorfastness!!

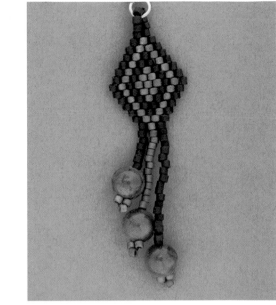

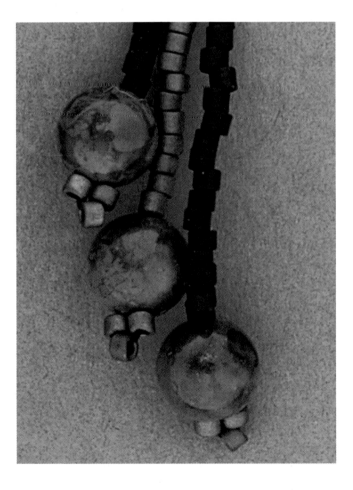

LEATHER AMULET BAG AND EARRINGS

NYMO™ THREAD, B & D
NEEDLES, SIZE 10 OR 12
LIGHTWEIGHT LEATHER SCRAP
ONE CLOISONNE FISH OR OTHER ACCENT
    BEAD (HINT: CHOOSE THIS FIRST TO
    DETERMINE OTHER COLORS)
DELICA™ BEADS, THREE COLORS
STONE AND/OR METAL ACCENT BEADS: CHIPS,
    4MM ROUND, 5MM ROUND, ETC.
SOFT FLEX WIRE, 1 YARD
TWO CRIMP BEADS
ONE NECKLACE CLASP
TWO EAR POSTS
BOND 527™ GLUE

PART I: AMULET BAG

1. Trace the pattern on the leather scrap. Cut out the pattern pieces.

2. Use a single, unknotted strand of thread. Leave a 10-inch tail. Create the start row of the beadwork.

Add beads as illustrated until the length of 20 beads is reached. Note the color pattern!

3. Reinforce the strip, by weaving back and forth through the piece, to the first bead.

4. Do brick stitch on both sides of the start row. Carefully note the color pattern.

5. Put a needle on the 10-inch tail.

String: three Delicas, the fish (or accent) bead and three more Delicas.

Pass the N & T through the opposite side of the Delica bead on the beadwork point.

Reinforce several times. Weave into the beadwork and trim.

6. Attach the beadwork to the leather -- Attach the beadwork to the flap of the bag by using a small amount of glue and stitches.

7. Stitch the bag together -- To form the bag, position the small piece of leather over the larger. Use **D** thread and begin 3-2-1 edge beading at the **X**.

Use the edge beading to stitch the two pieces together, as well as make the decorative edge.

8. Count the number of spaces between beads on the edge, from the **X** to the same point on the other side. This will determine the number of dangles.

9. String the dangles between the points of the edge.
String:

    six **A**
    two **B**
    six **C**
    two **B** (continued on next page)

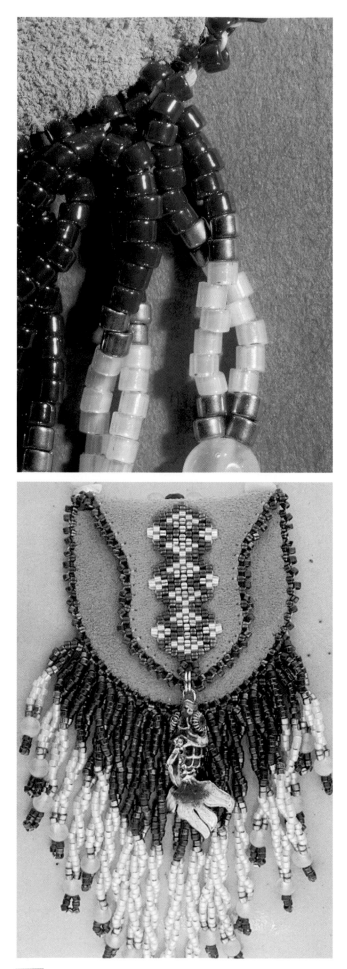

4mm
three **C**
one **B**
three **C**.
Pass the N&T through the 4mm.
String:

two **B**
six **C**
two **B**
six **A**.

Pass the N&T through the next point on the edge.

Note: Each dangle increases (or decreases) by two **A** *and two* **C**.

If twisted dangles are preferable, roll the thread between the middle finger and thumb until the desired number of twists are formed. Hold the twists as the N&T passes through the edge point.

10. For the necklace chain, poke four holes in the leather. Note the two marks on the pattern and two located next to the edge beading.

Thread one end of the soft flex wire down through the hole near the edge, then up through the next hole.

String beads (length to next hole).

Pass the wire down through the third hole and up through the last hole near the edge.

11. String beads on the soft flex wire (pattern - - your choice).

String a crimping bead and the necklace clasp.

Pass the wire back through the crimping bead and, if possible, a couple of other beads.

Close the crimping bead with crimping pliers. Repeat for the other side.

12. If desired, on the back side of the flap, glue a small strip of leather over the wire.

Part II: Earrings

1. Brick stitch one segment of the flap pattern. Weave in loose threads.

2. Glue the earring post to the center back of the beadwork segment. Allow to dry for 24 hours.

3. Repeat for the other earring.

Leather template referenced in #1, page 205.

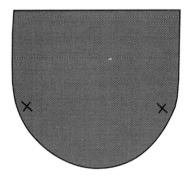

BEZELED CABOCHON SET

MATERIALS

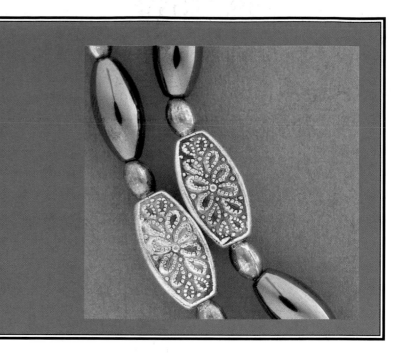

One 30 x 40mm cabochon
Two 15 x 20mm cabochons
24 12mm oval gemstone beads
49 5mm oval silver beads
Ten 12mm oval silver filigree beads
Seed beads, size 14 (Japanese), 2 colors
Seed beads, size 11, silver-lined gray
Thread: Nymo B and D
Needles: 10 and 13
Thin leather scrap
Tiger tail or soft flex wire, 30 inches
Bond 527 glue
Two crimping beads
Necklace clasp
Two ear posts

PART I: NECKLACE

1. Use Bond 527 to glue each cabochon to a small piece of leather. Allow to dry.

2. Use a single, unknotted strand of **B** thread and string two **A** beads.

Leaving a 4-inch tail, bring the N&T through the first bead.

Pull the N&T until the two beads are next to each other.

Pass the N&T through the second bead.

String another A bead and pass the N&T through the second bead again.

Bring the N&T back through the third bead.

3. Continue adding **A** beads in this manner until the strip of beads is 68 beads long (or long enough to go around the outside edge of the cabachon; must be an even number).

4. Connect the two ends of the bead strip and place the strip around the cabochon. The thread loops should be up. Tack the bead strip down around the cabochon.

5. Bring the N&T through a bead to the front side. Do a row of brick stitch. For example, pick up one bead with the N&T and pass the N&T under the first loop of thread.

Bring the N&T through the bead just picked up.

Connect the first and last bead of the row.

6. Do a row of 4-3-3-2 edge beading.

Pick up four beads to start, skip the first loop of thread, pass the N&T under the next loop of thread, and then through the fourth bead.

Continue by picking up three beads, passing the N&T under every second loop of thread, and back through the third bead.

At the end of the row, pick up two beads and pass the N&T through the FIRST bead of the row.

Catch a thread, then pass back through the first bead.

7. Gather the beads around the cabochon by running the N&T through all the points of the edged row. Pull tight. Bring the N&T to the back, knot and trim.

8. Carefully cut out the cabochon. Leave a scant 1/16 edge; don't cut the threads!

9. Cut an oval of leather the same size as the cabochon.

Fold the tiger tail (soft flex wire) in half.

Smear the back side of the cabochon with glue. Center the tiger tail in the glue, then cover with the leather oval. Allow to dry.

10. Mark the location of the dangles.

Using **D** thread and a 10 needle, start at one point and do 1-1-1 edge beading around the cabochon to the second mark for the dangles.

While working the 1-1-1 edge beading, tug after each bead addition to pull the bead to the top. The beads should be on the top edge of the leather close to the beadwork around the cabochon.

11. Do 3-2-2-1 edge beading where the dangles will be located.

Connect the two edges, then string the dangles. Bring the N&T out the first point of the 3-2-2-1 edge.

String:

> seven **A**
> one **C**
> seven **B**
> one **C**
> one oval
> one **C**
> four **B**
> one **C**
> four **B.**

Pass the N&T through:

> one **C**
> one oval
> one **C.**

String:

> seven **B**
> one **C**
> seven **A.**

Pass the N&T through the next point. Note that each dangle increases (or decreases) by two **A** and two **B** beads. If twisted dangles are desired, roll the

thread between the middle finger and thumb until the desired number of twists are formed. Hold the twists and pass the N&T through the next point on the edge.

12. Work a row of brick stitch on the 1-1-1 edge beading. The completed bezel should curve up toward the cabochon. Tie off, trim thread and hide knot.

13. String the tiger tail with:

    one silver oval
    one gemstone oval
    one silver oval
    one gemstone oval
    one silver oval
    one silver filigree.

Repeat the above pattern five times, then string:

    one silver oval
    one gemstone
    one silver oval
    one gemstone
    one silver oval
    one crimping bead
    necklace clasp.

Pass the tiger tail back through the crimping bead and through several beads. Pull tight and close the crimping bead. Trim the excess tiger tail. Repeat for the other side.

PART II: EARRINGS

1. Repeat steps 2, 3 and 4 EXCEPT make a strip of 32 beads.

2. Do 4-3-3-2 edge beading as in step 6.

3. Do steps 7 and 8.

4. Cut a leather oval the same size as the cabochon.

Sandwich an ear post between the cabochon and the leather backing with glue. Allow to dry.

5. Do 1-1-1 edging around the cabochon as in step 10.

6. Work a row of brick stitch on the edging.

Bring N&T to back, tie off and hide knot.

7. If desired, add dangles to the earrings.

See step 11.

PEARL AND CABOCHON NECKLACE AND EARRINGS

PART I: NECKLACE

1. Use Bond 527™ to glue the larger cabochon to the felt. Allow to dry.

2. Use a single, unknotted strand of **B** thread. String two seed beads. Leave a 4-inch tail.

Bring the N&T through the first bead. Pull the N&T until the two beads are next to each other.

Pass the N&T through the second bead.

String another seed bead and again pass the N&T through the second bead.

Bring the N&T back through the third bead.

3. Continue adding beads in the above manner until the strip of beads is long enough to go around the outside edge of the cabochon. *Note: This must be an even number.*

4. Connect the two ends of the bead strip and place the strip around the cabochon. The thread loops should be up. Tack the bead strip down around the cabochon.

5. Bring the N&T through a bead to the front side. Do a row of brick stitch.

For example, pick up one bead with the N&T and pass the N&T under the first loop of thread. Bring the N&T through the bead just picked up. At the end of the row, connect the first and last bead.

6. Create a row of 4-3-3—2 edge beading: Pick up four beads to start, skip the first loop of thread, N&T under the second loop of thread, then through the fourth bead.

Continue by picking up three beads, passing the N&T under every second loop of thread and back through the third bead.

At the end of the row, pick up two beads and pass

the N&T through the first bead of the row, catch a thread and continue back through the first bead.

7. Gather the beads around the cabochon by running the N&T through all the points of the edged row. Pull tight. Bring the N&T through the beads to the back.

8. Create a row of back stitching around the entire cabochon and "encircle" the row.

Note: This will even out the row and reinforce the beadwork.

9. Measure the cabochon and mark the location for the center pearls.

Sew a pearl next to the row of back stitching.

Use back stitch to outline the pearl on the remaining three sides.

10. Continue adding and outlining pearls in this manner until finishing all eight.

11. Fill in the remaining exposed felt with rows of back stitching.

Don't crowd; it should be flat, not bumpy.

12. Leave a 1/16-inch edge. Carefully cut out the beadwork.

13. Fold the soft flex wire in half. Center the wire on the back and baste into place.

14. Glue the beadwork to a piece of leather. Dry thoroughly on a flat surface and trim the leather.

15. Mark the location of the dangles. Use **D** thread and a size 10 needle. Begin at one point and do 1-1—1 edge beading around the cabochon to the second mark for the dangles. As the 1-1—1 edge beading is done, tug the thread after each bead addition. This pulls the bead to the top. That is, the beads should be on the top edge of the leather close to the beadwork around the cabochon.

16. Work 3-2-2—1 edge beading where the dangles will be located. Connect the two edges, then string the dangles.

Bring the N&T out the first point of the 3-2-2—1 edge.

String 25 beads, pearl and 11 beads.

Pass the N&T through the pearl and string 25 beads.

Pass the N&T through the next edge point.

Note: Each dangle increases (or decreases) by five beads.

17. To complete the 1-1—1 edging, work a row of brick stitch. Tie off, trim thread and hide knot.

18. String the soft flex wire with a combination of beads and pearls. Complete with the crimp bead and the clasp. Pass the wire back through the crimping bead and close with pliers. Trim excess wire.

Part II: Earrings

1. Use fewer beads and repeat steps 2, 3 and 4 on previous page.

2. Work 4-3-3—2 edge beading as in step 6 on previous page.

3. Work step 7 above and carefully cut out the beadwork. Leave 1/16-inch edge.

Cut a leather oval the same size as the beadwork. Use glue and position an ear post between the cabochon and the leather backing.

Allow glue to dry.

4. Create 1-1—1 edging around the cabochon.

5. Work a row of brick stitch on the edging. Bring the N & T to the back, tie off and hide knot.

6. Repeat for the other earring.

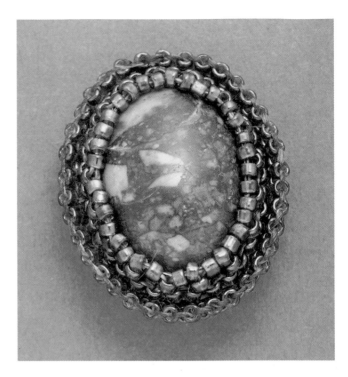

PART FIVE

PEYOTE STITCH TECHNIQUES

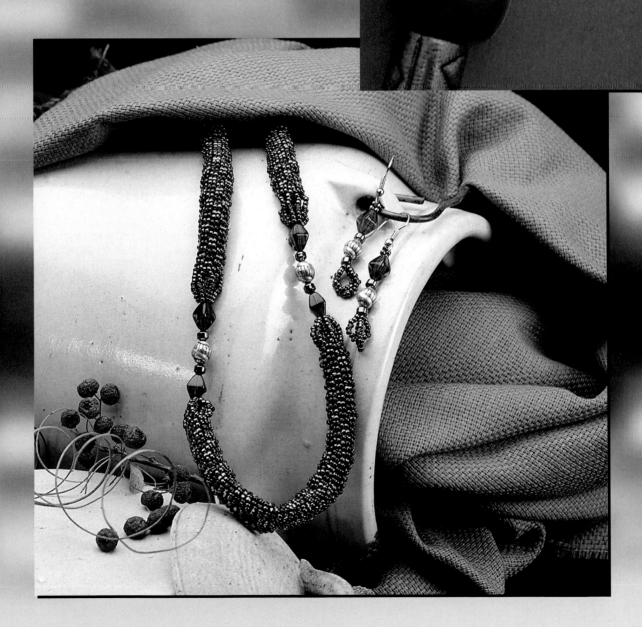

PEYOTE STITCH TECHNIQUES

Peyote stitch is a beadwork technique with several variations: tubular, flat and circular. The flexible "bead" fabric formed with this stitch has a twill pattern. This stitch is also referred to as gourd stitch. Both names are derivatives of the Native American custom of covering items used in their religious ceremonies.

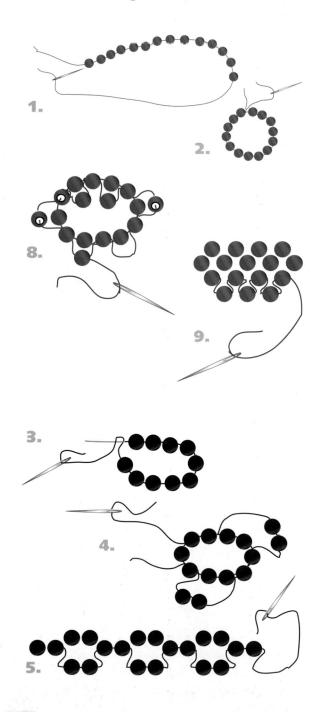

1. String the indicated number of beads.

2. Pass the N&T through all the strung beads and tie a square knot.

OR, use the loose end and the N&T end to tie a square knot.

3. Pass the N&T through the FIRST bead next to the knot.

4. String a single bead and pass the N&T through the third bead from the knot.

5. String another bead and pass the N&T through the fifth bead.

6. Continue in this manner until the entire row is complete.

7. If an UNEVEN number of beads was strung in step one, the stitch will spiral to the end.

8. If stringing an EVEN number of beads, pass the N&T through the LAST bead AND through the FIRST bead of the just completed row.

9. Fill in the spaces created by the previous row by stringing a single bead between each high bead.

10. Continue in this manner until the desired length is reached.

TWO-DROP PEYOTE

1. String an EVEN number of beads to form the base circle.

2. Pass the N&T through the first bead.

3. String two beads and pass the N&T through the 4th AND 5th beads.

4. String two more beads and pass the N&T through 8th and 9th bead.

5. Continue as above EXCEPT always string two beads and pass through two beads.

ADDING NEW THREAD

Use the end of the old thread and the end of the new thread and tie a square knot as close as possible to last bead. Put a very small dab of polish on the knot. Put a needle on each end and weave the tails into the beadwork, then trim.

TROUBLE-SHOOTING

1. **Beads "pop up" instead of laying flat** -- The N&T was not passed through EVERY OTHER bead, note steps 4 and 5. OR, the N&T was not passed through the first bead of the just completed row prior to starting the next row; note step 8.

2. **Holes in the "bead fabric"** -- High beads were skipped.

3. **The pattern is off** -- The beginning of each new row shifts diagonally by one bead across the pattern. Mark a diagonal line across the pattern.

ETHNIC-LOOK SET

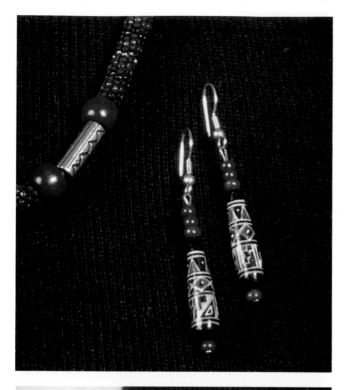

PART I: NECKLACE

1. Using a single, unknotted strand of **B** thread, string ten color **A** beads.

Leaving a 6-inch tail, tie the beads around the cord with a square knot about two inches from the middle of the cord.

2. Pass the N&T through the first bead.

3. Follow the pattern to complete the middle segment of the necklace:

     row 3: **A**
     rows 4 & 5: **B**
     rows 6 & 7: **A**
     rows 8 & 9: **C**
     rows 10 & 11: **A**
     rows 12 & 13: **B**
     rows 14 & 15: **A**
     rows 16 & 17: **D**
     rows 18 & 19: **A**
     rows 20 & 21: **B**
     rows 22 & 23: **A**
     rows 24 & 25: **C**
     rows 26 & 27: **A**
     rows 28 & 29: **B**

Then, do 35 rows of color **A** and repeat the above pattern from the bottom to the top. This measures about four inches.

4. Be sure to center the peyote stitch on the cord, then stitch through the cord and the beads a couple of times to secure. Put a needle on the loose tail and do the same.

5. String one crow, one metal, and one crow on EACH side of the tubular peyote.

6. String ten beads as in step 1 and start a new segment of tubular peyote close to the crow bead.

7. Do the peyote stitch pattern as above rows 3-29. Then start at rows 18-19 and reverse the pattern. The finished piece should be 2 inches long.

8. Secure both ends with stitching as in step 4.

9. Repeat steps 6-8 For the other side.

10. Repeat steps 5-9 again.

11. String one crow, one metal, and one crow on each side of the cord.

12. Put a piece of cellophane tape on each end of the cord to prevent fraying.

Cut the head off a head pin, push the pin halfway through the cord (1/4-inch from end) and twist one end of the pin around the cord several times.

Push a bell cap over the other end of the head pin.

Use round-nose pliers to form a loop in the head pin, while attaching the barrel clasp in the process. Repeat for the other side.

13. Put a knot in a single strand of **D** thread.

Push the N&T through the cord at the middle color **A** section of the tubular peyote.

Tug the thread to pull the knot into the cord.

Pass the N&T through the outermost bead of an 18-bead color **A** row.

14. String the dangles with:

    20 **B**

    pony

    four **D**

    one **C**

    four **D** .

Pass the N&T through one and string 20 B.

Pass the N&T up through the second bead of the 18-bead row.

Weave the N&T down the third bead of the 18-bead row and string another dangle. Note that the number of color **B** beads increases (or decreases) by three beads. There should be nine dangles.

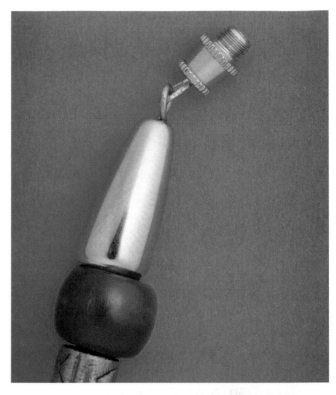

15. Weave the N&T so it's coming down out of the third bead of the 17-bead row above the 18-bead row with the dangles.

String:

> two **A**
> one **B**
> one **B**
> three **A**
> one **D**
> Peruvian
> three **D**.

Pass the N&T through the Peruvian and the one **D**. Then string:

> three **A**
> pony
> one **B**
> pony
> one **B**
> two **A**.

Pass the N&T up through the 15th bead of the 17-bead row.

16. Weave the N&T into the beadwork or cord and tie off.

PART II: EARRINGS

String a pleasing mix of pony beads and a Peruvian bead on a head pin. Use round-nose pliers to make a loop in the top. Attach ear wires. Repeat for the other earring.

LARGE-BEAD AMULET BAG SET

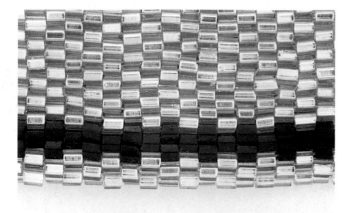

MATERIALS

THREAD: NYMO D
NEEDLES: 10
HEX BEADS, SIZE 8 (ALSO CALLED 3.3)
SEED BEADS, SIZE 11, ONE COLOR
FIVE PERUVIAN TEARDROP BEADS
15 6MM CZECH GLASS BEADS
TWO HEAD PINS
TWO EAR WIRES

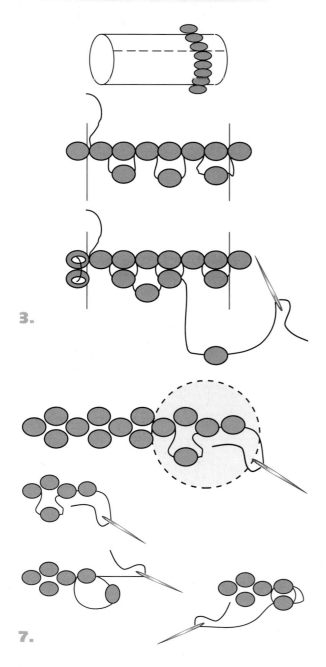

PART I: AMULET BAG

1. Using a double-strand of thread, string 42 color **A** beads.

Leaving a 4-inch tail, tie a square knot to form a circle of beads.

2. If desired, place the circle of beads over the cardboard center of a toilet paper roll. If necessary, cut the cardboard roll lengthwise to make it adjustable in size.

Pass the N&T through the first bead.

3. Do 28 rows of peyote stitch with color **A** beads. Then do three rows with color **B** beads. Finally, do three rows with color **A**.

4. Carefully flatten the beadwork. Flattened the beadwork so that the bottom beads fit together like zipper teeth.

5. Sew the bottom together by passing the N&T back and forth through the beads of the last row.

6. Weave the N&T to the top back of the bag. The side of the bag with ten high beads is the back of the bag. Weave the N&T so it is coming out the fourth high bead from the side edge.

7. Do ten rows (seven beads wide) of peyote stitch. Do six rows and decreased each by one bead to form the angle. Because there is an UNEVEN number of beads, it will be necessary to do this special weave stitch at ONE END OF THE ROW to get into position to do the next row:

8. Weave the N&T so it is coming out the fourth bead of the flap. String 1A, Peruvian, and three seed beads. Pass the N&T through the Peruvian and the 1A. Pass the N&T through the OPPOSITE side of the fourth flap bead. Reinforce.

PART II: CHAIN

9. Weave the N&T so it's coming out the outermost low bead on the top back of the bag.

10. String:

> one A
> Peruvian
> four seed beads
> 6mm
> four seed beads.

11. Do a 15-bead Commanche ladder (5A, 2B, 1A, 2B, 5A). Be sure to pull the ladder tightly next to the strung beads.

12. String four seed beads, 6mm and four seed beads.

13. Repeat steps 11 and 12 eleven times.

14. String Peruvian and one **A**. Pass the N&T through the other outermost bead on the top back.

15. Pass the N&T through the one **A** and the Peruvian bead.

String four seed beads and pass the N&T through the 6mm bead. String four seed beads and reinforce the 15-bead ladder by passing the N&T back and forth through the beads.

16. Continue adding seed beads and reinforcing ladders until the entire chain has been done.

17. Pass the N&T through the Peruvian and one **A** bead. Weave the N&T into the amulet bag, tie off and trim thread.

PART III: EARRINGS

String one **A**, Peruvian and 6mm on a head pin. Use round-nose pliers to form a loop in the head pin. Attach ear wire. Repeat for the other earring.

THREAD: NYMO B
NEEDLES: 13
SEED BEADS, SIZE 11, 3 COLORS
SIX 8MM SILVER BEADS
TEN 8MM CZECH GLASS BEADS
12 5MM GEMSTONE BEADS
ONE BARREL CLASP
TWO BEAD TIPS
TWO EAR WIRES

PART I: NECKLACE

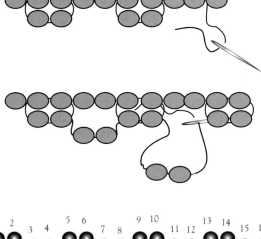

1. String 16 color **A** beads.

Leaving a 6-inch tail, tie a square knot to form a circle of beads.

2. If desired, place the circle of beads around a straw or pencil. Pass the N&T through the first bead.

3. Using two-drop peyote stitch, do 5 3/4 inches for the middle segment of the necklace. Be sure to follow the color pattern. Tie off and leave a remaining thread.

4. Repeat steps 1, 2, and 3 to make the two side segments. Each should be 3 1/2 inches in length. Tie off, but leave remaining thread.

5. Attach the middle segment to each of the side segments with 2 1/2 inches of strung beads: tie on (or use remaining threads, if long enough) using the loose tail of the middle segment. Weave the N&T until it is coming out a pair of the high points of the peyote stitch, as illustrated.

String:

    three **A**
    two **B**
    three **A**
    8mm
    5mm
    silver
    5mm
    8mm
    three **A**
    two **B**
    three **A.**

Pass the N&T through a pair of high points on the side segment.

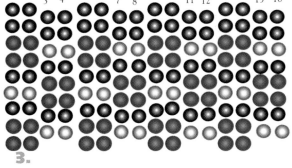

6. String 3A, 2B, and 3A.

Pass the N&T through the large beads and string 3A, 2B, and 3A.

Pass the N&T through the OPPOSITE side of the original high points.

Weave the N&T to the next pair of high points and repeat. Note that only seed beads will be strung and the N&T will pass through the large beads each time. Be careful not to twist the segments and be sure to keep it pulled tight.

Tie off and weave in loose ends.

7. Attach the side segments to the barrel clasp: tie on using the loose tail of a side segment. Weave the N&T until it is coming out a pair of the high points.

String:

> three **A**
> two **B**
> three **A**
> 8mm
> 5mm
> silver
> 5mm
> 8mm
> a bead tip.

String one **A** (with a large hole) and pass the N&T back through the bead tip and the large beads. Pull tight!

Continue as in step 6, except that seed beads are only strung on the peyote end and the N&T will pass through the large beads and the bead tip EACH TIME.

Tie off and weave loose ends into the beadwork.

8. Close the bead tips and attach the barrel clasp.

9. Use a single, unknotted strand of thread and string four **A** beads.

Leaving a 4-inch tail, pass the N&T through all four beads to form a loop.

10. String:

> 8mm
> 5mm
> silver
> 5mm
> three A
> two B
> six A
> two B
> three A.

Pass the N&T through the large beads, the four-bead loop, and back through the large beads.

> String:
>
> three **A**
> two **B**
> eight **A**
> two **B**
> three **A.**

Pass the N&T through the large beads and the four-bead loop again.

11. Use the loose tail and the N&T to tie off. Dab knot with polish and trim.

12. Repeat for the other earring.

13. Attach ear wires.

BUTTERFLY AMULET SET

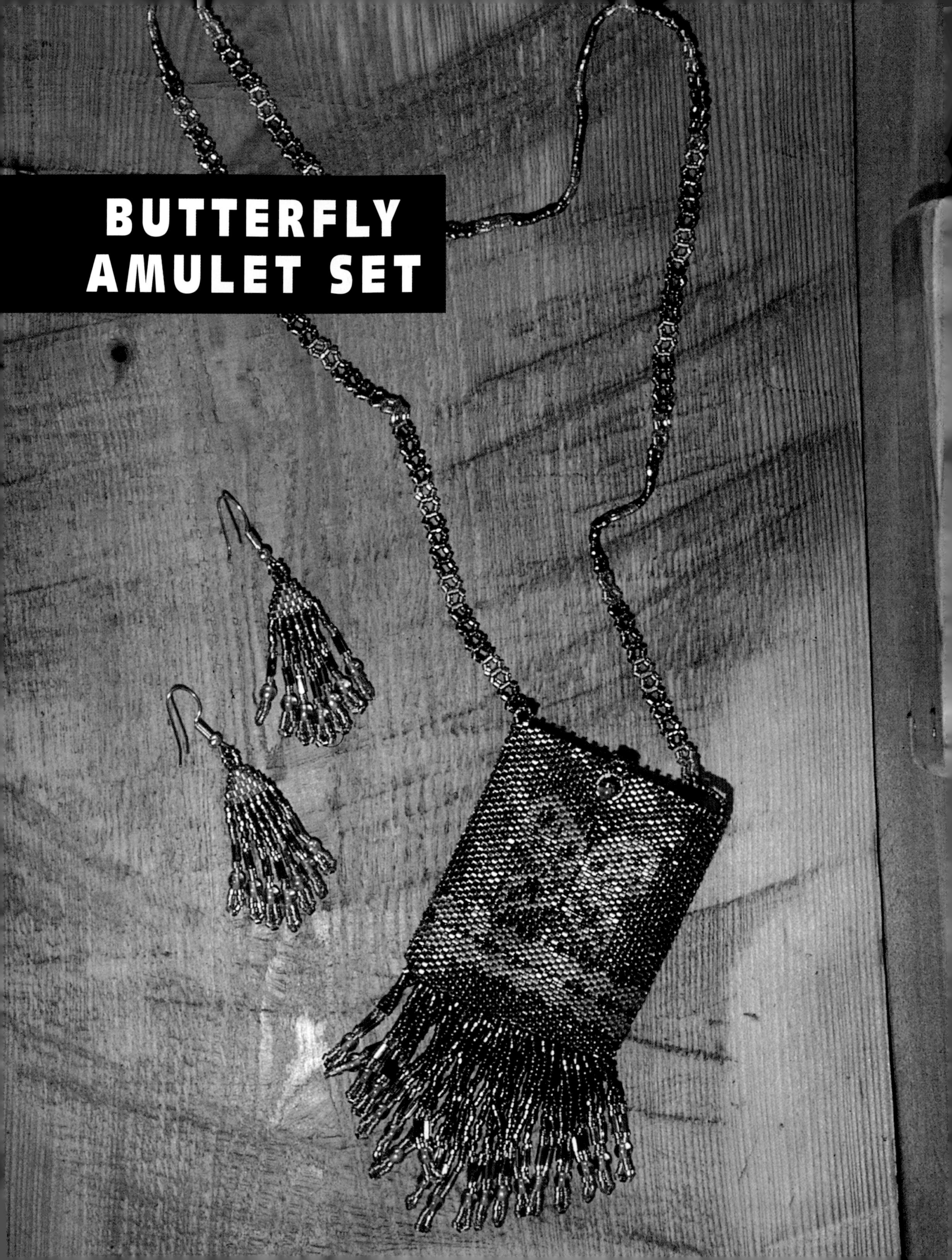

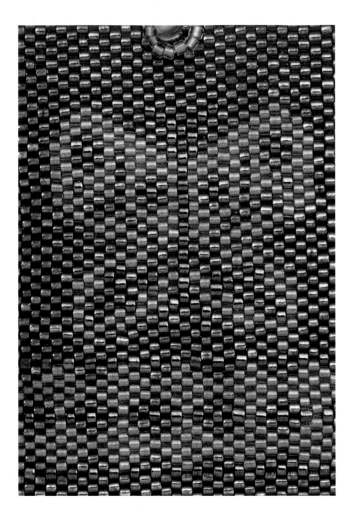

PART I: AMULET BAG

1. String 84 color **A** beads. Leaving a 4-inch tail, tie a square knot to form a circle of beads.

2. If desired, place the circle of beads over a cardboard toilet paper roll. If necessary, cut the cardboard roll lengthwise to make it adjustable. Pass the N&T through the first bead.

3. Starting at the bottom, follow the pattern and do 61 rows of tubular peyote stitch. Note that the back side of the bag does NOT have the butterfly motif; therefore, only the front side of the pattern is printed. Because the first bead in each subsequent row of tubular peyote stitch shifts by one, it is helpful to color a diagonal line across the pattern. Use this pattern as the starting point for each new row.

4. Do tubular peyote stitch with color **A** beads until the bag measures 2 1/2 inches.

Remove the beadwork from the cardboard roll and carefully flatten it and center the butterfly in the front.

3.

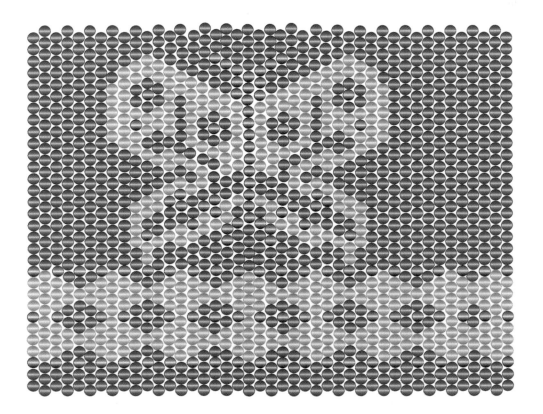

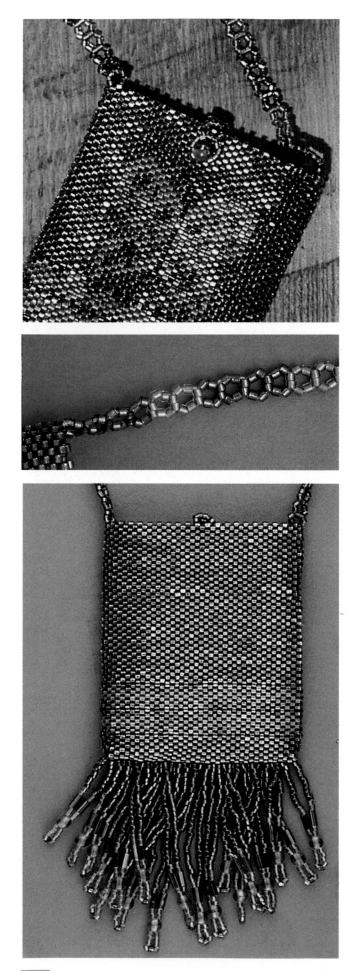

5. Top closure -- Weave the N&T so it is coming out the 11th high bead from the edge of the bag.

String six **A** and pass the N&T through the 12th high bead, the low bead and the 11th high bead again. Then pass the N&T through four strung beads.

String six **A** and pass the N&T through two beads on the first bead circle AND through four of the just strung beads.

String six **A** and repeat the preceding step.

String 11 **B** and pass the N&T through two beads on the third circle, as well as all 11 **B** beads. Weave the N&T through the bead circles to strength.

Weave the thread into the beadwork and tie off.

Sew on (as you would a button) a 4mm bead centered above the butterfly's head.

6. Chain -- Add enough new **D** thread to do the entire chain. Utilizing a high-low-high bead on the side of the bag, make the first bead circle as described and illustrated in step 5.

Continue making bead circles, until the chain is the desired length (pattern -- four color **A**, two color **B** circles).

Attach the end of the chain to high-low-high beads on the other side of the bag.

Weave the thread into the beadwork and tie off. Trim.

7. Bottom flap -- Use the loose tail to tie on new thread.

Weave the N&T so it's coming out the 20th bead from the front center line (marked with an * on the pattern).

Use color A beads and do eight rows of flat peyote stitch. Each row will be 19 beads wide.

8. Fold the bottom flap to the other side of the bag and stitch together.

Weave the N&T to the center row of the flap and add the dangles.

String:

> ten **A**
> two **B**
> bugle
> two **B**
> 4mm
> four **B**
> one **A**
> four **B.**

Pass the N&T through the 4mm and string 2B, bugle, 2B, and 10A.

Pass the N&T through the next bead in the peyote row.

Continue stringing dangles, noting that each increases (or decreases by 2A beads). There should be 19 dangles.

Weave the thread into the beadwork, tie off and trim.

PART II: EARRINGS
(WORKED WITH A BRICK STITCH)

1. Make a single-bead Commanche ladder that is seven beads wide (pattern – one **A**, five **B**, one **A**).

2. Follow the color pattern and brick stitch the top of the earring.

3. Add a six-bead loop for the ear wire.

4. Weave down the side of the earring and string the dangles.

String:

> five **A**
> two **B**
> bugle
> two **B**
> 4mm
> four **B**
> one **A**
> four **B**.

Pass the N&T through the 4mm, two **B**, bugle, two **B**, five **A** and the first bead in the Commanche ladder.

Weave to the next bead in the Commanche ladder and string another dangle. Note that the dangles increase (or decrease) by two **A** beads.

5. Weave the loose threads into the beadwork and trim.

6. Attach an ear wire.

7. Repeat for the other earring.

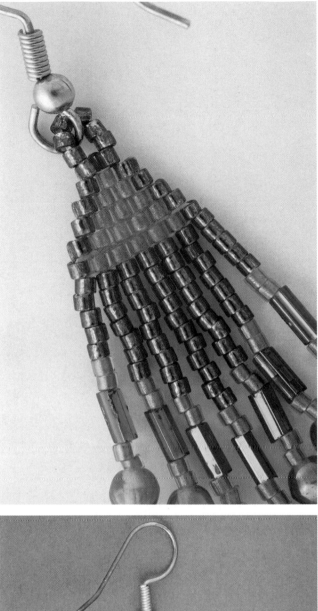

PART SIX
SPLIT-LOOM TECHNIQUES

Loomwork is significantly different than the other beadwork techniques in this book. The technique requires an additional piece of equipment, the loom, and uses two sets of threads, the warp threads and the weft thread. The warp threads are more-or-less attached permanently during the looming process. Use the weft thread to weave beads between the warp threads.

There are numerous looms available, from the metal or plastic kiddie looms to $100 adult versions. Don't even waste your money on the kiddie looms; they will not work for these split-loom necklaces. In looking at other looms, there are several points to consider. First, is the loom long enough? It should be at least 25 inches long to accommodate these necklaces. Second, does the loom utilize a spring to hold the warp threads in place? Some looms use strung beads instead of the coils of the spring. The problem with this is, whenever the loom is moved, the warp threads easily "jump" the beads resulting in a tangled mess. Third, does the loom have a solid piece of wood forming the base? This provides a very handy "table" for patterns and bead trays during the looming process. Fourth, is the length of the loom adjustable? This may or may not be a good thing. Adjustable looms are often so long that they're very cumbersome and awkward to work with. Note that it is easy to get the warp threads too tight, which causes the threads to stretch and results in puckered loomwork. Finally, does the loom cost an arm and a leg and your first-born? Frankly, why spend $80-100 when you can make your own for $8-10?

Materials to make a loom for these necklaces:
　　One 25" x 7" x 3/4" board (base)
　　Two 4" x 7" x 3/4" boards (sides)
　　Eight wood screws (1 1/2-inch long)
　　Two medium nails (1 1/2-inch long)
　　Two 6-inch springs
　　Four wood screws (1/2-inch long)

Pound each nail into the exact center of the sides. The nail should protrude about 1-inch. Fasten the sides to the base with the longer wood screws. Attach the springs to the top of the sides with the shorter wood screws. If desired, sand the edges a bit.

1. Once a loom has been procured, the first step in using it is stringing the warp threads.
  a. Use **D** thread for stringing the warp threads.
  b. If you are not stringing beads on the warp threads, tie the thread onto the nail. Leave about a 10-inch tail of thread.
  c. Place the thread in a coil on the spring, then across the loom to the corresponding coil on the OPPOSITE end of the loom.
  d. Wrap the thread around the base of the loom.
  e. Place the thread in an adjacent coil and continue with steps c & d until the desired number of warp threads have been strung.
  f. Tie the thread around the nail, leaving about a 10-inch tail.
  g. Remove the completed loomwork from the loom by cutting the warp threads under the base of the loom.
  h. If stringing beads on the warp threads, note that EACH warp thread will be cut to length (usually about 40 inches for these necklaces) and tied individually to the loom.
  i. Cut the indicated number of threads.
  j. Leaving a 10-inch tail, tie one end of the first thread around the nail.
  k. Put a needle (size 10) on the other end of the thread and string the indicated number and sequence of beads.
  l. Remove the needle, place the thread in the same coil at the opposite end of the loom, and tie the thread around the nail.

m. Repeat steps i, j, and k for the remaining warp threads.

n. Remove the completed loomwork from the loom by UNTYING the knots.

o. Try to string the loom so the warp threads are reasonably taut. Don't be concerned if the threads sag a bit. Be careful about getting the warp threads too tight; this could cause puckered loomwork!

p. It's important that the above stringing techniques be used. These necklaces require a considerable amount of thread on BOTH sides of the loomwork to accommodate the dangles and tying off the neck strap. Wrapping around the nail in the stringing process, or cutting the warp threads at the nail may not allow for enough thread.

2. The next step in loomwork is weaving with the weft thread. (If the terms warp and weft are confusing, remember weft and weave both begin with the letters w-e.)

a. Use 4-6 feet of **B** thread to begin.

b. Leaving a tail, tie a loose, single knot onto the outermost warp thread. The patterns indicate how far from the end of the loom to tie on the weft thread. It is also wise to tie on at the end with the longest thread tails. Use these tails to string the dangles.

c. Thread a 12 LONG needle onto the weft thread.

d. Use a post-it-note or a ruler to mark the first row of the pattern. Read the pattern from LEFT TO RIGHT and string the indicated number and sequence of beads.

e. Slide the beads down next to the knot.

f. Bring the N&T UNDER the warp threads and push the beads UP between the warp threads. There should be ONE bead between each warp thread.

g. Pass the N&T over the top of the warp threads (including the opposite outermost) through the row of beads. Note that the first row is the most difficult. It may be easier for beginners to pass the N&T through 5-6 beads at a time, rather than trying to do the entire row at once.

h. Move the row marker and continue with the above steps, looming the entire piece.

3. A couple of the necklaces require that the width of the row be decreased.

a. Pass the N&T through the number of beads in the previous row, which you will decrease in the new row.

b. Wrap the weft thread around the outermost warp thread of the new row.

c. String the indicated number and sequence of beads and weave with the weft thread as described above. However, note that the outer most warp thread has also shifted.

4. Upon removal of the loomwork from the loom, there will be 'zillions' of warp threads that have to be dealt with in some way. Often this means weaving the warp threads into the loomed piece.

a. Put a size 10 needle on the warp thread.

b. Weave the N&T back and forth vertically through ONLY that row as indicated. Weave through six-ten beads, depending on if the thread is a weight-bearing one.

c. Pass the N&T through six-ten beads in a horizontal row and trim the thread. Keep track of which horizontal rows are used; in other words, vary them or it will soon become impossible to get a needle through the beads. This could even result in a broken bead. Heaven forbid!

ADDING NEW THREAD

The only time to do this is after weaving a row of beads. Tie on a new weft thread as in 2b above, or if knots are not desirable, weave in a new weft thread by passing the N&T through 3-4 rows. Weave the loose ends into the loomwork and trim.

TROUBLE-SHOOTING

1. **The first bead falls off** -- The weft thread did not pass over the TOP of the outermost warp thread. Pull the weft thread out of the row of beads, string a new bead and try again.

2. **The loomwork is not flat and/or some beads sag** -- The weft thread did not go over the TOP of the warp threads. If there are only a few, correct the problem when weaving in warp threads at the end. Otherwise, redo the rows.

3. **The design is off** -- Remember to always read LEFT TO RIGHT; use something to mark the rows; be careful in noting number and sequence of beads per row.

4. **Skipped an entire row** -- Believe it or not, it is possible to add a row. Carefully cut the loop of weft thread around the outermost warp thread (next to where you are adding the row). Push the loomed rows apart to make enough space to add the row. Weave in a new weft thread and take care to go several times through the row with the cut loop. Loom the new row. Weave the weft thread into the loomwork and trim.

SEE PAGE 247 FOR ILLUSTRATIONS.

"STAINED GLASS" NECKLACE AND EARRINGS

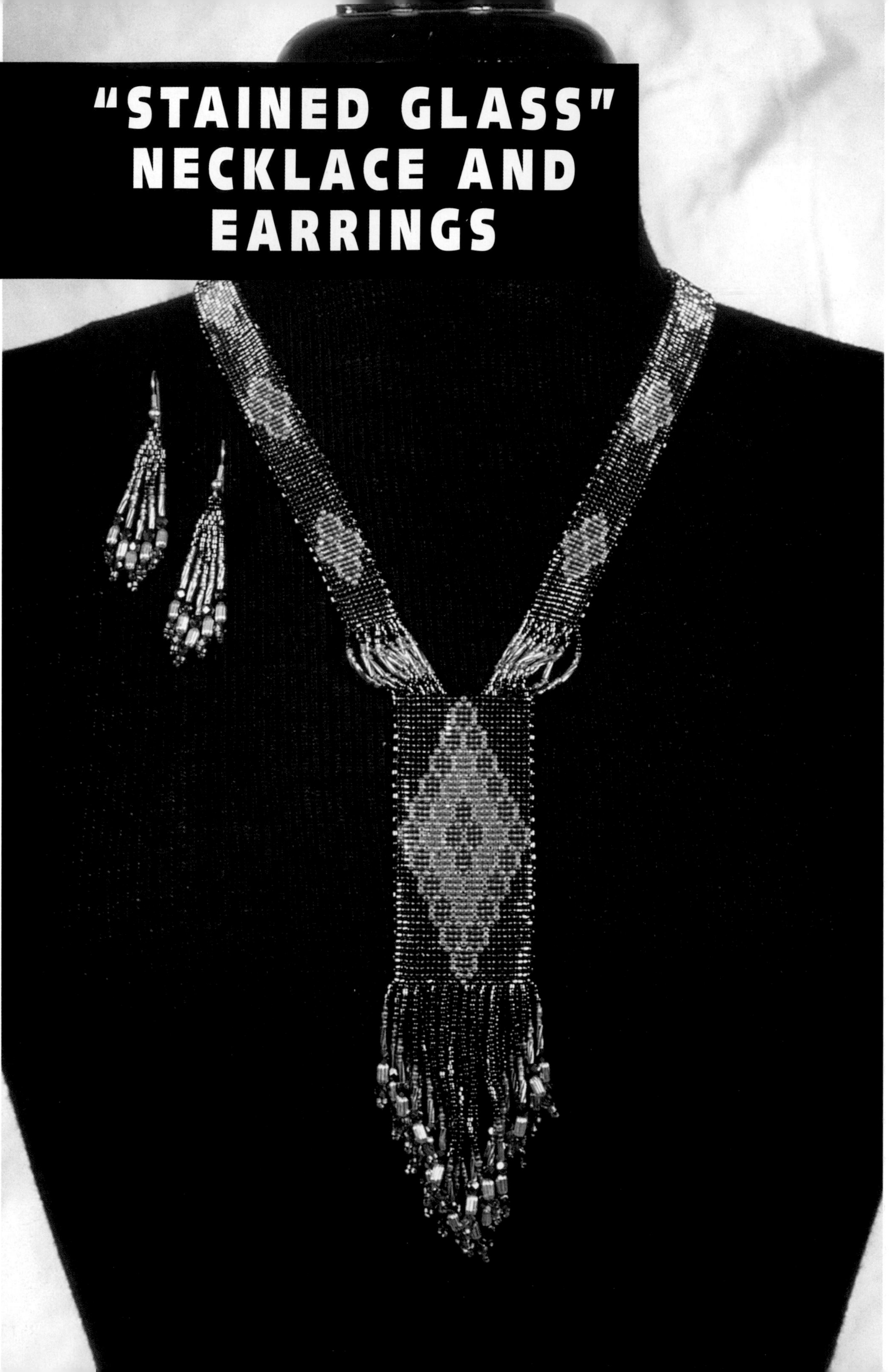

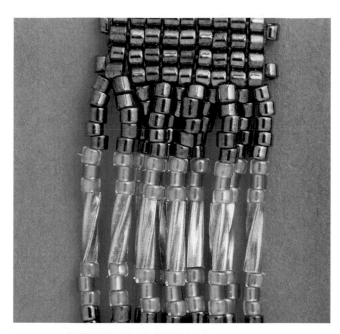

PART I: NECKLACE

1. Cut 20 pieces of **D** thread, each 40 inches long. On each of the first ten threads, string:

> five **A**
> one **B**
> one **C**
> one **B**
> bugle
> one **B**
> one **C**
> one **B**
> five **A**

Tie each thread onto the loom.

2. String six threads onto the loom with no beads. (Note: there is a total of 26 threads.)

Repeat the second part of step 1 with the remaining ten threads. Push the strung beads to one side.

3. Start at the other side about four inches from the end.

Tie on **B** thread and loom the large pattern (bottom to top). After completing the piece, loosen the tie-on knot and weave the loose tail into the loomwork.

4. Push the first set of strung beads (ten threads/17 beads) next to the completed loomwork.

Tie on **B** thread and loom the small pattern (bottom to top).

*Note: Repeat the pattern **five times**.*

5. Repeat for the other side. Loom the small pattern **six times**.

6. Edge the loomwork: This will strengthen the necklace, hide uneven edges and give a finished appearance. Weave in **new** thread.

Bring the N&T out the bottom row of the large pendant.

String one **A** and pass the N&T through the first two beads of the **next** row.

Pass the N&T up through the same two beads on the **third** row.

String another **A** bead and repeat the process. Continue until all the loomwork has been edged.

Move to the next piece of loomwork; pass the N&T through the strung beads between the loomed pieces.

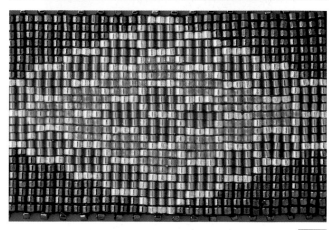

7. To remove the beadwork from the loom, **untie** the knots on the large pendant end. On the other end, cut the threads at the nail.

8. Weave the six plain threads into the loomwork and trim the threads.

9. **Attach the two ends of the neck chain** -- Put a needle on each of the outermost threads. In turn, weave each thread into the loomwork on the **opposite side**. Continue weaving all pairs of threads. Trim threads.

10. **String the dangles**: Put a needle on the outermost thread.

String:

> five **A**
> two **B**
> one **C**
> two **B**
> accent beads
> three **B.**

Pass the N&T through the accent beads, two **B**, one **C**, two **B**, five **A**.

Weave into the loomwork 1/2 to 3/4 inch. Trim thread.

Continue stringing dangles until finishing all 26. *Note: Each dangle increases (or decreases) by three **A**.*

11. *Optional: To set the knots and stiffen the beadwork, coat the back with a generous amount of clear nail polish. First test for colorfastness!*

PART II: EARRINGS
(WORKED WITH THE BRICK STITCH)

1. Leave a 4-inch tail. Create a five bead wide, single-bead Commanche ladder. Note the photograph.

2. Follow the color pattern and brick stitch three rows.

3. String four beads and form the ear wire loop as shown in photograph.

4. Weave the N & T to the first bead of the start row and string the dangles.

String:

> five **A**
> two **B**
> one **C**
> two **B**
> accent beads
> three **B** .

Pass the N & T through the accent beads, the seed beads and down through the second bead on the start row.

Continue stringing dangles.

*Note: The dangles increase (or decrease) by 2***A**.

5. Weave the thread ends into the beadwork and trim.

6. Repeat for other earring.

7. *Optional: To stiffen, coat the back with clear nail polish.*

8. Attach ear wires.

SNOWFLAKE SET

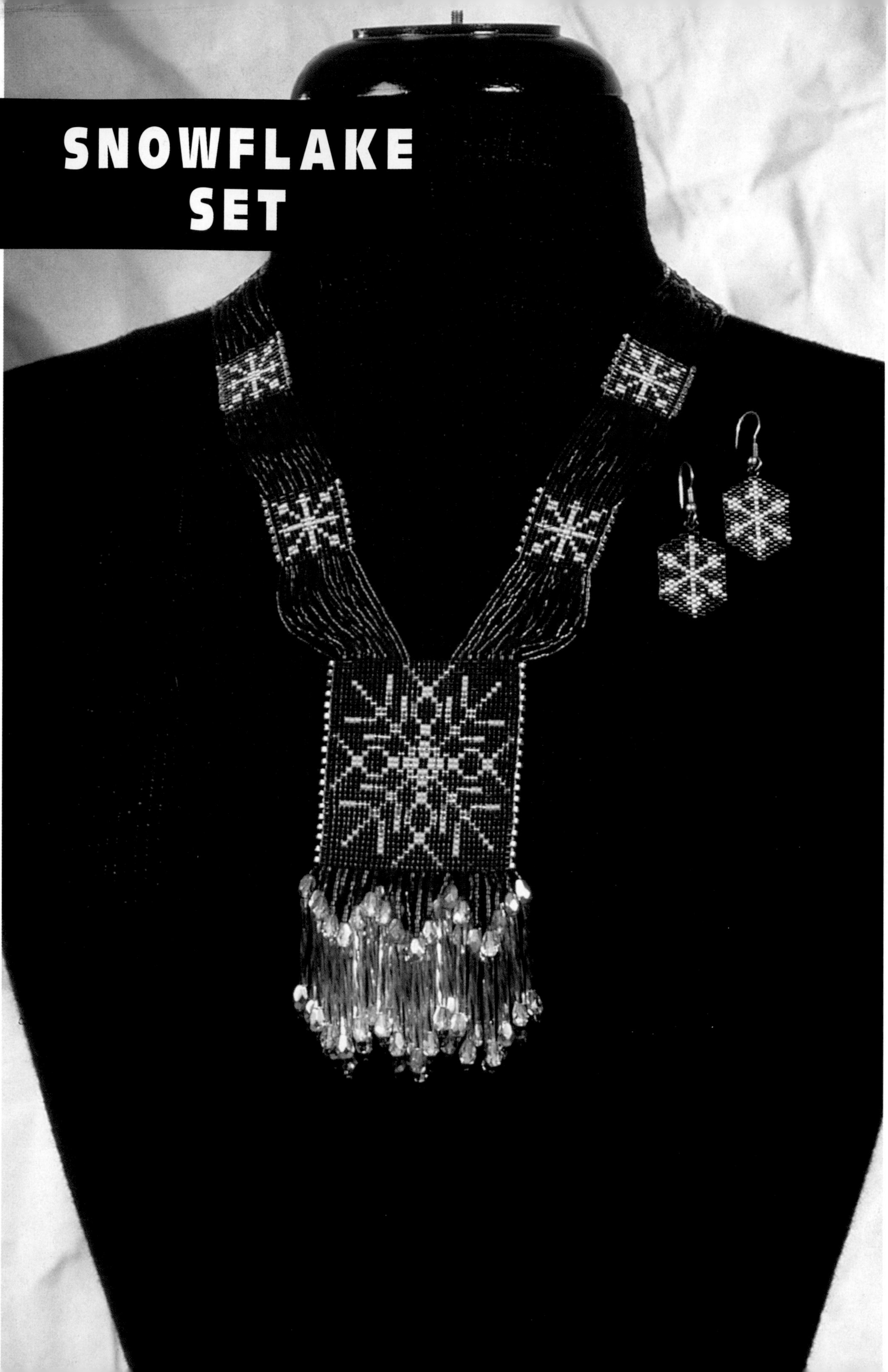

PART I: NECKLACE

1. Warp threads: cut 39 pieces of size **D** thread that are EACH 40 inches long.

On EACH of the first 16 threads, string 150 color **A** beads.

String seven threads with no beads.

String 150 color **A** beads on each of the last 16 threads. (Attach/tie one end of the thread to the loom, put needle on the other end, string 150 beads, remove needle, and attach/tie thread to the opposite end of the loom. Threads should be reasonably taut.)

Push the beads to one side.

(30 strung beads per warp thread)

    color **A**

    silver

    white

2. Starting at the other side, about five inches from the end, tie on **B** thread and loom the large snowflake pattern (bottom to top). After completing the piece, loosen the tie-on knot and weave the loose thread tail into the loomwork, as well as the weft thread.

3. Push the first set of beads (16 threads/30 beads each) next to the completed snowflake.

Tie on **B** thread and loom (bottom to top) a small snowflake. Repeat until looming all five small snowflakes.

Weave in loose threads.

4. Repeat for the other side, except ONLY LOOM four SMALL SNOWFLAKES.

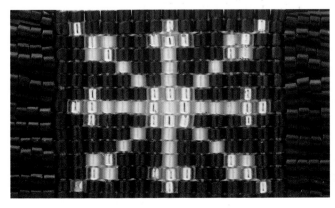

5. Edge the loomwork -- I like to do this because it strengthens the necklace, tends to hide uneven edges, and gives a finished appearance.

Weave in new thread, bringing the N&T out the bottom row of the large snowflake.

String one silver bead, and pass the N&T through the first two beads of the NEXT row.

Pass the N&T up through the same two beads on the THIRD row.

String another silver bead and repeat the process.

Continue edging until completing all the loomwork. To move from one snowflake to the next, pass the N&T through the strung beads between the loomed pieces.

6. Remove the beadwork from the loom by UNTYING the knots.

Tie a LOOSE temporary knot in each of the sides.

7. Weave the seven plain threads into the loom work and trim the threads.

8. Attach the two ends -- Put a needle on the outermost thread and pass the N&T through the beads to the loomwork.

Weave the N&T through several rows, tie a knot around a warp thread and pull the knot into the closest bead.

Weave the N&T into a couple more beads and trim the thread. Continue in this manner until all 32 threads on each side are complete.

9. String the dangles -- Put needle on the outermost thread, and string:

> three **A**
> 5mm
> bugle
> 5mm
> three **A**

Pass the N&T through the 5mm, bugle, 5mm and 3A.

Weave it into several rows of loomwork.

Knot around a warp thread, pull the knot into the closest bead, weave through a couple more beads and trim the thread. Follow the pattern, noting that the numbers indicate the number of color **A** beads strung each time, until all 39 dangles have been done.

10. If desired, coat the back with a generous amount of clear nail polish. This sets the knots and stiffens the beadwork.

Be sure to test for colorfastness!!

*The numbers are not here to indicate how many to string for each dangle.

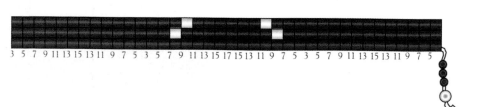

3 5 7 9 11 13 15 13 11 9 7 5 3 5 7 9 11 13 15 17 15 13 11 9 7 5 3 5 7 9 11 13 15 13 11 9 7 5

Part II: Earrings
(Worked in the Brick Stitch)

1. Leaving an 8-inch tail, make a single-bead Commanche ladder that is 17 beads wide. Note the color pattern.

2. Follow the pattern and brick stitch one side.

3. Weave the N&T down the side to the first bead of the ladder/start row.

4. Turn the beadwork over and brick stitch the other side.

5. Weave the thread into the beadwork and trim.

6. Put a needle on the 8-inch tail and string five beads.

Pass the N&T through the OPPOSITE side.

Reinforce, then weave into the beadwork and trim.

7. Attach an ear wire.

8. Repeat for the other earring.

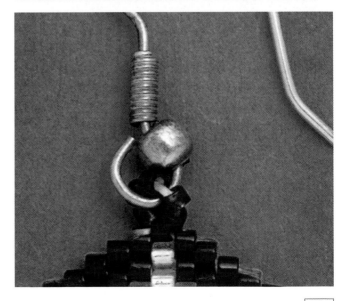

GEOMETRIC BUGLE SET

MATERIALS

BEADING LOOM, AT LEAST 25 INCHES LONG
THREAD: NYMO B & D
NEEDLES: 12 LONG
DELICA BEADS: 3 COLORS
6MM SILVER OR BASE METAL BUGLE BEADS
42 4MM CZECH GLASS BEADS
25 4MM SILVER MUSHROOM BEADS
SIX THAI-SILVER BEADS
TWO SILVER HEAD PINS
TWO SILVER EAR WIRES

PART I: NECKLACE

1. Measure your bugle beads in comparison to the Delica beads; number of Delicas equal one bugle. These directions presume that five Delicas equal one bugle.

2. String the loom with D thread: tie on, string five warp threads, skip five coils on the loom, string 18 threads, skip five coils again, and string five warp threads. There should be 28 total warp threads.

Determine the number of coils to skip by comparing the length of the bugle in comparison to the Delicas (step 1).

3. Leaving a 30-inch tail, tie on **B** thread about 8 inches from one end. Starting at the arrow, follow the pattern and loom (bottom to top) the square part of the pendant.

4. To do the point at the top, pass the N&T UNDER the outermost warp thread. Back through the beads in the last row until the N&T is at the first (*) warp thread of the shorter row. Loop the weft under and then over this outermost warp thread. String the beads for the shorter row and bring them under the warp threads and proceed as usual. Repeat for the other rows. Bring the N&T back into the loomwork and tie off. Trim thread.

5. Put a needle on the 30-inch tail at the bottom of the loomwork. Decreasing, add the bottom seven rows.

Weave the N&T back into the loomwork and tie off. Trim thread.

6. Attach a weft thread to the upper right and loom the neck chain. When completed, it should be about 13 inches long.

7. Reinforce the necklace by edging the outermost edge.

String one **C** bead and pass the N&T through two rows, string another **C** bead, and pass the N&T through two rows, etc.

Edge the ENTIRE right side.

8. Repeat steps 6 and 7 for the left side of the neck chain.

9. Weave loose ends into the loomwork and trim.

10. Remove the loomwork from the loom by cutting the warp threads close to the nails.

11. Connect the two ends of the neck chain by weaving each of the five threads on each side into the OPPOSITE side.

12. Except for one outermost thread on EACH side, weave the warp threads at the top of the pendant into the loomwork. Trim.

13. String:

> five bugles
> one 4mm glass
> one 4mm silver
> one 4mm glass

Repeat this sequence, to reach the desired length, on the remaining threads. It should be the same length as the loomed chain. If the threads are long enough, weave the ends into the loomwork and tie off. If they're too short, tie the two ends together and hide knots. Trim threads.

14. Note which of the warp threads at the bottom of the pendant will be used for dangles. Weave the remainder into the loomwork. Trim threads.

15. String the two outermost dangles on each side. String:

> three **A**
> one 4mm glass
> one 4mm silver
> one 4mm glass
> three **A**
> Thai-silver
> one **A**.

Pass the N&T back through the Thai-silver, 3A, 4mm, and 3A.

Weave the thread into the loomwork and trim thread. Note that the length of the longer dangles increases to four **A**.

16. String the loop dangles. Begin with the shortest thread and string 15 Delicas, one 4mm silver and 15 Delicas.

Weave the end into the loomwork.

Pass the other warp thread through the bead loop and weave the end into the loomwork. Trim thread. Note that the number of Delicas strung on EACH side of the 4mm increases by five beads.

String the following to form the largest loop:

> seven bugles
> one 4mm glass
> one 4mm silver
> one 4mm glass
> seven bugles

17. Coat the back side of the pendant with clear nail polish to set the knots and stiffen the loomwork. Test for colorfastness!

PART II: EARRINGS

String:
   Thai-silver
   4mm glass
   4mm silver
   4mm glass on a head pin.
Use round-nose pliers to form a loop in the head pin. Attach ear wire. Repeat for the other earring.

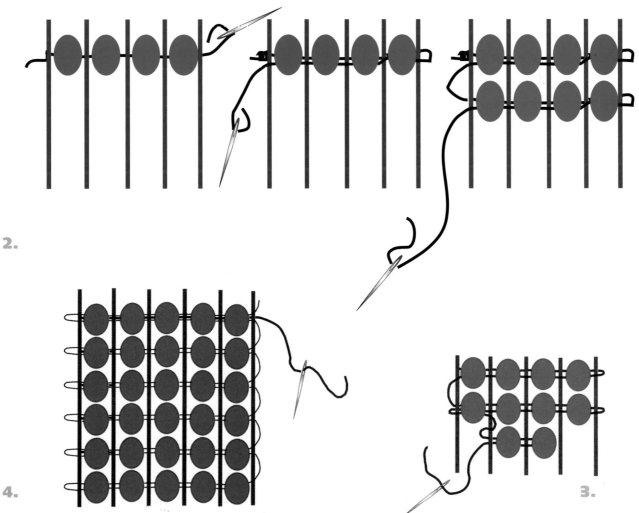

2.

4.

3.

PART SEVEN
GALLERY OF BEADWORK BY ALASKAN ARTISTS

The purpose of this chapter is to showcase the work of eight other Alaskan bead artists. The criterion for selection was simple; they are all friends and acquaintances whose work I admire. I asked each to submit one or two pieces, particularly those that reflect the use of Alaskan themes or materials.

Alaska, being somewhat isolated from the Lower 48, has a long, rich tradition of beadwork in its history. I believe modern Alaskan bead artists are producing many interesting and innovative pieces, which will inspire others.

"Butterfly Barrette"

untitled amulet bag

Inspired by the beadwork of Jane Hodson, Donna Affinito realized her passion for beads in 1993. Donna frequently shares her passion with students of Palmer High School, where she is a guidance secretary. Basketry is another interest, but she always goes back to beads, and often combines beads and basketry.

Donna's blue-ribbon-winning amulet bag was inspired by a new outfit that needed a piece of jewelry. The bag was done in tubular and flat peyote stitch with size 11 beads and accented with twisted fringe. The butterfly barrette was the product of an ugly, rainy, winter day, where an indoor activity, such as sorting beads seemed appropriate. All the bits and pieces that Donna discovered were used in the back-stitched barrette.

"Fire and Icicles"

"Sitting on the Dock of the Bay"

Nine years ago Ruby Brooke purchased a beaded amethyst bola from an artist named Wanda. That purchase fired her obsession with beads, which she happily shares with others at classes, retreats, and the newly formed Alaska Bead Society, Anchorage Chapter.

Lively, fiery beads purchased at Embellishment '96, a class taught by Jeannette Cook, and icicle-like fingers during early morning play with beads were the inspiring ingredients for "Fire and Icicles." The tranquil waters, teeming with oceanic life forms, of Homer, Alaska, as well as beads purchased from several Alaskan bead makers, resulted in "Sitting on the Dock of the Bay".

brown/ivory necklace

blue/green necklace

Jana Coffey's life typifies the "Alaskan Dream". She grew up on a homestead on the Kenai Peninsula, which was only accessible by floatplane. Her present home in beautiful Girdwood Valley is surrounded by seven awe-inspiring glaciers. In 1969 as an art student, Jana was first introduced to hot glass. Having been a serious bead collector for many years, it was only natural that the interest in hot glass and beads would eventually lead to handmade lampwork beads.

Both of these pieces combine seed beads worked in tubular peyote stitch with Jana's handmade beads. The brown and ivory beads are made of imported Italian Morreti glass. Seven large lampwork beads and 28 small multi-colored discs form the focal point of the blue/green necklace.

Moosehide Pouch

Tufted Jewelry Box

Originally from Koyukuk, Alaska, Lillian DeWilde, an Athabascan Indian, has lived in Fairbanks the past 12 years. She spends her summers at a fish camp called Bishop Mountain. Years ago Lillian's grandmother, Madeline Solomon of Galena, taught her to do beadwork. These days Lillian's beadworking skills supplement the family income. Her spouse Lee and three children, Shawn, Shelly and Rachel, are often found occupying the craft table with Lillian.

Lillian's penchant for combining traditional and contemporary materials is evident in these two pieces. Both are made of smoked moosehide and deer skin, accented with porcupine quilling and tufted caribou/reindeer hair. Note the use of the contemporary beads: Swarovski crystals, Czech glass, and cloisonné. The stitches include edging, couching, and back stitch.

untitled bracelet

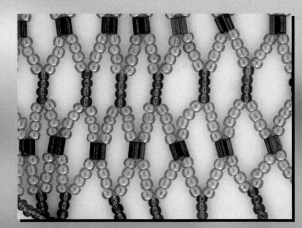

untitled collar

Since 1991 Jane Hodson, whose titles include spouse, homemaker, mother and grandmother, has filled her spare time with beads and basketry, particularly pine needle and antler-accented reed. Jane says she attends Jeanette's beading classes for the "lessons, laughter, and lots of beads." Jane's effervescent personality and hilarious tales definitely contribute to the ambiance.

Jane's bracelet was done on a loom using size 11 beads. The beadwork was then attached to a leather-backed metal bracelet cuff. The motif was inspired by the work of an elderly bead artist in Glenallen, Alaska. Size 11 beads and Czech glass crystals compose the collar, which combines a chevron chain with vertical netting.

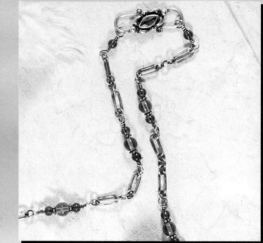

"Beaded Bead Necklace"

"Fairy Amulet Pouch"

Teri Packel has been buying beads as long as she can remember; she readily admits that she's hooked, addicted, obsessed. Good thing, that she works at Black Elk Leather and Beads, Alaska's largest bead store. For Teri beadwork is not only a time filler during long Alaskan winters, but also an outlet for her creative energies. After years of crafting, Teri finally feels she has the right to call herself an artist.

The "Beaded Bead Necklace" consists of Czech glass beads and three peyote-stitched wooden beads, connected with spiral rope and sterling silver chain. Inspired by her daughter Lesley's love of fairies, Teri created the "Fairy Amulet Pouch" depicting a tiny forest fairy. Done in two-drop peyote stitch, the pouch is accented with twisted fringe.

"1997 Love Stamp Amulet Bag"

"Tidal Pool Necklace"

Jacqueline Poston began beading in April 1995 and looks forward to pursuing this passion at all possible free moments. Jacqueline works as an environmental engineer and raises two sons. Jacqueline has lived in Alaska for the past ten years and believes doing beadwork is the best way to spend the long, dark winters!

The "1997 Love Stamp Amulet Bag" is a beaded replica of the US Postal Service stamp. It was completed in tubular peyote stitch with three layers of fringe work. The "Tidal Pool Necklace" consists of back stitching surrounding a lampwork bead by Andrea Guarino of Port Townsend, Washington. The free-form design represents the marine life typically found in a tidal pool.

"Baggin' Tourists"

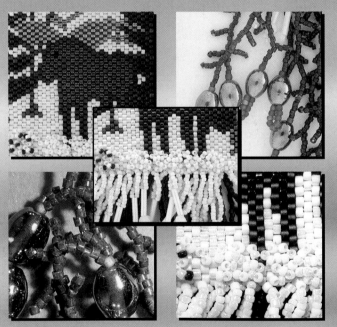

"Moose Nugget Factory"

Tourists flock to Alaska, lured by the certainty of seeing the whimsical puffin, the tail-flapping whale, the cute sea otter, and the soaring bald eagle. "Baggin Tourists," done with delica beads in tubular peyote stitch and spiral weave, echoes the wildlife and beauty of the Kenai Fjords.

Every Alaskan resident, even the urban ones, expects to share his property with the wildlife, especially the moose and bears. The neighborhood moose kindly leave behind droppings, which are gathered, lacquered, and sold to tourists as novelty items. It was tempting to accent this peyote-stitched amulet bag, entitled "Moose Nugget Factory," with real moose nuggets. However, I decided that nugget-shaped, brown glass beads would just be nicer to wear!

"In Full Bloom"

Although born in California, Rebecca Starry has lived in Alaska nearly 30 years. Through the creation of vivid, beaded floral expressions, Rebecca counters the rather long, cold winters of Alaska. She prefers labor-intensive pieces because of the meditative nature of the work. Eight years ago Rebecca was introduced to beadwork by her friend Ruby Brooke. Rebecca is vice-president of the Alaska Bead Society, Anchorage Chapter.

"In Full Bloom" was constructed with Czech seed beads, glass accent beads, and an ivory clasp, using thread and wire to do brick stitch and horizontal square stitch, a stitch which Rebecca developed. Michelle Waldren, an Alaskan bead maker, created the bead used at the center of the three-dimensional daisy.

The Complete Guide to
Beading Techniques

Photo by Myra Nunley

Jane Davis

Dedication

I dedicate this work to my mother, Marit Allgood Powell, who has always encouraged my many artistic endeavors since childhood. Thank you Mom. I love you.

Acknowledgments

Thank you and many warm thoughts to Sylvia Sur for pre-editing my text, especially for setting up the beginning organization of the patterns, the technical re-write of Chapters 5, 7, and 8, and the thread chart and information on beads in Chapter 1. This book would have fallen far short of its title without you.

Thank you to Ken Keyes Photography for the great photos that make this book a cut above.

Thank you to Carole Tripp of Creative Castle for the use of your store, your answers to all of my beading questions, moral support, and mostly for our wonderful friendship.

Thank you to Roger Tripp for dragging the slide projector out of your closet so I could preview the slides, and for carting miscellaneous beading items to your office so I could pick them up.

Thank you to Amy Tincher-Durik for your patience and understanding and your wonderful work on this book.

Thank you to all of the bead artists who have lent me their beautiful beadwork to photograph or sent me slides to include in this book. Your work beautifies these pages.

Thank you most of all to Rich, Jeff, Andrew, and Jonathan, who at times were strained but still supported my efforts, when this book spread throughout the house and put activities on hold so I could get it done and do it well.

In memory of Lynn Langford. Life is short, so make the most of if, and spread as much kindness as you can along the way.

Photo of beaded angel used with permission from *Art of Seed Beading*, by Elizabeth Gourley, Jane Davis, and Ellen Talbott, Sterling Publishing, N.Y., N.Y., 1999.

Table of Contents

Detail of the antique serving tray on page 365.

This antique steel-cut bag from France still shows the blue coating on the metal-faceted beads, although much of it has rusted or begun to flake away.

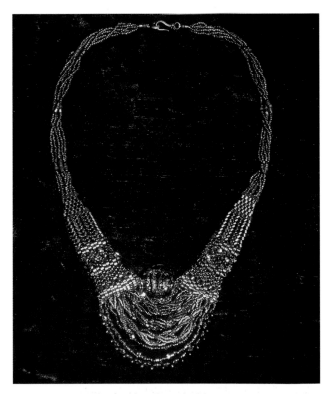

Ocean Waves, designed and stitched by Jane Davis. The use of various beading stitches adds texture to this piece.

Introduction

I was drawn to beadwork after seeing some amulet bags created by my friend Elizabeth Gourley and pulling out a treasured "some day I want to do this" article from 1986 on bead knitting by Alice Korach (the current editor of *Bead & Button Magazine*). Bead knitting was my first interest, and I searched out bead stores, magazine articles, and anything I could find to learn more. From there I progressed to peyote stitch and brick stitch. The first class I taught was the brick stitch Ladybug Box on page 294. I was extremely nervous at that first class, being very uncomfortable "on stage." But, my students were very gracious, and I'm still beading and teaching classes at Creative Castle in Newbury Park, California. During the same time period I entered a bead contest, and was amazed when my piece, Ocean Artisan, tied for the third place award. I was even more surprised when it was chosen for the cover of the companion book, *The Sea*. Since then, Liz Gourley, her twin sister Ellen Talbott, and I wrote *Art of Seed Beading*, and I have self-published three other beading books. I love all fine arts and crafts and find that my art background always helps with composition and color decisions.

This book is a result of my desire to try every possible handwork technique using beads. I have tried to make it as comprehensive as I could, all the time knowing it would be impossible to corral the ever-growing and ever-changing world of beads into one book. It is also my personal view of beading, which is a vast and varied creative field, with many different ways of doing the same thing. Because of this, I think of this book more as a sampling of beadwork, and so I have explained most techniques using a small sample first. A complete and creative project follows each how-to section. Several of the techniques, such as knitting, crochet, and tatting, assume the reader already has a skilled knowledge of the process, and so those sections do not cover the basics of that technique, but only how to use it incorporating beads. The final project, in Chapter 19, is a composite sampler using many of the techniques from the book. Throughout the book you will also find photos of beautiful antique beadwork and inspiring work of contemporary artists.

I hope you enjoy the projects in this book as much as I have enjoyed creating them.

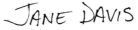

How to Use This Book

I wrote this book as both a reference and a project book. Before beginning a project in an unfamiliar technique, look over Chapter 1, The Basics, and then familiarize yourself with the new technique by making the learning sample that is provided before each project. For each sample, feel free to choose the color of beads and thread of your liking, unless otherwise noted. You can use these samples for small decorative projects like the ones shown here, or in Chapter 19, The Sampler, you can combine the learning samples into a sampler wall hanging.

The learning samples throughout the book can be used for a variety of small projects.

Chapter 1

The Basics

This chapter describes and illustrates the basic tools required for beadwork. Special tools such as bead looms are illustrated at the beginning of the chapters in which you learn how to use them with beads.

Beads

Technically, anything with a hole can be used as a bead. Most of the projects in this book use two types of glass beads, seed beads and Delica beads, but there are also other types available.

Seed beads are shaped like doughnuts and range from the tiny, antique size 24 beads used for miniature detail in projects, to the 1/8-inch tall by almost 3/16-inch wide size 6 beads used in the knitted pillow and right-angle weave basket projects (on pages 334 and 326, respectively). The higher the number, the smaller the bead.

Because of their curved sides, seed beads are well suited for techniques where the beads are arranged diagonally or at right angles, such as knitting, crochet, right-angle weave, flat circular peyote, and netting. The curved shape of the bead fits smoothly together in these stitches.

Delica beads, by Miyuki (and Toho Antiques, which are similar in size and appearance), are short cylinders with large holes relative to their size. They come in two sizes: small 1.5mm, about the same as a size 12 seed bead, and large, or 3.3mm, which is similar to a size 8 seed bead. There are more than 450 different colors of Delica. These beads are perfect for rectangular grid techniques such as loomwork, square stitch, peyote stitch, and brick stitch, where the beads fit tightly together in a stacking, block-like orientation.

Bead stores have an amazing variety of beads.

Seed beads.

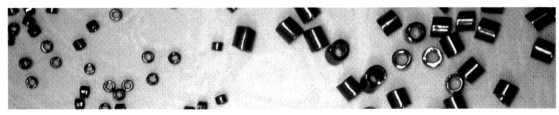

Delica beads.

Some other types of glass beads are:

Austrian Swarovski Crystals: Beads with a high lead content and precision faceting.

Bugle beads: Tube-shaped beads from 2mm to 30mm in length. These can be straight, hex cut, or twisted along their length.

Charlottes: These are seed beads that have been ground flat on one side.

Faceted beads: Seed beads ground with one or more flat surfaces. These include charlottes, three-cuts, and Austrian Swarovski Crystals.

Lampwork beads: Beads made one at a time by winding molten glass around a rod. The glass is heated using a small torch. In America, these beads are made as one-of-a-kind works of art. In Czechoslovakia, the same design of bead is made in larger quantities to sell, with apprentices spending much time learning to make beads exactly alike.

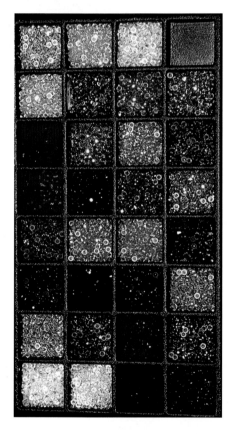

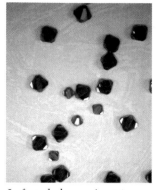

Left and above: Austrian Swarovski Crystals.

Bugle beads.

Charlottes.

Faceted beads.

Left and above: Lampwork beads.

Pressed glass: Beads pressed into a mold while the glass is soft. Common shapes are leaves, flowers, and drops, although many other shapes are available.

Three-cuts: Two-cut beads with random facets over their surface.

Two-cuts: Short bugle beads.

Any of the above beads can be made of different glass treatments such as:

Greasy: Semi-transparent beads.

Opaque: A solid-color bead commonly seen in traditional Native American beadwork.

Satin: Directional sheen due to tiny bubbles pulled through the glass as the bead is formed.

Transparent: Clear or colored glass that you can easily see through.

Pressed glass beads.

Pressed glass beads.

Three-cuts.

Two-cuts.

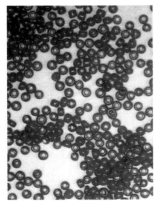

Greasy beads.

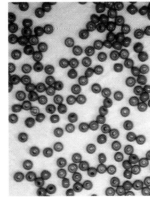

Opaque beads.

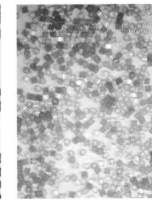

Satin beads.

Transparent beads.

Where Did Those Beads Come From?

Today, most beads are made in Japan, Czechoslovakia, or France. You can't always tell where the beads you have came from without verifying it with your place of purchase, but here are a few things of common knowledge among beaders. If it's on a hank, it's from the Czech Republic. It is the only country that does this right now; however, if it's in a bag or a tube, it may have been removed from a hank and bagged, so it could be from any manufacturer. If it's a Delica or antique bead, it's definitely from Japan. Finally, beads from France have muted colors, which was common in the late eighteenth and early twentieth centuries. White hearts are also from France. Other than that, there are no common indicators for French beads.

Glass beads can also be made with a variety of finishes. Some finishes are durable, while others wear off easily. Finishes can fade in the sun, wear off from water, heat, abrasion, or oils in your skin. To test a bead for durability, let it sit in the sun for a week (in a clear bag in your car is a good place), sew a strand to some fabric and put it through the washer and dryer, or wear a strand of beads on your wrist for a week. If you find that the bead finish wears off, you may choose not to use it, or to use it in a project where it isn't exposed to your skin, if that's its downfall, or isn't exposed to direct sunlight, etc. Beads with delicate finishes are sometimes the most beautiful or the perfect ones for your project. That's when you have to decide how much handling your piece will have, and whether it will hold up over time. Sometimes it's better to change bead colors to make a lasting project, but other times you may just want to use the beads you've found. The following page has a list of some common seed bead finishes in alphabetical order, noting possible wear problems.

Photo by Myra Nunley

Semi-precious stone cabochons and fused glass make great centerpieces for beading. These brooches were designed and beaded by Corinne Loomer.

Color and Beads

When choosing bead colors, there are a few things to consider. The color you see in a bag or tube of beads is not always the same color that ends up in your beadwork. This is because of the many different types of glass used for beads and the finishes applied to them. Finishes like Aurora Borealis (AB) color each bead a little differently, so unless you use the beads together in a large area, you will only have a small part of the color group in the AB beads. Also, loose beads in a bag or tube show both the side of the bead and the hole. In most beadwork, only the side of the bead shows; hence if the bead hole has more color or a different color than the side of the bead, you will have a different shade of color in your beadwork than what appears in the bag or tube. Finally, beads of the same shade look different depending on whether they are made from transparent, opaque, satin, or another glass process. For these reasons, it is very important to make a test swatch of the colors you plan to use in projects with small areas of a variety or gradation of colors, such as the face in the Sun Catcher project or the Floral Tray (see pages 304 and 282, respectively). This way, you can be confident from the beginning of your project that you will have a finished piece which is worthy of all of your time and effort.

Aurora Borealis (AB), iridescent beads, or oil beads: A permanent finish that gives a rainbow-like sheen to the glass. They look very different individually in beadwork from the color you see in the tube. These are good beads to use in large spaces, but use them judiciously in a complex color scheme, or they can mottle the design.

Galvanized metallic beads: Very shiny, attractive beads with a thin metallic coating. This coating quickly wears away from abrasion and contact with skin. Do not use in bracelets or any high-wear project. Coat with clear fingernail polish to help retain the finish after your project is completed.

Lined: Transparent glass with a color painted inside. May fade in sunlight.

Luster: A transparent colored coating. This is sometimes called a Ceylon or pearl finish if the coating is white, giving the bead a pearlized look. Good durability.

Matte: A dull finish achieved by tumbling or etching. Good durability.

Silver-lined: A silver lining in the hole of the bead gives a bright, shiny appearance and durable color to transparent-colored beads. The silver can wear off over time.

Surface dyed beads: Used on all types, from opaque to silver-lined, for making popular colors such as purples and pinks. These colors may rub off or will fade over time.

Many of the above finishes are combined to make a different type of bead such as a matte AB finish, which is a matte bead with the iridescent effect of an AB coating.

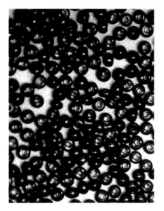
Beads with an AB finish.

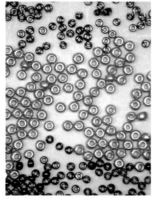
Galvanized metallic beads.

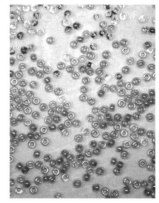
Color-lined beads.

Luster beads.

Matte-finished beads.

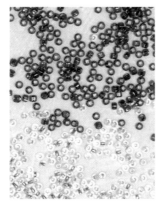
Silver-lined beads.

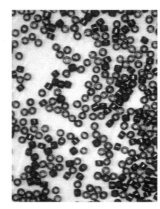
Beads with the color dyed onto the surface.

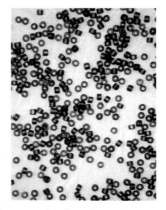
Matte beads with an AB finish.

These beads are in a category all their own!

Metal beads: Any bead made of metal.

Semi-precious stones: Beads of all shapes and sizes are made into semi-precious stone beads.

Steel cuts: Small metal beads, about a size 16, found in antique beaded bags. Some are round like seed beads, while some are faceted. Most are gold- or silver-toned. Some have a thin, metallic finish which is not very durable.

Triangles: Triangle beads are triangle-shaped as you look at them through the hole. In beadwork, the side showing is either one of the flat sides of the triangle, or one of the triangle edges, giving a distinct texture to the beadwork.

White hearts: A two-layer bead with a colored outer layer and a white inner glass layer. Originally, these beads were made to conserve on costly colored glass. Until recently, those available were all antique (they are being manufactured again).

Metal beads.

Semi-precious stone beads.

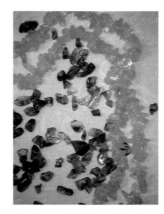
Semi-precious stone beads.

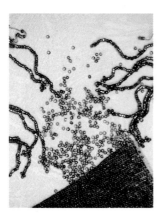
Steel cut beads.

Triangle beads.

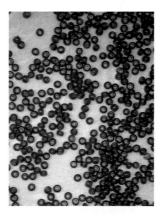
White heart beads.

Beading Terms

Here are a few general beading terms that appear throughout this book.

Beads can be packaged for sale in several ways. They are usually packaged by the bag or tube, by the hank or strand, or loose. Bags or tubes of beads are usually sold by weight, in grams and sometimes in ounces. A hank of beads is usually twelve 18- to 20-inch strands of beads with the ends tied together. Loose beads are usually large or specialty beads sold individually.

From left to right: loose beads, hanks of beads, and beads in bags and tubes.

Tools and Supplies

There is a variety of tools and supplies used in beading, with each beading technique having its own specific requirements and necessary tools and supplies. The following is an overview of the tools and supplies needed for the projects in this book.

Findings

Findings are metal parts used to put a piece of jewelry together, such as jump rings, clasps, earring posts, bead tips, and purse clasps. They are available in inexpensive base metals, as well as more expensive silver and gold. Taking time to choose a clasp or other finding that suits your project can greatly enhance the finished product. I recommend that you use quality findings that will not discolor, break, or cause skin allergies for the wearer. Be sure to ask for hypoallergenic findings when you purchase them if you have sensitive skin.

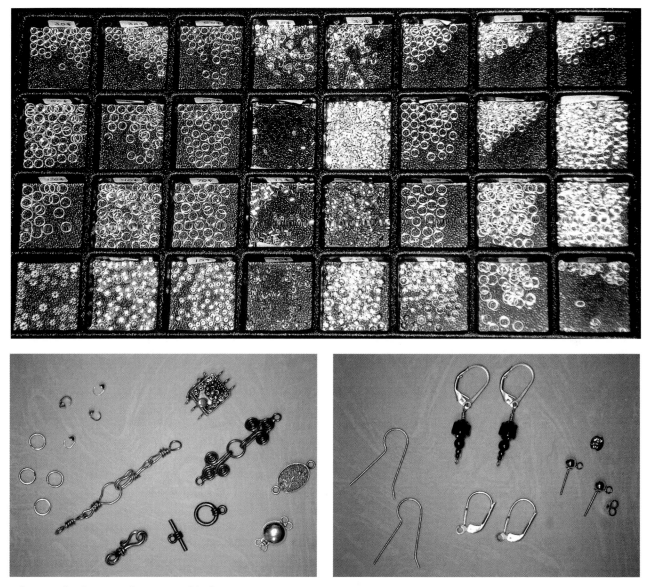

Above and right: A wide variety of findings.

Pliers

Pliers are used to shape wire and findings. There are three types commonly used with beadwork.

Needle nosed pliers are small pliers with pointed ends that look like a semi-circle from the end. They have small ridges on the inside face for a good grip. They are good all-purpose pliers for anything from bead knotting to just pulling a needle through a tough piece of suede.

Flat nosed pliers are like needle nosed pliers except that they do not have ridges and the nose end does not taper down to points. They are good for bending wire at right angles and gripping loops to wind wire around.

Round nosed pliers are thin, tapered pliers with small, round ends. They are used for winding wire into loops.

Wire Cutters

Any wire cutter will do for beginning wirework, but as you become more adept, you will want better tools. The best wire cutters for jewelry close together parallel on one side, so you can make a clean cut through the wire, making a straight edge, rather than one tapered to a center ridge.

Wire

Wire comes in many colors, sizes, and metals. The sizes are determined by the gauge; the lower the number, the thicker the wire. Wire can be soft, hard, or somewhere in between. Soft wire is easily bent and hardens somewhat the more it is bent. Hard wire is more difficult to bend, so it is good for adding structure to a piece. Wires come in many shapes, including round, half round, square, triangle, and beaded. Square and triangle wire are often twisted to give added detail to a wirework piece.

Purse Frames

There is a variety of purse frames, both antique and contemporary, used for making beaded purses and bags. The majority has holes along the bottom of the frame to sew beadwork in place.

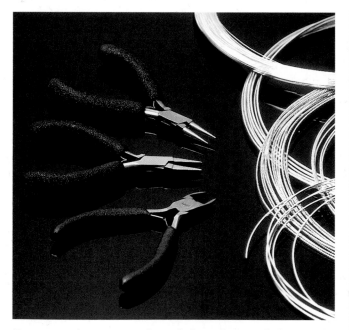

From top to bottom: round nosed pliers, flat nosed pliers, and wire cutters and beaded, round, and square sterling silver wire.

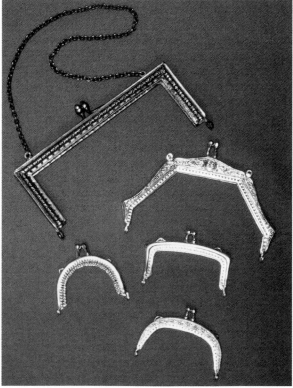

Antique and contemporary purse frames used in making beaded bags.

Needles

Any needle that can fit through your bead holes can be used for beading; however, thin needles, which easily slide through small bead holes, and long needles, which can pick up many beads at a time, are preferred. Here are several types of needles that make beading easier.

Beading needles are longer and thinner than sewing needles, so they fit through bead holes and allow you to pick up several beads at one time. Most beading needles have sharp ends. They range in size from the very thin size 16 to the thick size 10; these numbers correspond loosely to the bead size the needle will fit through.

Loomwork beading needles are 3 inches, or more, long, so that you can pass through a wide width of loomed beads.

Wire beading needles are a thin piece of wire, folded in half and twisted. The eye is the folded loop which collapses when pulled through a bead. Wire needles are used for threads which are too thick to thread in a standard beading needle, such as silk cord for knotted necklaces.

Bead embroidery needles are short like a cross stitch needle and have a blunt end, but are thin enough to accommodate size 11 beads.

Sharps needles are short, pointed needles with a small eye, used for appliqué and general hand stitching.

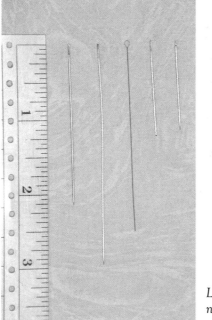

Left to right: Beading needle, loomwork needle, wire beading needle, bead embroidery needle, and sharps needle.

Threads and Cords

Beading thread can be any thread you can thread your needle with and get through a bead hole; however, glass beads get heavy as you add them to large projects. You should use the strongest thread you can find, which still gives you the drape you want. Some say that no thread can compare to the drape silk allows, but I have found that tension plays just as large a role in how a beaded fabric drapes.

About Thread Size Labeling Systems

Various systems have been used to designate thread thickness, resulting in a confusing set of numbers and letters to refer to the similar units of measurement.

Denier is an old French term for the weight in grams of 9000 meters of thread. Different fibers have different weights, so 40 denier nylon is not the same thickness as 40 denier silk. Denier is relevant only when used to compare the same fiber and it is only used for extruded fibers like silk and nylon and not spun fibers such as cotton or wool. For this reason, the European Union has banned the use of denier, and the new unit of measure is grams per kilometer of thread. The term denier still remains in use in the United States.

Common Thread Thickness Units

Nymo	Denier	Other threads that are the same thickness
OO	50	Silk size 50
O or A	60	Silamide twisted tailoring nylon
B		Silk size 380
D	1000	Upholstery Conso or Coats twisted nylon
E, F, FF		Gudebrod silk stringing twist with the same letter designations

Nymo

This is the most popular all-purpose beading thread currently available. Made of non-twisted bonded nylon filaments, Nymo comes in many colors and thicknesses. The number of filaments determines the thickness of the thread. Although Nymo has become the generic term for nylon beading thread, the brand name Nymo thread, by Belding Cortecelli, is generally the best quality. Nylon does not mildew or rot and makes a very durable thread for beadwork pieces.

Silk Cord

I like to use this thread for knitting, crochet, and beadweaving. It is very important to wax silk before beadweaving, or it will knot and kink. Silk is sized both by letters, as Nymo, and by denier, as shown in the table on the previous page. For knitting and crochet, 1000 denier is good and corresponds to about a size D Nymo.

Pearl Cotton

Sizes 12 and 8 are used for bead knitting, beaded knitting, and tubular crochet projects. This is a cotton thread and has its own numbering system. Size 12 is comparable to an E and size 8 is about as thick as F cord in silk. Pearl cotton tends to fray from the beads sliding on it, so it is not good for flat or round crochet or tatting where much of the cotton shows. If you wax the pearl cotton, it is a good thread for beadweaving with the larger size 8 and 6 beads.

Cebelia or Manuela

A tightly twisted cotton cord is better than pearl cotton for bead knitting, bead crochet, and tatting. The tight twist keeps the cord shiny and clean. There are many brand names available; however, they are not as readily available as pearl cotton. (For mail ordering, see the Supply Sources.)

Thread Conditioners

The traditional thread conditioner is beeswax. Slide the thread through the wax several times to apply an even, light coating. Then, slide the thread between your fingers several times to soften the wax and press it into the thread. If you use too much wax, the eye of the needle can close from wax build-up and even the bead holes can get filled with wax. To remove a wax plug from a needle, hold the needle between your thumb and forefinger to warm the wax in the eye. Also, it is better to use a thicker thread instead of heavily waxing a thinner one to give body to the bead fabric.

Pearl cotton.

There is a growing variety of tightly twisted cotton cords suitable for bead knitting, bead crochet, and tatting.

Nymo thread.

Silk cord.

Beeswax and Thread Heaven.

274

Thread Heaven is a newer, silicon-based thread conditioner that is lighter than beeswax and causes the end of the thread to be repelled from the working length. If you have lots of knotting problems involving the end of your thread, this can help you. Apply to the thread the same as beeswax. Use lightly and repeat if necessary.

Fray Check is an old sewing standby. It is useful for stiffening the end of the thread for easier threading into the eye of the needle. A light coating of glue will also work to create a stiff thread end that can function like a self-needle.

Basic Techniques

Beginning and Ending Threads

No matter how long a thread you use, eventually you have to end and restart your thread. For the best results, be sure to:
• Hide the threads invisibly in the work.
• Secure them in the work with a small knot or by weaving around in a circle so the thread cannot come out.
• Bury the new end in the beads so it does not show.

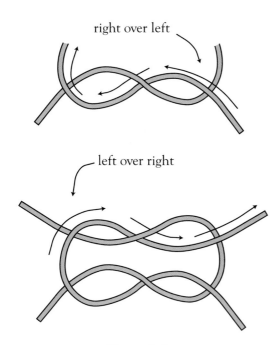

right over left

left over right

Figure 1-1

Stop Bead

A stop bead is used at the beginning of a project to prevent the beads from falling off the tail and provide tension for the first row of strung beads against which to weave.

To make a stop bead, pick up a bead and tie a square knot 6 inches from the tail, catching the bead in the knot. You will need to untie the bead later to weave in the tail thread. You can also wrap the tail around one of your fingers several times instead of using a stop bead.

Square Knot

The square knot (**Figure 1-1**) is my favorite knot in beadwork. Always remember: right over left, then left over right. This means cross the thread in your right hand over the thread in your left hand and around and through to tie a knot. Then, cross the thread that's now in your left hand over the thread in your right hand and around and through to tie a knot again. This makes a secure knot that won't slip out as easily as others. You may also want to put a small amount of clear nail polish on the knot to make sure it stays tied.

Overhand Knot

An overhand knot (**Figure 1-2**) is a good knot to use when weaving in threads. It catches the thread on itself, giving added protection against unraveling. To make an overhand knot, take a small stitch over a thread in the work and pull through until there is just a loop. Pass through the loop and pull tight. This knot is not as secure as the square knot but works well when used twice along with weaving the thread through several beads.

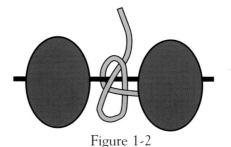

Figure 1-2

Weaving in Thread Ends

Weaving in thread ends means to pass the thread back through the beads, or fabric, knotting the thread and hiding it so that it is invisible.

For beadwork which is supported or will not get much handling, such as the Peyote Stitch Sun Catcher (on page 304), I just pass through adjacent beads several times.

For pieces that are handled often, such as the Herringbone Pinch Purse (on page 318), I tie an overhand knot, then pass through several beads in the stitch pattern and tie another overhand knot, then pass through several more beads and cut the thread close to the beadwork.

In knitted, crocheted, and tatted projects where there are non-beaded areas, make overhand knots in the non-beaded thread areas to secure the ends, then pass through the non-beaded area, encasing the thread in the stitches invisibly. Cut close to the needlework.

Bead Fabric

Large pieces of flat beadwork are sometimes referred to as bead fabric.

Breaking a Bead

Sometimes you will have a bead in the wrong place, and it is easier to break the bead rather than undo your work to correct the error. For example, when stringing beads for knitting, crocheting, or tatting, you may have added two blue beads and the pattern only calls for one, or, in netting, you find you've put six beads in a loop that's supposed to have five and you don't want to pull all of the beading out to get back to that point.

You can easily break a glass bead with flat nosed or needle nosed pliers, but if you do it the wrong way, you will cut your thread every time. You need to wrap the thread tightly around your index finger and carefully grab the bead (**Figure 1-3**). Turn your face away and squeeze the pliers until the bead breaks. You may also want to slide your hands between a folded towel so you can easily clean up the glass chips. Never break the bead by squeezing the pliers on the bead as shown in (**Figure 1-4**). This will cause the breaking bead to cut the thread.

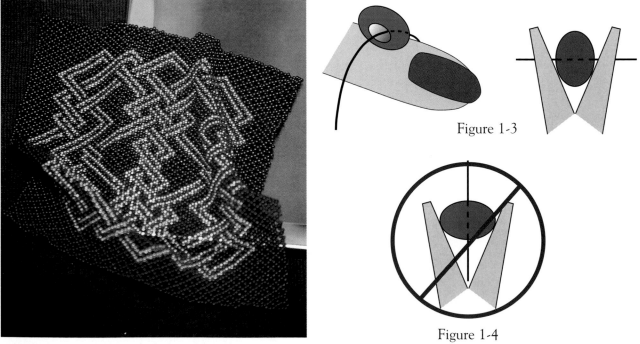

This bead netted piece shows the fluid drape of the beading; this is why it is sometimes called "bead fabric."

Figure 1-3

Figure 1-4

Sculptural beadwork is three-dimensional bead-work in any medium.

One Grecian Urn Perfume Nectar Necklace, designed and stitched by Delinda V. Amura. This sculptural vessel pendant is stitched in peyote with size 15 seed beads.

Antique loomed steel-cut purse made in France.

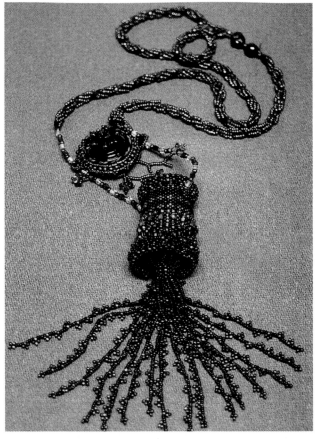

Heart Locket Gone Wild, by Marlin Beads, is constructed with a combination of brick stitch and sculptural peyote stitch, using a variety of bead types.

This neckpiece shows how changing bead sizes and random increases and decreases transforms peyote stitch. Collared Elegance in freeform peyote stitch, by Marlin Beads.

Beaded Vessel, designed and stitched by Sylvia Sur. Sculptural beadwork like this small container can be even more beautiful when viewed with back lighting.

Chapter 2
Loomwork

Beaded loomwork is a very old craft, used in the United States by Native Americans for generations. This technique of making a fabric of beads with thread is suitable for a large variety of items, from purses to belts and necklaces. There are many ways to add to the flat loomed piece, from adding fringe while the piece is on the loom to adding three-dimensional beading, giving depth to the finished piece.

Weaving beads on a loom is one of the quickest methods of beading, because a whole row of beads can be woven at one time. You give back some of the speed of weaving in setting up the loom in the beginning, and in hiding or decorating the warp threads at the end.

First, you start warping the loom, which means looping the warp thread back and forth across the loom, laying down equally spaced, parallel rows of thread. Next, you string the beads according to a design on a separate thread called the weft, and weave them between the warp threads. When you finish weaving the design, you cut the warp threads near the loom. Finally, you hide the cut ends of the warp ends at the back of the work or weave them up into the work.

There is a variety of looms available. The following sample is made on an inexpensive, small metal and wood loom sold in most craft stores. The following will show you how to warp the loom and create a sample.

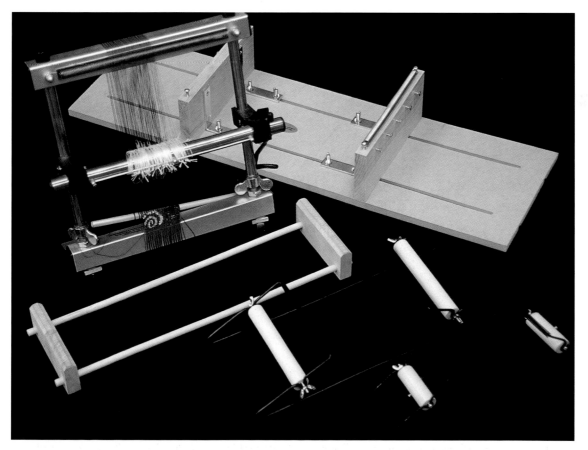

Several types of looms.

Loomwork Sample

You Will Need

Delica beads, in the colors shown in
   the Loomwork Sample design chart
Size D Nymo

Size 10 beading needle
Beading loom
Glue

To warp the loom:

1. Roll the loom's dowels so the screws are facing away from the loom. Tighten the wing nuts.

2. Pull the thread from the spool, but do not cut it. Tie a square knot around the screw on one of the dowels.

3. Guide the thread up over the springs, around the screw on the other dowel (**Figure 2-1**).

4. Guide the thread back over the springs again so that it rests in the next slot between the springs (**Figure 2-2**). Continue looping the thread back and forth, over the springs and around the screws until there are 21 threads across the loom, each in its own slot. Keep the tension even.

5. Tie the thread to the screw and cut the thread from the spool. These are your warp threads. You always use one more warp thread than the number of beads in the width of the bead design chart.

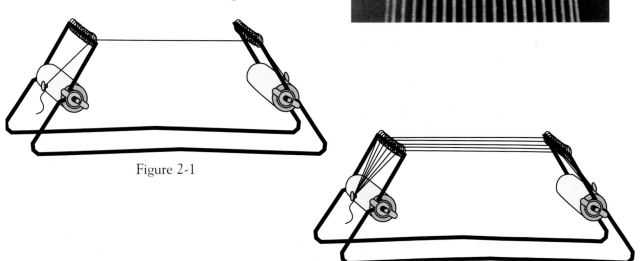

Figure 2-1

Figure 2-2

To begin weaving:

1. Tie an 8-foot length of thread to the bottom leftmost warp thread, leaving a 12-inch tail to weave in later. Thread the needle.

2. Pass the needle under the warp threads to the right. Read the Loomwork Sample design chart from the bottom to the top, left to right. Pick up beads for Row 1 (all cream beads), and push them up against the warp threads so that each bead sits between two warp threads.

3. Pass the needle back through the beads, holding the beads against the warp with your index finger so the needle passes above the warp threads, locking the beads in place.

4. Repeat Steps 2 and 3 for each row of the design chart.

To make a thread selvage:

1. Weave in and out of the warp threads without beads for about 1/4 inch (**Figure 2-3**).

2. Put a dab of glue along the last two or three rows of thread weaving. Let dry.

3. Thread the 12-inch tail at the beginning of the weaving and repeat Steps 1 and 2.

4. Cut the beadwork from the loom 1/8 inch beyond the thread selvages.

5. Fold the woven thread selvages under. Glue them to the beads in place with a small amount of glue.

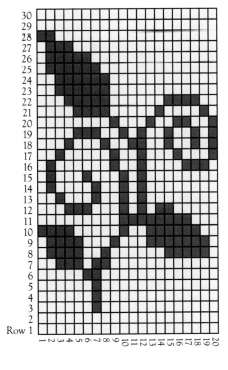

■ #859
□ #157

Loomwork Sample
design chart

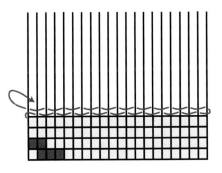

Figure 2-3

Here's how the small loom looks after you've bent the ends up. They are almost perpendicular to the table so you can weave a larger piece without winding the beading.

Beaded Loomwork Floral Tray

You Will Need

Sudberry House Petite Serving Tray #6565
Delica beads, as shown in the Color Key
    for Floral Loomwork Tray
1 large spool size D Nymo

1 small spool size B Nymo
Size 10 or 12 loom beading needle
Loom
Glue

The idea for a beadwork tray came from the beautiful antique beaded needlepoint tray on page 365. I chose some of my favorite flowers for the design and made the graph from my watercolor painting. Then, I took the pattern from the loom-work sample and repeated it randomly in white and mint to add texture to an otherwise plain background.

Unless you own a loom that is wide enough for 177 warp threads, you will need to make this piece in sections, as I did. I have written the instructions so you can make this piece in strips on a small loom. If you use a larger loom, you will need to adjust the number of warp threads to the most you can fit for each section.

Finished size: 7 by 10 inches (beadwork area only)

I learned a trick from Delinda Vannebrightyn Amura, a national teacher and author of The Illuminated Beading Manuscripts Book II The Loom, *to make the loom big enough to bead a larger area without having to wind the growing beadwork onto the dowels. To fit the 7-inch height of beading onto your small loom, before beginning, pull the ends so they are almost perpendicular to the bottom wire. Adjust the loom so that all of the corners lie flat on the table.*

1. Warp the loom as described for the sample of loomwork on page 280 using size D Nymo, until you have filled it with warp threads. Use size B Nymo for the last warp thread so the seams will not show on the finished piece.

2. Count how many warp threads you have and then subtract 1. This is the number of beads you will be weaving for this section of the tray. Use sticky notes on the Beaded Loomwork Floral Tray design chart to isolate the section you will be weaving.

3. Beginning in the bottom left corner, weave the section of the pattern you have isolated. Make thread woven selvages as described for the sample on page 281. Cut from the loom.

4. Repeat Steps 1 to 3 for the next sections of the design, each time moving the sticky notes to show only the part of the design you are weaving.

5. When all of the sections are completed, stitch them together by weaving through three or four beads in each row along the adjoining selvages (**Figure 2-4**).

6. Place the finished beadwork into the tray following the manufacturer's instructions.

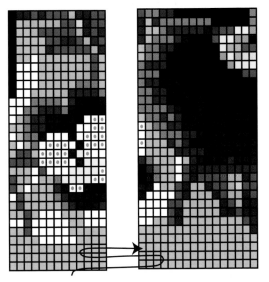

Figure 2-4

Color Key for Floral Loomwork Tray

- Background #829, 50 grams
- Background #211, 9 grams
- Pansy leaves #372, less than 1 gram
- Pansy leaves #724, less than 1 gram
- All leaves #663, 3 grams
- Violet leaves #374, less than 1 gram
- Violet leaves #373, 2 grams
- Violet leaves #859, 3 grams
- Violet and Pansy leaves #275, 3 grams
- Sweet Pea leaves #733, less than 1 gram
- Sweet Pea leaves #877, 3 grams
- Sweet Pea leaves #372, less than 1 gram
- Sweet Pea leaves #380, less than 1 gram
- Sweet Pea leaves #724, 3 grams
- Flower centers #160, less than 1 gram
- Johnny Jump-up #053, less than 1 gram

- Sweet Pea #234, less than 1 gram
- Sweet Pea #245, less than 1 gram
- Sweet Pea #855, less than 1 gram
- Sweet Pea #1371, less than 1 gram
- Sweet Pea # 362 , less than 1 gram
- Red Pansy #295, less than 1 gram
- Red Pansy #296, 2 grams
- All Flowers # 80 , 2 grams
- All Flowers #881 , 2 grams
- All Flowers #661, 2 grams
- All Flowers # 216 , 2 grams
- Pansies #880, 2 grams
- All Flowers #1379, 1 gram
- Pansies #464, 2 grams
- Pansies #278, 1 gram
- Pansies #310, less than 1 gram

Rows

Columns

Beaded Loomwork Floral Tray design chart

285

Chapter 3
Square Stitch

Square stitch is visually very close to loom-work, because the beads are aligned in the same straight rectilinear grid pattern of rows and columns.

In square stitch, the beads are added to the beginning row of beads one bead at a time. You put on a bead, then loop through the bead below on the first row, then come back up through the new bead. You add each bead this way to the end of the row, then repeat the process starting on the opposite side.

Because you follow the pattern back and forth in a zigzag, you have to pay attention to the direction of the work with non-symmetrical designs.

Square stitch creates a very elastic fabric, with a great deal of drape. The first row is awkward, and you'll need to keep the beads in place as you stitch. Once you complete about three rows, it is easier.

Square Stitch Sample

You Will Need

Delica beads, in the colors shown in the Square Stitch Sample design chart	Size B or D Nymo
	Size 10 beading needle

Finished size: 1-1/8 inches by 2-1/8 inches

1. Thread the needle with a 4-foot length of thread and add a stop bead.

2. String 18 cream-colored Delicas; this is the first row of the Square Stitch Sample design chart, from bead 1 to bead 18.

3. String one cream-colored bead. This is bead number 18 in the second row of the design chart.

4. Pass through the 18th bead from the first row (**Figure 3-1**).

5. Pass through the 18th bead from the second row (**Figure 3-2**). The first row is very flexible. Pull each stitched bead tight, holding the beads in place so they stay parallel to the same number bead in the previous row. Use the stop bead to keep the beads in the first row snug.

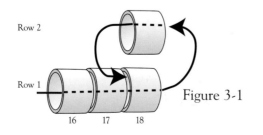

Row 2

Row 1

16   17   18

Figure 3-1

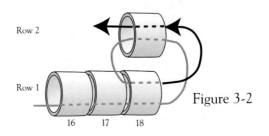

Row 2

Row 1

16   17   18

Figure 3-2

6. String the 17th bead in Row 2 on the design chart.

7. Pass through the 17th bead from the first row (**Figure 3-3**).

8. Pass through the 17th bead from the second row (**Figure 3-4**).

9. Continue adding beads, looping through the adjacent bead in the previous row, then back through the new bead until the end of the row.

Repeat in the opposite direction, adding beads 1 through 18 of Row 3. Continue in this manner for each row.

10. When you've finished the pattern, weave in the working thread and cut close to the beading.

11. Untie the stop bead and remove it from the thread. Thread the needle with the 12-inch tail and loop through the first row (**Figure 3-5**). This evens out the tension in the first row so it has the same elasticity as the rest of the piece. Weave in this thread and cut close to the beading.

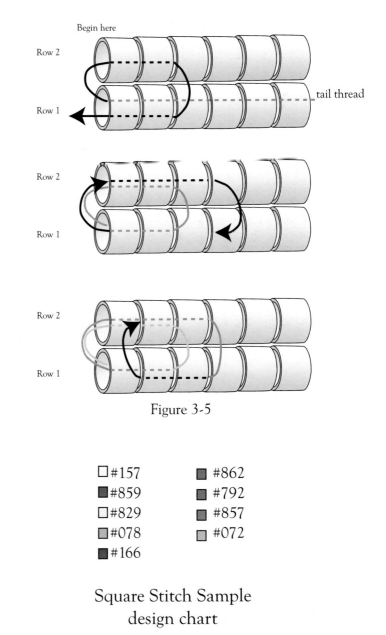

Figure 3-3

Figure 3-4

Figure 3-5

□ #157	■ #862
■ #859	■ #792
□ #829	■ #857
▨ #078	▨ #072
■ #166	

Square Stitch Sample
design chart

287

Square Stitch Table Setting

You Will Need

Wooden salt and pepper shakers, milk can
style, 3-3/16 inches high by 1-3/4-inch
diameter
Wooden napkin ring, colonial style, 1-1/4
inches tall by 1-3/4 inches wide
Size 8 seed beads
16 grams or 3/4 oz. of green

6 grams or 1/4 oz. of pink
6 yellow
77 grams or 2-3/4 oz. white
Size D white Nymo
Size 10 beading needle
White craft paint and brush or enamel
spray paint

This table setting is
quick to make in size 8
seed beads. The beaded
covers for the salt and
pepper shakers are bead-
ed flat, then attached
around the middle of the
wooden shakers. The
napkin ring is worked in
the round on a wooden
base. The coaster is a flat
piece of beadwork which
can be stitched to a
padded fabric base or
used alone.

Finished sizes:
Coaster: 3-3/4 inches
square
Salt and pepper shakers:
1-1/4-inch high beaded
area on 3-3/16-inch high
by 1-3/4-inch diameter
shakers
Napkin ring: 3/4-inch
wide beaded area on a 1-
3/4-inch diameter wood-
en napkin ring

Paint
1. Paint the wooden salt
and pepper shakers and
napkin ring with white
paint. Let dry.

288

To make the coaster:

1. Thread the needle with a 8-foot length of Nymo. Tie a stop bead 18 inches from the tail.

2. String Row 1 of the Coaster design chart.

3. Bead the coaster following the pattern. Weave in the end and cut close to the beading.

4. Thread the 18-inch tail and loop through the first and second rows as described for the Square Stitch Sample (on page 286) to even out the tension of the first row. Weave in the tail and cut close to the beading.

5. If desired, cut a piece of felt 1/8 inch smaller than the finished coaster and stitch along the edges to the beads.

Note: The coaster is shown on its side.

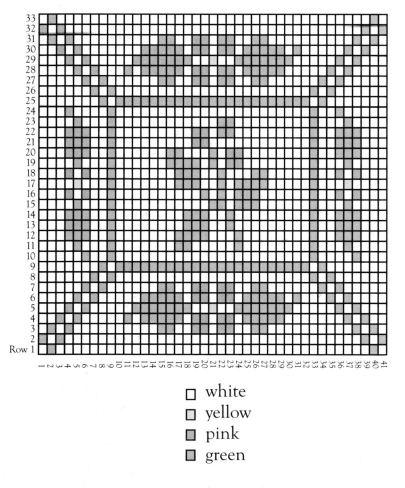

□ white
□ yellow
■ pink
□ green

Coaster design chart

To make the salt and pepper shakers:

1. Thread the needle with a 8-foot length of Nymo. Tie a stop bead 12 inches from the tail.

2. String Row 1 of the Salt and Pepper Shaker design chart.

3. Bead the design following the pattern.

4. Stretch the beadwork around one shaker and stitch through the adjacent beads of the first and last rows to close the beadwork around the shaker (**Figure 3-6**).

5. Weave in the tail and working thread and cut close to the beadwork.

6. Repeat Steps 1 to 5 for the pepper shaker, using the "P" in place of the "S."

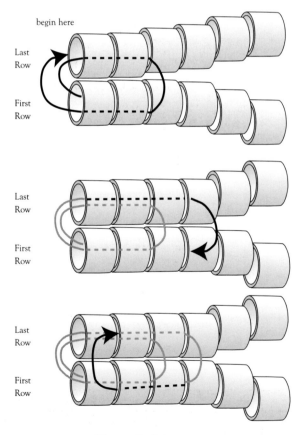

Figure 3-6

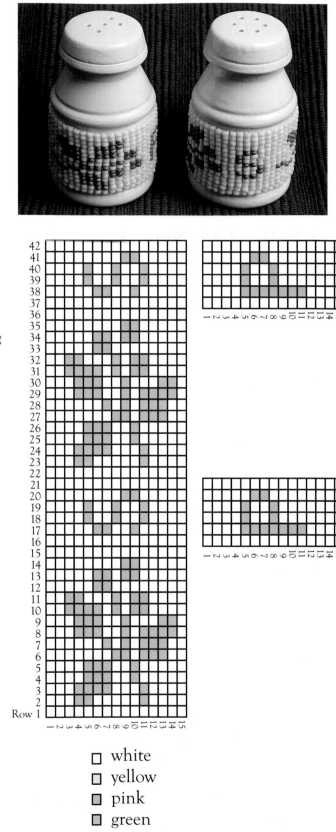

☐ white
☐ yellow
☐ pink
☐ green

Salt and Pepper Shaker
design chart

To make the napkin ring:

1. Thread the needle with a 8-foot length of Nymo. String 65 white beads and pass through them again to form a circle (**Figure 3-7**).

2. Tighten the circle of beads over the indentation on one end of the wooden base. Tie the tail and working thread into a square knot, leaving a 6-inch tail to weave in later. This is the first row of the design. The visible gaps between the beads will be evened out as you bead the next rows.

3. Bead Row 2 of the Napkin Ring design chart. The first and last row will be tight in the groove of the napkin ring. All of the other rows will be loose and elastic.

4. When you finish the round, pass through the first and last beads of the first two rows to attach the first and last beads of Row 2 together (**Figure 3-8**). Repeat this for each row.

5. Stitch Row 3 in the opposite direction around the napkin ring.

6. Continue stitching around, alternating the starting direction of the stitching with each row until you finish the beadwork. Pass through the last row of beads again and pull tightly, so the last row fits into the indentation on the napkin ring. Knot the thread. Weave in the ends.

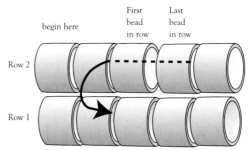

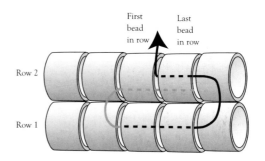

Figure 3-8

□ white
□ yellow
■ pink
□ green

Napkin Ring
design chart

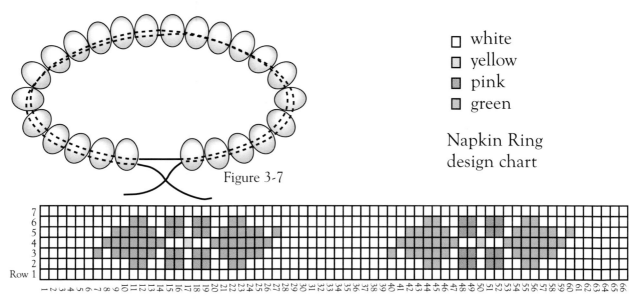

Figure 3-7

291

Chapter 4
Brick and Ladder Stitch

Brick stitch is well named, because the beads are arranged like a brick wall, with each row offset by half a bead width. The bead holes sit vertically, and each bead is added by attaching it to the loop between two beads in the previous row.

Ladder stitch is the most common way to begin the brick stitch, because it provides a row of beads with loops of thread between the vertical bead holes, ready for brick stitch. Brick stitch is sometimes called Comanche or Cheyenne stitch due to its usage by Native American tribes of the same names.

Brick stitch box in progress.

Brick Stitch and Ladder Stitch Sample

— You Will Need —

Delica beads, in the colors shown in the Brick Stitch Sample design chart	Size B or D Nymo
	Size 10 beading needle

Finished size: 1-1/8 by 2-1/4 inches

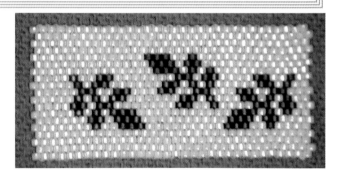

To make the first row in ladder stitch:

1. Thread the needle with a 6-foot length of thread. Tie a stop bead 6 inches from the tail and pick up 32 cream-colored beads. This is Row 1 on the Brick Stitch Sample design chart.

2. Hold the beads in your left hand (**Figure 4-1**) and pass through the second bead from the needle, toward the needle. Pull tight so the bead closest to the needle and the bead you passed through tighten together about 6 inches from the stop bead (**Figure 4-2**).

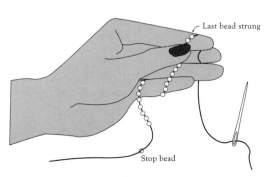

Last bead strung

Stop bead

Figure 4-1

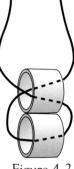

Figure 4-2

3. Pass the needle through the next bead away from the needle, toward the two beads just stitched, and pull the thread through, letting the three beads hang just before you pull them tight so they can twist into place on the growing ladder of beads (**Figure 4-3**).

4. Repeat Step 3 until all 32 beads are stitched together. Pass back through the second to last bead. Untie and remove the stop bead and tie the tail and working thread into a square knot (**Figure 4-4**). This is Row 1 of the Brick Stitch Sample design chart stitched into ladder stitch.

To make the sample in brick stitch:
1. Continuing with the ladder-stitched beads, pick up bead 1 and bead 2 in Row 2 on the design chart.

2. Pass through the thread between the last two beads on the ladder stitch piece (**Figure 4-5**).

3. Pass down through bead 2 on Row 2 (**Figure 4-6**). Pull tight.

4. Pick up the next bead in the row. Pass through the next loop between the next two beads in the previous row. Pass down through the bead just strung.

5. Repeat Step 4 across the row.

6. Continue each row the same as Steps 1 through 5, working back and forth across each row of the design chart. Weave in the ends.

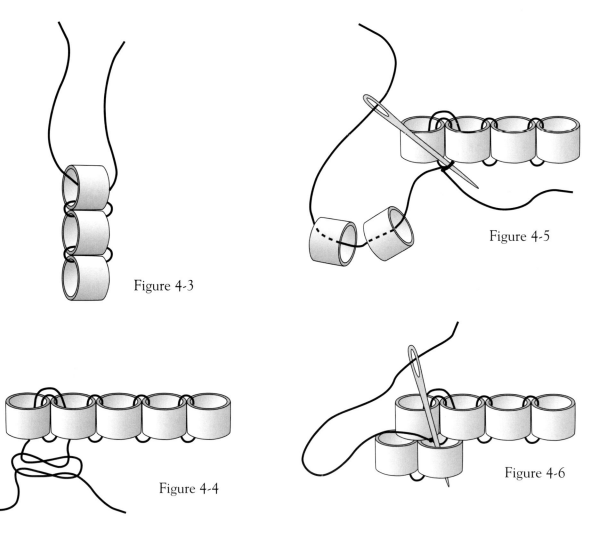

Figure 4-3

Figure 4-5

Figure 4-4

Figure 4-6

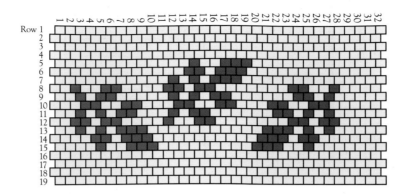

■ #859

□ #157

Brick Stitch Sample
design chart

Ladybug Box

You Will Need

Wooden, round "pumpkin" box, 2 inches wide
  by 1-1/2 inches high
Small amounts of black and white acrylic
  paint and brush
Clear gloss acrylic spray

Size B Nymo
Size 10 beading needle
Delica beads, in the colors shown in the
  Ladybug Box design chart

This box is special to me, because it is the first project I ever taught. It was a big step for me because I am much more comfortable alone in a room with my needlework than standing in front of a class. I'll always remember those polite students, who really knew more about beading than I did at the time.

This is a fun box to make, although the first three rows are a bit of a struggle. It is important to pay close attention to the increases, so that the pattern lines up properly from the beginning, so you can stitch the rest of the box trouble-free.

Finished size: 2 inches wide by 1-1/2 inches high (beaded area is 1-1/4 inches high)

To paint the wooden box:

1. Paint the area you will bead over in white.

2. Paint the rims, bottom, and lid in black. Let dry.

3. Spray with a clear gloss finish. Let dry.

How to read the Ladybug Box design chart:

1. Each colored rectangle is one bead. The color matches the bead color to use.

2. White rectangles with diagonal lines indicate where you increase or decrease your bead count to shape the beaded cover so it fits snugly around the curved box.

3. You start at the upper left corner and work left to right and down.

How to increase:

Increase beads have arrows pointing to the left. When you get to one of these beads in the chart, put on one bead and pass the needle through the same thread loop as the bead before. You have two beads in the same thread loop (**Figure 4-7**).

How to decrease:

Decrease beads have arrows pointing to the right. When you get to one of these beads in the chart, put on one bead and skip the next thread loop. Pass through the second thread loop over. You decreased by one bead (**Figure 4-8**).

To work Row 1:

1. Thread the needle with a 6-foot length of thread. Start 2 feet in from the end and make a tight ladder stitch 82 beads long using the light blue beads. You will use up some of the tail in making the ladder, and the rest will be for weaving in once you have stitched about three rows on the box.

2. Make sure your ladder is not twisted (straighten out any twists). Join into a circle by passing through the first bead (**Figure 4-9**).

3. Put the loop of ladder stitch in the indentation below the box's top rim. Tie a square knot with the tail and working thread.

To work Row 2:

1. Pick up two light blue beads and start to brick stitch around the box, following the color placement in the design chart.

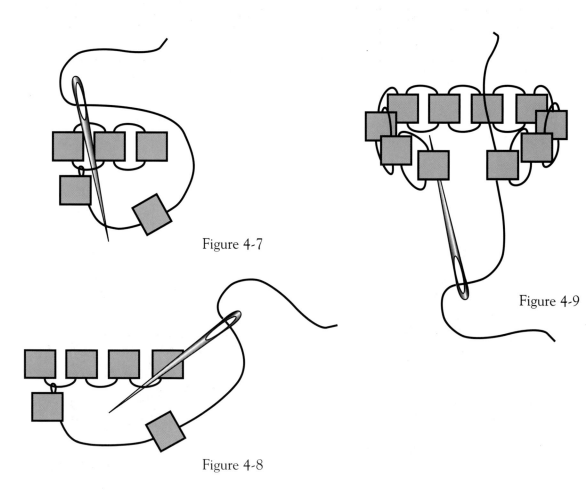

Figure 4-7

Figure 4-8

Figure 4-9

2. At the end of the row, pass through the first bead in the row (**Figure 4-10**), then back through the last bead in the row to close the round (**Figure 4-11**).

To work Row 3:

1. Pick up two beads. Pass through the thread loop between the first and second beads in Row 2. Pass through the second bead and continue around the box, following the chart.

2. Increase where the arrows indicate by stitching the bead marked with an arrow in the same space as the stitch before it.

3. Close the round by passing up through the first bead in this row and one bead in Row 2 (**Figure 4-12**).

4. Pass down through one bead in Row 2 and the first bead in Row 3 (**Figure 4-13**).

To work Row 4:

1. Pick up two beads. Pass through the thread loop between the second and third bead in Row 3.

2. Continue around, finishing as you did Row 3.

To finish the box:

Work brick stitch around the box. On odd rows, stitch between the first and second beads of the previous row. On even rows, stitch between the second and third beads of the previous row. Watch how the beginning beads line up to make sure that you are starting your rows correctly.

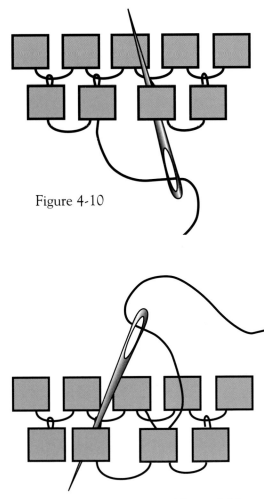

Figure 4-10

Figure 4-11

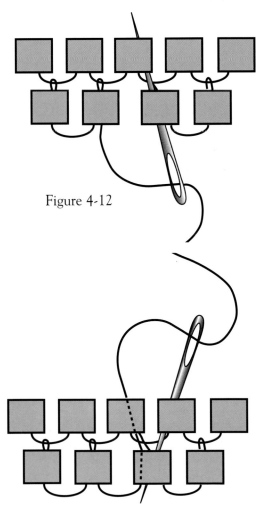

Figure 4-12

Figure 4-13

Ladybug Box
design chart

- ☐ #879
- ■ #683
- ■ Black
- ☐ #107
- ☐ #916
- ■ #656
- ■ #797
- ■ #275

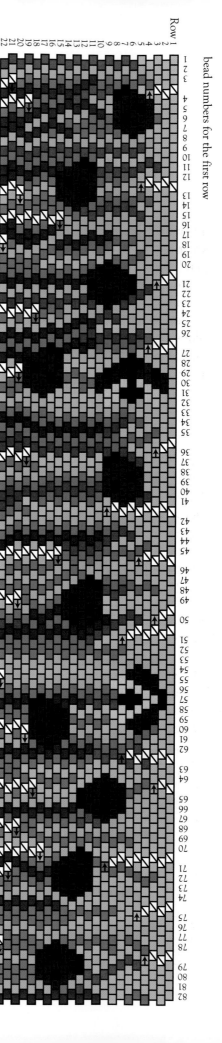

Chapter 5

Peyote Stitch

The stitch commonly known as peyote in North America is the basis for all netting stitches, and versions of it exist from beading samples from the Middle East dating back 2,000 years. The name peyote comes from a version of this stitch that is used by Native Americans to make religious items such as rattles and fan handles for peyote-based ceremonies. The Native American version of peyote (which is also known as gourd stitch when used for non-religious items) is different from the popular symmetrical version. For a comprehensive discussion of that technique, refer to *Native American Beadwork*, by Georg Barth (see the Bibliography).

The popular version of peyote has become the stitch of choice for many beaders because it is quick, easy, and versatile when compared to most other beading stitches. There are three main variations to the single bead version of this stitch:

• **Flat peyote:** Odd or even count. These are the versions you will learn in this book.
• **Tubular peyote:** Odd or even count.
• **Circular flat peyote:** You will learn this version in Chapter 6, Bead Netting.

Other variations use two or three beads instead of one; these are known as two-drop and three-drop peyote. These are faster and easier to work than the one-drop version. The only difference from standard peyote stitch is that two or three beads are picked up instead of one for each stitch.

Because the grid for this stitch is not based on a square, and you put on every other bead to make a row, reading peyote stitch charts takes some getting used to. I like to use a sticky note to cover all of the rows except the ones I've completed and the one I am working on, so I can easily find my place.

In working a flat piece of peyote with an odd bead count, at the end of odd numbered rows, your needle is not coming out of the correct bead to put the next bead on. So, you have to learn to make a figure-eight turn at the end of odd rows of flat peyote pieces to position your needle for the next bead.

In tubular even peyote, you have to learn to recognize the first bead you put on at the beginning of a row because you need to step up through it to start the next row. "Step up" means going through the last bead of the previous row, then up through the first bead of the row you are finishing. This shifts each new row over by one bead. Charts for circular peyote stitch are sometimes marked with a diagonal line indicating the first bead in each row.

Tubular odd peyote does not have turns so you do not have to position your needle at the end of rows, nor do you have a step up; you keep spiraling around.

Idele Gilbert is adept at miniatures stitched using peyote stitch and Delica beads, like these fish swimming in a pearl stream.

Amulet bags, such as this peyote-stitched example designed and beaded by Carole Tripp in 1997, helped the current popularity of beading. Beading has steadily grown in popularity since the late 1980s when magazine articles such as Alice Korach's bead knitting and Virginia Blakelock's fabulous loomwork neckpieces were published. When Alice founded Bead & Button Magazine in 1994, she established beading as a craft form.

Prairie Dawn, by Shonna Neuhart, in peyote stitch.

Sculptural peyote stitch around a ceramic molded face, designed and beaded by Carole Tripp.

Peyote-stitched beads strung into a necklace and loose beads are shown with a brooch made of beads stitched around a cabochon. Designed and beaded by Sylvia Sur.

Peyote stitch figure, by Marlin Beads.

This little circus monkey is made in two-drop peyote, where two beads are picked up for each stitch. Circus Monkey was designed and beaded by Elizabeth Gourley.

Flat Odd Count Peyote Stitch Sample

Finished size: 1-1/8 inches by 2-1/8 inches

1. Thread the needle with a 6-foot length of thread. Tie a stop bead 6 inches from the tail and pick up 39 cream-colored beads. This is Row 1 and Row 2 on the Peyote Stitch Sample design chart.

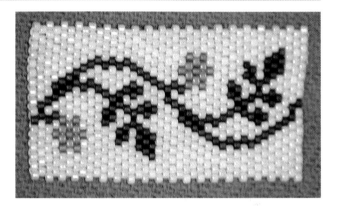

2. Pick up bead 39 in Row 3 and pass through the third bead from the needle (bead 38 in Row 2) (**Figure 5-1**). Pull tight.

3. Pick up the next bead in Row 3, skip the next bead on the thread, and pass through the following bead on the thread (bead 36 in Row 2) (**Figure 5-2**). Pull tight.

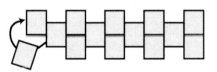

4. Repeat Step 3 across the row, picking up a bead from the chart, skipping a bead on the thread, and passing through the next bead on the thread.

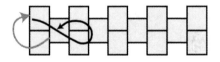

5. Pick up the last bead. Follow the thread path in **Figure 5-3** to add the last bead in Row 3 and position the needle to begin Row 4. You make this turn at the end of every odd-numbered row.

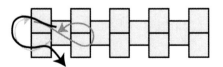

6. Continue following the design, working peyote stitch back and forth.

Figure 5-3

7. Weave in the ends.

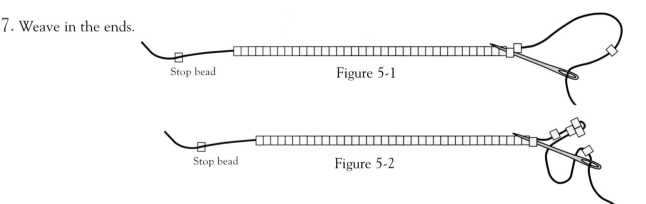

Stop bead   Figure 5-1

Stop bead   Figure 5-2

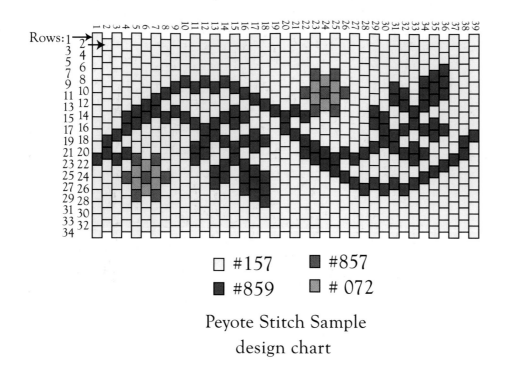

Rows: 1

□ #157　■ #857

■ #859　■ # 072

Peyote Stitch Sample
design chart

Peyote Stitch Beaded Sun Catcher

You Will Need

Floating glass picture frame, at least 5 by 7
inches with a landscape orientation and
enough space between the two pieces of
glass to fit the width of the beads (check
this by actually putting a bead between the
two pieces of glass)

Delica beads, in the colors shown in the
Sun Catcher design chart
Delica beads in two contrasting colors (light
and dark) for a starter strip
Size B or D white Nymo
Size 10 beading needle

This project uses a floating glass picture frame
in a whimsical wire stand to display the peyote
stitch panel, rather than a traditional sun catcher
which hangs in a window. The transparent and
opaque beads contrast as sunlight glistens through
the beadwork, and white beading thread keeps the
true color of the beads.

You will start this project by making a reusable
starter strip of peyote stitch. This is a wonderful
tool for starting peyote stitch projects without
struggling with the first three rows and the uneven
beginning tension common to peyote work. You

first bead a false row onto this foundation and
then remove it after you finish several rows of the
project. This separates the reusable starter strip
from the project. The process creates a smooth
beginning to the beadwork, so the tension is uniform throughout. The starter strip is well worth
the time and effort because it can be used again
for starting other flat peyote stitch projects.

Finished size: 5-1/2 inches wide by 5 inches tall
in a 5- by 7-inch horizontal frame

The colors in this piece change when the light shines through the beads, illuminating the translucent beads.

To make the starter strip:

1. Thread the needle with an 8-foot length of thread and tie a stop bead 6 inches from the tail. String 120 Delica beads, consisting of 24 repeats of four light beads and one dark bead.

2. Work five rows of flat peyote, making a vertical stripe with the dark beads so you have a five-bead repeat. This helps, because now you can easily count by fives when you add your project beads. There will be 60 beads in each of the two rows.

3. Weave in the ends and cut close to the beadwork.

To make the sun catcher:

1. Thread the needle with a 6-foot length of thread. Loosely anchor the thread in the starter strip. Bead one row of 56 beads to the starter strip. This is your temporary row and can be a contrasting color. You will remove this row after you bead three or four more rows. Be very careful not to split the thread in the starter strip with the needle while beading this row and the next.

2. Bead the first three to five rows of the pattern from the Sun Catcher design chart.

3. Separate the starter strip from the project by unthreading the beads from Step 1. Once you begin to separate the row, it pulls apart easily.

4. Remove all of the beads on the thread from the first temporary row and weave the thread into the sun catcher. Cut close to the beading.

5. Continue beading the pattern in peyote stitch until complete. Weave in the thread ends among the opaque beads so the threads will not show through the transparent beads in the sunlight.

6. Insert the finished beadwork into the picture frame and place on a counter or window sill, or in a window box, so the sunlight filters through the beads.

Sun Catcher
design chart

Row 1

■ # 216

■ #785 inside star

■ #177

■ #905

■ #651

□ #854

■ #781

■ #777

■ #769

■ #734

306

Chapter 6

Netting

Making a net with beads is just a matter of adding more beads to peyote stitch; the basic structure of both techniques is the same. Netting usually has an odd number of beads in loops, and each loop is attached by passing through the center bead in a loop on the previous row. Similar to peyote, odd count and even count flat netting have different turns at the ends of rows, and round netting has the shifting first stitch, as in tubular peyote.

A flat bead netted piece can be described by the number of beads in each stitch, such as three-bead netting, which is when you pick up three beads for every stitch. You can increase the width of the work by adding more beads in each stitch, such as progressing from three-bead netting to five-bead netting to seven-bead netting. Lowering the number of beads in each stitch decreases the width of the fabric. This makes it is easy to shape netting around curved jars and balls.

Because netting is made of loops of beads, it is a very loose stitch, which is dramatically affected

Detail of a skirt from Bali. The bead-netted pattern is made using tiny size 16 seed beads.

by anything placed beneath it because of the space between the stitches. When stitching a pattern in netting and using a lining, use a background fabric which blends with the background beads in the pattern.

Bead Netting Sample

You Will Need

Size 11 seed beads, in the colors shown in the Bead Netting Sample design chart

Size B Nymo
Size 11 or 12 beading needle

Finished size: 1-1/8 inches by 2-1/8 inch

1. Thread the needle with a 6-foot length of thread. Tie a stop bead 6 inches from the tail.

2. String 21 beads. This is Row 1 on the Bead Netting Sample design chart.

3. String three beads and pass through the eighth bead away from the needle, including the three

beads just strung, toward the tail end of the thread (**Figure 6-1**).

Figure 6-1

4. String three additional beads and pass the needle through the fourth bead away from the last stitch (**Figure 6-2**).

5. Repeat Step 4 across the row.

6. Tighten the beads together across the row, then pick up five beads and pass through the center bead in the last three-bead loop, going in the opposite direction (**Figure 6-3**) to make the turn around to the next row.

7. Repeat Step 4 across the row. After the last three-bead loop is added, repeat Step 6 to make the turn around to the next row.

8. Continue as in Step 7, following the color pattern in the design chart below. Weave in the ends.

Bead Netting Sample
design chart

Figure 6-2

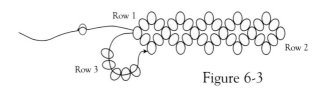

Figure 6-3

cream

green

blue

308

Bead Netted Knot Design

You Will Need

Picture frame 5 inches square or larger*
21 grams or 3/4 oz. size 11 dark-colored seed
   beads
14 grams or 1/2 oz. size 11 light-colored seed
   beads
Size B beading thread

Size 11 beading needle

*If you plan to use the finished piece as a trivet, be sure
to choose a picture frame that can withstand heat. Also,
make sure the frame has enough excess room to fit a 5-
1/2 inch square to accommodate the beadwork.

Many ethnic beadwork pieces, such as the detail of the skirt from Bali on page 307, use rich patterns in bead netting. Here is a flat beaded knot pattern using the same technique for a trivet, coaster, or wall decoration. Bead netting easily lends itself to Celtic knot patterns because of the strong diagonal lines in its construction.

Finished size: 5-1/2 inches square

1. Thread the needle with an 8-foot length of thread. Tie a stop bead 6 inches from the tail and string 113 dark beads. This is Row 1 on the Netted Knot design chart.

2. Follow Steps 3 through 6 of the Bead Netting Sample (on pages 307 and 308), then continue as in Step 7, following the color pattern in the design chart. Weave in the ends.

3. Place the beadwork in the picture frame to use as a coaster, trivet, or hang on the wall.

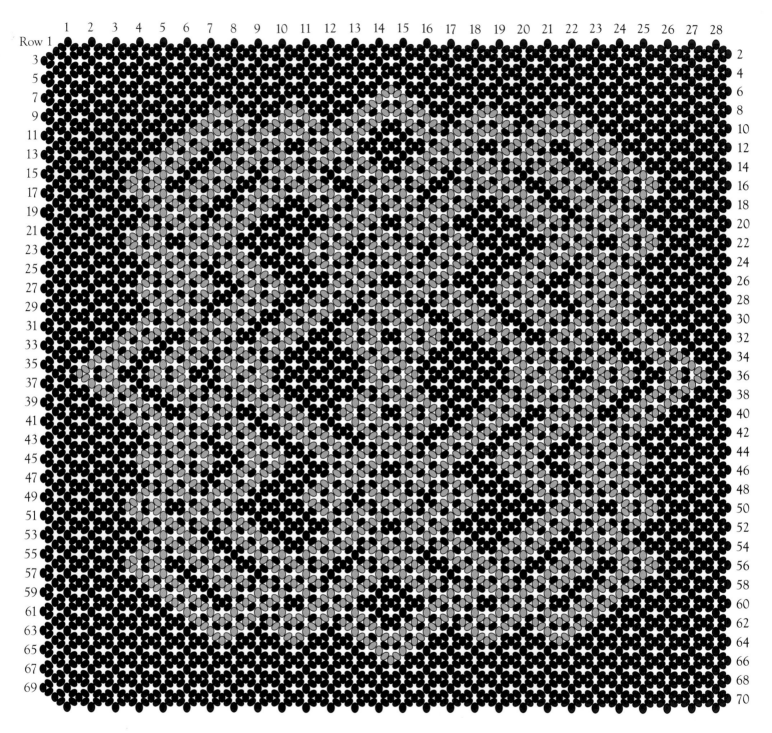

Row 1
3
5
7
9
11
13
15
17
19
21
23
25
27
29
31
33
35
37
39
41
43
45
47
49
51
53
55
57
59
61
63
65
67
69

2
4
6
8
10
12
14
16
18
20
22
24
26
28
30
32
34
36
38
40
42
44
46
48
50
52
54
56
58
60
62
64
66
68
70

1 2 3 4 5 6 7 8 9 10 11 12 13 14 15 16 17 18 19 20 21 22 23 24 25 26 27 28

 light beads

dark beads

Netted Knot
design chart

Bead Netting Christmas Ornament

You Will Need

Size 15 seed beads, white and blue, 3 grams or 1/8 oz. of each
Size 0 Nymo to match the blue beads
Size 13 beading needle

12 inches of 26 gauge wire
Round nosed pliers
Flat nosed pliers

This project truly shows the connection between peyote stitch and bead netting. The ornament is stitched in the round, beginning with flat circular peyote stitch and progressing to netting. The snowflake pattern is made by repeating a specific color sequence six times around the piece. Finally, thin wire is strung through the center bead of each three-bead loop on the last row to keep the piece flat. You can make this pattern in any size seed beads to change the piece's finished size. You can also make earrings by only stitching the first 10 rounds in size 15 beads. Use the thickest wire which will fit through the beads to form the finished piece into shape.

Finished size: 2-1/8 inches in diameter

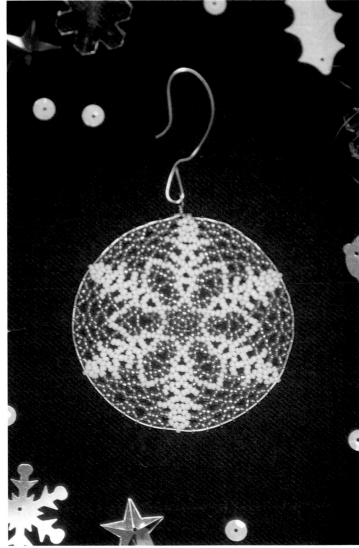

1. Thread the needle with an 8-foot length of thread. String three blue beads and tie into a circle with a square knot. Row 1 (a circle) is now completed on the Bead Netted Ornament design chart. Pass through the first bead to prepare for Row 2 (**Figure 6-4**).

2. Pick up two blue beads and pass through the next bead on Row 1 (**Figure 6-5**). Repeat twice. Pass through the first bead in the row to prepare for Row 3 (**Figure 6-6**).

Darker beads show current stitch

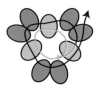

Figure 6-4

Figure 6-5

Figure 6-6

3. Pick up one blue bead and pass through the next bead from Row 2. Repeat four times. Pick up one blue bead and pass through the last bead in Row 2 and the first bead in Row 3 (**Figure 6-7**). Row 3 is now completed, six beads around.

4. Now follow the pattern in the Bead Netted Ornament design chart, adding beads as indicated for each round and passing through the beads of the previous row. Weave in the ends after the last round.

5. Carefully pass the wire through the center bead in each three-bead set on the last row. When the wires meet, adjust the wire to make a smooth circle. Then bend the ends up (**Figure 6-8**) with the flat nosed pliers and bend one end so it has a 1/8-inch neck.

6. Grab the end with two bends with the round nosed pliers (**Figure 6-9**) and make a loop.

7. Grab the loop and the straight end with the flat nosed pliers and grab the end of the loop with the round nosed pliers; wind three times around the neck of both ends (**Figure 6-10**). Cut both ends.

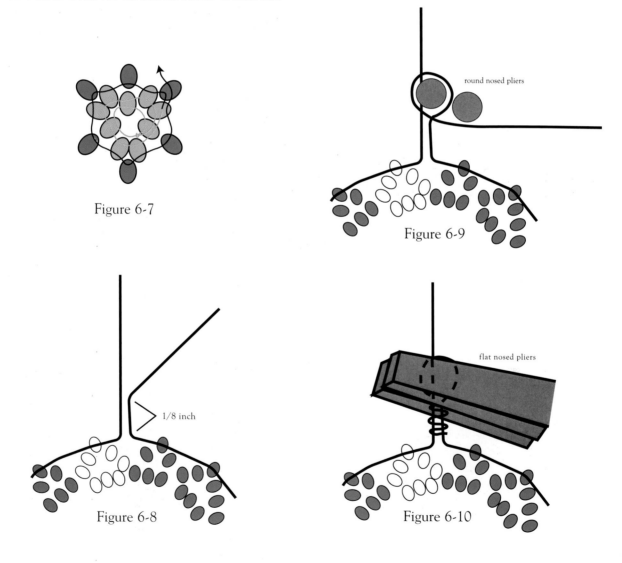

Figure 6-7

Figure 6-9

Figure 6-8

Figure 6-10

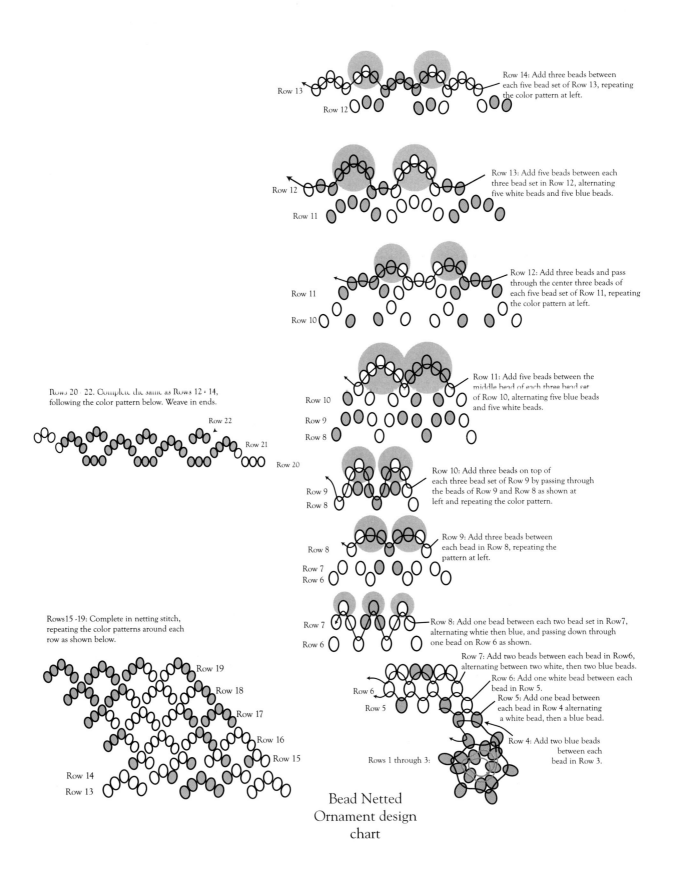

Row 14: Add three beads between each five bead set of Row 13, repeating the color pattern at left.

Row 13

Row 12

Row 13: Add five beads between each three bead set in Row 12, alternating five white beads and five blue beads.

Row 12

Row 11

Row 12: Add three beads and pass through the center three beads of each five bead set of Row 11, repeating the color pattern at left.

Row 11

Row 10

Row 11: Add five beads between the middle bead of each three bead set of Row 10, alternating five blue beads and five white beads.

Row 10

Row 9

Row 8

Row 10: Add three beads on top of each three bead set of Row 9 by passing through the beads of Row 9 and Row 8 as shown at left and repeating the color pattern.

Row 9

Row 8

Row 9: Add three beads between each bead in Row 8, repeating the pattern at left.

Row 8

Row 7

Row 6

Row 8: Add one bead between each two bead set in Row 7, alternating whtie then blue, and passing down through one bead on Row 6 as shown.

Row 7

Row 6

Row 7: Add two beads between each bead in Row 6, alternating between two white, then two blue beads.

Row 6: Add one white bead between each bead in Row 5.

Row 6

Row 5

Row 5: Add one bead between each bead in Row 4 alternating a white bead, then a blue bead.

Row 4: Add two blue beads between each bead in Row 3.

Rows 1 through 3:

Rows 20 - 22. Complete the same as Rows 12 - 14, following the color pattern below. Weave in ends.

Row 22

Row 21

Row 20

Rows 15 -19: Complete in netting stitch, repeating the color patterns around each row as shown below.

Row 19

Row 18

Row 17

Row 16

Row 15

Row 14

Row 13

Bead Netted
Ornament design
chart

Circling in the Fourth Dimension, by Marlin Beads. An elegant neckpiece can be fashioned by creating a textural cord with a Zepher brand glass art bead accent. This neck chain is stitched using the quadruple helix stitch, a variation of netting in which the loops of beads are attached to the previous row by passing through the thread between the beads, instead of passing through a bead.

Using the same basic graph as the Christmas Ornament project, a variety of designs can be achieved, like this Celtic knot pattern (Odin's Glory, by Jane Davis).

Beaded Beauty, designed and beaded by Dorianne Neuhart, uses netting to encase a Cameo.

Hollyhocks amulet bag in bead netting, designed and beaded by Jane Davis.

This lacy lamp is bead netted over a fabric shade. Designed and beaded by Delinda V. Amura.

Chapter 7

Herringbone Stitch

Herringbone stitch is also known as *Ndebele* (pronounced: en dah BELL ee) stitch, named for the South African tribe that invented and uses it extensively. It is also called herringbone because of its resemblance to the chevrons of herringbone fabric.

There are two common ways to begin this stitch:
• Start with a strip of ladder stitch in larger beads than the beads for herringbone. This makes a firm, straight beginning edge to the piece as in the Pinch Purse project (on page 318).
• Start with herringbone stitch directly. This provides a beginning edge that has the same fluid drape as the rest of the bead fabric made with herringbone stitch.

The Herringbone Stitch Sample explains the direct starting method. You string cream beads for Row 1 and blue beads for Row 2. Next, you bead the third row in herringbone stitch in green beads. The beading pulls to half the width of the strung beads of Rows 1 and 2 as the blue beads move up to sit in the second row above the cream beads. You need to leave some slack in the thread as you make the first three rows so the beads can slide into the proper position. After the fourth row, it is easy to bead herringbone stitch.

Victorian Fantasy, by Jane Davis, is a gate purse in circular netting and herringbone stitch, with the floral pattern taken from the antique purse shown on the title page.

Herringbone Stitch Sample

You Will Need

Size 11 cream seed beads, 3-1/2 grams or 1/8 oz.	size 11 seed beads
Small amounts of light green, blue, and purple	Size B Nymo
	Size 11 beading needle

Finished size: 1-1/8 inches by 2-1/8 inches

To make the herringbone sample:

1. Thread the needle with an 8-foot length of thread. Tie a stop bead 6 inches from the tail.

2. Pick up one blue bead, then pick up five repeats of two cream beads and two blue beads. Pick up two cream beads.

3. You have 23 beads for Rows 1 and 2 of the Herringbone Sample design chart. Pick up one blue bead and one green bead. Pass back through the blue bead (**Figure 7-1**).

4. Skip the two cream beads, and pass through the next blue bead. Pick up two green beads, and pass through the next blue bead (**Figure 7-2**). Push the beads on both threads so they sit in rows of the same color (**Figure 7-3**).

5. Repeat Step 4 to the end of the strand. You have finished the first three rows.

6. Pick up one green bead and one cream bead. Pass back through the green bead you just picked up and the next green bead in the row (**Figure 7-4**).

7. Pick up two cream beads and pass through the next two green beads (**Figure 7-5**).

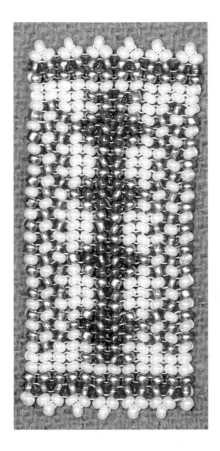

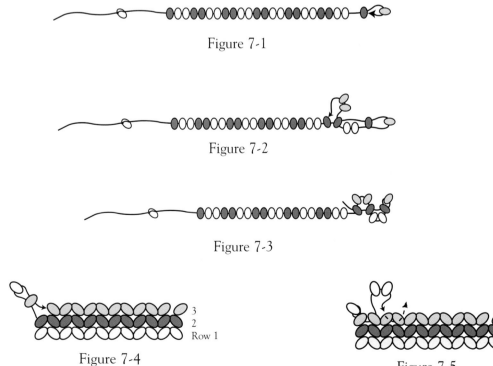

Figure 7-1

Figure 7-2

Figure 7-3

Figure 7-4

Figure 7-5

8. Continue beading as in Step 7, then turning as in Step 6, and following the color pattern in the design chart.

To add a nice finish to the ends, complete the end rows as follows:

1. On Row 1, use the tail thread and work one more row, adding one bead for each stitch instead of two.

2. On Row 33, use the working thread and work one more row, adding one bead for each stitch instead of two (**Figure 7-6**).

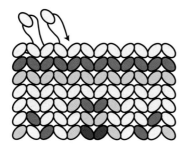

Figure 7-6

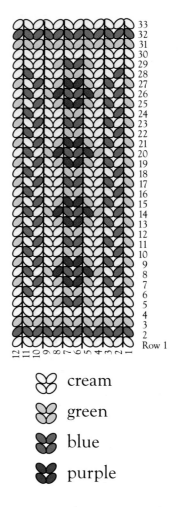

⚘ cream

⚘ green

⚘ blue

⚘ purple

Herringbone Sample

design chart

Herringbone Stitch Pinch Purse

You Will Need

Pinch purse frame, 3-1/8 inch
Size 11 seed beads, in the colors shown in the Pinch Purse design chart
42 bronze twisted bugle beads size 9 (1/8 inch long)
Brown suede: 1 piece 3-1/8 by 8 inches and 4

pieces each 1/2 by 3/4 inch
Size O brown Nymo
Size 11 beading needle
Size 12 sharps needle for sewing suede
Thimble
Knife and needle nose pliers

The soft drape of herringbone stitch makes it a good choice for purses and bags. This little pinch purse, with its curling ferns and suede lining, is as elegant as it is functional.

Finished size: 3-1/2 by 3-1/2 inches

To bead the ladder stitch and starting row:

1. Thread the beading needle with an 8-foot length of thread. Make a 42-bead ladder stitch

strip as shown on page 292, using the size 9 twisted bugle beads. Pass back through the second to last bead and make a square knot with the tail thread and working thread to hold the strip together. Pass back through the last bead.

2. Pick up bead 1 and bead 2 on Row 1 of the Pinch Purse design chart. Pass down through the second bead and up through the third bead on the ladder stitch strip (**Figure 7-7**).

3. Pick up the next two beads on Row 1 of the design chart and pass down and up through the next two ladder stitch beads.

4. Repeat Step 3 across the ladder stitch strip, following the color pattern of the design chart. One side of the first row of the purse is complete.

5. Pass through the loop between the second and third size 9 beads (**Figure 7-8**). Pass back through the last size 9 bead (**Figure 7-9**).

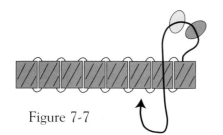

Figure 7-7

Figure 7-8

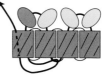

Figure 7-9

6. Repeat Steps 2 and 3 across the ladder stitch strip along the other side. Repeat Step 5.

You have finished Row 1 of the design chart once for the front and once the back of the purse. You are now ready to begin beading in the round in herringbone stitch.

To bead the herringbone stitch purse:
1. Pass up through the first bead (**Figure 7-10**). Pick up bead 1 and bead 2 in Row 2 of the design chart and pass through bead 2 and bead 3 of Row 1 (**Figure 7-11**).

2. Continue in herringbone stitch to the end of one side of the purse, then repeat the pattern on the other side. When you get to the beginning of the row, step up by finishing the last stitch and then passing through the first bead in the current row (**Figure 7-12**).

3. Continue beading, following the design chart color pattern. For the last row, add just one bead for each stitch, instead of two. This makes a nice edging. Weave in the ends.

To assemble the purse:
1. Using the knife edge, bend back the metal flap that holds the pin in the hinge on one side of the purse frame and remove the pin so the purse frame opens flat for easier assembly.

2. Cut a rectangle from each of the corners of the 8-inch long piece of suede (**Figure 7-13**).

3. Fold one short side of the 8-inch piece of suede over 3/4 inch and stitch in place (**Figure 7-14**). Repeat for the other side. Stitch 1/8 inch side seams. Slip this lining onto the purse frame, reinsert the hinge, and fold down the metal flap with the pliers.

4. Stitch the four small strips of suede to the inside and outside of the beading to pad the beading, along the sides of the purse where the hinge will be.

5. Slip the beading onto the suede lining and blind stitch to the top of the suede lining.

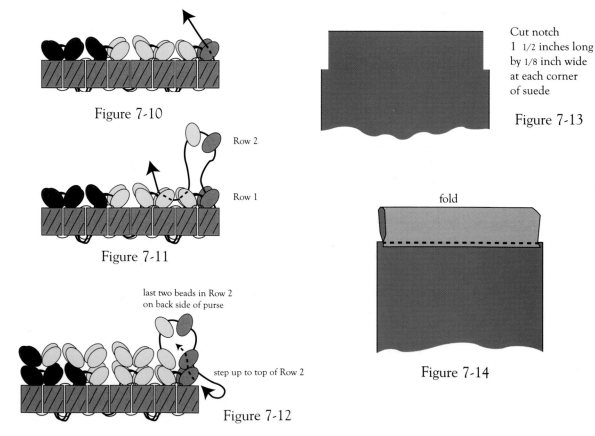

Figure 7-10

Row 2

Row 1

Figure 7-11

last two beads in Row 2 on back side of purse

step up to top of Row 2

Figure 7-12

Cut notch
1 1/2 inches long
by 1/8 inch wide
at each corner
of suede

Figure 7-13

fold

Figure 7-14

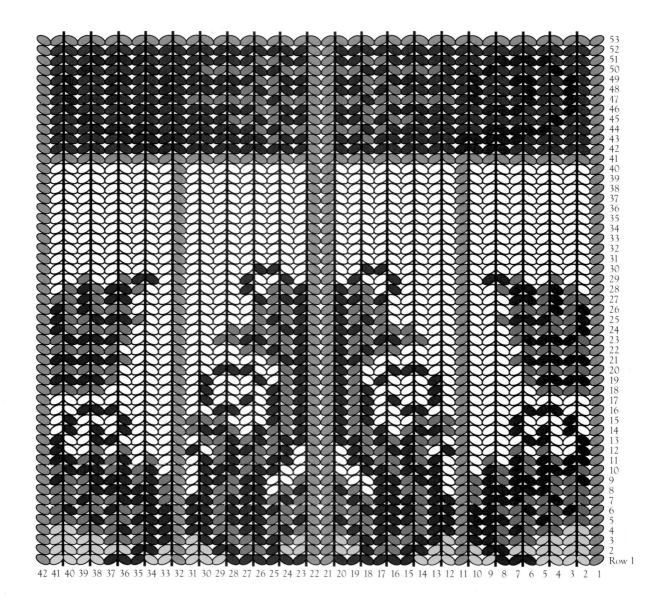

53
52
51
50
49
48
47
46
45
44
43
42
41
40
39
38
37
36
35
34
33
32
31
30
29
28
27
26
25
24
23
22
21
20
19
18
17
16
15
14
13
12
11
10
9
8
7
6
5
4
3
2
Row 1

42 41 40 39 38 37 36 35 34 33 32 31 30 29 28 27 26 25 24 23 22 21 20 19 18 17 16 15 14 13 12 11 10 9 8 7 6 5 4 3 2 1

🦋 Dull white, 20 grams or 3/4 oz.

🦋 Lime green, 10 grams or 3/8 oz.

🦋 Hunter green, 10 grams or 3/8 oz.

🦋 Mustard, 1 gram

🦋 Bronze, 10 grams or 3/8 oz.

🦋 Matte brown, 5 grams or 3/16 oz.

Pinch Purse
design chart

Chapter 8

Right-angle Weave

R ight-angle weave is an old beading technique commonly done around the world
with two needles. The single-needle version
popularized in the United States by bead artist
David Chatt uses a figure-eight thread path to
hold beads together in a square grid. The single-
needle version is explained in this book.

The name right-angle weave describes the
stitch: beads are placed at right angles to each
other. Because the needle is first going clockwise
to put on a set of beads, then counterclockwise to
put on the next set of beads, this is a difficult
stitch to work correctly at first. But, once you get

the rhythm of the turns, it becomes a fun stitch to
bead.

You start with a square of four beads. Make the
first row by adding three beads to the end of the
four-bead square, then passing through the beads
to come out of the center bead of the three beads.
Then, you add another three-bead set and continue connecting squares in a row. You work the following rows by attaching to the first row to make
a grid of interconnected four-bead squares.

Because the thread goes through the beads several times, it is important to use a thinner thread
and beads with large, regular holes.

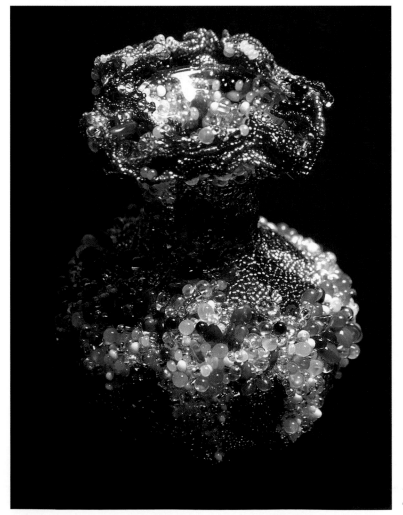

*Right-angle weave and a variety of bead types
add texture to this piece, by Susan Hilyar.*

This intricate design, by Marlin Beads, combines several stitches, including right-angle weave, to make a fun, complex piece.

Right-angle Weave Sample

Finished size: 1-1/8 inches by 2-1/8 inches

1. Thread the needle with an 8-foot length of thread. Pick up four cream beads and tie the tail and working thread into a square knot 6 inches from the tail. Pass through one bead. These are the first four beads of Row 1 on the Right-angle Weave Sample design chart.

2. Pick up three cream beads and pass through the bead the thread is coming out of and through two beads of the three-bead set (**Figure 8-1**).

3. Pick up three cream beads and pass through the bead the thread is coming out of and through two beads of the three-bead set (**Figure 8-2**).

4. Repeat Steps 2 and 3 three more times. You have nine interconnected squares making up the first row on the design chart.

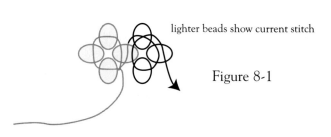

lighter beads show current stitch

Figure 8-1

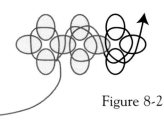

Figure 8-2

5. Pass through the next bead, pick up three cream beads, and pass through the bead the thread is coming out of and through the first of the three beads just strung (**Figure 8-3**).

6. At the beginning of each row, you put on three beads at a time to make the turns. You put on two beads at a time for the rest of the row.

7. Pick up two cream beads and pass through the beads as shown (**Figure 8-4**).

8. Pick up two cream beads and pass through the beads as shown (**Figure 8-5**).

9. Repeat Steps 6 and 7 across the row. Turn as in Step 5. Two rows are completed.

10. Continue in right-angle weave, adding beads and following the color sequence from the design chart. Weave in the ends.

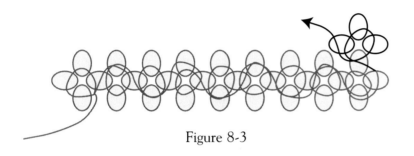

Figure 8-3

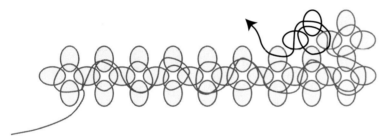

Figure 8-4

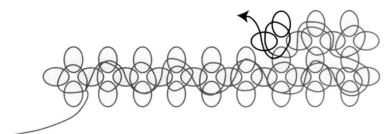

Figure 8-5

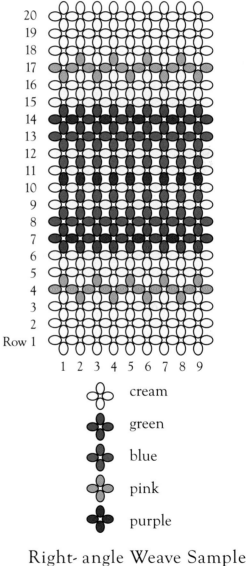

Right-angle Weave Sample design chart

Right-angle Weave Band on a Wicker Basket

You Will Need

11-1/2-inch diameter wicker basket with at least a 3-inch section of straight sides
Size 6 seed beads, 16 oz. of cream and 8 oz. of green
Size 8 DMC brown pearl cotton to match the basket color
Size 10 beading needle
Beeswax
Rubber band large enough to go around the basket or 2 feet of elastic

Large beads and a meandering vine design complement the rough woven texture of this basket. To prevent the pearl cotton from fraying as it slides through the beads, wax it well. The thick pearl cotton fills the holes of the large beads, keeping the correct tension in this loose stitch.

Finished size: 3-inch wide band around an 11-1/2-inch diameter basket

1. Cut a 9-foot length of pearl cotton, apply beeswax, and thread the needle.

2. Following the Beaded Band design chart, bead the pattern twice in flat right-angle weave, following the instructions from the Right-angle Weave Sample (on page 324).

3. Join the first and last rows together by adding one bead at a time, maintaining the color pattern and passing through beads from each end (**Figure 8-6**). Weave in the ends.

4. Slip the beadwork on the basket and hold in place with a large rubber band or a piece of elastic thread to tie the beadwork to the basket.

5. Sew the beadwork to the basket along the top edge first, passing through an edge bead and then through the weave of the basket.

6. Remove the elastic or rubber band and stitch the bottom edge of the beadwork to the basket the same as for the top.

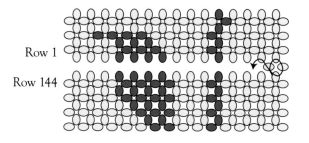

Row 1

Row 144

Figure 8-6

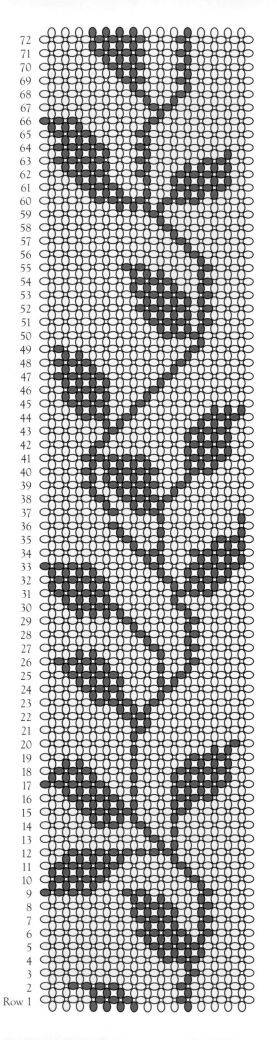

72
71
70
69
68
67
66
65
64
63
62
61
60
59
58
57
56
55
54
53
52
51
50
49
48
47
46
45
44
43

cream

green

42
41
40
39
38
37
36
35

Beaded Band
design chart

34
33
32
31
30
29
28
27
26
25
24
23
22
21
20
19
18
17
16
15
14
13
12
11
10
9
8
7
6
5
4
3
2

Row 1

Chapter 9

Knitting

Techniques for Prestrung Beads

To work beads into a crocheted, knitted, or tatted project, you must string the beads on the thread first. This means that you have no loose beads to worry about and can take projects that use prestrung beads on trips with ease. Because it is important to string all of the beads in the correct color order, the preparation for starting these project takes extra time and careful attention.

Note: For the techniques in Chapters 9 through 11, you will require a previous knowledge of knitting, crochet, and tatting.

Basic Techniques for Stringing Beads

To Slide Prestrung Beads on Project Thread or Yarn

This technique is used when you have purchased beads in hanks and all of the beads in the project are the same.

1. Pull one strand of beads from the hank and tie a knot around the bead at one end of the strand to prevent the beads from falling off.
2. Tie an overhand knot at the other end of the strand around the project thread or yarn so that the project thread or yarn folds in half inside the knot.
3. Carefully slide about 1 inch of beads at a time from one thread to the other. This takes some practice. The thread used for bead hanks is easily broken if you pull hard; the knot may get loose and your project thread can slip out. Beads that are misshapen or with holes that are too small to slide over the knot have to be discarded. When any of these problems occur, if there are still plenty of beads on the strand, retie the strand to the project thread and continue sliding the beads.

To String Beads Following a Design

If the beads are not in hanks, or they need to be strung in a color order according to a design, use a needle small enough to fit through the bead holes. If the project thread is too thick to fit the bead needle, tie a 10-inch piece of beading thread to the project thread and thread the needle with the beading

---

Correcting Errors

Beads in the Wrong Place

If a bead is knit into, or between, the wrong stitches, it must be removed or reworked. If all of the beads are one color, you can break the bead, if it is an extra bead; otherwise, you must rip back to that section and knit or crochet it again. For tatting, it's best just to cut it out and redo the section. Make sure to take your time and carefully check each row or section before beginning the next.

Beads in the Wrong Color Sequence

Because the beads in a color pattern are all strung in a specific order, it's very important to work each row correctly, because any error will throw off the pattern for the rest of the work. Always check the pattern after knitting or crocheting each row to make sure you have completed the row correctly. Knitting or crocheting a pattern using paper row markers helps you find errors quickly. If you get to the end of a row and have beads left over, or you get to the marker and haven't finished the row, you know you have made a mistake. (For example, you may have strung the wrong number of beads for that row, or stitched too many or too few into the row.) Correct the error before continuing, then tear off the row marker and begin the next row.

thread, or use a wire needle with a collapsing eye (**Figure 9-1**).

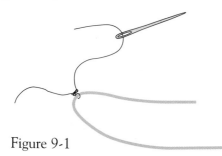

Figure 9-1

String the beads according to the design chart. When stringing beads following a design chart, separate each row with a small piece of paper. This helps you in double-checking for errors. I use 3/8-inch squares of paper I have already pierced with a large needle so that they fit easily over the needle and thread or yarn.

To Clear the Working Thread

About every four rows, you will use up the yarn or thread and need to slide the beads away from the project to clear some more thread to continue. Keep the thread ball in a basket and slide about 4 to 6 inches of beads along the yarn or thread at a time, until there are about 4 feet of yarn or thread without beads near your project. If you have beads for a row in progress, leave those up near the work.

To Keep Track of Beads Per Row

In patterns where the bead count changes from row to row, the number in parentheses following the row number tells you how many beads are needed for the row. Slide that number of beads up near your project before beginning each row. The paper row marker makes this easy to find.

To Attach New Thread or Yarn

When you run out of beads or thread, or need to correct a stringing error, you will need to attach a new thread.
- In knitting, change at the end of a row.
- In tatting, change threads after a ring.
- In crochet, anywhere is okay.
- Cut the working thread to about 6 inches.
- For knitting and tatting, tie the tail and new thread into a knot as close to the work as possible.
- For crochet, pull a loop of the new thread through

the loop on the hook and pull the old thread as tight as possible.
- Continue working as before using the new thread.
- When the piece is finished, bury the ends into the back of the work for about 1-1/2 inches and cut the excess yarn or thread.

Knitting

There are two types of knitting with beads, both of which you will use in this book.

Beaded Knitting

For this type, one or more beads are slid between stitches on the thread or yarn. The bead lies on the front or back of the knitting based on the stitches beside it. A bead bordered by knit stitches lies on the back of the fabric, while purl stitches on either side of the bead cause it to stay on the front of the fabric. The beads lie horizontally in the fabric, or hang in a swag or loop if many beads are slid between stitches.

Bead Knitting

Here, a bead is pushed into a stitch as it is made. This technique is more difficult than beaded knitting, because there must be tension on the thread and the bead must be positioned properly so it can be pushed into the stitch. It was traditionally accomplished in twisted stockinette stitch and more recently in plaited stockinette stitch. These tight stitches are needed so that the knitting locks the beads on the right side of the fabric.

Twisted stockinette stitch: All of the stitches are made by knitting into the back of the stitch. This technique causes all of the beads to slant in the same direction and the fabric to have a strong bias slant.

Plaited stockinette stitch: The knit stitches are made by knitting into the back of the stitch and wrapping the thread or yarn clockwise around the needle. The purl stitches are made by purling into the front of the stitch and wrapping the thread or yarn counterclockwise around the needle (standard purl stitch). The beads alternately slant to the right in one row, and then to the left in the next, and the finished fabric has no bias slant. Plaited bead knitting was developed in the 1980s by Alice Korach, the founder of *Bead & Button Magazine*. It is the technique used for projects in this book.

Bead-knitted scarf, designed and knitted by Jane Davis for Linda Niemeyer and Blue Sky Alpacas, using size 6 pearl beads, size 5 knitting needles, and sport-weight Blue Sky Alpacas alpaca yarn. Pattern available from Blue Sky Alpacas (see Supply Sources).

Beaded Knitting Sample

You Will Need

300 size 11 cream seed beads
Size 12 cream pearl cotton

Size 000 or 0000 knitting needles
Size 11 beading needle

Finished size: 1 inch by 1-3/4 inches at the widest point

Note: You may wish to practice first with size 6 beads using a sport-weight yarn and size 5 knitting needles. It takes time to get used to the small needles.

String the beads onto the pearl cotton.
Cast on 12 stitches.
Rows 1-3: Knit.
Row 4: Knit two stitches, slide one bead next to the second stitch, knit two more stitches, and slide one bead next to the second stitch. Repeat the pattern to the end of the row, knitting the last two stitches.
Rows 5-7: Knit the same as Row 4.
Rows 8-11: Knit the same as Row 4 except slide two beads between the stitches instead of one.
Rows 12-22: Knit the same as the previous rows, increasing the number of beads between stitches by one every four rows.

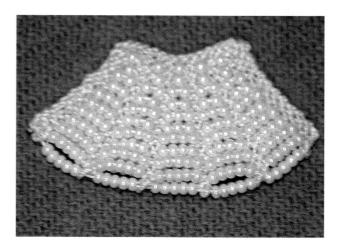

To cast off on row 23, slide five beads up to the needle. Cut the thread 12 inches from the beads and thread the beading needle. Pass through the first two stitches and slide them off of the knitting needle. Pick up five beads, slide them next to the knitting, and pass the beading needle through the next two stitches, sliding them off of the knitting needle. Repeat to the end. Weave in the tail thread.

Bead Knitting Sample

You Will Need

Size 11 seed beads, in the colors shown in
the Bead Knitting Sample design chart
Size 8 cream pearl cotton or size 20 cream

Cebelia
Size 000 or 0000 knitting needles
Size 11 or medium wire beading needle

Finished size: 1-1/8 inches by 2-1/8 inches

Note: You may wish to practice first with size 6
beads using a sport-weight yarn and size 5 knitting
needles. It takes time to get used to the small needles.

Beginning at the top row, string the beads onto
the thread from right to left or left to right (the
design is symmetrical), following the Bead
Knitting Sample design chart.
Cast on 24 stitches.
Row 1: Knit into the back of each stitch, wrapping
the thread or yarn around the needle clockwise.
Row 2: Purl two stitches, then purl the next
stitch, sliding a bead into the stitch as it is made.

To put a bead in a purl stitch:
1. Keeping the tension tight on the thread, insert
the right needle into the front of the stitch on the
left needle as to purl.

2. Slide one bead about 3/8 inch (about 1/2 inch
for size 8 or size 6 beads) from the stitch. Wrap
the thread or yarn around the right needle counterclockwise.

3. Pull the right needle toward you and the left
needle away from you to create a gap between the
stitch, and slide the bead through the gap to the
right side of the knitting (facing away from you).

4. Finish the stitch.

Bead purl the next 21 stitches. Purl the last two
stitches.

Row 3: Knit two stitches. Knit the next stitch,
sliding a bead into the stitch as it is made.

To put a bead in a knit stitch:
1. Keeping the tension tight on the thread, insert
the right needle into the back of the stitch on the
left needle as to knit.

2. Slide one bead about 3/8 inch (about 1/2 inch
for size 8 or size 6 beads) from the stitch. Wrap
the yarn around the right needle clockwise.

3. Pull the right needle toward you and the left
needle away from you to create a gap between the
stitch, and slide the bead through the gap to the
right side of the knitting (facing you).

4. Finish the stitch.

Bead knit the next 21 stitches. Knit the last two
stitches.

Rows 4-9: Repeat Rows 2 and 3 above.
Row 10: Purl. Cast off.

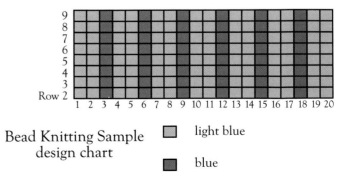

Bead Knitting Sample
design chart

☐ light blue

■ blue

Beaded Knitting Pillow

You Will Need

2 skeins of Crème Brulee by Knit One Crochet Two (each approx. 50 grams, or 131 yards or 120 meters), 100% wool, color #294

40 grams or 1-1/2 oz. size 6 pearl-toned beads

Size 5 circular knitting needle, 24 inches or 60cm long

Size F and I crochet hooks

Size 10 beading needle and 10 inches of beading thread to string beads on yarn

21 inches by 16-1/2 inches cotton fabric to blend with the yarn color

Stuffing

Making a pillow is a great way to try a new technique; it is small enough to complete easily, yet large enough to get comfortable with the technique.

Here is a quick project to get you accustomed to knitting with beads. I was inspired by the small repeating patterns of Fair Isle knits from the Shetland Islands and the rich cable textures of Aran sweaters of the Aran Isles.

Only the front of the pillow is knitted, then you sew it to a fabric pillow casing and stuff. You will be knitting flat, alternately using one skein strung with beads and one skein without beads. This minimizes wear on the yarn from sliding the beads. Circular needles are used so you can pick up the type of yarn you need at the beginning of either end of the row.

Finished size: 10 inches by 15-1/2 inches

String all of the beads onto one skein of yarn. Using the non-beaded skein, cast on 80 sts. The numbers in parenthesis at the beginning of the row are the total number of beads you will knit in that row.

Row 1: (0) (K1, P1) repeat across
Row 2: (0) (P1, K1) repeat across
Rows 3-8: alternate Row 1 and Row 2
Row 9: (0) (K1, P1) x 3, K68, (K1, P1) x 3
Row 10: (0) (P1, K1) x 3, P68, (P1, K1) x 3
Row 11: (0) (K1, P1) x 3, K68, (K1, P1) x 3
Row 12: (0) (P1, K1) x 3, K68, (P1, K1) x 3
Row 13: (0) (K1, P1) x 3, K68, (K1, P1) x 3
Attach and begin using beaded yarn.
Row 14: (17) (P1, K1) x 3, K2, B, (K4, B) x 16, K2, (P1, K1) x 3
Row 15: (51) (K1, P1) x 3, (P1, B, P1, B, P1, B, P1) x 17, (K1, P1) x 3
Row 16: (17) (P1, K1) x 3, K2, B, (K4, B) x 16, K2, (P1, K1) x 3
Begin at the opposite end of needle, using non-beaded yarn.
Row 17: (0) (K1, P1) x 3, P68, (K1, P1) x 3
Row 18: (0) (P1, K1) x 3, P68, (P1, K1) x 3
Row 19: (0) (K1, P1) x 3, P68, (K1, P1) x 3
Change to beaded yarn.
Row 20: (33) (P1, K1) x 3, (P2, B) x 33, P2, (P1, K1) x 3
Begin at the opposite end of the needle, using non-beaded yarn.
Row 21: (0) (K1, P1) x 3, K68, (K1, P1) x 3
Row 22: (0) (P1, K1) x 3, K68, (P1, K1) x 3
Row 23: (0) (K1, P1) x 3, K68, (K1, P1) x 3
Change to beaded yarn.
Row 24: (17) (P1, K1) x 3, (P2, K1, B, K1) x 17, (P1, K1) x 3
Row 25: (17) (K1, P1) x 3, K1, P1, B, P1, (K2, P1, B, P1) x 16, K1, (K1, P1) x 3
Row 26: (17) (P1, K1) x 3, (K1, B, K1, P2) x 17,(P1, K1) x 3
Begin at the opposite end of the needle, using non-beaded yarn.
Row 27: (0) (K1, P1) x 3, P68, (K1, P1) x 3
Row 28: (0) (P1, K1) x 3, P68, (P1, K1) x 3
Row 29: (0) (K1, P1) x 3, P68, (K1, P1) x 3
Row 30: (0) (P1, K1) x 3, K68, (P1, K1) x 3
Row 31: (0) (K1, P1) x 3, P68, (K1, P1) x 3
Row 32: (0) (P1, K1) x 3, P68, (P1, K1) x 3

Row 33: (0) (K1, P1) x 3, P68, (K1, P1) x 3
Change to beaded yarn.
Row 34: (14) (P1, K1) x 3, (P1, B, P1, K3) x 13, P1, B, P1, K1, (P1, K1) x 3
Row 35: (14) (K1, P1) x 3, P1, (K1, B, K1, P3) x 13, K1, B, K1, (K1, P1) x 3
Row 36: (14) (P1, K1) x 3, (P1, B, P1, K3) x 13, P1, B, P1, K1, (P1, K1) x 3
Row 37: (27) (K1, P1) x 3, (K1, B, K2, B, K1, P1) x 13, K1, B, K2, (K1, P1) x 3
Row 38: (67) (P1, K1) x 3, (P1, B) x 67, P1, (P1, K1) x 3
Row 39: (40) (K1, P1) x 3, P1, K1, (B, K2, B, K1, B, K2) x 13, B, K1, (K1, P1) x 3
Row 40: (27) (P1, K1) x 3, P2, B, P1, (K1, P1, B, P2, B, P1) x 13, (P1, K1) x 3
Row 41: (14) (K1, P1) x 3, P1, (K1, B, K1, P3) x 13, K1, B, K1, (K1, P1) x 3
Change to non-beaded yarn.
Row 42: (0) (P1, K1) x 3, K68, (P1, K1) x 3
Row 43: (0) (K1, P1) x 3, K68, (K1, P1) x 3
Row 44: (0) (P1, K1) x 3, K68, (P1, K1) x 3
Row 45: (0) (K1, P1) x 3, P68, (K1, P1) x 3
Row 46: (0) (P1, K1) x 3, K68, (P1, K1) x 3
Row 47: (0) (K1, P1) x 3, K68, (K1, P1) x 3
Row 48: (0) (P1, K1) x 3, K68, (P1, K1) x 3
Begin at the opposite end of the needle, using beaded yarn.
Row 49: (14) (K1, P1) x 3, (P1, B, P1, K3) x 13, P1, B, P1, (K1, P1) x 3
Row 50: (27) (P1, K1) x 3, (K1, B, K2, B, K1, P1) x 13, K1, B, K2, (P1, K1) x 3
Begin at the opposite end of the needle, using non-beaded yarn.
Row 51: (0) (K1, P1) x 3, P68, (K1, P1) x 3
Row 52: (0) (P1, K1) x 3, P68, (P1, K1) x 3
Row 53: (0) (K1, P1) x 3, P68, (K1, P1) x 3
Change to beaded yarn.
Row 54: (13) (P1, K1) x 3, P1, (B, P1, K7, P1, B, P1) x 6, B, P1, K6, (P1, K1) x 3
Row 55: (13) (K1, P1) x 3, (P5, K1, B, K2, B, K1) x 6, P5, K1, B, K1, P1, (K1, P1) x 3
Row 56: (13) (P1, K1) x 3, K2, (P1, B, P1, K3) x 13, P1, (P1, K1) x 3
Row 57: (14) (K1, P1) x 3, K1, B, K1, P1, K1, B, K1, P5) x 6, K1, B, K1, P1, K1, B, K1, P3, (K1, P1) x 3
Row 58: (14) (P1, K1) x 3, K4, (P1, B, P1, B, P1, K7) x 6, P1, B, P1, B, P1, K1, (P1, K1) x 3

Begin at the opposite end of the needle, using non-beaded yarn.
Row 59: (0) (K1, P1) x 3, K68, (K1, P1) x 3
Row 60: (0) (P1, K1) x 3, K68, (P1, K1) x 3
Row 61: (0) (K1, P1) x 3, K68, (K1, P1) x 3
Change to beaded yarn.
Row 62: (13) (P1, K1) x 3, (P3, K1, B, K1) x 13, P3, (P1, K1) x 3
Row 63: (39) (K1, P1) x 3, K2, (P1, B, P1, B, P1, B, P1, K1) x 13, K2, (K1, P1) x 3
Row 64: (39) (P1, K1) x 3, P2, (K1, B, K1, B, K1, B, K1, P1) x 13, P2, (P1, K1) x 3
Row 65: (13) (K1, P1) x 3, (K3, P1, B, P1) x 13, K3, (K1, P1) x 3
Change to non-beaded yarn.
Row 66: (0) (P1, K1) x 3, P68, (P1, K1) x 3
Row 67: (0) (K1, P1) x 3, P68, (K1, P1) x 3
Row 68: (0) (P1, K1) x 3, P68, (P1, K1) x 3
Row 69: (0) (K1, P1) x 3, K68, (K1, P1) x 3
Row 70: (0) (P1, K1) x 3, P68, (P1, K1) x 3
Row 71: (0) (K1, P1) x 3, P68, (K1, P1) x 3
Row 72: (0) (P1, K1) x 3, P68, (P1, K1) x 3
Begin at the opposite end of the needle, using beaded yarn.
Row 73: (17) (K1, P1) x 3, K2, B, (K4, B) x 16, K2, (K1, P1) x 3
Change to non-beaded yarn.
Row 74: (0) (P1, K1) x 3, K68, (P1, K1) x 3
Row 75: (0) (K1, P1) x 3, K68, (K1, P1) x 3
Row 76: (0) (P1, K1) x 3, K68, (P1, K1) x 3
Row 77: (0) (K1, P1) x 3, P68, (K1, P1) x 3
Row 78: (0) (P1, K1) x 3, K68, (P1, K1) x 3
Rows 79-86: (0) Same as Rows 1-8

Bind off loosely.
Block to 10 inches x 15-1/2 inches. Weave in the tails and working yarn.

To make a crocheted edging for pillow:

1. Using one strand of yarn and the size F crochet hook, single crochet loosely around the edges of the knitting, making three single crochet in the corners.

2. Using two strands of yarn and the size I crochet hook, single crochet, loosely, backwards into every other single crochet stitch. At each corner, single crochet in the two stitches before and after the corner stitch.

To make the pillow casing:

1. Fold the fabric, right sides together, to 10-1/2 inches x 16-1/2 inches.

2. Stitch the edges using a 1/2-inch seam allowance, leaving a 4-inch gap on the 16-1/2-inch edge for filling with stuffing. Clip corners, turn right side out, and press.

3. Stitch the knitting to one side of the pillow so that the crochet edging extends beyond the pillow edge.

4. Stuff the pillow and whip stitch the opening closed.

Blue Thistle Beaded Purse

You Will Need

3-inch clasp as pictured, inside dimensions, closed: 2-1/4 inches x 1-1/8 inches

60 yards of YLI silk cord 1000 denier, Corn Flower Blue

2 hanks of blue pearlized size 11 seed beads

Size 11 white pearl-toned seed beads, 4 grams or 1/8 oz.

Size 000 or 0000 double pointed knitting needles

Size 10 or 11 beading needle

This little purse uses the knitting techniques of the antique beaded purses made at the turn of the nineteenth century. The thistle pattern idea at the top is a new touch I added to update this style.

Finished size: 5 inches x 4 inches at the widest point

Slide seven strands of the blue beads onto the silk cord. Thread the needle and string the thistle pattern on the Blue Thistle Beaded Purse design chart, from Row 12 to Row 1, right to left or left to right (the design is symmetrical), separating each row with a small piece of paper.

Cast on 32 stitches.
Row 1: Knit
Row 2: Knit
Row 3: K4, (B1, K1) x 25, K3
Row 4: Knit
Row 5: K3, (B1, K1) x 27, K2
Rows 6-26: alternate Rows 4 and 5
The thistle pattern is completed. Only blue beads remain on the silk cord.
Rows 27 and 28: K2, (B1, K2) x 15
Rows 29 and 30: K2, (B1, K2, B2, K2) x 7, B2, K2
Rows 31 and 32: K2, (B1, K2, B3, K2) x 7, B1, K2
Rows 33 and 34: K2, (B1, K2, B4, K2, B1, K2, B2, K2) x 3, B1, K2, B4, K2, B1, K2

Rows 35 and 36: K2, (B1, K2, B5, K2, B1, K2, B1, K2) x 3, B1, K2, B5, K2, B1, K2
Rows 37 and 38: K2, (B1, K2, B6, K2, B1, K2, B1, K2) x 3, B1, K2, B6, K2, B1, K2
Rows 39 and 40: K2, (B1, K2, B6, K2, B1, K2, B2, K2) x 3, B1, K2, B6, K2, B1, K2
Rows 41 and 42: K2, (B1, K2, B5, K2, B1, K2, B3, K2) x 3, B1, K2, B5, K2, B1, K2
Rows 43 and 44: K2, (B1, K2, B4, K2) x 7, B1, K2
Rows 45 and 46: K2, (B1, K2, B3, K2, B1, K2, B5, K2) x 3, B1, K2, B3, K2, B1, K2
Rows 47 and 48: K2, (B1, K2, B2, K2, B1, K2, B6,

K2) x 3, B1, K2, B2, K2, B1, K2

Rows 49 and 50: K2, (B1, K2, B1, K2, B1, K2, B7, K2) x 3, B1, K2, B1, K2, B1, K2

Rows 51 and 52: K2, (B1, K2, B2, K2, B1, K2, B7, K2) x 3, B1, K2, B2, K2, B1, K2

Rows 53 and 54: K2, (B1, K2, B3, K2, B1, K2, B6, K2) x 3, B1, K2, B3, K2, B1, K2

Rows 55 and 56: K2, (B1, K2, B4, K2, B1, K2, B5, K2) x 3, B1, K2, B4, K2, B1, K2

Rows 57 and 58: K2, (B1, K2, B5, K2, B1, K2, B4, K2) x 3, B1, K2, B5, K2, B1, K2

Rows 59 and 60: K2, (B1, K2, B6, K2, B1, K2, B3, K2) x 3, B1, K2, B6, K2, B1, K2

Rows 61 and 62: K2, (B1, K2, B7, K2, B1, K2, B2, K2) x 3, B1, K2, B7, K2, B1, K2

Rows 63 and 64: K2, (B1, K2, B8, K2, B1, K2, B1, K2) x 3, B1, K2, B8, K2, B1, K2

Rows 65 and 66: K2, (B1, K2, B8, K2, B1, K2, B1, K2) x 3, B1, K2, B8, K2, B1, K2

Rows 67 and 68: K2, (B1, K2, B7, K2, B1, K2, B2, K2) x 3, B1, K2, B7, K2, B1, K2

Rows 69 and 70: K2, (B1, K2, B6, K2, B1, K2, B3, K2) x 3, B1, K2, B6, K2, B1, K2

Rows 71 and 72: K2, (B1, K2, B5, K2, B1, K2, B4, K2) x 3, B1, K2, B5, K2, B1, K2

Rows 73 and 74: K2, (B1, K2, B4, K2, B1, K2, B5, K2) x 3, B1, K2, B4, K2, B1, K2

Rows 75 and 76: K2, (B1, K2, B3, K2, B1, K2, B6, K2) x 3, B1, K2, B3, K2, B1, K2

Rows 77 and 78: K2, (B1, K2, B2, K2, B1, K2, B7, K2) x 3, B1, K2, B2, K2, B1, K2

Rows 79 and 80: K2, (B1, K2, B1, K2, B1, K2, B8, K2) x 3, B1, K2, B1, K2, B1, K2

Rows 81 and 82: K2, (B1, K2, B1, K2, B1, K2, B8, K2) x 3, B1, K2, B1, K2, B1, K2

Rows 83 and 84: K2, (B1, K2, B2, K2, B1, K2, B7, K2) x 3, B1, K2, B2, K2, B1, K2

Rows 85 and 86: K2, (B1, K2, B3, K2, B1, K2, B6, K2) x 3, B1, K2, B3, K2, B1, K2

Rows 87 and 88: K2, (B1, K2, B4, K2, B1, K2, B5, K2) x 3, B1, K2, B4, K2, B1, K2

Rows 89 and 90: K2, (B1, K2, B5, K2, B1, K2, B4, K2) x 3, B1, K2, B5, K2, B1, K2

Rows 91 and 92: K2, (B1, K2, B6, K2, B1, K2, B3, K2) x 3, B1, K2, B6, K2, B1, K2

Rows 93 and 94: K2, (B1, K2, B7, K2, B1, K2, B2, K2) x 3, B1, K2, B7, K2, B1, K2

Rows 95 and 96: K2, (B1, K2, B8, K2, B1, K2, B1, K2) x 3, B1, K2, B8, K2, B1, K2

Rows 97 and 98: K2, (B1, K2, B9, K2, B1, K2, B1, K2) x 3, B1, K2, B9, K2, B1, K2

Rows 99 and 100: K2, (B1, K2, B10, K2, B1, K2, B1, K2) x 3, B1, K2, B10, K2, B1, K2

Rows 101 and 102: K2, (B1, K2, B10, K2, B1, K2, B1, K2) x 3, B1, K2, B10, K2, B1, K2

Rows 103 and 104: K2, (B1, K2, B10, K2, B1, K2, B1, K2) x 3, B1, K2, B10, K2, B1, K2

This is one half of the bag. To make the other half, continue knitting, following the directions in reverse order from Row 98 to Row 27. Cut the silk cord 6 inches from the knitting. Thread the needle onto a new silk cord and string the thistle pattern on the design chart, from Row 12 to Row 1, right to left or left to right. Attach to the knitting and knit one row, then knit following the instructions for Row 26 to Row 1 in reverse order. Bind off. Weave in the ends.

Finishing:
Carefully stitch each end of the bag to the sew holes in the clasp, pulling tight to hide the holes. Stitch the sides together, beginning 3/8 inch below the sew holes for the clasp hinge to open and close.

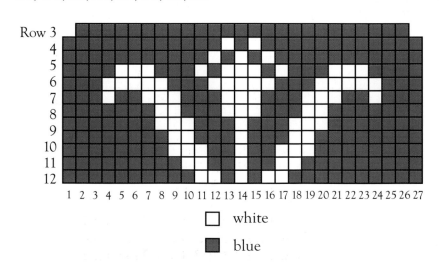

white

blue

Blue Thistle Beaded Purse

design chart

Daisy Scissors Case

You Will Need

1 ball #8 DMC pearl cotton in a color to match the background beads
Size 000 or 0000 knitting needles
Size 11 seed beads, in the colors shown in the Daisy Scissors Case design chart
1 large oval bead for the closure
Scraps of suede to fit the lining patterns in

Figure 9-2
Leather needle
Beading needle
Thimble (for pushing the needles through the leather)
Size 0 beading thread

This scissors case is easier to make than it looks. Once you string the beads accurately onto the pearl cotton, you can enjoy the project. If you haven't worked with such small needles before, knit a small practice swatch, with or without beads. If you like to knit, you will enjoy this once you get the hang of the beads and needles.

Knitting the back:

Following the pattern in the Daisy Scissors Case design chart, string the size 11 seed beads beginning at Row 90, and working down to Row 4, from either left to right or right to left (the design is symmetrical) onto the pearl cotton. The design chart only shows the bead pattern of the scissors case. The first three rows of knitting do not have beads and are not shown on the design chart, nor are two stitches on the sides of the chart.

Cast on 8 sts
Row 1: knit
Row 2: purl
Row 3: knit
Row 4: P2, PB4, P2
Row 5: K2, KB5, inc 1. 9 sts total
Row 6: P2, PB6, inc 1. 10 sts total
Row 7: K2, KB7, inc 1. 11 sts total
Row 8: P2, PB8, inc 1. 12 sts total

Row 9: K2, KB9, inc 1. 13 sts total
Row 10: P2, PB10, inc 1. 14 sts total
Row 11: K3, KB9, K2
Row 12: P2, PB10, P2
Row 13: K2, KB11, inc 1. 15 sts total
Row 14: P2, PB12, inc 1. 16 sts total
Row 15: K2, KB13, inc 1. 17 sts total

Row 16: P2, PB14, inc 1. 18 sts total
Row 17: K3, KB13, K2
Row 18: P2, PB14, P2
Row 19: K2, KB15, inc 1. 19 sts total
Row 20: P2, PB16, inc 1. 20 sts total
Row 21: K3, KB15, K2
Row 22: P2, PB16, P2
Row 23: K2, KB17, inc 1. 21 sts total
Row 24: P3, PB16, P2
Row 25: K2, KB17, K2
Row 26: P2, PB18, inc 1. 22 sts total
Row 27: K2, KB19, inc 1. 23 sts total
Row 28: P3, PB18, P2
Row 29: K2, KB19, K2
Row 30: P2, PB20, inc 1. 24 sts total
Row 31: K2, KB21, inc 1. 25 sts total
Row 32: P2, PB22, inc 1. 26 sts total
Row 33: K3, KB21, K2
Row 34: P2, PB22, P2
Row 35: K2, KB23, inc 1. 27 sts total
Row 36: P3, PB22, P2
Row 37: K2, KB23, K2
Row 38: P2, PB24, inc 1. 28 sts total
Row 39: K3, KB23, K2
Row 40: P2, PB24, P2
Row 41: K2, KB25, inc 1. 29 sts total
Row 42: P3, PB24, P2
Row 43: K2, KB25, K2
Row 44: P2, PB26, inc 1. 30 sts total
Row 45: K3, KB25, K2
Row 46: P2, PB26, P2
Row 47: K2, KB27, inc 1. 31 sts total
Row 48: P3, PB26, P2
Row 49: K2, KB27, K2
Row 50: P2, PB28, inc 1. 32 sts total
Row 51: K3, KB27, K2
Row 52: P2, PB28, P2
Row 53: K2, KB29, inc 1. 33 sts total
Row 54: P3, PB28, P2
Row 55: K2, KB29, K2
Row 56: P2, PB30, inc 1. 34 sts total
Row 57: K3, KB29, K2
Row 58: P2, PB30, P2
Row 59: K3, KB29, K2
Row 60: P2, PB30, P2
Row 61: K2, KB31, inc 1. 35 sts total
Row 62: P3, PB30, P2
Row 63: K3, KB29, K1, K2tog. 34 sts total
Row 64: P3, PB28, P1, P2tog. 33 sts total

Row 65: K2, KB29, K2
Row 66: P3, PB28, P2
Row 67: K3, KB27, K1, K2tog. 32 sts total
Row 68: P2tog, P1, PB26, P1, P2tog. 30 sts total
Row 69: K2tog, K1, KB25, K2. 29 sts total
Row 70: P2tog, P1, PB24, P2. 28 sts total
Row 71: K2tog, K1, KB23, K2. 27 sts total
Row 72: P2tog, P1, PB22, P2. 26 sts total
Row 73: K2tog, K1, KB21, K2. 25 sts total
Row 74: P2tog, P1, PB20, P2. 24 sts total
Row 75: K2tog, K1, KB19, K2. 23 sts total
Row 76: P2tog, P1, PB18, P2. 22 sts total
Row 77: K2tog, K1, KB17, K2. 21 sts total
Row 78: P2tog, P1, PB16, P2. 20 sts total
Row 79: K2tog, K1, KB15, K2. 19 sts total
Row 80: P2tog, P1, PB14, P2. 18 sts total
Row 81: K2tog, K1, KB13, K2. 17 sts total
Row 82: P2tog, P1, PB12, P2. 16 sts total
Row 83: K2tog, K1, KB11, K2. 15 sts total
Row 84: P2tog, P1, PB10, P2. 14 sts total
Row 85: k2tog, K1, KB9, K2. 13 sts total
Row 86: P2tog, P1, PB8, P2. 12 sts total
Row 87: K2tog, K1, KB7, K2. 11 sts total
Row 88: P2tog, P1, PB5, P1, P2tog. 9 sts total
Row 89: K2tog, K1, KB4, K2. 8 sts total
Row 90: P2tog, P1, PB3, P2. 7 sts total
Row 91: purl
Row 92: K2tog, K3, K2tog. 5 sts total
Cast off

Photo by Myra Nunley

Front:
String the size 11 seed beads beginning at Row 52 on the design chart, and working down to Row 1, from either left to right or right to left (the design is symmetrical) onto the pearl cotton. Knit following the same directions as for the back through Row 52. Knit the next row. Purl the next row. Cast off.

Finishing:

1. Align the front and back, bead sides together, and stitch the seam close to the beads so there is no gap in the beads at the seam. Turn right side out.

2. Trace and then cut the front and back lining from leather (**Figure 9-2**). With right sides together, hand stitch together with a running stitch and using a leather needle, then stitch back the other way, filling in the spaces left from the first pass of running stitches (**Figure 9-3**).

3. Slip the suede lining inside of the bead knitting. To attach the flap to the leather and encase the edge with beads, anchor the beading thread at the base of the flap. Using the beading needle, string three to five beads and overcast stitch through the leather and the knitted selvage, covering the edge

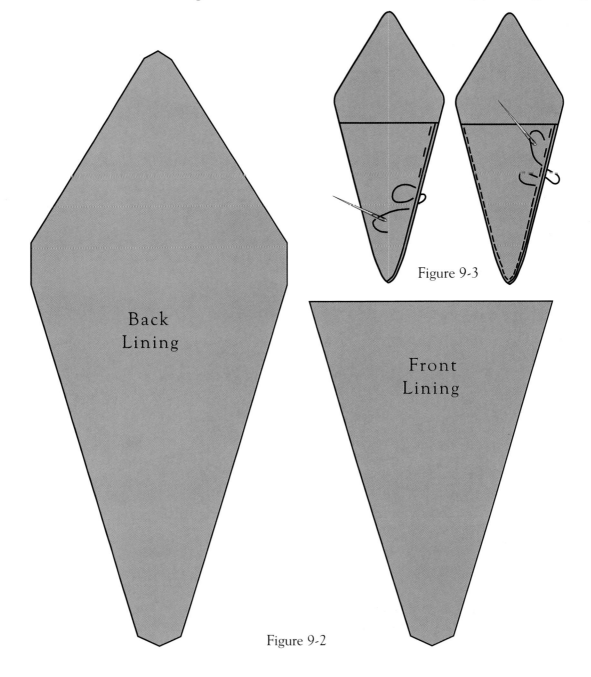

Figure 9-3

Back
Lining

Front
Lining

Figure 9-2

of the leather and the knitted selvage with beads. There should be no gap between the knitted beads and the beads on the overcast stitches (**Figure 9-4**).

4. Using the leather needle and pearl cotton, overcast stitch the front of the bead knitting to the edge of the leather (**Figure 9-5**).

5. Using the beading needle and beading thread, make a picot edge as shown in **Figure 9-6** at the top of the front, stitching in and out along the top row of beads in the knitting.

Closure:

1. Using the beading needle and beading thread, make two or three loops of seed bead strands on the front, just big enough so the large oval bead can slip through. Stitch several times through the leather and beads for a strong closure.

2. Using the beading needle and beading thread, sew the large oval bead to the point of the flap, stitching through the leather and creating a neck of seed beads long enough so the oval bead can be tilted to slide through the loop on the front (**Figure 9-7**).

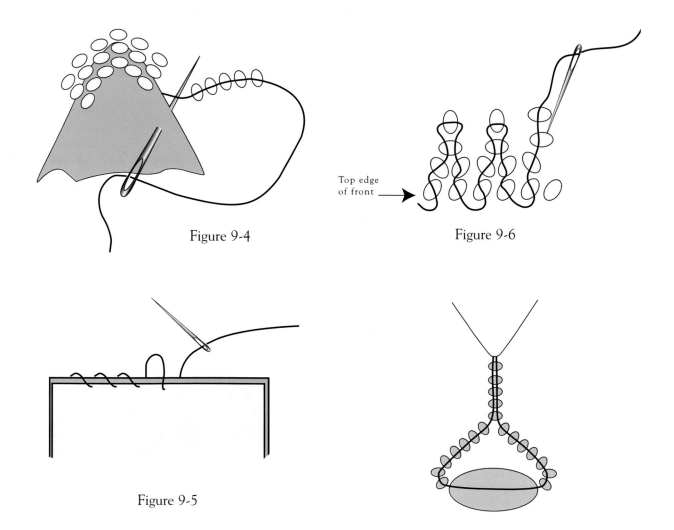

Figure 9-4

Figure 9-6

Top edge of front ⟶

Figure 9-5

Figure 9-7

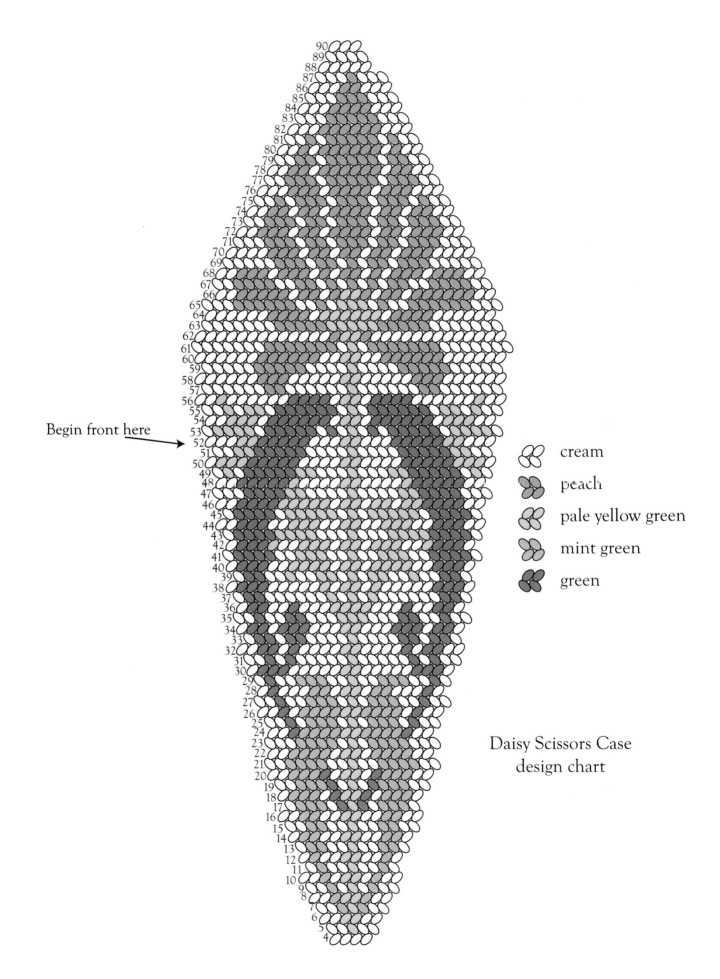

Begin front here →

90
89
88
87
86
85
84
83
82
81
80
79
78
77
76
75
74
73
72
71
70
69
68
67
66
65
64
63
62
61
60
59
58
57
56
55
54
53
52
51
50
49
48
47
46
45
44
43
42
41
40
39
38
37
36
35
34
33
32
31
30
29
28
27
26
25
24
23
22
21
20
19
18
17
16
15
14
13
12
11
10
9
8
7
6
5
4

cream

peach

pale yellow green

mint green

green

Daisy Scissors Case
design chart

Chapter 10
Crochet

This chapter teaches you two methods of using beads in single crochet:

• Bead crochet in the round with the beads in the back of the work.

• Flat bead single crochet with the beads in the front of the work. On alternate rows you work beads into the back of the work to keep the beads all on the same side.

Traditionally, bead crocheted projects were almost always crocheted in the round. It is easy to slide beads into the back of single crochet stitches, so the back side of the work becomes the beaded front of the finished piece.

Several bead crocheters have recently developed techniques for pulling the beads to the front of a crochet stitch so that we can now bead crochet on a flat piece, crocheting rows back and forth and always keeping the beads on the same side.

Before these developments, crocheters broke the thread at the end of each row and started a new one, beginning each row at the same side in order to stitch a flat beaded piece. I use the method developed by Elizabeth Gourley, one of my co-authors for the book *Art of Seed Beading*, for crocheting beads to the front of the stitch. When sliding a bead into the back of a stitch, the beads slant to the left if the bead is added at the beginning of the stitch, and they slant to the right if the bead is added after the stitch is started.

I like adding the beads at the beginning of the stitch for a consistent leftward slant in both flat and round beaded crochet. In flat front bead crochet, the beads also slant to the left in the method I use.

This flapper bag from the 1920s is crocheted and fabric-lined.

These are antique and contemporary bead crochet projects. The best way to find out which crochet technique was used is to look at a piece's back.

To make a beaded single crochet (BC):

1. Slide the hook into the stitch.

2. Slide a bead down to the work.

3. Thread around the hook clockwise.

4. Pull the thread through the stitch. The bead is in the stitch on the back of the work.

5. Thread around the hook clockwise.

6. Pull the thread through both loops on the hook.

7. The bead lies on the back side of the work. It will slant to the left.

To make a front beaded single crochet (FBC):

1. Slide the hook into the stitch.

2. Wrap the thread around the hook clockwise.

3. Pull the thread through the stitch, sliding a bead down to the hook and pushing the bead through the stitch as well, so it comes to the front.

4. Wrap the thread around the hook clockwise.

5. Pull the thread through both loops on the hook.

Abbreviations for this chapter

SC: single crochet
BC: single crochet with a bead in the back of the stitch
FBC: single crochet with a bead in the front of the stitch
CD: double crochet
st(s): stitch(es)
ch: chain

Bead Crocheted Star Sample

You Will Need

252 size 11 cream seed beads
Size 20 light blue DMC pearl cotton or

Cebelia
Size 8 crochet hook

This example teaches you how to slide the bead in place at the beginning of the stitch so the bead sits on the back of the stitch. You may want to practice in size 6 beads, using a sport-weight yarn and size H hook first, then try it with the smaller beads, thread, and hook once you get used to working with the beads.

Finished size: 2-1/4 inches in diameter

String 252 beads onto the thread (see page 329 in the knitting section).
Chain 3. Join into a ring.
Round 1: 7 SC in ring. 7 stitches.
Next you begin the continuous spiral rounds.
Round 2: BC and SC into the next stitch. Repeat around. 14 stitches.

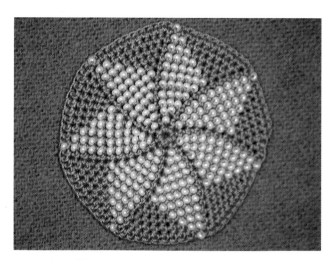

Round 3: (BC into next st, BC and SC in next st) x 7. 21 stitches.
Rounds 4 through 6: BC into each beaded stitch.

346

BC and SC in each stitch without a bead. Each round will increase by 7 stitches.

Make the points of the star:
Round 7: (BC into the next 5 sts, sc in next st, 2 sc in next st) x 7. 56 stitches.
Rounds 8 through 12: (BC 1 less than the round before and 1 more sc, then 2 sc in last st) x 7. The last round has no beads and 91 stitches.

Front Beaded Flat Crochet Sample

------------------------------ *You Will Need* ------------------------------

144 Size 11 seed beads
Size 8 DMC pearl cotton or size 20 Cebelia

Size 8 crochet hook

This sample teaches you how to make a flat front beaded single crochet panel. You may want to practice in size 6 beads, using a sport-weight yarn and size H hook first, then try it with the smaller beads, thread, and hook once you get used to working with the beads.

Finished size: 1 1/4 inches x 2 1/4 inches

String the beads onto the thread.
Ch 20.
Row 1: Ch1, SC in each chain, turn.
Row 2: Ch1, SC in each st, turn.
Row 3: Ch1, SC in first st, BC in each st to the last st. SC in last st, turn.
Row 4: Ch1, SC in first st, FBC in each st to the last st. SC in last st, turn.
Rows 5-10: alternate Row 2 and Row 3.
Row 11 and 12: SC in each st. End.

Ocean Waves Bead Crochet Bag

You Will Need

1 ball size 20 Manuela blue variegated cotton crochet cord
60 grams size 11 clear glass Japanese seed beads
1 yard 1/8-inch cord for drawstring
2 small shells, with one drilled hole to fit a sewing needle

2 large shells with two drilled holes to fit the cord
Blue sewing thread and needle
Size 8 crochet hook
Clear craft glue for stabilizing the drawstring's cut ends

This is an easy beaded bag for avid thread crocheters. The fun closure with small shells to open the bag, and large shells to close it, add to the ocean theme of the wave pattern. I chose blue variegated thread with the colors aligning in a swaying pattern, showing through the clear glass beads. The closure idea is from a bag one of my students, Sherri Atkins, brought to class one day.

This bag is worked in continuously spiraling rounds. You may find it helpful to mark the beginnings of the rounds with a knit marker or a small safety pin while making the increases.

Finished size: 8 inches high by 11-1/2 inches around

To crochet the bag bottom and the side up to the wave pattern:
Slide 20 grams of beads onto the cotton crochet cord (see page 329).
Using a size 8 crochet hook, chain 3. Join into a ring.
Round 1: 7 SC in ring.
Round 2: BC and SC into the next st. Repeat around. 14 stitches.
Round 3: (BC into next st, BC and SC in next st)

x 7. 21 stitches.
Round 4: BC into each beaded st. BC and SC in each st without a bead.
Continue as in Round 4 until there are 17 beads

and 1 SC without a bead, 7x around the edge. 126 stitches.

BC without increasing in every st. You are now crocheting the side of the bag. Continue until the bag measures 4-1/2 inches from the center bottom up to the working edge.

To crochet the sides with the wave design:

Begin following the Wave design chart, from right to left, bottom to top, making a SC for each blank square and a BC for each blue square. The beaded design will be reversed from the chart. Repeat the design chart 7x for each round of the bag.

SC in all stitches until the bag is 2 inches taller than the bead crochet waves.

To make the drawstring cord casing and shell stitch edging:

Reverse direction, so that the right side of the bag is facing you.

Row 1: Ch 3. DC in the next 2 sts. ch 1. (DC in the next 3 sts. ch 1) x 31, increasing 2 sts evenly around the bag. Slip stitch in third ch at beginning of the row. 128 sts.

Row 2: Ch 3. (DC in each DC, ch 1) x 32. 128 sts.

Rows 3 and 4: Ch 1, then SC in every st. Slip stitch in ch at beginning of the row. 128 sts.

Row 5: (7 treble crochet in fourth ch. Slip stitch in eighth ch.) x 16. End.

To add the drawstrings:

1. Apply glue to a 1/2-inch section of the center and ends of the drawstring cord to prevent raveling. When dry, cut the cord in half (for two 18-inch lengths).

2. Weave one length of cord through the openings in the bottom double crochet row and the other length of cord through the top double crochet row so that the cord tails meet at opposite ends of the rows (**Figure 10-1**).

3. Using sewing thread and a needle, stitch a small shell to the center of each cord and through to the double crochet, anchoring the cord to the bag at that point. These are now handles for opening the bag.

4. Thread the tail cords through the large shells and tie a square knot above the shell, so that the cords extend at least 1 inch beyond the bag when it is fully open.

5. Tie a knot in each tail close to the square knot. Cut the tails 1 inch from the knot and unravel to make a fringe. Cut the fringe evenly to about 3/4 inch.

Figure 10-1

Wave
design chart

Floral Belt Bag

You Will Need

1 tan-colored ball of size 10 DMC Cebelia
Size 8 seed beads in the colors shown in
    the Belt Bag design chart
1/2 oz. or 14 grams size 8 tan or brown seed
    beads for back of design
63 size 8 seed beads for flap
20 grams of size 15 green seed beads for flap
    edge

1 large accent bead
Various fringe beads to make a fringe of 21
    dangles (see Figure 10-2)
Size 5 crochet hook
Size 12 beading needle and thread
Chenille needle to weave in ends of crochet
    cotton

This small belt bag is a composite of ideas from two sources that inspired me: the beautiful brown bag on page 300 by Shonna Neuhart and the pattern on the antique purse on the title page. I used size 8 beads and a crochet technique in adapting these ideas to my belt bag. When crocheting in the round, the rows slant somewhat. To counteract this for this bag, crochet loosely and block the bag before adding the fringe.

Finished size: 2-1/4 inches x 5-1/4 inches, including fringe

String the 63 green size 8 beads for the flap. Then, string the pattern as shown in the Belt Bag design chart onto the cotton, following the pattern from right to left, top to bottom for each row. See page 329 for stringing instructions.

To make the bag:

1. Chain 44. Join into a ring with a slip stitch.

2. BC into each chain. 44 sts.

3. Continue BC spiraling around the bag, until all of the beads are crocheted.

To make the flap:

1. Reverse direction. Ch 1. SC in next 20 sts. Turn.

2. Ch 1. Skip next st. FBC in next 18 sts. Skip next st. SC in next st. Turn. 20 sts.

3. Ch 1. Skip next st. BC in next 16 sts. Skip next st. SC in last st. Turn. 18 sts.

4. Ch 1. Skip next st. FBC in next 15 sts. SC in last st. Turn. 17 sts.

5. Ch 1. Skip next st. BC in next 14 sts. SC in last st. End.

With the sewing thread and beading needle, stitch strands of size 15 seed beads along the edge of the flap as for the Knitted Scissors Case flap (on page 342). Sew the large accent bead in place.

To block the bag:

Wet the bag with water and pat off any excess with a towel. Shape the bag so it lies in a rectangle. Place a dishtowel on a cookie sheet and put the bag on it. Heat up your oven to 200 degrees. Place the cookie sheet with the beadwork in the oven and turn it off. This will set the shape of the bag with heat and water. Let the bag dry overnight.

To make the fringe:

Sew the bottom of the bag together. Thread the beading needle and alternate Fringe A and Fringe B with suggested beads across the bottom of the bag (**Figure 10-2**).

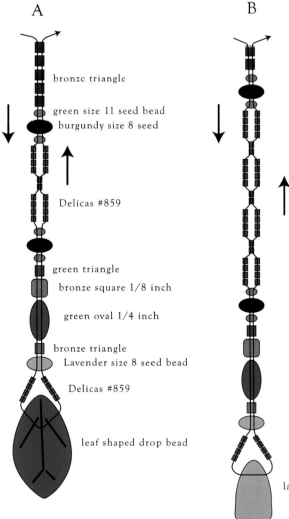

A

B

bronze triangle

green size 11 seed bead
burgundy size 8 seed

Delicas #859

green triangle
bronze square 1/8 inch

green oval 1/4 inch

bronze triangle
Lavender size 8 seed bead

Delicas #859

leaf shaped drop bead

lavender drop bead

Figure 10-2

351

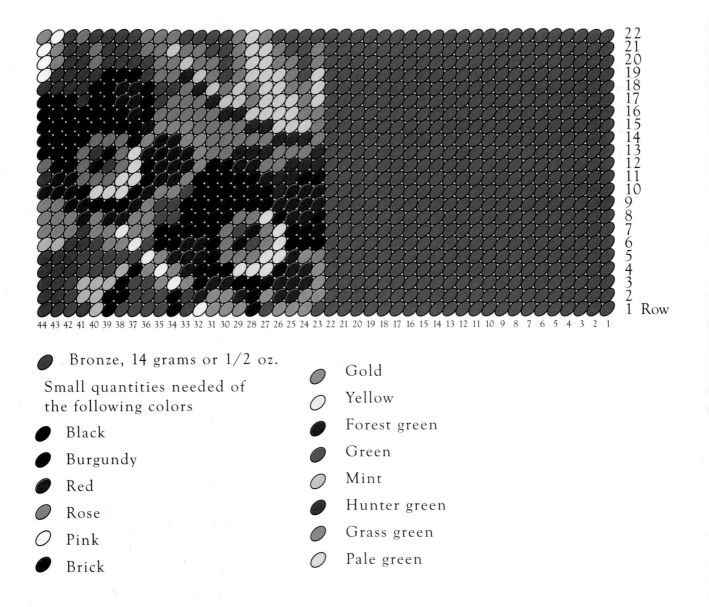

Bronze, 14 grams or 1/2 oz.

Small quantities needed of the following colors

- Black
- Burgundy
- Red
- Rose
- Pink
- Brick

- Gold
- Yellow
- Forest green
- Green
- Mint
- Hunter green
- Grass green
- Pale green

Belt Bag
design chart

Purple Vine Crocheted Bracelet

You Will Need

20 yards 1000 plum denier silk cord
6 grams size 15 plum seed beads
2 grams size 15 lavender seed beads
2 large accent beads
Clasp
4 size 8 spacer beads

2 spacer disks
2 silver cones
Size 10 crochet hook
Plum beading thread
Size 12 beading needle

The firmness of this beaded rope comes from the number of beads in each round. The small beads, silk, and silver create an elegant design.

Finished size: 9 inches long

String the beads onto the silk, following the Crochet Bracelet design chart from right to left, top to bottom for each row. String Row 7 through Row 9, 43 more times. String Row 1 through Row 4 again.

Leave a 15-inch tail at the beginning for adding the accent beads.

1. Chain 12, putting a bead into each chain (**Figure 10-3**).

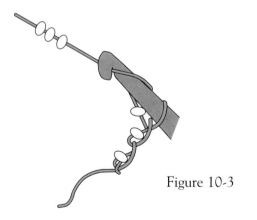

Figure 10-3

Tip: The first round of bead crochet tubes is very difficult because it is easy to lose track of which stitches to put your hook through. If you thread the first and last st in the beginning chain, each with a 3-inch length of contrasting thread and also the first st you make to join the chain into a loop, you will easily be able to know which stitch is which.

2. Slide the hook under the thread of the first chain stitch with a bead, to the left of the bead (**Figure 10-4**).

3. Slide a bead down to the hook, wrap the thread around the hook clockwise, and pull through both threads on the hook (**Figure 10-5**).

4. Repeat Steps 2 and 3, spiraling around, making a beaded slip stitch in every st, until all of the beads are crocheted. End.

5. Sew the cones, beads, and clasp. Using the tail thread, string the beads as shown in **Figure 10-6**. Pass through the clasp at the back and through the beads. Repeat and anchor into the crochet work; weave in all. Repeat for the other end of the bracelet, adding the other end of the clasp.

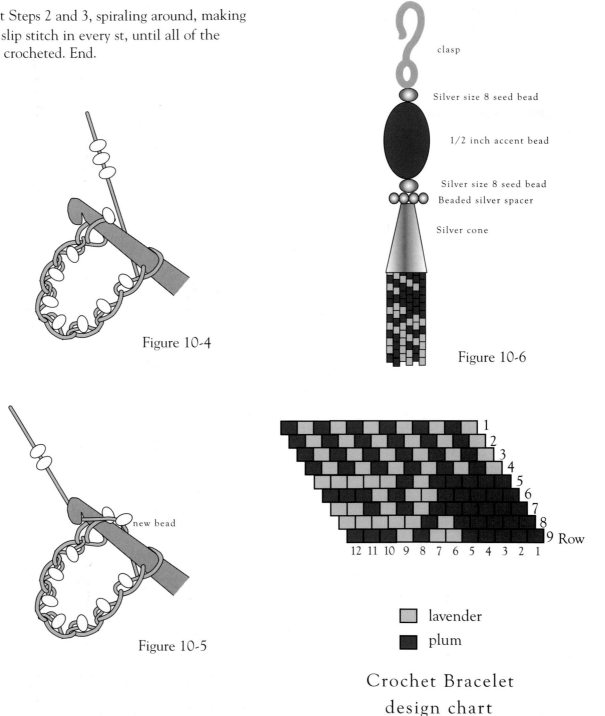

Figure 10-4

Figure 10-5

new bead

clasp

Silver size 8 seed bead

1/2 inch accent bead

Silver size 8 seed bead
Beaded silver spacer

Silver cone

Figure 10-6

1
2
3
4
5
6
7
8
9 Row

12 11 10 9 8 7 6 5 4 3 2 1

☐ lavender

■ plum

Crochet Bracelet
design chart

Chapter 11
Tatting

The easiest way of incorporating beads into tatting is to string one type and color of bead onto the tatting thread and then slide them into all of the pattern's picots. This has the added advantage of providing uniform picots for beginning tatters. All picots end up the correct size, based on the number of beads used.

Unjoined picots look best with an odd number of beads so there is a point at the center of the picot. Picots that you join to other design elements can have an odd or even number of beads depending on the effect you want. The photograph below shows some of these possibilities.

You can use either needle or shuttle tatting with most patterns. Shuttle tatting limits you to using beads small enough to fit on the bobbin for tatting from the bobbin. You can get around this by stringing larger beads onto the ball and tatting off of the ball instead. Needle tatting has the advantage of letting you add larger beads onto the needle while tatting. (You will use both techniques in this book.)

I prefer tatting with beads close in size and color to the cord. I also like to incorporate plain picots with beaded picots to keep the delicate look of tatting.

Bead Tatted Sample With Shuttle or Needle

You Will Need

Size 20 cream DMC Cebelia cotton cord
Tatting needle or shuttle

137 size 11 cream seed beads
Size 11 beading needle

Finished size: 2-1/4 inches by 5/8 inch

To make a sample of beaded needle tatting:

1. Thread the beading needle with the Cebelia and string all of the beads.

2. Remove the beading needle and thread the Cebelia onto the tatting needle and work from the ball.

3. Follow the diagram (**Figure 11-1**), sliding the number of beads as shown between chains instead of picots. Close the ring.

4. Slide nine beads up to the completed ring. This is the chain between rings.

5. Begin another ring, joining to the picot of the first ring. To join to a beaded picot, hold the tension tight on the thread, insert the needle into the picot so that there are two beads on either side, and pull the thread through, so that the loop of thread is between the two pairs of beads (**Figure 11-2**).

6. Finish the ring. Continue until there are six rings and five chains. Weave in the ends.

To make a sample of shuttle beaded tatting:

1. Thread the beading needle with the Cebelia and string all of the beads.

Sample made using size 30 cebelia and charlottes.

2. Remove the beading needle with the beaded Cebelia and wrap onto the bobbin.

3. Slide 18 beads into the ring.

4. Tat following the diagram in **Figure 11-1** to make the first ring, sliding the number of beads indicated into the picots.

5. Slide nine beads up to the completed ring. This is the chain between rings.

6. Make the next ring, joining to the first ring at the first picot. To join to a beaded picot, hold the tension tight on the thread, insert the hook or tip of the shuttle into the picot so that there are two beads on either side and pull the thread through, so that the loop of thread is between the two pairs of beads (**Figure 11-2**).

7. Continue until there are six rings and five chains. Weave in the ends.

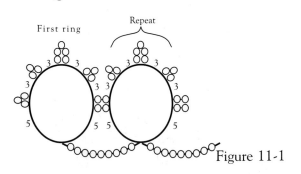

Figure 11-1

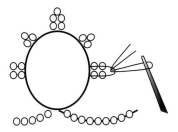

Figure 11-2

356

Needle Tatted Lampshade Fringe

Blue and white is my mother's favorite color combination. So this little lamp, with its blue and white color scheme, is perfect for decorating her new home.

Finished size: Will fit around a shade 6 inches in diameter at the bottom.

1. Thread the beading needle with the Manuela cotton; do not cut it from the ball.

2. String 37 repeats of the bead pattern (**Figure 11-3**). Change to the tatting needle.

3. Tat the pattern (**Figure 11-4**).

4. Weave the ends together to form a circle.

5. Pin to the lampshade, then carefully glue in place. When the glue is dry, remove the pins.

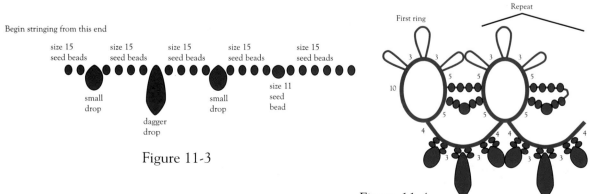

Figure 11-3

Figure 11-4

Needle Tatted Mirror Case

You Will Need

2-3/4-inch pocket mirror with an opening on the back for inserting needlework
Tan-colored tatting thread
3-inch circle of sage-colored linen
155 size 15 cream-colored seed beads

10 cream-colored Delica beads
5 size 8 matte silver-lined gold beads
Size 7 tatting needle
Tan sewing thread and needle

This is a good example of the advantage of needle tatting with beads over shuttle tatting. Here, you have a needle to add beads as you work.

Finished size: 2 inches of tatting on a 2-3/4-inch mirror back.

1. Make one ring following **Figure 11-5**.

2. Close the ring.

3. Slide four beads up to the ring and string one Delica, one size 8 bead, and one Delica, then make another ring joining to the first (**Figure 11-6**).

4. Make a total of five rings, joining the last to the first. Weave in the ends.

5. Begin a new thread at one of the four bead picots on the ring. Following **Figure 11-7**, make the large chain, adding plain picots and beaded picots as shown. Repeat around the first round, attaching at each of the four remaining bead picots. Attach to the beginning picot and weave in the ends.

6. Sew the tatted piece to the linen, taking care to form the shape evenly. Insert the linen into the mirror back following the manufacturer's instructions.

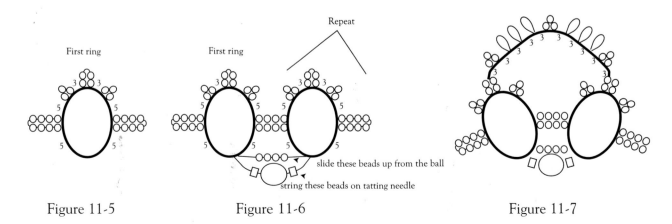

Figure 11-5

Figure 11-6

Figure 11-7

Shuttle Tatted Pin Cushion

You Will Need

Sudberry House Etcetera Pincushion #15761
10-inch circle of hunter green cotton
   velveteen
260 size 12 cream-colored charlottes
234 sea green-colored size 15 seed beads
26 gold charlottes

Cream-colored tatting thread
Tatting shuttle
Cream-colored sewing thread and needle
Large blunt needle
Size 12 beading needle
Sewing needle

Although you can also make this pattern with needle tatting, shuttle tatting creates a tighter stitch, making it easier to weave the second tatted section into the first.

Finished size: 4-inch circle of tatting on a 3-3/4-inch wide by 3/4-inch thick pin cushion, not including the wood base

To make the first row:

Using the beading needle, string the cream-colored charlottes onto the tatting thread.

Make 26 repeats of **Figure 11-8**, joining the last to the first, creating a circle.

Cut from the ball and weave in the ends.

To make the second row:

Using the beading needle, string 26 repeats of one gold charlotte and nine of the green beads onto the tatting thread. Make 26 repeats of **Figure 11-9**. Do not join into a circle. Cut from the shuttle, leaving a 6-inch tail.

To assemble the pin cushion:

1. Cover the pincushion with the velveteen, following the manufacturer's instructions. Pull the fabric only tight enough so the cushion is about 3/4 inch thick.

2. Pin the first row of tatting on the velveteen and stitch in place, going through only the picots and closing point of the rings.

3. Thread the large blunt needle with the tail of the second row of tatting and weave through the first row of tatting as in the project photo.

4. Use the sewing needle to hide the tails in the tatting.

5. Stitch the second row of tatting to the velveteen at the gold-beaded picots.

6. Follow the manufacturer's instructions for gluing the pincushion to the wood base.

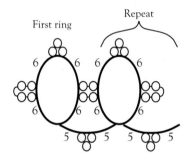

Figure 11-8

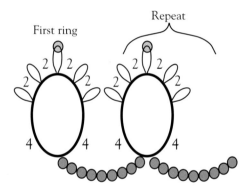

Figure 11-9

360

Chapter 12
Tambourwork

Tambour embroidery is the process of chain stitching with a tambour needle on fabric pulled tight in an embroidery hoop. The tambour needle is a hook similar to a crochet hook with a point at the tip to pierce the fabric. Different colored threads are used to make decorative chain stitches across the surface of the fabric. The hoop needs to be in a stand, because you need both hands free: one to hold the tambour needle on the topside of the hoop and the other to guide the thread on the underside.

When doing tambour embroidery with beads, the chain stitch is merely functional, and the beads carried on the thread on the right side of the fabric are the decorative feature.

Use a thin thread that blends with the color of the fabric so you can work the beads close together. A soft fabric such as velvet makes it easy to make the chain stitches.

The design for the tambourwork is drawn on the backside of the fabric which is stretched in the

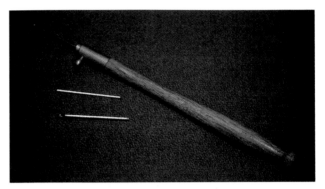

Tambour needles and handle.

hoop with the right side of the fabric facing down. Each bead is slid up to the fabric and caught in the underside of the chain stitch as it is made on the top of the fabric. The technique is simple, but practice is important so that the stitches are uniform. Each stitch should be just a little bit longer than the length of the bead you are using; hence stitch length varies according to the bead size.

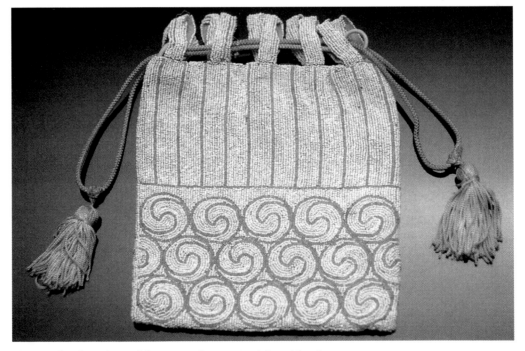

Antique bead tamboured drawstring bag in size 16 seed beads.

Tambourwork Sample

_____ *You Will Need* _____

14-inch square of muslin
12-inch embroidery hoop and stand
Tambour needle size 90
DMC tatting thread size 80

Size 11 green seed beads
Tracing paper, transfer paper, and pencil
Size 11 beading needle
Size 10 crochet hook

Finished size: 2 inches by 3 inches

1. Transfer the design in the Tambourwork Sample design chart onto the back of the muslin with the tracing paper, transfer paper, and pencil. Stretch in the embroidery hoop with the design facing up. Put in the stand.

2. String about 15 inches of beads onto the tatting thread, keeping the thread on the ball. Insert the tambour needle in the tambour handle so that the hook faces the screw. Screw tight.

3. Holding the needle in your dominant hand, push it through the fabric at the beginning of the stem line.

4. With the other hand under the hoop, hold the thread about 6 inches from the end and loop it around the needle hook. Pull the needle up through the fabric, keeping tension on the thread below, and sliding the needle away from the hook side (the screw shows where the hook side is), so it glides back through without catching on the fabric. You should have pulled a loop up to the top side of the fabric (**Figure 12-1**).

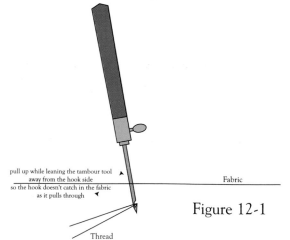

pull up while leaning the tambour tool
away from the hook side
so the hook doesn't catch in the fabric
as it pulls through

Fabric

Thread

Figure 12-1

5. Pull the thread tail through to the top. Make a second stitch without a bead, close to the first. Thread the tail through the loop and pull tight to anchor the thread.

To add beads to the stitches:

1. Slide about 10 beads up the thread so that they are between your hand and the fabric. Practice moving one bead at a time up to the fabric without seeing what you are doing. You can also position a mirror below the work to see what you are doing, keeping in mind it will be a reverse image.

2. When you are comfortable sliding the beads, slide one bead up to the fabric and insert the tambour hook into the fabric about one bead's width away from the last stitch. Holding your hand

under the hoop (**Figure 12-2**), guide the thread onto the hook and finish the stitch, catching the bead in the stitch.

3. Continue stitching with beads until you reach the end of the design. Take a small stitch without a bead and pull a loop of thread up to the back of the fabric.

4. Cut the thread, leaving about a 6-inch tail. Using the size 10 crochet hook, weave the tail through about five loops on the fabric to anchor it. Cut close to the fabric. Repeat for the beginning thread.

5. Repeat the process for each line of the design.

begin here

Tambourwork Sample
desing chart

Figure 12-1

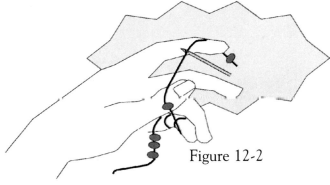

Figure 12-2

Bead Tamboured Needle Tool Box

You Will Need

Sudberry House Needle Tool Box #1595C
#90 Tambour needle and handle
8-inch embroidery hoop and stand
DMC tatting thread size 80

Size 11 blue, green, and turquoise seed beads
Size 11 beading needle
Tracing paper, transfer paper, pencil

Tambour embroidery is more fun when each color is a long, continuous line. That way, you tambour more and begin and end less. This small, easy project is a fun one to make. The thick pile of the velveteen hides the chain stitches and accents the beads nicely, giving the project an elegant look.

Finished size: 1-5/8-inch by 3-1/2-inch beaded area

1. Transfer the design in the Needle Tool Box design chart onto the back of the velveteen, using the tracing paper, transfer paper, and pencil.

2. Stretch the fabric, design side up, into a free-standing needlework frame.

3. String about 4 inches of one color beads onto the tatting thread, leaving the thread attached to the spool. Take the needle off of the thread.

4. Tambour embroider with beads along the first pattern line. End the thread and remove any excess beads.

5. Repeat Steps 3 and 4 for the other stitching lines, using different colored beads. Remove the fabric from the frame and follow the manufacturer's instructions for inserting it into the needle tool box.

Needle Tool Box design chart

Chapter 13

Needlepoint and Cross Stitch

Using beads in needlepoint and cross stitch projects adds texture and dimension to the design. The beads are easily added by making a half cross stitch, or tent stitch, with a bead picked up on the thread before completing the stitch.

You need to use a needle small enough to fit the bead hole and use beads that fill the stitch size of the evenweave fabric.

You can use beads sparingly as in the top of the Sampler shown on page 397, to accent the foreground design as in the Needlepoint Glasses Case on page 366, or throughout the piece as the antique beaded tray below. You can also add more dimension by using strands of beads across the surface.

Traditionally, beads are stitched using a neutral colored thread, but I like to match the thread to the bead colors to fill the space with the same color. Transparent beads are enhanced when you choose a thread color to match or brighten the hue.

Beaded purses and bags, such as this antique needlepoint drawstring floral bag, have gone in and out of style since the seventeenth century.

This beautiful antique serving tray was made using size 11 seed beads and gold-toned steel-cut beads, in needlepoint, on Penelope canvas.

Needlepoint Glasses Case

You Will Need

10 by 10 inches of 18-count Aida cloth
8- by 8-inch lining fabric
Needlework frame
Size 8 seed beads, in the colors shown in the Glasses Case design chart
Size 8 DMC pearl cotton to match beads (use royal blue background thread to stitch the

beads on the butterfly)
Two skeins of Impressions by Caron needle-work thread, 50% silk/50% wool, medium blue # 7044
2 feet of 1/4-inch dark blue cord
Size 22 and 26 needlepoint needles
Sewing thread and needle to match lining

I was inspired by a carved soapstone butterfly to create this case. I chose 18-count Aida cloth because it has the correct spacing to fit size 8 seed beads. First, I stitched the beads across two stitches with the Aida stretched on a frame. Then, I began the needlepoint stitches.

Work the leaf stitch and Florentine stitch on a frame using a laying tool to make the two strands of Impressions thread lie flat. You can work the other single-strand stitches in the hand without a frame.

Finished size: 7-1/4 by 4 inches

To stitch the design:

1. Following the Glasses Case design chart, stitch the beads with matching colors of pearl cotton and the size 22 needlepoint needle using the tent stitch.

2. Using two strands of Impressions, stitch the leaf stitch, Florentine stitch, and tent stitch sec-

tions, following the numerical sequence in the stitch diagrams **(Figures 13-1, 13-2, and 13-3)**.

3. Stitch the fern stitch using a single strand of Impressions, following the diagram **(Figure 13-4)**. Stitch the dark blue background in fern stitch, using the royal blue pearl cotton you used to stitch the butterfly beads on.

4. Stitch the running cross stitch variation using a single strand of Impressions, following the diagram **(Figure 13-5)**.

To make the case:
1. Trim the raw edges of Aida cloth to 1/4 inch from the needlework. Turn under and press. Blind hem stitch the bottom and side edges together to make the glasses case.

2. Fold the lining fabric in half with right sides together. Stitch a 1/2-inch seam on the long side and one short side. Trim the seam to 1/4 inch and slip inside the glasses case.

3. Fold the raw edge of the lining over to line up with the top edge of the glasses case. Blind hem stitch in place.

4. Blind hem stitch the cord around the sides and bottom of the case and make a loop at the side and tie in a knot. Knot the tail and cut 1-1/2 inches from the knot. Unravel the cord up to the knot to make a fringe. Cut to 1 inch.

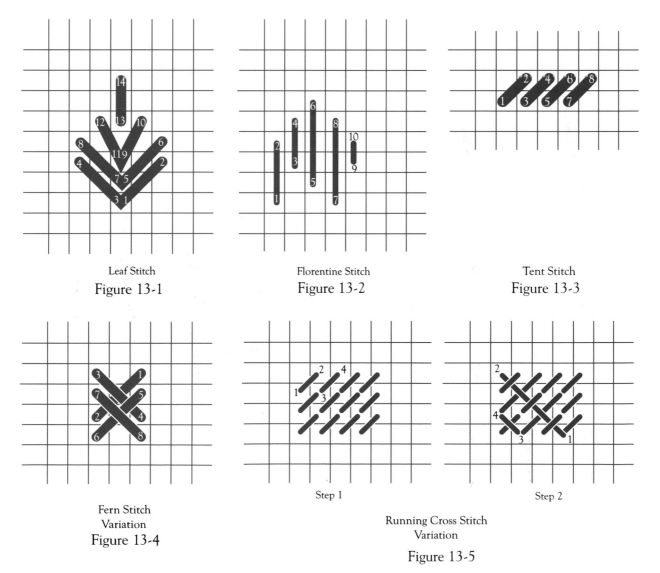

Leaf Stitch
Figure 13-1

Florentine Stitch
Figure 13-2

Tent Stitch
Figure 13-3

Fern Stitch
Variation
Figure 13-4

Step 1

Step 2

Running Cross Stitch
Variation
Figure 13-5

367

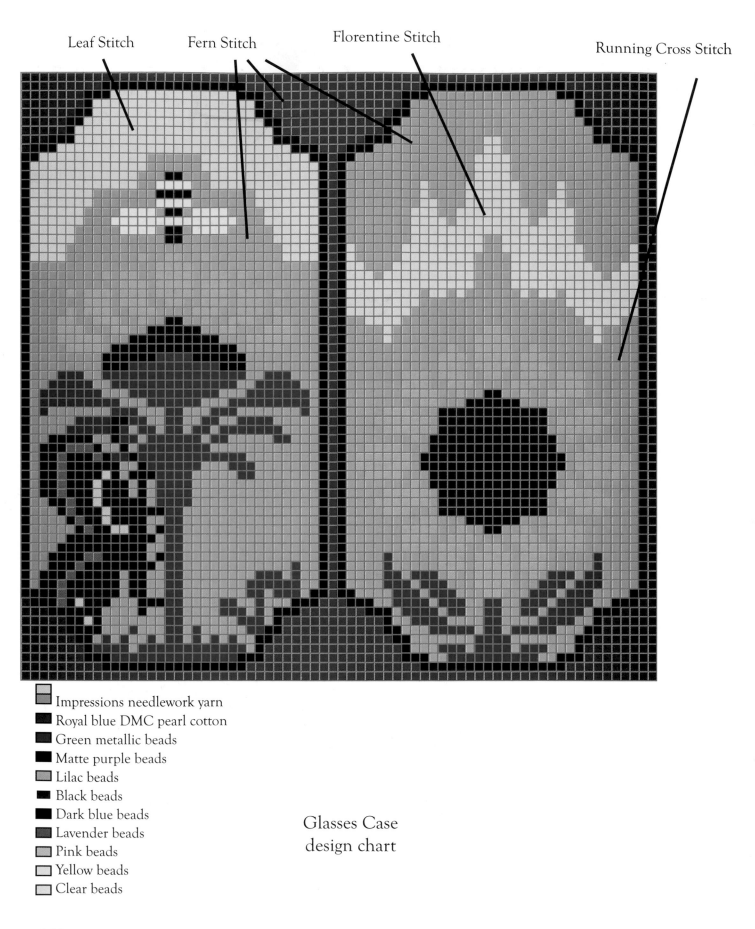

Leaf Stitch   Fern Stitch   Florentine Stitch   Running Cross Stitch

■ Impressions needlework yarn
■ Royal blue DMC pearl cotton
■ Green metallic beads
■ Matte purple beads
■ Lilac beads
■ Black beads
■ Dark blue beads
■ Lavender beads
■ Pink beads
□ Yellow beads
□ Clear beads

Glasses Case
design chart

Cross Stitch and Beads Business Card Holder

You Will Need

3- by 4-inch 14-count Aida cloth in a dark, neutral color

DMC six-strand floss:
  # 815 dark red
  # 820 royal blue
  # 918 brown
  # 3787 dark mushroom
  # 712 cream
  # 310 black

Size 11 seed beads to match each of the floss

colors above

4- by 9-inch piece of dark red Ultra Suede

4- by 5-1/4-inch piece of dark blue Ultra Suede

Size 26 needlepoint needle

Size 10 bead embroidery needle

Size 12 sharps needle

Size B Nymo

Thimble

Heavy, double-sided fusible interfacing

This design was inspired by the beautiful rugs my mother's friend, Albert Desrosiers, collects. I was privileged to sit in on their weekly quartet gatherings, listening to live chamber music, in a home where the floors, walls, and tables were covered with outstanding Persian and oriental rugs, antique molas, stained glass windows, and brilliant cut glass. It was a wonderful, inspiring setting.

Finished size: 2-3/4 by 3-1/2 inches

To make the cross stitch and beadwork:

1. Using three strands of floss and no beads, cross stitch all of the dark red following the Business Card Holder design chart. Stitch the black border in the same way.

2. Stitch the rest of the design using beads and two strands of floss the same color as the beads. Make half cross stitches with beads, the same direction as the first half of the cross stitch used in Step 1.

3. Turn under the edges of the Aida cloth so only the stitching shows. Press.

To make the case:

1. Cut the interfacing 1/16 inch smaller than the beadwork. Press the beadwork onto the blue suede **(Figure 13-6)**.

Figure 13-6

2. Cut another piece of interfacing 1/16 inch smaller all around than the blue suede and another piece 1-3/4 by 3-3/4 inches. Stack **(Figure 13-7)**. Press in place.

3. Bead the edge design **(Figure 13-8)** and stitch all of the pieces together, using black beads, the beading thread, beading needle, and a thimble.

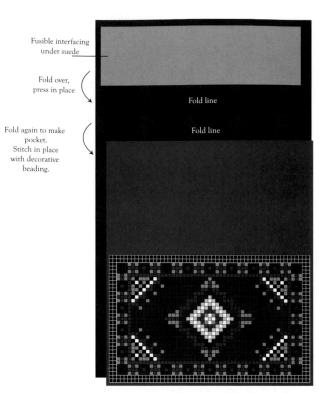

Fusible interfacing under suede

Fold over, press in place

Fold line

Fold line

Fold again to make pocket. Stitch in place with decorative beading.

Figure 13-7

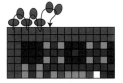

Figure 13-8

Business Card Holder
design chart

Chapter 14

Embroidery

Using beads in embroidery by stitching short strands of beads on fabric opens up a whole world of freedom in surface embellishment. The bead size and placement do not have to conform to a grid. And, if you find you need more color in an area you have completed, you can simply stitch on a few more beads; you don't have to undo rows of beadwork before you can make color or design changes.

Beaded edgings also give you a lot of creative freedom. You can use edgings to join two pieces of fabric while embellishing a piece. Edgings can be simple, like that shown on the Bead Embroidered Chatelaine (on page 375), or very elaborate, such as the fringe on the amulet bag by Delinda V. Amura on page 372. They can add greatly to the quality of the piece just by giving it a clean finish as in the Sage Jewelry Bag project on page 373.

Photo by Myra Nunley

This elegant bag, made by adding beads to a ribbon, was designed and beaded by Carole Tripp.

Embroidered butterfly on a velvet bag, designed and beaded by Delinda V. Amura.

Photo by Myra Nunley

Sage Jewelry Bag

You Will Need

One 6- by 4-inch and two 3-1/2- by 4-1/2-
   inch pieces of dusty green Ultra Suede
20 4mm round aventurine beads
Size 11 dark, medium, and light green seed
   beads, 3 grams or 1/8 oz. of each

40 size 8 green triangle beads
Frog closure
Beading thread to match suede
Size 11 beading needle
Paper clips

This easy beaded edging adds elegance to a simple project. All suede sections are double thickness for a sturdy bag. You stitch a beaded edging around the two front pieces and then join the beaded edging to the two back pieces. Then you bead the edges of the flap and attach a frog closure.

Finished size: 4 by 3 inches closed

1. Cut the front of the bag from the large piece of Ultra Suede folded in half, using **Figure 14-1** as a pattern and folding the suede along the fold on the pattern.

2. Use paper clips to hold the fold together.

3. Stitch the edging pattern (**Figure 14-2**) around the raw edges of the folded front, stitching through both front pieces to join them together.

4. Stitch the top edging (**Figure 14-3**), 1/8 inch from the fold.

5. Cut two of pattern **Figure 14-1** from Ultra Suede.

6. Paper clip the back and flap pieces as one to the front beaded piece. Stitch all around (**Figure 14-4**).

7. Stitch the frog closure parts to the flap and body of the bag.

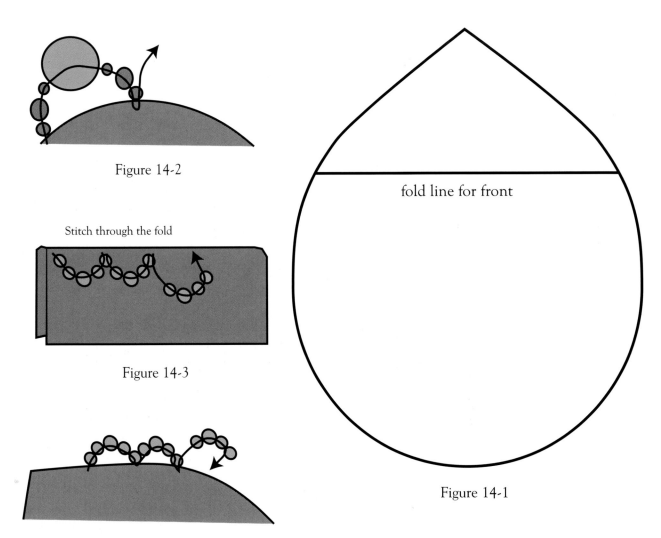

Stitch through the fold

Figure 14-2

Figure 14-3

fold line for front

Figure 14-1

Figure 14-4

Bead Embroidered Chatelaine

You Will Need

Two 4-1/2- by 2-1/4-inch pieces of emerald green Ultra Suede

5 grams or 1/4 oz. size 15 silver lined pale aqua seed beads

7 grams or 1/4 oz. size 11 aqua AB seed beads

Size 8 silver lined pale aqua triangle beads

Various accent beads for the neck chain and

chatelaine edging (see Figure 14-9 for design ideas and to calculate the quantities needed)

Size 11 and 13 beading needles

Beading thread to match Ultra Suede

Paper clips

Tracing paper and pencil

This project combines beaded edgings, bead embroidery, and bead stringing to create an elegant accessory for a special pair of scissors.

Finished size: 3-3/4 by 2-1/4 inches, not including chain

To make the chatelaine:

1. Cut two of the pattern (**Figure 14-5**) from Ultra Suede.

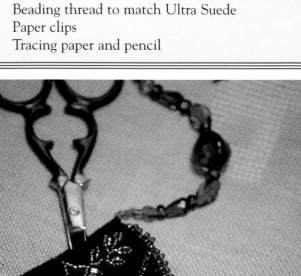

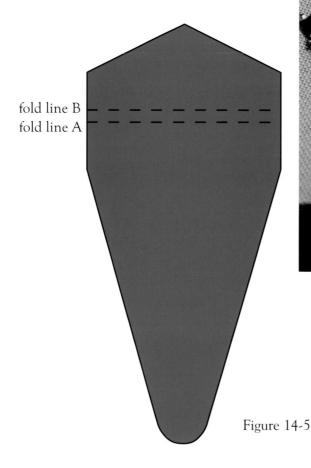

fold line B
fold line A

Figure 14-5

2. Trace the designs in **Figure 14-6**. Pin the top pattern to one side of one piece of Ultra Suede and the bottom pattern to the other side. Embroider through the tracing paper. Use back stitching for the vine and straight stitches for the leaves. Tear the tracing paper off.

3. Fold the beaded piece at fold line "A" as shown in **Figure 14-5** and the plain piece at fold line "B." Hold together with paper clips with the folds (wrong side) facing out.

4. Use size 11 beads and stitch the sides together following the pattern (**Figure 14-7**). Stitch the

beads closer together at the curve, adding the accent bead (**Figure 14-8**).

5. Use size 15 beads and stitch the same edging along the bottom of the flaps.

To make the neck chain:

1. Thread the needle with a doubled thread long enough to make a neck strap plus 12 inches for sewing the ends to the bag.

2. Attach to one side of the bag going through 1/2 inch of the Ultra Suede.

Stitch on the back side of the suede

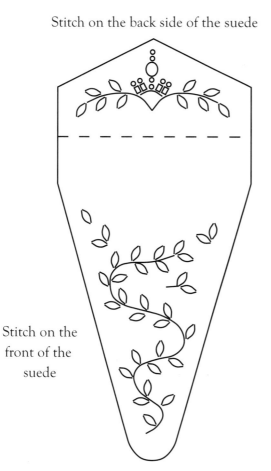

Stitch on the front of the suede

Figure 14-6

Figure 14-7

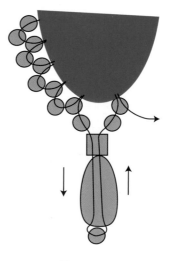

Figure 14-8

376

3. String the beads on the doubled thread in the suggested order (**Figure 14-9**).

4. Stitch down the second end of the neck chain about 1/2 inch through the Ultra Suede to attach it securely to the chatelaine.

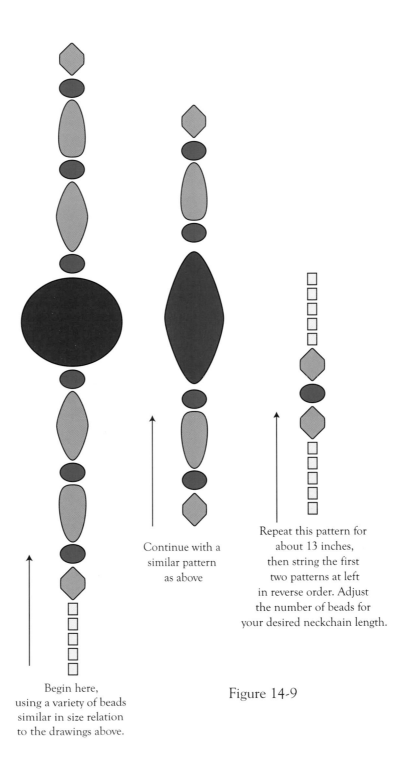

Begin here,
using a variety of beads
similar in size relation
to the drawings above.

Continue with a
similar pattern
as above

Repeat this pattern for
about 13 inches,
then string the first
two patterns at left
in reverse order. Adjust
the number of beads for
your desired neckchain length.

Figure 14-9

Chapter 15
Knotted Silk

Necklaces of strung beads separated by knots have always been the hallmark of fine jewelry. Originally, the knots were there to keep the expensive beads from falling to the ground should the thread break. They also protected the beads from the abrasion of rubbing against each other.

Silk or nylon cord with a wire needle is the preferred medium for stringing a bead-knotted necklace. Use the thickest cord that will fit through the smallest bead you plan to string. Specialty knotting tools are available just for making knotted bead necklaces, but a small-sized round nosed pliers will also hold the forming knot close to the bead for a nice, tight placement.

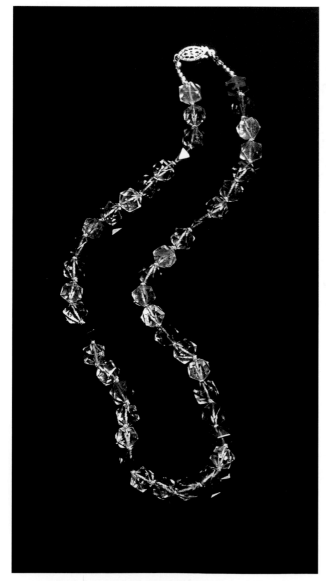

Faceted Fluorite bead-knotted necklace, designed and constructed by Cheryl Council.

Multi-strand freshwater pearl and glass bead necklace, designed and constructed by Cheryl Council.

Silk Beaded Knotted Necklace

You Will Need

78 4mm aventurine round beads
Size 3 card of nylon or silk beading cord in
   color to match the beads with needle
Two 4mm bead tips

Two 1/4-inch jump rings
Clasp
Round nosed pliers
Glue or clear fingernail polish

To practice knotting, string some size 11 seed beads onto size 20 Cebelia and knot between each bead until you can get the knots close to each bead.

Finished size: 18 inches

1. Unwind the beading cord with the wire needle attached. Tie an overhand knot 1 inch from the end and string through one bead tip (**Figure 15-1**). Put a dab of glue on the knot. Let dry, then cut the tail close to the glued knot inside the bead tip.

2. Make another overhand knot on the outer side of the bead tip. Hold the cord with the round nosed pliers (**Figure 15-2**) so the knot will tighten next to the bead tip. This is how all the knots are made in this necklace.

3. String all of the beads onto the cord and tie a slipknot near the needle so the beads won't fall off. Push the first bead up to the knot next to the bead tip. Tie a knot as in Step 2, close to the bead. Try to make the knots with enough room for the bead so that the growing necklace hangs smoothly, but without any excess cord showing between the beads, only the knot.

4. Slide the next bead up toward the first, holding

it next to the knot, and make another knot to hold the new bead in place. Repeat until all of the beads are held between knots.

5. Pull out the slipknot near the needle and pick up the other bead tip and tie a knot inside the bead tip. Put a dab of glue on this knot and let dry. Cut the excess thread close to the glued knot. Let dry.

6. Slip a jump ring onto the hook of one of the bead tips and roll the hook into the bead tip with the needle nosed pliers. Repeat for the other bead tip.

7. Slide one side of the clasp onto each jump ring.

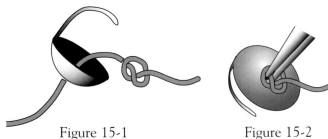

Figure 15-1   Figure 15-2

Chapter 16
Stranding

Stranding is a term I've chosen for techniques involving stringing strands of beads without knotting. The beads are strung into loops or strands and then twisted or woven to create three-dimensional effects. These techniques are quick ways to work with beads and create complex looking effects.

It is important to make the strands tight, so there are no gaps of thread, before twisting or weaving; otherwise, the thread will lock together between the beads as you try to pull one strand through another. Before weaving with a strand of beads, always pass through the last bead strung, pushing it up to the other beads so they are locked in place (**Figure 16-1**).

Many projects can be made by stringing large numbers of one type of bead. An easy technique I use for picking up five or more of the same bead is to pour a pile of beads on a mat and scoot the needle through the pile until it is almost filled, then slide the beads onto the thread in groups of five. This becomes a very quick process with practice.

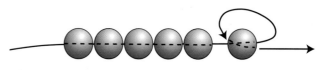

Figure 16-1

Beaded boxes from the book Beaded Boxes, *by Jane Davis.*

Blue and Copper Bracelet

You Will Need

20 grams or 3/4 oz. blue size 11 seed beads (A)	36 carnelian chips (F)
140 size 11 silver-lined brown seed beads (B)	2 round 1/4-inch beads (G)
12 oval 3/16-inch long copper beads (C)	Clasp
26 rounded square 1/8-inch copper beads (D)	Size 11 beading needle
18 size 6 transparent brown beads (E)	Size B black Nymo

This is a fun bracelet to make, with many possibilities for different looks if you change some of the beads. I have assigned letter codes to the types of beads in the materials list so you can easily change the design to suit your color preferences. The only consideration is that the beads at each end of the bracelet have holes large enough to allow at least 11 passes of the thread. I use one long strand of thread so I don't have to pass through the end beads more than necessary.

Finished size: 8 inches long.

Note: To adjust the size of this bracelet, add or subtract three of the (A) beads from each strand for each 1/4-inch adjustment.

1. Cut three yards of Nymo. Thread through the clasp and tie the ends in a square knot so that the clasp is in the middle of the thread.

2. Thread the needle with one of the thread ends. Pick up one bead (G) and one bead (D). String the following sequence of beads:
   a. 20 (A)
   b. 1 (B), 1 (C), 1 (B)
   c. 20 (A)
   d. 1 of each (B), (D), (B), (E), (B), (D), (B)
   e. 20 (A)
   f. 1 of each (B), (F), (B), (F), (B), (F), (B)
   g. 1 (E)
   h. 1 of each (B), (F), (B), (F), (B), (F), (B)

3. Repeat stringing e through a in reverse order.

4. Pick up one bead (D) and one bead (G). Pass through the other side of the clasp and back through beads (G) and (D). One strand is completed.

5. Repeat the stringing sequence in Steps 2 and 3. Pass through beads (D) and (G) and the clasp, then back through beads (D) and (G) again (**Figure 16-2**). Two strands are now completed.

6. Make four more strands as in Step 5, always passing through the two beads at the end, through the clasp, then back through the two beads at the

end again, ready to string more beads. Six strands are now completed. Knot the thread at the clasp and weave back into one of the strands for about 1-1/2 inches. Cut excess.

7. Thread the remaining tail and make two more strands only with bead (A), stringing on beads until the strand is the same length as the completed strands. Eight strands are now completed.

8. String a repeat of 10 of bead (A) and one of bead (B) until the strand measures the same as the other strands. Repeat. Ten strands are now completed.

9. Knot the thread and weave back into one of the strands for about 1-1/2 inches. The bracelet will be more than 9 inches long at this point, but will tighten up in the following steps.

10. Now split the strands into two sections, five on each side, and pass one end through the opening (**Figure 16-3**). Repeat three more times.

11. Make new openings by pulling two or three strands over to the other five-strand section. Pass one end of the bracelet through this opening (**Figure 16-4**). Repeat at the other end, and several times more, experimenting until you are happy with the shape of the bracelet.

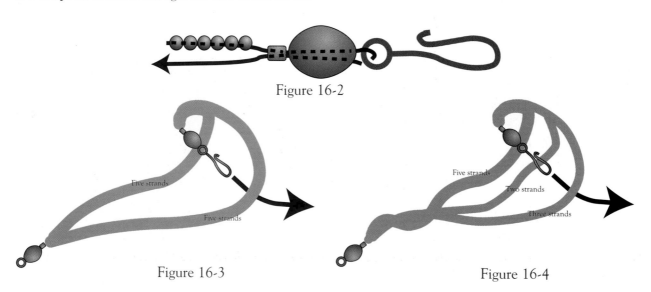

Figure 16-2

Figure 16-3

Figure 16-4

Using the stranding idea and the same beads as the Blue and Copper Bracelet project on page 381, this necklace, by Jane Davis, was made with a lampwork bead by Blue Meeler Glass as the centerpiece.

Forest Glen bracelet, designed and stitched by Jane Davis. A herringbone embellished centerpiece is flanked by twisted strands of beads to make this unusual bracelet.

Chapter 17

Wirework

To watch a skilled wire artist take a straight piece of wire and wind it into a beautiful work of art is an amazing thing, like watching a clown at the fair magically transform a few balloons into a poodle. It's one of those skills that needs quite a bit of practice because the wire needs to be bent into the desired shape the first time for a clean, smooth form.

There are several styles of wirework. Designs in wire can be carefully planned with a great deal of measuring, marking, and taping, or they can be free and wild, with little uniformity; however, most wirework takes planning, no matter how random it appears. Beads used in wirework need to have holes big enough for the wire to pass through. By combining different gauges of wire, a larger variety of beads can be added to a wirework project, without sacrificing strength in the piece's structure.

Wire and beads can be used for simple projects like these nifty key chains, by Kathy Henjyoji.

Wire and beads can also be used for elegant jewelry like this necklace and earrings, by Cheryl Council.

Wirework Beaded Bracelet

You Will Need

1 roll of 24-gauge gold-tone wire	16 size 11 green seed beads
6 6mm green glass beads	Round nosed pliers
6 4mm oval green pearls	Flat nosed pliers
24 size 11 bronze seed beads	Wire clippers
2 size 8 bronze seed beads	

This bracelet is a good introduction to wirework techniques. It helps if you practice wrapping the basic loops until you are comfortable with the technique before making the bracelet.

Finished size: 7-1/2 inches long

1. Cut a 2-1/2-inch piece of wire.

2. Grab the wire about 1 inch from one end with the round nosed pliers and bend to a 45-degree angle. Without letting go of the wire, take the flat nosed pliers and bend the 1-inch end tightly around the pliers, until you've made a loop with the excess wire sticking beyond the loop (**Figure 17-1**).

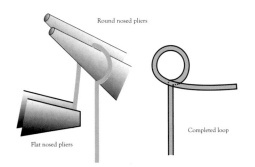

Figure 17-1

3. Because the round nosed pliers are tapered, the size of the loop will be determined by where you hold the wire on the pliers. Experiment until you like the loop size you make, then try to hold the wire at the same place every time. Don't make this first loop smaller than 1/8 inch because it is the loop part of the clasp.

4. Take the flat nosed pliers and hold the loop tightly. Wrap the 3/8-inch tail tightly around the straight wire three times with the round nosed pliers (**Figure 17-2**). Cut close to the wrap.

5. String one bronze size 11 bead, one pearl, and one bronze size 11 bead onto the wire.

6. Grab the wire with the round nosed pliers about 1/8 inch from the last bead, make a loop as described in Step 2, and wrap the tail around the wire as in Step 3, ending next to the beads. The first style of wire link is complete (**Figure 17-3**).

7. Repeat Steps 1 and 2 with another wire, then slide the first beaded wire section into the loop.

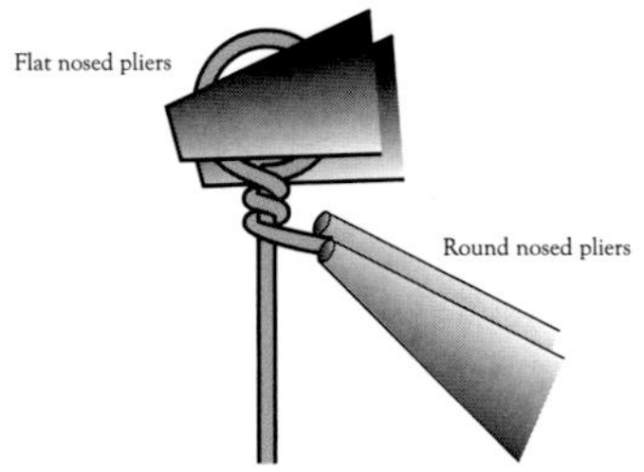

8. Repeat Step 4.

9. String one green size 11 bead, one bronze size 11 bead, one 6mm bead, one bronze size 11 bead, and one green size 11 bead onto the wire. Repeat Step 6. The second style of beaded wire link is complete.

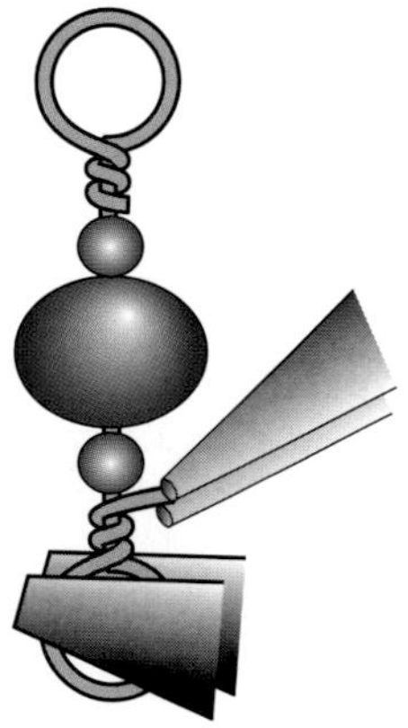

10. Continue making the two styles of links, until there are ten completed beaded wire links, five of each kind.

11. The last link includes a hook. Cut a 4-inch piece of wire. Fold down 1-1/2 inches and pinch tight with the flat nosed pliers (**Figure 17-4**).

12. Grab the folded wire 3/4 inch from the fold with the needle nosed pliers and grab the small tail with the round nosed pliers. Wrap the small tail around the long tail three times. Cut excess (**Figure 17-5**).

13. Bend the folded section into the shape of a hook. This is the hook part of the clasp. Slide the same bead pattern as the first link made onto the long tail and make the loop, sliding the last link made into the loop to complete the bracelet.

14. To make a safety catch, make five more small links and attach them to the links as shown (**Figure 17-6**).

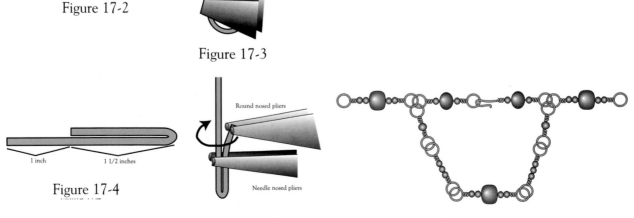

Flat nosed pliers

Round nosed pliers

Figure 17-2

Figure 17-3

1 inch   1 1/2 inches

Figure 17-4

Round nosed pliers

Needle nosed pliers

Figure 17-5

Figure 17-6

Beads and Wire Floral Detail

You Will Need

12 inches of 20-gauge wire
45 inches of 26-gauge wire
Small amounts of size 11 seed beads, three
    shades of green, three shades of purple, gold
Small amounts of green triangle beads or size
    8 seed beads

Size 15 green seed beads
Round nosed pliers
Flat nosed pliers
Size 11 beading needle
Green size B beading thread

Use this little ornament to decorate a special package, as a pin to wear, or as an accent on a wreath as shown in the photo below. The combination of wire and threadwork give the piece structure as well as the ability to increase beading detail.

Finished size: 3-inch long leaf and stem

To make the leaf:

1. Bend the 20-gauge wire (**Figure 17-7**), stringing the triangle or size 8 beads.

2. Cut an 8-foot length of beading thread and thread the needle. Tie the thread between the first and second bead on the center wire of the leaf (**Figure 17-8**).

3. Pick up one medium green size 11 seed bead and wrap around one of the leaf's side wires, between two large beads. Pass back through the size 11 bead (**Figure 17-9**).

4. Pick up another medium green bead and wrap around the center wire, between the second and third large bead. Pass back though the medium green bead (**Figure 17-10**).

5. Repeat Step 3. Now pick up three medium beads and wrap around the center wire, then pass back through the last bead strung (**Figure 17-11**).

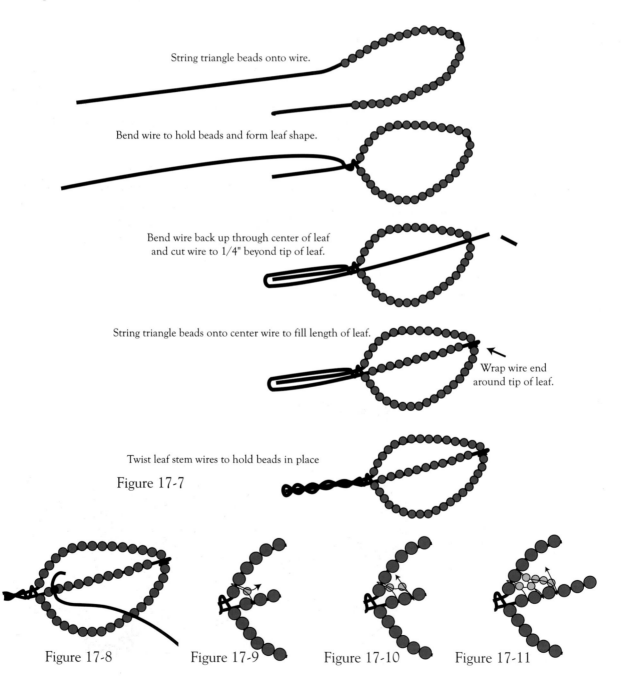

String triangle beads onto wire.

Bend wire to hold beads and form leaf shape.

Bend wire back up through center of leaf and cut wire to 1/4" beyond tip of leaf.

String triangle beads onto center wire to fill length of leaf.

Wrap wire end around tip of leaf.

Twist leaf stem wires to hold beads in place

Figure 17-7

Figure 17-8   Figure 17-9   Figure 17-10   Figure 17-11

6. Pick up three more beads, wrap around the side wire, and pass back through the last bead strung (**Figure 17-12**).

7. Repeat Step 6, stringing enough beads to fill the space between the two wires and each time passing around the wire between the next two beads along the wire. Choose bead colors to make the leaf show highlights and shadows. You will increase the number of beads in each pass to the widest point of the leaf, and then begin decreasing, until you get to the tip or end of the leaf. The strands of beads will be doubled across the leaf, one for the pass to the side of the leaf and one for the pass to the center of the leaf.

8. Repeat for the other side of the leaf, working back to the base of the leaf. Knot the thread and pass through several strands, then cut close to the beadwork. Repeat for the tail thread.

To cover the stem with beads:
1. Cut 12 inches of the 26-gauge wire and wrap one end tightly around the base of the leaf.

2. String 5 inches of the size 15 beads onto the 26-gauge wire and wrap it tightly around the stem (**Figure 17-13**).

3. Add or take off beads so there are just enough beads to cover the 20-gauge wire. Tuck the 26-gauge tail into the stem and cut the wire close to the beadwork.

To make the flowers:
1. Pick up three gold beads on the remaining 26-gauge wire and twist together (**Figure 17-14**), leaving a 3-inch tail.

2. Pick up 15 of one color of the purple beads and twist into a loop close to the gold beads (**Figure 17-15**).

3. Repeat Step 2 until there are seven or eight purple loops on the wire. Twist the beginning and ending wires (**Figure 17-16**). Arrange the purple loops around the gold beads to create a flower.

4. Make two more flowers, each about 1/2 inch apart, using a different color purple for each one. Wrap the wire around the stem of the leaf, positioning the flowers on one side of the leaf. Use the excess wire to attach the finished beadwork to a ribbon, bow, or pinback.

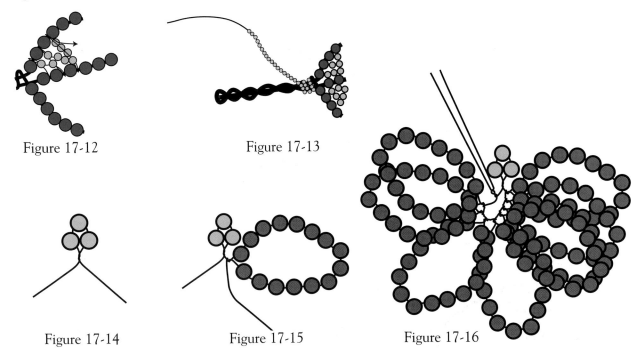

Figure 17-12   Figure 17-13

Figure 17-14   Figure 17-15   Figure 17-16

Kathy Henjyoji designed and finger-knotted this choker, adding the interesting treatment of the beads with wire.

Beaded Wire Pansy, designed and worked by Arlene Baker. This pansy is made in the method used for beaded wire flowers from the nineteenth century.

Twisted square wire adds detail to wire and bead projects. Brooch designed and constructed by Cheryl Council.

This dancing figure, by Cheryl Council, shows how a few beads and some wire can be transformed into a familiar image.

Lapis and gold-filled wire bracelet, designed and constructed by Cheryl Council.

391

Chapter 18
Mosaics

osaics use small pieces of color to create a picture or design; most beadwork is actually mosaic by definition. This chapter looks at a few ways to design with beads using glue, rather than thread.

It's not a new technique; the Huichol Indians of Mexico have been making such mosaics for years using beads for colored tile and beeswax for glue. They lay the beads into the wax coated on an armature carved out of wood in a magical animal shape, or inside a gourd, so the holes face upward like a doughnut. They arrange the beads tightly together, so they create a hexagonal grid. The Star Christmas Ornament and the Mosaic Beaded Lampshade projects use these elements of embedding beads in an adhesive to create beaded mosaics.

Contemporary Huichol beaded lizard.

Star Christmas Ornament

You Will Need

3-1/2-inch papier mâché star
Tacky glue
Toothpicks
5 grams each or 1/4 oz. each of size 15 seed

beads in blue and silver
5 grams or 1/4 oz. of size 11 seed beads in
silver

This project takes the idea of placing beads with the hole facing up from the Huichol Indians. It takes some planning. Without the Huichol technique of keeping the beads in line in a hexagonal grid, it's easy to end up with gaps where a bead won't quite fit. So, as you glue the beads down, you need to think about the spaces you are leaving and whether a bead will fit between the others. The spirals used in this project are a per-fect practice piece for learning how to plan your bead placement. If you start in the middle of a spiral, remember to leave a space for each color so the two colors of beads can wind around each other. You can also incorporate the year or your name, or use traditional seasonal motifs, to decorate the star.

Finished size: 3 inches

1. Squeeze a thin line of glue along two edges of the star. Rub the tip of a toothpick in beeswax or the glue, just to make it tacky enough to pick up a bead. Using the toothpick, place the size 11 silver beads in the glue along the edge of the star (**Figure 18-1**). Let dry, then glue another section of the size 11 beads along the edge of the star until all of the edges are lined and dry.

2. Begin a spiral pattern at the center of the star. Squeeze a pea-sized drop of glue on the star. Smooth to about a 1/16 inch thick, making a round glue section about the size of a penny. Using the toothpick as in Step 1, begin making a spiral of silver beads with blue beads as the background. See **Figure 18-2** for the beginning placement.

3. When one spiral is complete, surround it closely with blue beads and begin another spiral starting at the outer edge of the spiral and working in to the center (**Figure 18-3**).

4. Continue adding new glue sections as you fill in current ones. Take time to stop and look at the spirals and vary the direction and size, placing a silver bead in large blue gaps, building the design as you go.

5. Repeat the design on the other side of the star, or use a design of your choosing.

Figure 18-1

Figure 18-2

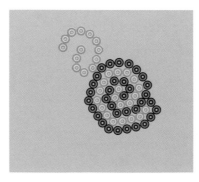

Figure 18-3

Meandering Vine Beaded Lampshade

You Will Need

Table lamp or candle lamp with a glass shade   One hank of size 11 green seed beads
Tacky glue   Pencil

Another way to glue with beads is to keep them in strands while placing them into glue and then sliding the thread out from the beads. This helps you keep the beads in a tight line, with all of the beads on their sides, and create flowing linear patterns with the beads. This project uses this technique with beads from the Czech Republic, which are packaged in hanks.

Finished size: Varies according to lampshade

1. Transfer the design (**Figure 18-4**) lightly onto the outside of the glass shade with the pencil.

2. Squeeze a line of glue along the vine and carefully place the beads on the line as close together as possible. Slide the thread from the beads in the glue. Let dry.

3. Squeeze glue in one leaf area at a time and place the beads, laying them in directionally (by holding a section of beads on the shade and draping them to the shape of the leaf's edge), as in the project photo. Repeat until all of the leaves are covered in beads. Let dry.

Figure 18-4

Chapter 19
Sampler Project

You Will Need
(for top section of design, described by use)

Base fabric: Cream-colored 28 count even-weave fabric 14 inches by 20 inches
House: DMC six-strand cotton floss # 712 cream
Roof and fence: 1/16-inch brown suede
Door and windows: DMC pearl cotton size 8, #415 silver gray
Tree trunk: Rainbow Gallery Pebbly Perle brown
Tree leaves: Needle Necessities Spring II,

#372 green
Tree leaves and background hills: Impressions by Caron, #208 Meadow
Hills and plants: Leah's hand-dyed size 12 pearl cotton, # 215 and # 217
Flowers: Size 15 rose, lavender, and white seed beads
Bead embroidery needle
Size 24 and 26 needlepoint needle
Needlework frame and stand

This project combines many of the techniques in this book, pulling from the samples described in the technique sections. The Beadwork Sampler design chart shows the layout and references where each technique is found in the book.

Finished size: 12 inches by 18 inches

To cross stitch the design:

1. Follow the House design chart. Begin with the house. Match up the center of the fabric, 4 inches below the top selvage, with the mark on the design chart. Using two strands of the cream floss, cross stitch the house, using a laying tool so the threads lie flat and parallel to each other.

2. Stitch the roof and fence using the brown suede and size 24 needle, following the stitching lines on the design chart.

3. Stitch the tree trunk and tree. Note that the stitching lines for the leaves are a mix of a half cross stitch over one or two threads in a random design.

4. Stitch the background hills with half cross stitches.

5. Stitch the branches to the rose bushes and fox-gloves, then add the beads, using one strand of the cream floss and the bead embroidery needle.

To complete the Sampler:

1. Use the Beadwork Sampler design chart to make each sample. Arrange them below the cross stitch design according to the layout in the design chart or in your own arrangement.

2. Blind stitch in place.

3. Place the Sampler in a frame, being careful to have a space between the glass and the finished piece so that it will not be crushed.

397

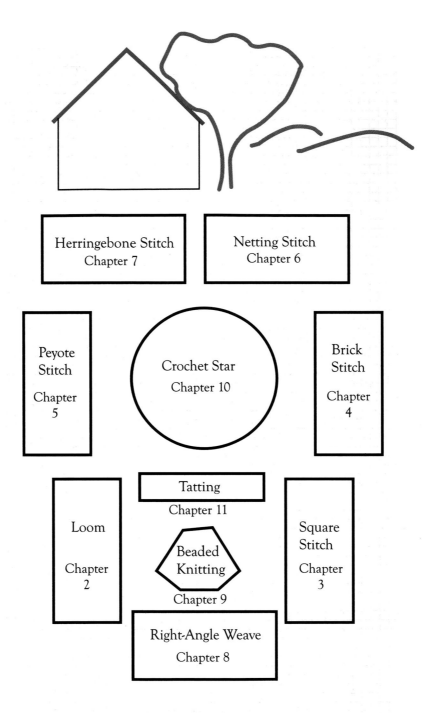

Beadwork Sampler
design chart

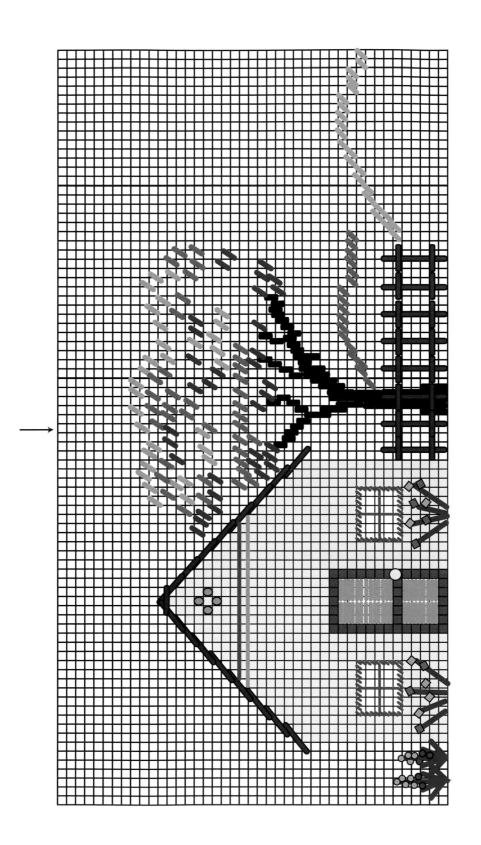

House
design chart

Graph Papers

Here are blank graphs for all of the graphed techniques in this book. In my opinion, this is one of the most valuable sections of this book, because you now have a resource to create your own designs. Many of the stitches, such as herringbone and right-angle weave, have not been used for patterns as extensively as peyote and brick stitch in most books, and this is the first printing of graph paper for these techniques. Just copy them, color them in, and enjoy!

Loom and Square Stitch Graph

Brick and Peyote Graph

Herringbone Graph

Five Bead Netting Graph

Right-Angle Weave Graph

Bead Knitting Graph

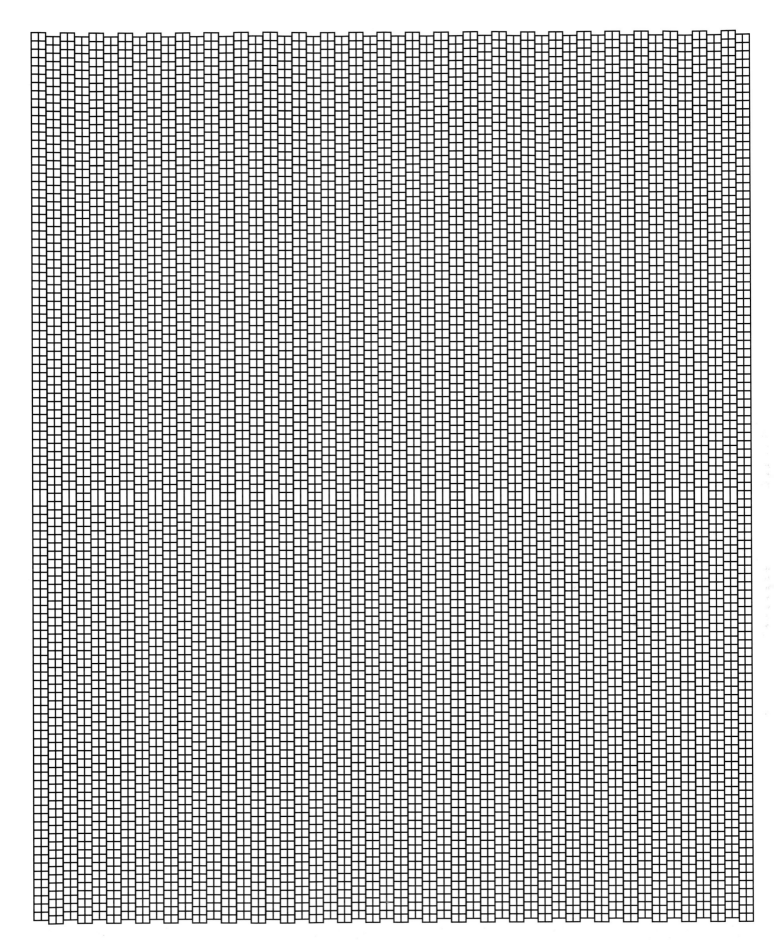

Two-Drop Peyote Graph

bead numbers for the first row

Blank graph to cover 2" pumpkin box (Ladybug box)

Ladybug Brick Stitch Graph
(project on page 294)

Supply Sources

Whenever possible, I encourage you to seek out local sources for your supplies. Local stores need to be supported so they can continue to provide the valuable opportunity for us to peruse through their stock in person. This is something that can't compare to mail order; however, if you are unable to find supplies locally, here are some mail-order sources for products in this book.

Beadcats
Universal Synergetics Inc. Bead Store
P.O. Box 2840
Wilsonville, OR 97070-2840
(503) 625-2323
Fax: (503) 625-4329
www.beadcats.com
Owned by Carol Perrenoud and Virginia Blakelock, two of the first bead artists in this current interest of beading, this is a wonderful mail-order source, and the catalog is an information resource in itself about beads.

Blue Sky Alpacas
P.O. Box 387
St. Francis, MN 55070
(763) 753-5815
www.blueskyalpaca.com
My pattern for the bead knitted scarf on page 331 is distributed by Blue Sky Alpacas. The web page lists retail stores which carry the company's yarns and patterns.

Caravan Beads, Inc.
449 Forest Ave.
Portland, ME 04101
(800) 230-8941
Fax: (207) 874-2664
www.caravanbeads.com
Home of the Miyuki Delica Challenge—the bead contest that gave me the courage to pursue beading as a career—this is a great bead source for Miyuki products, from size 15 seed beads and Delicas to the large size 6 seed beads and triangles.

Creative Castle
2321 Michael Dr.
Newbury Park, CA 91320
(805) 499-1377
www.creativecastle.com
This store carries beads, beads, and more beads, as well as wire, findings, tools, and basic supplies for all things bead-wise. It also carries the wood bases for the napkin rings, salt and pepper shakers, and pumpkin boxes used for projects in this book.

Handy Hands
577 N. 1800 E
Paxton, IL 60957
(217) 379-3802
Fax (800) 617-8626
www.hhtatting.com
e-mail: tatthands@aol.com
This is the mail-order source for all things tatting. The company also carries several brands of cotton cord which are wonderful for bead crochet. Definitely worth looking into.

Weavers Needle and Frame
1610-2 Newbury Road
Newbury Park, CA 91320
(805) 499-7979
e-mail: weavlady@gte.net
Here you'll find all of the needlepoint and cross stitch supplies for this book, including Sudberry House wood products. Also does custom framing.

Artists in This Book

Arlene Baker

Arlene is an artist and teacher of Victorian ribbon and beadwork. She gets inspiration and learns techniques for her designs by studying her large collection of Victorian-era ribbon and beadwork. You can call Arlene to find out about her classes and kits at (562) 928-3583 in Downey, California.

Designs on pages: 390

Cheryl Council

Cheryl formerly worked as a designer in the aerospace industry. She is now a jewelry designer and teacher of wire jewelry making techniques. Cheryl has won numerous competitions, both local and in the state of California, with her artistic creations.

Designs on pages: 378, 384, 391

Marcia DeCosta and Linda Parker

Marcia and Linda teach under the name of MarLin Beads. They have been bead partners for the last six years and share a passion for beadwork and an enthusiasm for instructing others. Many of their pieces are inspired through collaboration, with each bringing their own unique design and color perspective to the finished work.

Designs on pages: 278, 302, 314, 323

Idele Gilbert

Idele Gilbert is an off-loom bead artist, designer, and teacher. She is currently creating original, three-dimensional designs in beadwork. In her pre-bead life, she was a needlepoint designer, miniaturist, and needle artist/teacher. She also is a mola maker and a designer of pop-up card patterns for rubber stampers.

Designs on pages: 299

Elizabeth Gourley

Elizabeth is co-author of *Art of Seed Beading* (Sterling Publishing, 1999). She loves writing, painting, doing all forms of needle art, and creating miniatures. She is currently working with her sister on a miniatures beading book. When she isn't beading, Elizabeth tends to her many animals and spends time with her family.

Designs on pages: 302

Kathy Henjyoji

Kathy loves to "fiddle" and has taught herself a lot. Her designs usually include a couple of different jewelry-making techniques. A dancer with a business degree, she works and teaches at Creative Castle in Newbury Park. Kathy also manages her husband's auto brokerage HARDYmotorsports and performs with costumes she has designed and made for Ajiva Dance Theatre in the Ventura County, California, area.

Designs on pages: 384, 390

Susan Hilyar

Susan is a nationally known teacher and bead artist. She is the publisher of *A River Flows*, a beadwork newsletter. Her work is shown in galleries and is frequently featured in *Bead and Button Magazine*.

Designs on pages: 322

Corinne Loomer

Corinne teaches beading classes and collects antique beadwork. She has won awards for her needlework and is always inspired by new techniques.

Designs on pages: 268

Dorianne and Shonna Neuhart

Dorianne and Shonna are a mother and daughter team of avid bead artists who began beading in the late 1990s. They have sold their work in boutiques and create custom orders of beaded jewelry. You can see their current pieces on display on their web page at www.ebetterbeads.com.

Designs on pages: 300, 314

Sylvia Sur

A lifelong interest in needlework and sewing led Sylvia to beads around 1994 when the popularity of beads had started to grow. "I enjoy the process of design and invention as much as wearing or displaying the product. I have learned a lot about using color in beads, which is the hardest part of learning to bead. Colors in glass do not act the same way as they do in paint, fiber, or fabric." When not beading, she designs websites and climbs mountains. Her work is on changing display at: http://home.att.net/~ssur/home.htp

Designs on pages: 278, 301

Carole Tripp

Carole creates designs for a line of bead kits and has had her designs published in several books. She teaches beading classes and is an avid promoter of beadwork, hosting a bi-weekly bead night at her store, Creative Castle, in Newbury Park, California. When not beading, Carole enjoys all types of needlework, softball, and spending time with her family.

Designs on pages: 300, 301, 371

Delinda Vannebrightyn Amura

Delinda is a nationally known instructor, whose work is shown in galleries and museum collections, including several pieces in the beadwork collection at the Smithsonian. She strives to incorporate antique techniques, workmanship, and materials into her intricate designs. She has a line of beadwork kits and imports silk thread for beadwork which can be found on her web page, www.delinda-v-amura.net.

Designs on pages: 277, 315, 372

Bibliography

Amura, Delinda Vannebrightyn. *The Illuminated Beading Manuscripts Book II The Loom*. Taos, New Mexico: Fairy Wing Press, 1997.
Delinda has presented more information on loomwork in this book than in any other loomwork book I have seen.

Barth, Georg. *Native American Beadwork*. Stevens Point, Wisconsin: R. Schneider Publishers. 1993.
Contains detailed information on peyote stitch.

Blumqvist, Gun and Elwy Persson. *Tatting Patterns and Design*. Mineola, New York: Dover. 1988.
This book shows clear illustrations for shuttle tatting and presents a large selection of patterns, though none include beads. It was originally published in Swedish in 1967.

Borjay, Genevieve. *The Basics of Bead Stringing*. Santa Monica, California: Borjay Press. 1998.
This is an excellent book on the basics of bead stringing with straightforward, clear illustrations and instructions.

Davis, Jane. *Beaded Boxes*. Ventura, California: Davis Designs Press. 1998.
This book presents several methods for using strands of beads to cover the same pumpkin boxes as in the brick stitch ladybug box (see page 294).

——— *Bead Netted Patterns*, Ventura, California: Davis Designs Press, 1999.
Here you will find more patterns in bead netting, including instructions for Odin's Glory on page 314 and Hollyhocks on page 315.

Foster, Barbara. *Needle Tatting Book I and Book II*. Paxton, Illinois: Barbara Foster. 1995.
These two little books were written by the owner of Handy Hands; I learned how to needle tat from them. Both have clear, simple photos and instructions.

Gourley, Elizabeth, Jane Davis, and Ellen Talbott. *Art of Seed Beading*. New York, New York: Sterling Publishing Co., Inc. 1999.
This book has information about many techniques for working with beads, including a photo step-by-step and 30 projects to make.

Korach, Alice. *Bead and Button Magazine*. Norwalk, Connecticut: Conterie Press. April, 1994 No. 2, pps 22 and 23.
Alice Korach, editor of *Bead and Button Magazine*, describes in detail her method of bead knitting, which is the technique I use for all of my bead knitting.

Paludan, Lis. *Crochet History and Technique*. Loveland, Colorado: Interweave Press, 1995.
This is an excellent resource of crochet history and styles. It includes a small section on bead crochet.

Reader's Digest. *Complete Guide to Needlework*. Pleasantville, New York: The Reader's Digest Association, Inc. Fifth printing. 1981.
I learned how to knit and crochet from this book after my mother taught me how to cast on. There are also sections on tatting, needlepoint, embroidery, and quilting, all of which are informative, even if the projects are dated.

Sanders, Julia E. *Tatting Patterns*. New York, New York: Dover Publications. 1977.
This is a wonderful reprint of a 1915 tatting book, showing unusual treatments for tatting, including several projects using beads.

Stessin, Nicolette. *Beaded Amulet Purses*. Seattle, Washington: Beadworld Publishing, 1995.
David Chatt's right-angle weave amulet bag is on the cover of this book.

Wells, Carol Wilcox. *Creative Bead Weaving*. Asheville, North Carolina: Lark Books. 1996.
This has become the standard for learning beading stitches such as peyote, brick, square, and right-angle weave stitches.

Glossary

Accent bead: A bead larger than other beads in a project, often with an unusual shape, color, or pattern used to contrast from the rest of the project.

African Helix Stitch: A spiraling beading stitch in which strands of beads are stitched together by passing around the thread of a strand on a previous round.

Antique bead: A bead more than 90 to 100 years old. Also, the brand name of cylindrical beads made by the Toho company of Japan.

Aventurine: A green semi-precious stone resembling green jade.

Bead: Anything with a hole for stringing or threading.

Bead crochet: Crocheting with beads strung onto the crochet thread and slid into the crochetwork as it progresses.

Bead fabric: A piece of beadwork.

Bead knitting: Knitting with beads strung onto the knitting thread and slid into stitches as they are made.

Bead knitting: Stringing beads onto silk or nylon cord and tying overhand knots between the beads.

Beaded knotting: Knitting with beads strung onto the knitting thread and sliding beads between stitches.

Beading needle: Needles made especially for beadwork which are longer and more slender than sewing needles. Some are made from twisted wire with a collapsible eye.

Blocking: To wet a finished piece of needlework, arrange it into the desired finished shape, and let it dry. This "sets" the threads in the piece, improving the overall appearance. You can also steam block by pressing with a hot iron at the steam setting.

Brick stitch: A beading stitch in which the beads are sewn together so that they resemble a brick wall.

Bugle bead: A bead shaped like a long tube.

Cabochon: A stone ground and polished so that the underside is flat and the topside is smooth and domed.

Charlotte: A round bead with a facet ground on one side. These beads sparkle in beadwork.

Comanche stitch: Another name for brick stitch.

Cone bead: A bead shaped like a cone.

Cross stitch: An embroidery technique in which colored threads are stitched in an "x" pattern on evenly woven fabric.

Delica: The brand name of cylindrical beads made by the Miyuki company of Japan.

Denier: A unit of measure used for silk thread.

Drop bead: A bead which is wider at one end. The hole can be through the length of the center of the bead or at the small end, perpendicular to the bead.

Facet: A flat section ground onto the side of a bead. Beads can have one or more facets. Charlottes have one facet, three-cuts have many random facets, and Swarvorski Crystals have precision-cut facets, like a diamond.

Finding: Components for making jewelry, usually metallic, including clasps, earring parts, pins, and jump rings.

Fringe: Long strands of beads along the edge of a project.

Gourd stitch: Another name for peyote stitch.

Hank: A number of strands of beads (usually twelve strands, each 20 inches long), folded in half with the ends tied together.

Herringbone stitch: A beading stitch in which the beads are sewn together so that they make a texture resembling the chevrons in herringbone fabric. Also known as Ndebele (pronounced en-d-Bell-ee) stitch after the Ndebele tribe of Africa which invented the stitch and uses it extensively.

Huichol (pronounced WEE-chul) Beadwork: A beading technique in which beads are pressed into warm beeswax, which has been coated on a wooden form or inside a dried gourd. This technique was invented and is used extensively by the Huichol Indians of Mexico.

Ladder stitch: A beading stitch used often as the first row in brick stitch in which a row of beads is sewn together, one bead on top of the other, resembling a ladder.

Lampwork bead: A bead made individually by melting glass and forming the bead on a rod using a small torch.

Leather needle: A needle with the sides near the pointed end ground flat on three sides so the needle can pierce through leather.

Loomwork: A type of beadwork in which beads are woven together on a loom.

Mosaic: An image created by using small colored components glued or drawn on a surface.

Needlepoint: An embroidery technique in which colored yarn or thread is sewn in a pattern onto a canvas.

Ndebele stitch: Another name for herringbone stitch.

Netting stitch: A beading stitch in which strands of beads, usually three or more, are sewn together in a loose fabric resembling a net.

Nymo: The brand name for a synthetic beading thread.

Peyote stitch: A beading stitch in which beads are stitched in an undulating pattern. Peyote stitch turned on its side looks just like brick stitch.

Picot: In tatting, a loop of thread between stitches. Sometimes beads are slid into the picots.

Right-angle weave: A beading stitch in which beads are sewn at right angles to each other.

Seed bead: A bead which is round like a doughnut and small. Seed beads range in size from the tiny sand-sized antique size 24 to the almost 1/4-inch size 5.

Shuttle: In tatting, a shuttle is the device which holds the thread as your work.

Spacer bead: A flat disk-shaped bead usually used as a decorative element in bead stringing.

Square stitch: A beading stitch in which beads are sewn together in regular rows and columns. Square stitch looks the same as loomwork.

Stranding: A beading technique in which strands of beads are manipulated to create jewelry or to decorate surfaces.

Tambourwork: An embroidery stitch in which beads are strung onto thread and a hooked needle fastened into a wooden handle (called a tambour needle) is used to make chain stitches on fabric as beads are slid into the stitches underneath the fabric.

Tatting: A lace making technique in which beads are strung onto thread and the thread is made into lace by making a series of half knots called half hitches, and beads are slid between stitches or into loops of thread. Tatting can be done with a tatting needle or a shuttle.

Tatting needle: A long blunt needle with a large eye used in tatting.

Triangle beads: Beads shaped like a triangle as seen looking through the hole.

Ultra Suede: A synthetic fabric made to feel like suede, but is easier to cut and sew through.

Vintage bead: A bead which is no longer manufactured but is not old enough to be an antique.

Warp: The vertical threads stretched on a loom which beads are then stitched between.

Weft: The thread which is threaded with a needle, then strung with beads and woven perpendicular to the warp threads on the loom.

Woof: Another name for weft.

Wirework: Bending wire into creative designs, including jewelry and decorative items, in which beads are often added.

French-Beaded Flowers
New Millennium Collection

Dalene Kelly

Without the constant help and support of my husband, Van,

it probably would have taken me years to complete this book.

Thank you for taking over so many of my duties.

Thank you for keeping my nose to the grindstone.

Table of Contents

Introduction

The technique is referred to as French Beading. It's commonly recognized that French and other European peasants created this art when they collected discarded glass beads and used them to create arrangements and flowered memorial wreaths. Although it's listed along with other beading techniques, French Beading is more like sculpting than sewing. The beads are first strung onto a spool of wire. The wire is then bent and twisted into the flower shapes.

Therefore, even with a pattern, the French-Bead artist has to have some knowledge of flowers. Patterns will give you a pile of parts, but it's up to you to assemble them in the right direction. What is the RIGHT direction?

The next time you receive one of those beautifully photographed seed catalogs, file it with your beading supplies. No pattern or explanation can compare to a photo or the live plant. Since most companies are trying to sell the exquisite blooms, the catalogs are excellent references for beading.

When French Beading, some patterns are quite lifelike while others are created in a manner that merely suggests reality. In most cases, large flowers are beaded to depict more detail than the smaller varieties.

As you begin accumulating a pile of flower parts, it's easy to forget exactly what you are creating. Therefore, this simple diagram of common names (fig. 1) can be used as a quick reference. If a pattern doesn't have all these parts, don't panic. This is an art, not a science. A rose is a rose.

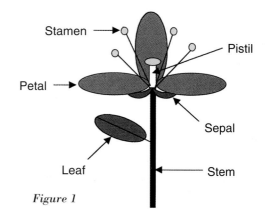

Figure 1

Typical Assembly

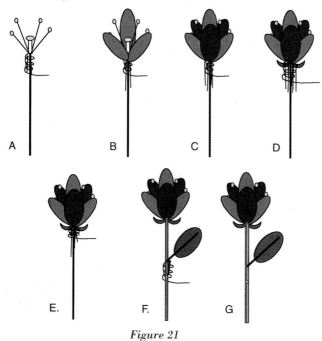

Figure 21

(Lightly, tape the stem wire.)

A. Use light-gauge wire to secure the pistil and stamens in place.

B. and **C.** Add the petals either one at a time or in groups. Wire them in place.

D. Position and wire the sepals in place.

E. Trim the wires to different lengths so the stem will have a smooth appearance. Tape over the exposed construction wire.

F. Position the leaf at the desired level. Wire it in place.

G. Tape over the exposed construction wire.

Materials, Tools, and Supplies

Beads

Finish

Begin by choosing only glass seed beads that appear uniform in size and shape. They can be found in transparent, opaque (shiny, silk, or matte), pearl (painted), and lined finishes. Although the first three are used interchangeably, lined beads can produce some special problems. The lining materials in these beads can deteriorate over a period of time. Sunshine, cleaning products, and sometimes even the act of stringing the beads can ruin the color.

Shape

Round seed beads are the beads of choice. However, particularly on very large flowers, cut seed beads can produce a very elegant effect.

Size

To reproduce the flowers in this book, choose either a size 10/0 or size 11/0. Size 10/0 is easier to work with, while size 11/0 produces a somewhat more delicate petal. All of the flowers photographed in this book are done with size 10/0.

Quantities

All of the quantities given are estimates. It's usually safest to buy extra, as some will inevitably end up escaping to the floor.

Seed beads are available either loose or strung. For ease and speed, you will probably be much happier finding a supplier that carries strung beads (mostly Czechoslovakian). If you can't find them locally, many are available on the Internet. However, loose beads can also be used easily if you invest a little more money and purchase a bead spinner (or stringer).

The quantities for the patterns in this book are based on these approximate figures:
- 16–17 beads per inch
- 18" per strand
- 12 strands per hank
- 20–24 hanks per kilo (2.2 lbs)

Wire

Finish

Wire is metal, and metal rusts. Therefore, my first choice is always a painted or coated wire. A wide range of colors, as well as gold and silver, can be found in the jewelry and bead departments of your local craft store. For a more economical source of green, black, and white, check out the paddle wire in the floral and bridal departments. I really like 30-gauge floral paddle wire for all of my assembly. It's cheap, and it won't show once the flower is taped.

Sizes

You will use a 26- or 28-gauge wire for most flower parts. The 28-gauge wire is easier to use, but 26-gauge makes a more durable flower. If you are using color-coated copper wire, switch to 24- or 26-gauge. These "craft" or "artistic" type wires are very flexible. On long spear-shaped leaves, try a 22-gauge wire for stiffness. Use 30- to 34-gauge wire for assembly and lacing. If you have trouble handling the wire, experiment with different sizes and materials. The ultimate decision on wire is up to your personal preference.

Stem wire is available in pre-cut painted lengths in the floral department. Listed here are suggested sizes:

Small flowers—18-gauge

Medium to large flowers—14- to 16-gauge

Large or un-balanced flowers (like orchid plants)—1/8" round rod stock, threaded rod stock, cut up coat hangers, or any really stiff wire or rod

Floral Tape

In the floral department, look for regular, wax-coated paper tape. When your flower is completed, smoothly wrap the entire stem with floral tape, and then rub the stem to seal the wax on the tape. This will provide a waterproof seal.

Tools

Wire cutters—Choose comfortable-to-use, sharp, hobby or jewelry front-cutters. Side-cutters are more difficult to handle.

Flat, long-nosed pliers—Excellent for stretching and straightening bent wire.

Needle-nosed pliers—Choose ones with cutters, and save your regular cutters from having to cut heavy stem wire.

Scissors—Small, sharp, and comfortable to use.

Hem gauge or ruler—The hem gauge is preferred because it can be set to the size needed, thereby insuring that all of the petals are uniform.

Darning needle—Use this to lace large leaves and petals.

Divided or flat lunch tray (optional)—Lay or glue felt inside the sections. It makes a wonderful work area, and it keeps your loose beads off the floor.

Hemostats—These are available in medical, hardware, or sporting goods (hook removers) stores. In my opinion, this is your most important tool.

Seed Bead Sizes	
7/0	4mm
8/0	3.1mm
9/0	2.7mm
10/0	**2.3mm**
11/0	**2.1mm**
12/0	1.9mm
13/0	1.7mm
14/0	1.6mm

Wire Gauges		
Gauge	**Inches**	**mm**
—	.125 (⅛)	3.2
16	.063	1.6
18	.048	1.2
20	.035	.88
22	.029	.73
24	.023	.58
26	.018	.46
28	.016	.41
30	.014	.36
32	.013	.33
34	.012	.30

General Instructions

Basic Method

1. Begin by transferring your beads onto the spool of wire. If using strung beads, hold the string taut and slide the wire through several inches at a time. If using loose beads, "spear" them onto the wire one at a time, or use a bead spinner. Put enough beads on the wire to complete the entire petal or leaf. It can be very difficult to make up for a shortage of beads. Err on the side of excess.

2. Determine (from the pattern) the size of your "basic" beaded row. Count (or measure) the required amount of seed beads; slide them toward the tip, leaving several inches of bare basic wire. Hold the beads in place by pinching the wire below them. Wrap the wire loosely around your hand, forming the "basic loop." Bring the wire up under the beads, and twist several times (fig. 2). If you have trouble keeping your basic row on the wire, try bending the tip of the wire into a tight loop before beginning. (You will now be wrapping beads up one side and down the other side of the first basic row.)

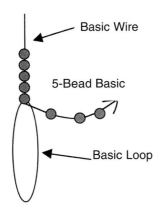

Figure 2

3. Keep your basic wire straight at all times! Push some beads forward, and bring the wire to the top of the basic row. Cross OVER then UNDER the basic wire; pull the wire tight (fig. 3). Follow the same procedure, going down the other side. Rows are counted straight across the center, so you have now completed three rows (fig. 4).

4. Proceed in the same manner, until you have the desired number of rows.

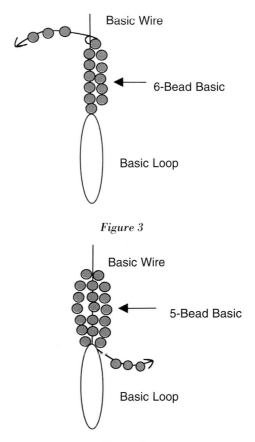

Figure 3

Figure 4

To form a rounded petal: Keep the wire very close and straight across the previous row when crossing the basic wire.

To form a pointed petal: Cross the basic wire at a 45° angle, leaving a very slight space before your over-and-under twist.

To make even more of a point: Add an extra bead to the top of your basic wire, between the rows (fig. 5). This is not mentioned in most patterns, but it can be

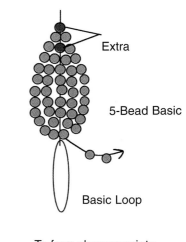

To form sharper points, add extra beads to the basic wire between rows.

Figure 5

used to accomplish the desired effect. Long, narrow, pointed leaves and petals are especially enhanced by the use of extra beads.

5. To end the flower, check the pattern to determine the number of wires you should have remaining. Use one of the methods below to cut the wire from the spool. The bulkiness of the wires during construction and the support needed for each petal will determine how you should cut the piece from the spool. The more wires you leave, the stiffer it will be.

3 Wires (stiff)—Cut the basic loop open at the bottom, and pull out some spool wire. Cut the spool wire and twist the three wires (fig. 6).

Cut both wires at arrows.

Figure 6

2 Wires (medium)— Cut the spool wire 1/2" from the bottom of the piece. Cut the bottom of the basic loop open, and twist (fig. 7).

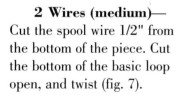

Cut both wires at arrows.

Figure 7

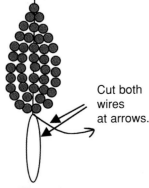

Cut both wires at arrows.

Figure 8

1 Wire (light)—Cut both the spool wire and one side of the basic loop 1/2" from the piece, and twist (fig. 8).

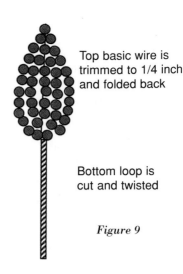

Top basic wire is trimmed to 1/4 inch and folded back

Bottom loop is cut and twisted

Figure 9

6. Cut the top section of the basic wire to a 1/4" length. Fold it down tightly against the back of the piece (fig. 9).

7. Twist the bottom wires with the hemostats. When twisting wires, grab the wire tips with the locking hemostats, hold the flower part in one hand, and put the middle finger of your other hand through one of the handle loops. Pull tight, rotating your wrist. The result is a smooth, even stem that will not fall apart later. CAUTION! Twist only until smooth and even (fig. 10). If you get carried away, you'll lose your stem!

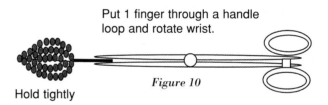

Put 1 finger through a handle loop and rotate wrist.

Hold tightly

Figure 10

8. On long or wide pieces, it's necessary to Lace the rows together in order to get a smooth and neat appearance.

Lacing

Thread a piece of 30-gauge (or finer) wire through a darning needle. Twist the needle to secure the wire, and then use one of the two methods below.

Method 1

Beginning in the center of the back of the piece, use an over-and-under motion to weave the wire to the outside edge. Then turn (running stitch), and use the same stitch to weave back across to the far edge. Turn, and weave back to the center. Pull the ends together, twist, and cut (fig. 11).

Method 2

Beginning at the edge of the back, twist the loose end of the wire around the outside row of beads. Working on the back side, use a backstitch to work across to the far edge. Twist the end around the last row again to secure and trim (fig. 11).

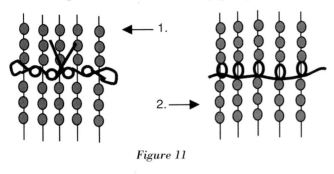

Figure 11

Stem Stiffening

Method 1

For long, slender leaves that are meant to stand up straight, incorporate an additional stem wire into the construction. After you measure your basic row of beads, hold the extra, light-gauge stem wire against the back of the beads. On each round, wrap the bead wire around both the extra and the basic wires. When the leaf is finished, trim and twist the extra wire right along with the basic wire (fig. 12).

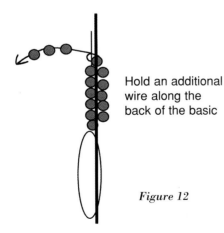

Hold an additional wire along the back of the basic

Figure 12

Method 2

For large, round leaves that just need support at the base, add only enough wire to thicken the short, twisted stem. After the leaf is completed, but before you twist the stem wire, cut a piece of wire that is twice as long as the distance from the bottom of the basic wire to the top of the lower, wrapped area.

Fold the cut piece of wire in half. From the right side of the leaf, insert one end of the folded wire, at the bottom, between rows 1 and 2. Insert the other end, at the bottom, between rows 1 and 3. Lightly twist the entire length of the cut wire. Then, combine the twisted wire with the stem wires and twist again (fig. 13).

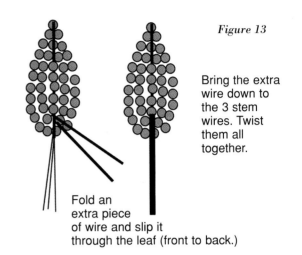

Figure 13

Bring the extra wire down to the 3 stem wires. Twist them all together.

Fold an extra piece of wire and slip it through the leaf (front to back.)

Taping

To finish the piece, tape the exposed wire with floral tape. You may also choose to bead, floss, or otherwise cover the stems. However, be sure to tape them first. It waterproofs the wire and provides a good non-skid base for anything you may choose to add.

Floral tape is usually found in 1/2" widths. Use as is or, for ease in handling when working on small pieces, remove a length of tape, cut it in half lengthwise, and use the 1/4" tape for taping small stems and leaves.

Lightly stretch the tape to activate the wax. Hold the tip against the bloom end of the wire; twirl the

Figure 14

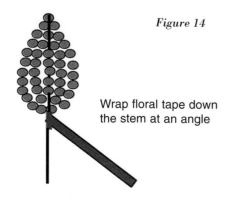

Wrap floral tape down
the stem at an angle

wire between your fingers as you move the tape downward. This will create a tight, smooth spiral. Once the entire area is covered, tear off the tape. Then pinch, smooth, and rub the stem so that the tape edges fuse together (fig. 14).

Flossing Stems

This is done just like, but over the top of, your tape. The most elegant type of floss to use is untwisted silk. Because this is somewhat expensive and hard to find, feel free to experiment with a range of different materials.

Beading Stems

This is most impressive on large flowers and branches. Make sure to tape the stem first, and then string at least five feet of beads. Do the buds and small branches first. Allowing about 2" of bare wire to trail down the stem, hold the bare end of the wire tight against the bottom of the bud. Wrap tightly twice around the stem. Slide the beads forward on the wire, and hold them tightly in place while wrapping them around and down the stem (just like taping).

I keep my other thumbnail tight against the previously wound row. Then, as I wrap the next time around, the new row actually pushes my thumbnail down the stem. When you get to a leaf, pull the leaf downward. Bead tight into the crevice. Pull the leaf back up and bead around until you meet the leaf again.

At this time, let the beads slide back, and wrap the bare wire once around the base of the leaf. Push the beads back up the wire, and continue to wrap the beads down to the point where the stems (branches) meet.

End here by wrapping the bare wire several times around the stem, as close to the beads as possible. Then spiral the bare wire down a few inches before cutting. Do the same thing to the rest of the small stems and branches. Then, after wiring the branches together, proceed in the same manner to do the large flower stems.

Here are two tips to help the process along: 1) If you have enough room, start your wrapping by putting the first row of beads between the petals and the sepals. Wrap the bare wire around each sepal, just as you did the leaf on the bud stem. 2) DON'T cut the wire when you reach the joints. Wrap the bare wire once around each joint and continue downward. Stop at least 1" to 3" from the bottom. End as before. Cut the wire, and cover all exposed ends with floral tape.

Other Commonly Used Techniques

Continuous Loops

Without a basic wire, form a loop of beads in the desired length, cross the wires, and give one full twist. Beginning at the base of the loop just completed, repeat the process for the desired number of loops (fig. 15).

Figure 15

Use at least 1 full twist at the bottom of each loop. (Always twist all of the loops in the same direction.)

Continuous Double Loops

Use the same technique as the Continuous Loops to form the first loop. Then wrap the beads around the outside of the loops a second time. Twist and move on to the next loop (fig. 16).

Figure 16

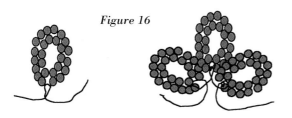

When you apply the second row of beads around the outside of the first, wrap the wire around the bottom. Do not try to twist again.

Continuous Crossover Loops

Beginning with the Continuous Loop technique, make the loop, twist to secure, and then bead up the front of the loop and down the back. Twist, and move on to the next loop. This makes a 4-row crossover loop. For the 3-row crossover, bead up the front and leave bare wire down the back. Twist and move on to the next loop (fig. 17).

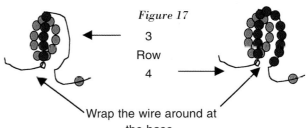

Figure 17

3

Row

4

Wrap the wire around at the base.

Three completed Continuous Crossover Loops

Beehive (Cup)

This technique is accomplished by bending the basic wire, the basic loop, or both, backwards, at a set angle, while continuing to add rows. A slight bend of both wires will form a type of raised-button shape, similar to the center of a daisy. A sharp bend of one wire will create a tapered cup (snapdragon petal). A sharp bend of both basics will create a thimble shape (coneflower center). See illustration for side views (fig. 19).

Weaving or Basket Bottom

This technique looks just as it sounds. However, you don't actually weave over and under the wires. Instead, every time you come to one of the spread wires (spokes), you wrap the wire around it, as if it were the basic wire.

Cut a determined number of wires. Hold them together in a bundle, and wrap the bare end of the beaded wire twice, tightly around the centers. Spread the wires open, like the spokes of a wheel, and bead around the center. (Some patterns will tell you how many beads to put between the spokes, others will not.) These are counted as rounds, instead of rows (fig. 20).

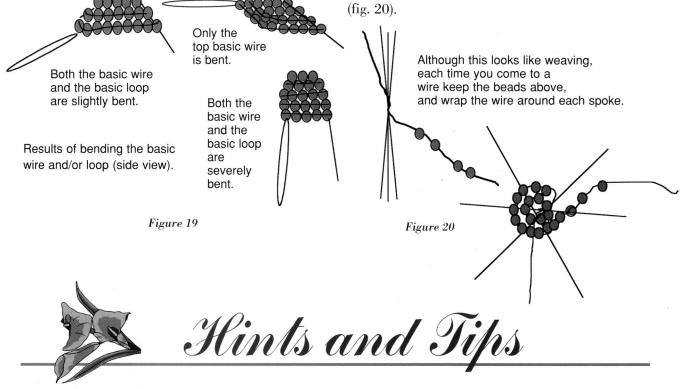

Both the basic wire and the basic loop are slightly bent.

Only the top basic wire is bent.

Both the basic wire and the basic loop are severely bent.

Results of bending the basic wire and/or loop (side view).

Figure 19

Although this looks like weaving, each time you come to a wire keep the beads above, and wrap the wire around each spoke.

Figure 20

Hints and Tips

How many beads should I string at a time?

If you're making multiple petals with the same color beads, be sure to string enough to complete at least the part you are making. Always err on the side of too many. If you do run short, over estimate the amount of wire you will need, cut it from the spool, and add the beads onto the cut end.

Never try to attach a second wire in the middle of a petal. It may look fine when you're finished, but you will have lost the overall integrity of the piece. Strange and unusual twists are bound to appear in years to come. Personally, I like to get most of my stringing done at the beginning, so I can continue moving from petal to petal without interruption.

What is a bead spinner, and why should I use one?

Many bead stores, craft shops, and Internet craft sites carry a nifty little item called a bead spinner (or stringer). It's a small wooden or plastic bowl with a center shaft. When you spin the shaft, the beads are forced out against the sides in a whirling mass. Although a curved needle is usually supplied with the spinner, a French Beader can go one better on the concept. All you have to do is bend the tip of your beading wire into a hook and lower it into the spinning beads. The beads will literally jump onto the wire. This not only allows you to easily use loose beads, but it's also an absolute blessing when mixing colors for variegated leaves and petals. If you intend to do a lot of beading, a bead spinner is worth its weight in gold!

How should I clean my French-Beaded flowers?

If you are not sure whether or not the beads have a lined or dyed finish applied to them, the safest way to clean your flowers is to simply run them under hot water. If you are sure that they are "color safe," a mild spray cleaner can also be used. The most important thing is to make sure that they are dried thoroughly! On hot sunny days, set them in the sun for an hour or two. On cool days, place them in the oven on the COOLEST setting for several hours, or use a hair dryer to blow them dry.

What kind of container should I use to display my flowers?

French-Beaded flowers are very heavy! Everyone who lifts one for the first time is amazed by the weight. This can create some unique problems when trying to assemble a bouquet. In other words, don't place a bouquet in Grandma's antique, bone china vase and walk away. It will, most likely, come crashing down.

Make sure that you choose containers that are extremely stable and have rather broad, flat bottoms. It's often necessary to have enough room to also add some material to the vase for added weight. A display that continually crashes to the floor is not only nerve wracking, but it usually ends up all bent and twisted.

How do I add extra weight to my vase?

There are many ways to add extra weight to a favorite vase or container. One way is to fill your containers with marbles, stones, or BBs. Although rather messy, floral clay can also add enough extra weight to hold the flowers. If the bouquet is to stay in the vase "forever," floral clay can even be melted (gently) and poured in after the bouquet is complete. In most cases, floral foam will NOT work. The flowers are just too top heavy to remain secure in Styrofoam®.

If all else fails, make your own pot. Tape over the drainage hole, and fill a clay pot with wet plaster of Paris. Leave enough empty room at the top to later add camouflage. Lightly wrap a piece of paper around a flower stem several times, and tape it. Push it all the way down into the pot. Then, pull out the stem, leaving the paper behind. Once the plaster becomes firm, twist the paper and pull it out. If some remains, use tweezers or hemostats to reach in and pull it out.

Using the same plaster method, you can cut lengths of plastic drinking straws, tape the ends, and insert them into the plaster. Add a couple extra to each pot, for future use. Once the plaster hardens, cut the straws off even with the surface. Disguise the plaster by covering its surface with moss or shredded bark.

Can I add scent to my French-Beaded flowers?

To give your flowers that extra touch of reality, scented oils can be added to the pot. However, NEVER put scented oils on your beads! The ingredients can discolor the beads!

How do I keep the dogs and kids from knocking over my projects?

Check out second-hand sources for a small computer cart on wheels. Not only will you have several shelves for your supplies, but the keyboard shelf is just the right size for your beading tray.

Long-stemmed Sweetheart Rose

This is my most often requested ready-made flower. Nature provides us with every shade of white, pink, orange, lavender, and bi-color bloom. However, for a great contemporary look, try making these with black petals and either clear or metallic leaves. The result is quite dramatic! This time, I chose the patriotic look.

Materials Needed

- 1 hank of petal-color beads
- 1/2 hank of green beads
- 26-gauge beading wire
- 30- to 34-gauge assembly wire
- 18" of 14- or 16-gauge stem wire
- 1/2" green floral tape

Petals (round top, round bottom)

Make 5 (petal color)
8-bead basic, 3 rows (Reduce to 1 wire.)

Make 5 (petal color)
4-bead basic, 7 rows (Reduce to 1 wire.)

Make 5 (petal color)
4-bead basic, 9 rows (Reduce to 1 wire.)

Make 5 (petal color)
5-bead basic, 11 rows (Reduce to 1 wire.)

Make 5 (petal color)
5-bead basic, 13 rows (Reduce to 1 wire.)

Sepals (pointed top, round bottom)

Make 5 (green)
3-bead basic, 7 rows (Reduce to 1 wire.)

Leaves (pointed top, round bottom)

Group #1

Make 1 (green)
8-bead basic, 11 rows (Leave 3 wires, and twist.)

Make 2 (green)
8-bead basic, 7 rows (Leave 3 wires, and twist.)

Group #2

Make 1 (green)
8-bead basic, 13 rows (Leave 3 wires, and twist.)

Make 2 (green)
8-bead basic, 9 rows (Leave 3 wires, and twist.)

Assembly

1. Lightly tape the stem wire.

2. Starting with the smallest petals, hold a single petal so that the base is even with the top of the stem wire. Using the thin assembly wire, tightly wrap the petal in place (2-3 passes). One at a time, position each petal around the stem and secure in the same manner.

3. When all five petals are added, go on to the next size, and repeat the procedure. Make sure to place each row tightly against the previous row. Failure to do so will leave unsightly gaps in your bloom.

4. When all 25 petals have been added, arrange the sepals in the same manner. Secure the sepals, and cut the assembly wire.

5. Turn the rose upside down, pull the wires slightly away from the stem, and cut them all to the same length, 1/2" from the bloom.

6. Tape the entire stem again, making sure to wrap the assembly area with several layers, thereby producing the rose-hip effect.

7. Leaf Group Assembly:

Group #1

a. After twisting the wires, cut a length of floral tape in half (lengthwise). Beginning at the base of the beads, tape about halfway down each leaf.

b. With the largest leaf at the top and the two small ones opposite each other (fig. 23), hold the leaves together, and twist the wires together.

c. Tape the twisted area, and slightly flatten the lower half. This will lessen any bulges on the flower stem.

d. Position this group several inches below the bloom, and tape it in place.

Group #2

Assemble as above, and place this group several inches below and opposite Group #1.

Figure 23

Cymbidium Orchid

For many years, my youngest brother brought me an Easter corsage. I would wear it for a day and then mourn its demise. Last year I decided to immortalize it. Now I can remember the sentiment all year long. Thanks Darrell.

Materials Needed

2 1/2 hanks of petal-color beads

1/2 hank of contrasting-color beads

2 strands of yellow (matte) beads

1 hank of green beads

1/2 hank of brown beads (optional for beading the stem)

26-gauge beading wire

30- to 34-gauge wire (for lacing and assembly)

Two 18" pieces of 18-gauge green stem wires, cut in half (to stiffen leaves)

14" of 1/8" rod stock, or very heavy stem wire

1/2" green floral tape

1/2" brown floral tape

Petals

Make 15 (petal color) (pointed top, round bottom)

1 3/4" basic, 13 rows

    a. Add an extra bead to the basic wire on each row after row 5.

    b. Leave 3 wires, and twist.

Make 3 (contrasting color) (round top, round bottom)

1 3/4" basic, 7 rows (Leave 3 wires, and twist.)

Make 3 (Mix equal parts of petal-color and contrasting-color beads on the wire, about 1 1/2 strands of each color per petal.) (pointed top, round bottom)

1-bead basic, 23 rows

    a. Use 6 beads each for rows 1 and 2. Push them down against the basic bead, and then bead around this until you reach a total of 7 rows.

    b. On each additional row, add an extra bead to the basic wire until the petal is completed.

    c. Leave 3 wires, and twist.

Pistil

Make 3 (yellow)

    a. String 6" of beads, make a loop, and twist twice.

    b. Pinch the loop closed, twist beads (3"), and fold in half (1 1/2").

    c. Put one basic stem wire through the tip of the loop.

    d. Finish by twisting the wires.

Bud (pointed top, round bottom)

Make 2 (1 green, 1 petal color)

1 1/2" basic, 11 rows (Leave 3 wires, and twist.)

Leaves (pointed top, round bottom)

Make 4 (green)

6" basic, 9 rows

    a. After measuring the basic wire, use Stem Stiffening Method 1 to reinforce the leaf.

    b. Leave 3 wires, and twist.

Assembly

1. Lace all petals across the center.

2. Lace the leaves twice, 2" from the top and 2" from the bottom.

3. Working with the large, multicolored petal, bring the sides up to form a cone at the base of the petal. Use lacing wire to tack the sides together, about 1" from the base.

4. Slip the pistil into the cone. Hold the bases even, and twist the wires together several times. Bend the tip of the cone down slightly.

5. Position the contrasting-color petal (back side down) directly over the top of the cone. Using assembly wire, wrap the stem several times. Bend the petal into a gentle curve toward the cone.

6. Add 5 (contrasting-color) petals, one at a time, securing each with the same assembly wire. Tape with green floral tape. Assemble the other two blooms in the same manner.

7. Place the 2 buds with their back sides together. Twist the petals to form a bi-colored spiral. Twist the wires together, and tape with green floral tape. Tape the remainder of the plant in brown floral tape.

8. Allowing about 1 1/2" of green to show, wire the bud to the top of the stem. Now add each of the blooms in the same manner, leaving about 2" between them. Continue spiral wrapping the wire down to within 3" of the bottom.

9. Add two leaves, opposite each other, and wire in place. Add the last 2 leaves directly below the first 2, and finish by taping the entire stem again.

10. Hold the stem firmly. Put a distinct bend in the stem where each bud and bloom connects to the stem.

11. Optional: If you choose to bead the stems, use green for the individual bloom stems and brown for the main stem.

Large Moth Orchid

Every time another orchid blooms, I'm haunted by the fact that the flowers will soon fade away. French beading is my solution. Out come the beads, and another flower is captured.

Materials Needed

3 hanks of petal-color beads
3 hanks of green beads
1 strand of yellow beads
26-gauge beading wire
30- to 34-gauge wire (for lacing and assembly)
18" of 1/8" rod stock, or very heavy stem wire
1/2" green floral tape
1/2" brown floral tape

Centers (pointed top, round bottom)

Make 3 (petal color)

3-bead basic, 9 rows, and 2 loops

    a. After completing row 5, add 4 beads to the basic wire.

    b. Each time you cross the "extra beads," pinch the tip to form a point.

    c. Once the rows are complete, leave 5" of bare wire, and cut the wire from the spool.

    d. Add 18 yellow beads, and form two 9-bead loops at the base of the petal.

    e. Fold the loops towards the back of the petal (fig. 24).

    f. Leave 3 wires, and twist.

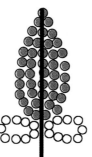

Figure 24

Make 6 (petal color)

1-bead basic, 7 rows

    a. After completing row 3, add 3 beads to the basic wire.

    b. Each time you cross the "extra beads," pinch the tip to form a point.

    c. Leave 3 wires, and twist.

Petals

Make 6 (petal color) (pointed top, round bottom)

1-bead basic, 23 rows

    a. Use 9 beads each for rows 2 and 3 (fig. 25).

    b. After completing row 9, add one bead to the basic wire for the next 4 rows.

Flatten the long rows down against the short basic.

Figure 25

c. Each time you cross the "extra bead," pinch the tip to form a point.

d. Leave 3 wires, and twist.

Make 3 (petal color) (pointed top, round bottom)

20-bead basic, 13 rows (Leave 3 wires, and twist.)

Make 6 (petal color) (round top, round bottom)

16-bead basic, 11 rows (Leave 3 wires, and twist.)

Pistils

Make 3 (petal color)

a. Leave 3" of bare wire. Use 1" of beads for the first loop and then complete the Double Crossover Loop.

b. Leave 3" of bare wire, cut, and twist.

c. Twist beaded loops.

Buds (pointed top, round bottom)

Make 1 (petal color)

12-bead basic, 13 rows (Leave 3 wires, and twist.)

Make 1 (green)

12-bead basic, 11 rows (Leave 3 wires, and twist.)

Make 2 (green)

10-bead basic, 9 rows (Leave 3 wires, and twist.)

Leaves (round top, round bottom)

Make 3 (green)

2" basic, 19 rows

a. Leave 3 wires.

b. Use Stem Stiffening Method 2 to stiffen.

Make 3 (green)

2 1/2" basic, 21 rows

a. Leave 3 wires.

b. Use Stem Stiffening Method 2 to stiffen.

Make 3 (green)

3" basic, 23 rows

a. Leave 3 wires.

b. Use Stem Stiffening Method 2 to stiffen.

Assembly

1. Lace the 9 leaves and the 6 large petals.

2. Large Bud

a. Hold the petal-color bud and the largest green bud back-to-back. Twist the beads into a spiral.

b. Twist the wires, and tape with green floral tape.

3. Small Bud

a. Hold the 2 small, green buds together, and twist into a spiral.

b. Twist the wires, and tape with green tape.

4. Centers

a. Cup 3 of the center pieces (1 large with loops and 2 small) backwards.

b. Hold them together with all cups facing inward. Place the large one at the bottom, a small one at each side, and add a pistil at the top.

c. Twist all the wires together. Do the same for the other 2 sets.

5. Using assembly wire, attach two large petals on either side of the center assembly.

6. Add 2 small petals to the bottom and 1 medium petal to the top.

7. Secure all the parts with assembly wire. Tightly twist all the wires together. Tape the bloom stem with green tape. Assemble the other two blooms in the same way.

8. Using brown tape, lightly tape the 1/8" rod.

9. Position the small bud at the very tip, and wire it in place.

10. About 1 1/2" from the beads, bend the stem of the large bud at a 90° angle. Wire this about 1 1/2 to 2" from the small bud. Bend the green stems of the blooms, and attach them in the same manner, alternating them on opposite sides. You should have 2 blooms on one side; there should be 1 bloom and 1 large bud on the other side. Spiral the assembly wire down the rod.

11. About 3" from the bottom of the stem, attach the 3 small leaves at the same level. Next, directly below the first group, add the 3 medium leaves, then the 3 large leaves. Secure with wire and tape.

12. Bend the rod into a gentle arc, and make sure all of the blooms are right side up.

Snapdragon

The reason for making this design was simple. I couldn't find a pattern for a snapdragon anywhere. The more of these you add, the more fabulous your bouquet becomes.

Materials Needed

1 1/2 hanks of petal-color beads
1 1/2 hanks of green beads
26-gauge beading wire
30-gauge assembly wire
18" of 18-gauge stem wire
1/2" green floral tape

Petals *(round top, round bottom)*

Make 18 small cups (petal color)

1-bead basic, 13 rows

    a. After completing row 3, bend the top basic wire back to about an 80° angle. As you continue beading, you will be making a slanted cup.

    b. After you trim and twist the wires, lightly pinch the cup near the twisted wire, while tugging the other side outward. You should end up with a Beehive shape similar to Little Bo-Peep's bonnet (fig. 19, page 430).

    c. Reduce to 1 wire.

Make 18 large cups (petal color)

3-bead basic, 9 rows

    a. Bend the basic wire back to an 80° angle after row 3.

    b. Reduce to 1 wire.

Buds *(Pinch loops together, and twist wires.)*

Make 6 (petal color)

Leaving 2" of bare wire at the beginning and end, make two 12-bead Continuous Loops.

Make 6 (petal color)

Leaving 2" of bare wire at the beginning and end, make three 16-bead Continuous Loops.

Make 1 (green)

Leaving 2" of bare wire at the beginning and end, make five 16-bead Continuous Loops.

Sepals

Make 30 (green)

Leaving 2" of bare wire at the beginning and end, make five 12-bead Continuous Loops.

Leaves *(pointed top, round bottom)*

Make 15 (green)

2" basic, 5 rows (Leave 3 wires, and twist.)

Assembly

1. To make the blooms, hold a single small-cup petal and a single large-cup petal together with front sides facing. Make sure the bases are even. Twist twice to hold them together. Position a sepal (Continuous Loop) assembly at the base, with the open side facing down (under the large cup). Twist all the wires together. Trim wires to 2" and tape.

2. Position a petal-color bud in each of the remaining sepals. Twist the wires together, and tape.

3. Lightly tape the large stem wire.

4. Position the green bud tightly against the tip of the large stem wire, and wire in place. Keep the wire connected. Wire down 1", and secure 3 small buds at equal distances around the stem.

5. Tape down 1". Attach the next 3 small buds in the same manner, making sure that they are positioned below the empty spaces of the previous row.

6. Tape down 1". Attach the large buds, all of the blooms, and all of the leaves in the same manner (1" between rows, 3 per row, all spaced under the empty spaces of the row above). Tape the entire stem.

Hanging Fuchsia

Use your imagination. Make these in white, pink and white, pink and purple, or red and blue. It really doesn't matter whether you stay with one color or mix them up. They are just adorable!

Materials Needed

1 1/2 hanks of petal-color beads (If you use 2 colors, the ratio of petal to contrasting color is 50/50.)

1 1/2 hanks of light green beads

26-gauge beading wire (Colored is best for the pistil and stamens.)

30-gauge assembly wire

Three 18" pieces of 18-gauge stem wire

1/2" green floral tape

1/2" colored floral tape or silk floss to match the large petals (optional)

Cup Petals (round top, round bottom)
Make 8 (petal or contrasting color)
4-bead basic, 5 rows (Reduce to 1 wire.)
Make 10 (petal or contrasting color)
3-bead basic, 7 rows (Reduce to 1 wire.)
Make 12 (petal or contrasting color)
2-bead basic, 9 rows (Reduce to 1 wire.)

Outer Petals (pointed top, round bottom)
Make 8 (petal color)
3/4" basic, 9 rows (Reduce to 1 wire.)

Buds (pointed top, round bottom) (DON'T cut top basic wire.)
Make 3 (petal color)
3-bead basic, 5 rows (Reduce to 1 wire.)
Make 3 (petal color)
4-bead basic, 7 rows (Reduce to 1 wire.)

Leaves (pointed top, round bottom)
Make 2 (green) (seed pods)
1/2" basic, 5 rows (Leave 3 wires, twist, and tape.)
Make 2 (green)
3/4" basic, 7 rows (Leave 3 wires, twist, and tape.)
Make 6 (green)
1" basic, 9 rows (Leave 3 wires, twist and tape.)

Pistil and Stamens
Make 7 (petal color)
a. Cut 4" of bead wire.
b. Add 1 bead to the center.
c. Fold in half, and twist the entire length.
Make 1 (petal color)
a. Cut 5" of bead wire.
b. Add 3 beads to the center.
c. Fold in half, and twist the entire length.

Assembly

1. Lightly tape the 3 stem wires.

2. Using assembly wire, attach the pistil and 7 stamens about 1/2" from the bottom of one of the stem wires. (This flower is upside down.)

3. One at a time, and still using assembly wire, attach 4 small petals with the wrong sides facing the stamens. Keeping each row tight against the previous one, add 5 medium petals and then 6 large round petals in exactly the same manner.

4. Next, with the wrong side facing out, add 4 large pointed petals. Wrap tightly. About 1/2" above the last petals, trim all the wires to the same length. Tape and bead over the 1/2" of wires. Or, using colored or white tape, tape the bundle of wires and tape 1" up the stem. (If you were not able to obtain tape to match the petals, tightly wrap the bundle with untwisted silk floss.) Using green tape, make a neat line around the top of the bundle, and cover the rest of the colored tape. Set this aside, and repeat the procedure to assemble the next blossom.

5. Using the 3 small bud petals, hold the tips together, and twist the top basic wires. Cut the top basic twist to 1/2", and bend it down between the petals. Cup the petals. Bring the bottoms together, twist, and tape. Create the large bud in the same manner.

6. Using the smallest green leaves (seed pods), twist the beads into a spiral, and tape the stems.

7. On the bottom of the last 18" of stem wire, use assembly wire to attach the 2 buds and the 2 smaller green leaves (the buds hanging down, leaves facing up). Tape over the assembly wire, and tape up the stem.

8. Hold all three large stems together. Position them so that the buds are 3" below the first flower and the second flower is 1" above the first.

9. Move up 3", add 2 leaves (facing up), and wire all the stems together.

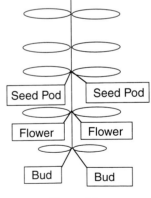

Figure 26

10. Wire up 3", and add 2 leaves and the 2 seedpods. Wire them in place. Wire up another 3". Position the last 2 leaves, and wire the rest of the stem. Tape over the entire stem (fig. 26).

11. Cup all of the small petals toward the stamens, and bend the large petals upwards.

*W*hen I first saw a photo of this unusual flower, I was entranced by the dramatic petal arrangement. This is an excellent choice for the contemporary home. It's also an impressive choice for the beginner.

Materials Needed

1 hank of red beads
1 hank of green beads
1 strand of yellow beads
26-gauge beading wire
30- to 34-gauge wire (for lacing and assembly)
18" of 16-gauge stem wire (or heavier)
1/2" green floral tape

Petals (pointed tops, round bottoms)

Make 4 (red)

2" basic, 11 rows (Leave 3 wires, and twist.)

Make 2 (red)

2 1/2" basic, 7 rows (Leave 3 wires, and twist.)

Stamens

Make 6 (yellow and red) (Use unpainted craft or beading wire.)

   a. Using yellow, make two 10-bead Continuous Loops.

   b. Measure 6" of spool wire, and cut. Cut the short end of the wire to 1/2".

   c. Put 2" of red beads on the 6" wire.

   d. Hold the short wire tight against the long wire, and push the beads up over both. Make sure the beads are tight against the bottom of the loops.

   e. Shape the loops so that the stamen forms a "T."

   f. Add 1" of yellow beads, and set aside.

   g. Make the other 5 stamens. Next, make the pistil.

Pistil

Make 1 (yellow and red)

   a. Using red beads, make three 8-bead Continuous Loops.

   b. Cut the spool wire to 6".

   c. Cut the short wire to 1/2".

   d. In the same manner as the stamens, add 2" of red beads and 1" of yellow beads to the wire.

   e. Bend the loops down against the stalk to form a knob on the end of the pistil.

Leaves (pointed top, round bottom)

Make 12 (green)

6" basic, 3 rows (Leave 3 wires, and twist.)

Assembly

1. Lace all leaves and petals.

2. Lightly tape the 18" stem wire.

3. Hold all the stamens and the pistil together in a bunch. Twist the bare wires until the beads are tight.

4. Twist the 1" of yellow beads into a spiral, leaving the red portion loose. Wrap a single strand of assembly wire around the group, placing it where the red and yellow beads meet. Twist tightly, trim to 1/4", and tuck the end into the spiral.

5. Stack 3 of the large petals (facing up), and twist the wires together. Slide the petals into a fan shape. Using a finger, hold down the center of the middle petal, and squeeze the petal into a trough. Put the stamen-pistil assembly in this trough, match the bases, and twist the wires. Curl the petals back.

6. Stack the 3 remaining petals with the large one in the center. Twist the wires. Slide the petals into a fan shape. Using assembly wire, attach the 2 petal groups to the end of the stem wire. Use the photo to determine proper petal placement.

7. Holding 3 green leaves together, twist the wires. Repeat with the rest, so that you have 4 groups of 3 leaves each. Six inches from the bottom of the stem wire, position the 4 groups of leaves around the stem, and wire them in place. Tape the entire stem.

8. Bend the large stem wire down until the blossom hangs in a drooping position.

Dutchman's Breeches

Although this flower is very easy to construct, it adds a definite point of interest to your bouquet.

Materials Needed

1 hank of white beads
3 strands of light green beads
1 strand of yellow beads
26-gauge beading wire
30-gauge assembly wire
18" 16-gauge stem wire
1/2" green floral tape

Petals (round bottom, pointed top)

Make 22 (white)

6-bead basic, 9 rows (Reduce to 2 wires, and twist.)

Stamens

Make 11 (yellow)

    a. Leave 3" of bare wire. Make three 1/2" Continuous Loops.

    b. Leave 3" of wire, and cut.

Leaves

Make 1 (green)

    a. Leave 1" of bare wire. Make one 16-bead loop.

    b. Thread the 1" of bare wire through the loop, and pull it tight. Thread it through again, and trim the short wire close to the loop.

    c. Push 4 beads up tight against the loop.

    d. Make 2 more 16-bead loops. Push forward another 4 beads. Repeat until you have completed a total of 17 loops with 4-bead spacers between the pairs of loops.

    e. Leave 2 beads on the wire, measure 3" of bare wire, and cut.

Make 2 (green)

Make these in exactly the same manner. However, in step d., make a total of 15 loops.

Assembly

1. Lightly tape the 18" stem wire.

2. Put two petals together, front sides facing, and lightly twist the wires. Open the petals to a flat ("T") position. Where they are joined, insert a 3-loop stamen through the petals, so that one bare wire goes between the first two beaded rows of each petal. Twist the stamen wire once or twice tight against the back of the petals. Hold all the petal and stamen wires together, twist tightly, and tape.

3. Hold a thin, flat object (such as a wooden ruler) with the edge against the center back of a petal. Fold both sides of the petal back sharply, and pinch them. Repeat the procedure on the second petal. Bend both petals backwards toward the stem.

4. Open the sepal loops so that 1 loop is back against each petal and the center one points straight outward. Repeat until you have completed all 11 blossoms.

5. Using assembly wire, attach one blossom to the tip of the stem wire. Place the next blossom at a distance, so that its sepal fits right into the V-shape of the previous one, and wire it in place. Continue until all blossoms have been wired to the stem.

6. Lightly arch the stem wire. Pull the blossoms out and down to alternate sides of the wire.

7. Stack the 3 leaves with the bases together. Twist the wires, and tape. Fan the pieces slightly so they still have the appearance of a single leaf. Pinch the uppermost loops flat. Bend them towards the tip to create a tapered effect. Tape this assembly 1" below the lowest blossom.

8. If you feel that your bouquet needs more greenery at its base, make and add more leaves. Tape them at the same level as the first.

Common Flax

Materials Needed

1/2 hank of light blue beads
5 strands of medium green beads
1 strand of yellow beads
26-gauge beading wire
26-gauge gold beading wire
12" of 16-gauge stem wire
1/2" green floral tape

The branching nature of this small-blossomed plant adds depth and symmetry to any arrangement.

Flowers

Make 9 (blue)
a. Leave 4" of bare wire. Make five 3-row 1" Continuous Crossover Loops.
b. Leave 4" of bare wire, and cut. Don't twist or tape.

Buds

Make 3 (blue)
a. Leave 4" of bare wire. Make two 8-bead Continuous Loops.
b. Measure 4" of wire, and cut.

Make 3 (blue)
a. Leave 4" of bare wire. Make two 12-bead Continuous Loops.
b. Measure 4" of wire, and cut.

Make 3 (blue)
a. Leave 4" of bare wire. Make two 16-bead Continuous Loops.
b. Measure 4" of wire, and cut.

Stamens

Make 9 (yellow beads on gold beading wire)
a. Measure 4" of bare wire. Make five 1/2" Continuous Loops of wire containing 1 bead per loop.
b. Measure 4" of wire, and cut.
c. Holding the bead at the top of the loop, twist each loop into a tight stalk.

Sepals

Make 9 (green)
a. Leave 4" of bare wire. Make four 8-bead Continuous Loops.
b. Measure 4" of wire, and cut.

Leaves

Make 18 (green)
a. Leave 1" bare wire. Measure 1" of beads.
b. Make a single loop. Twist, but don't tape.
c. Pinch the loop closed.

Make 9 (green)
a. Leave 1" bare wire. Measure 1 1/2" of beads.
b. Make a single loop. Twist, but don't tape.
c. Pinch the loop closed.

Make 12 (green)
a. Leave 1" bare wire. Measure 2" of beads.
b. Make a single loop. Twist, but don't tape.
c. Pinch loop closed.

Assembly

1. Lightly tape the stem wire.

2. Put a stamen group in the center of each flower. Pull the wires down tight. Twist all 4 wires (stamen and flower) together. Cut a length of floral tape to 1/4" wide. Beginning at the blossom, tape down 1". Add a small leaf, and tape down 1". Add a medium-sized leaf. Tape down 1". Set aside.

3. Cup a sepal assembly around each of the 9 buds. Pull the pieces tight against each other. Twist all 4 wires (bud and sepal) together. Tape down 1". Add a small leaf, and tape down 2".

4. Hold 1 bud and 1 flower together. Twist the bare portion of the wires, and tape down 1/2". Repeat with the remaining pieces (9 units).

5. Hold 3 units together. Twist the bare portion of the wires, and tape down 1/2". Add 2 large leaves, and tape down 1/2". Repeat twice more for 3 large units.

6. Tape one large unit to the top of the stem wire. Tape down 1", and add the second. Tape down 1", and add the third. Tape down the rest of the stem, adding large leaves at 1/2" intervals. Bend the large and small stems until most of the blossoms are at approximately the same level and the branch has a lifelike appearance.

Large Ox-eye Daisy, Black-eyed Susan & Coneflower

These flowers are so similar that you can use the same pattern, with just a few variations, to make a multicolor bouquet.

Materials Needed

6 strands of white beads (yellow for Black-Eyed Susan, pink for Coneflower)

1 strand of yellow beads (brown for Black-Eyed Susan and Coneflower)

6 strands of green beads

26-gauge beading wire

30-gauge assembly wire

16" of 16-gauge stem wire

1/2" green floral tape

Petals

Make 1 (white)

 a. Leave 3" of bare wire. Using 4" of beads per loop, make 12 Continuous Crossover Loops (4 row).
 b. Once completed, leave 4" of bare wire. Cut the bare wire, and bring it up between the first two petals made.
 c. Pull it back down between two petals on the opposite side of the flower.
 d. DON'T twist.

Center (round)

Make 1 (yellow)

1-bead basic, 14 rows

 a. Since you have an even number of rows, you will end at the top basic wire. Leave 4" of bare wire, and cut from spool.
 b. DON'T cut the top basic wire.
 c. Bend all of the wires backwards 90°.
 d. DON'T twist.

Sepals

Make 1 (green)

Make 8 continuous 1/2" loops.

Leaves

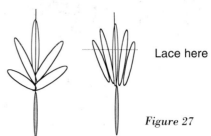

Lace here

Figure 27

Make 2 (green)

2" basic, 11 rows

 a. Make the first 3 rows as usual.
 b. Take row 4 up the side, but stop 1/2" from the top.
 c. Turn and bead down to the bottom, then up the other side. Turn 1/2" from the top.
 d. Repeat, but this time stop 1/2" from the previous row.
 e. Leave 3 wires, twist, and tape.
 f. Lace the leaf, and then bend the loose tips outward (fig. 27).

Assembly

Large Ox-Eye Daisy

1. Lightly tape the stem wire.

2. Place the flower center over the middle of the petals. Push the center down, with the wires passing between petals. Pull the wires to the middle of the back, and twist several times with the petal wires.

3. Using assembly wire, attach the flower to the end of the stem wire. Cut the petal wires to different lengths. Push the sepals up under the blossom. Wire the sepals in place.

4. Arrange the leaves at attractive places on the stem. Wire them in place.

5. Tape the entire stem.

Black-Eyed Susan

1. Petals (yellow)—Make the same as the daisy.

2. Center (dark brown or black)—1-bead basic, 10 rows. Make the same as the daisy.

3. Stamens—Make the same as the daisy.

4. Leaves—2" basic, 11 rows, (pointed top, pointed bottom).

Coneflower

1. Petals—(pink) Make the same as the daisy.

2. Center—(brown) 1-bead basic, 20 rows.

After completing row 7, bend both wires backwards to about 80°. Continue beading, positioning each row so that you are forming a cup (fig. 19, page 430). End the same as the daisy.

3. Stamens—Make the same as the daisy.

4. Leaves—2 1/2" basic, 11 rows (pointed top, pointed bottom).

Coral Bean

This tall spike of blooms is a great way to add height to your bouquet. If you can find colored floral tape, a red stem adds even more interest to this piece.

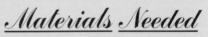

Materials Needed

2 hanks of red or deep coral pink beads

1/2 hank of green beads

1 strand of yellow beads

26-gauge beading wire

28-gauge gold wire (for the stamens)

30- or 34-gauge wire (for lacing and assembly)

18" of 16-gauge stem wire

1/2" green floral tape

Buds

Make 4 (red)
    a. Leaving 2" of bare wire before and after, make two 1" Continuous Loops.
    b. Twist the loops into a spiral.

Make 4 (red)
    a. Leaving 2" of bare wire before and after, make two 2" Continuous Loops.
    b. Twist the loops into a spiral.

Make 4 (red) (pointed top, round bottom)
1/4" basic, 7 rows (Twist into a spiral.)

Make 4 (red) (pointed top, round bottom)
1/2" basic, 7 rows (Twist into a spiral.)

Petals (round top, round bottom) (Lace all of the petals.)

Make 4 (red)
1/2" basic, 13 rows (Leave 3 wires, and twist.)

Make 4 (red)
3/4" basic, 13 rows (Leave 3 wires, and twist.)

Make 4 (red)
1" basic, 13 rows (Leave 3 wires, and twist.)

Make 4 (red)
1 1/4" basic, 13 rows (Leave 3 wires, and twist.)

Sepals

Make 16 (red)
Leaving 2" of bare wire before and after, make four 8-bead Continuous Loops (buds)

Make 8 (red)
Leaving 2" of bare wire before and after, make four 12-bead Continuous Loops (small petals)

Make 8 (red)
Leaving 2" of bare wire before and after, make four 16-bead Continuous Loops (large petals)

Stamens

Make 48 (yellow)
    a. Cut 6" of gold wire.
    b. Add 3 beads.
    c. Fold it in half, and twist the entire length.

Leaves (pointed top, round bottom)

Make 3 (green)
3-bead basic, 15 rows
    a. Add 1 bead to the basic wire on each row after row 7.
    b. Leave 3 wires, twist, and tape.

Assembly

1. Lightly tape the stem wire.

2. Apply a sepal to the base of each bud, and twist the wires.

3. Hold a pencil along the back basic wire, and bend each petal into a tube. Where the two laced edges meet, use lacing wire to connect the edges and secure the tube.

4. Slip 3 stamens into each tube. Position them so that they extend about 1/4" past the tip. Add the appropriate size sepal, and twist the wires.

5. Begin at the tip of the stem wire. Use assembly wire to attach the 4 smallest buds.

Allowing 1" between rows, attach the rest of the buds and blooms (4 at a time). Bend the two upper rows upward. Bend the rest of the rows downward.

6. Stack the 3 leaves together. Beginning 1/2" from the beads, twist the stems together. Slide the leaves into a fan shape. Tape the twisted area. Wire this in place 2" to 3" below the bottom bloom.

7. Tape the entire stem with green floral tape.

Queen Anne's Lace

Late summer in Ohio provides us with acres of this delicate beauty. Who can resist the lacey appearance and the aromatec smell of wild carrots?

Materials Needed

1/2 hank of white beads

4 strands of light green beads

1 red bead

30-gauge white wire

26-gauge beading wire

30- to 34-gauge wire (assembly)

18" of 16-gauge stem wire

1/2" green floral tape

Flowerets

Make 35 (white beads on white wire)
a. Leaving 4" of bare wire, make four 7-bead Continuous Loops.
b. Leave 4" of bare wire, and twist lightly.
c. On the last floweret, thread a single red bead onto the wire. Bring the wire over the top of the flower. Center the red bead.
d. Bring the wire back down, and twist lightly.

Sepals

Make 4 (green)
a. Leave 3" of bare wire.
b. Make 3 Continuous Loops. The first is a 1/2" loop. The second requires 1" of beads. And, the third is 1/2" again.
c. Leave 3" of bare wire, and cut.
d. Put 1/2" of beads on each wire, and twist.

Make 4 (green)
a. Leave 3" of bare wire.
b. Make 3 Continuous Loops. The first is a 1" loop. The second requires 2" of beads. And, the third is 1" again.
c. Leave 3" of bare wire, and cut.
d. Put 1" of beads on each wire, and twist up to the loops.

Leaves

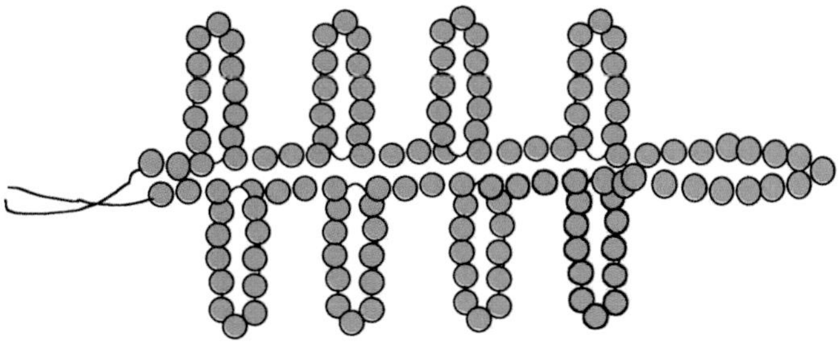

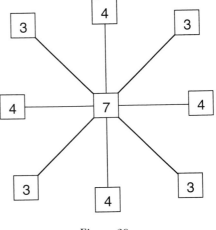

Figure 28

Make 2 (green)
a. Leave 3" of bare wire.
b. Make a 1" loop.
c. Leave 1/2" of beads.
d. Make another 1" loop.
e. Repeat until you have 4 loops with 1/2" of beads between them.
f. Make a 2" loop (tip of leaf).
g. Make a 1" loop. Leave 1/2" of beads, and then make the next 1" loop. Continue until you have another set of 4 loops with 1/2" beaded spacers.
h. Cut 3" bare wire, and add 1/2" of beads to each bare end (fig. 28). Twist the wires.
i. Pinch all of the loops closed, and twist the beads on all of the loops and stem. This gives them a lacier appearance.

Assembly

1. Lightly tape the stem wire.

2. This is a flat-topped flower. Therefore, when assembling flower groups, put the flowerets face down on a smooth surface. Bring the wires toward the center, and adjust the length of each wire to insure that the flowerets remain flat. Once they are in position, twist the wires lightly. Make 4 groups of 3 flowerets. Make 4 groups of 4 flowerets. Make 1 group of 7 flowerets (the one floweret with the red bead should be in the center, and the other six should completely surround it).

3. Arrange the groups as shown in fig. 29. Bring the wires together, and twist. Use assembly wire to attach the flower to the end of the stem. Pull the wires away from the stem, and cut them to different lengths, so that they will taper when pulled back down. Tape this area lightly.

4. Attach the 4 large sepals directly below the flower. Bend them upwards. Attach the 4 small sepals in the spaces between the large sepals. Bend them downwards.

5. Wire the two leaves at attractive distances from the flower. Tape the entire stem.

Figure 29

Harvest Lily

This little wild lily blooms so late in the season its leaves often whither before the blooms appear. Therefore, the leaves are done in either tan or transparent gold beads.

Materials Needed

7 to 8 strands of medium or dark purple beads
2 strands of green beads
3 strands of tan beads
1 strand of white beads
1 strand of yellow beads
26-gauge beading wire
30- to 34-gauge assembly wire
Four 18" pieces of 18-gauge stem wire
1/2" green floral tape

Petals (pointed top, round bottom)
Make 18 (purple)
1" basic, 5 rows (Reduce to 2 wires.)
Make 9 (white)
4-bead basic, 3 rows (Reduce to 2 wires.)

Buds (pointed top, round bottom) (After completion, twist the petal into a spiral.)
Make 1 (purple)
3/4" basic, 7 rows (Reduce to 2 wires.)
Make 1 (green)
3/4" basic, 7 rows (Reduce to 2 wires.)
Make 1 (green)
1/2" basic, 5 rows (Reduce to 2 wires.)

Pistil
Make 3 (yellow)
Leaving 2" of bare wire, make one 1" 4-row Crossover Loop, cut wires, and twist.

Leaves (pointed top, round bottom)
Make 2 (tan)
1" basic, 11 rows (Leave 3 wires, and twist.)
Make 2 (tan and green)
3" basic, 3 rows
    a. String the tan beads, leaving 4" of bare wire, and make your basic loop.
    b. String 3" of green beads on the basic wire.
    c. Complete the next 2 rows with tan (green center, tan on the outside).
    d. Leave 3 wires, and twist.

Assembly

1. Cut one of the stem wires into three 6" pieces (bud stems). Lightly tape the top 4" of all 6 stem wires.

2. Tape a bud to the end of each short wire.

3. Use assembly wire to attach 1 pistil, 3 small white petals, and 6 purple petals to the end of each long wire. Tape each down to the previous tape line.

4. Hold all 6 stems together with the flower and bud bases even. Tightly wrap them together with assembly wire, 1" above the tape line. Attach the two tan leaves at the same point. Tape down the stem about 6", and attach the two bi-color leaves opposite each other. Finish taping.

5. Bend the flowers and buds outward. Twist the bi-color leaves into spirals, and bend them into "withered" shapes.

$\mathcal{B}$leeding $\mathcal{H}$eart

My grandfather's garden always included several of these delicate beauties. To this day, I have carried on the same tradition. Now I will never be without one, regardless of the season.

Materials Needed

1 hank of pink or white beads
4 strands of white beads
   (inserts)
5 strands of green beads
26-gauge beading wire
30-gauge assembly wire
18" of 16-gauge stem wire
14" of 16-gauge stem wire
1/2" green floral tape

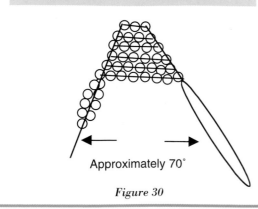

Approximately 70°

Figure 30

Petals (round top, round bottom)

Make 20 (pink or white)

1-bead basic, 13 rows

a. After row 3, bend the basic wire and the basic loop backwards to an approximate 70° position (fig. 30). Continue beading until you complete row 12. (You will be forming a cup.)

b. At the end of row 12, you will be at the top basic wire. Add 4 beads to the basic wire. Bead up and back down these beads. (This will form a 3-row tab on the lip of the cup.) Complete row 13.

c. Reduce to 1 wire, and twist lightly. You now have a "coonskin cap."

d. Find something small and flat—like a Popsicle® stick—and place it inside the cup.

e. Hold it tightly against the basic wire, and pinch the cup flat.

f. Bend the tab and the tip of the cup outward.

Inserts (round top, round bottom)

Make 10 (white)

1/2" basic, 5 rows

    a. After completing row 4, add 4 beads to the basic wire.

    b. Bead up and then down the 4 beads, as in the petals.

    c. Complete row 5.

    d. Reduce to 1 wire, and twist lightly. This is shaped like an elongated figure 8.

Buds

Make 1 (pink and white)

    a. Cut 8" of wire. Center 2" of pink beads, and make a loop.

    b. Add more beads to form the Crossover Loop. Begin with 3/4" of pink, add 1/2" of white, and end with 3/4" of pink. Position the beads so that the bud is white on the tips.

    c. Twist it into a spiral.

Make 1 (pink and white)

    a. Cut 8" of wire. Center 1 1/2" of pink beads, and make a loop.

    b. In the same manner, form the next Crossover Loop. Begin with 1/2" of pink, add 1/2" of white, and end with 1/2" of pink. Position the beads so that the bud is white on the tips.

    c. Twist it into a spiral.

Make 1 (pink)

    a. Leaving 2" of wire before and after, form a 1" Crossover Loop.

    b. Twist it into a spiral.

Leaves (pointed top and bottom)

Make 2 (green) (right)

1" basic, 9 rows

    a. After row 7, bead up the right side to 1/2" from the top.

    b. Turn and bead back down to the bottom.

    c. Reduce to 2 wires, and twist.

    d. Lace the leaf, 1/2" below the folded tip.

    e. Bend the tip outward.

Make 2 (green) (left)

1" basic, 9 rows

    a. After completing row 7, bead up the left side to 1/2" from the top.

    b. Turn and bead back down to the bottom.

    c. Reduce to 2 wires, and twist.

    d. Lace the leaf 1/2" below the folded tip.

    e. Bend the tip outward.

Make 2 (green) (center)

1" basic, 11 rows

    a. After row 7, bead up the right side to 1/2" from the top.

    b. Turn and bead back down to the bottom.

    c. Bead up the left side to 1/2" from the top.

    d. Turn and bead back down to the bottom.

    e. Reduce to 2 wires, and twist.

    f. Lace the leaf 1/2" below the folded tips.

    g. Bend the tips outward.

Assembly

1. Lightly tape the stem wires.

2. Using 2 flattened petals and one insert, slide a pink petal over each "shoulder" of the white insert. Hold all 3 wires together, and twist. Tape lightly. Assemble each of the 10 flowers in the same manner.

3. On the 18" stem wire, tape the smallest bud to the tip. Tape down 1 1/4", and add the next largest bud. Tape down 1 1/4", and add the last bud. Continue in the same manner, adding 5 flowers to the stem. Set aside.

4. On the 14" stem, tape 5 flowers at 1 1/4" intervals.

5. Put the 2 stems together, and secure the lower 4" with wire.

6. Form 2 leaf groups. Stack 1 each of all 3 leaf types. About 1" from the beads, twist the wires and tape the stem.

7. Adjust them so that the large (center) leaf is in the middle and the right and left leaves have their bent tips on the outside of the group.

8. Position them below the "V" of the main stem, and wire them in place. Tape the stem.

Garden Tulip

There is something so neat and pretty about these little Dutch beauties. I think every arrangement deserves a couple!

Materials Needed

1 hank of petal-color beads

1 hank of green beads

1/2 strand of yellow beads

6" of black or brown beads

26-gauge beading wire

30- to 34-gauge wire (for lacing)

Two 9" pieces of 18- or 20-gauge stem wire (to stiffen leaves)

16" of 16-gauge (or heavier) stem wire

1/2" green floral tape

Petals (round top, round bottom)
Make 6 (petal color)
1/2" basic, 21 rows (Leave 3 wires, and twist.)

Leaves (pointed top, round bottom)
Make 2 (green)
4" basic, 19 rows
a. Use one of the 9" pieces of wire, and then use Stem Stiffening Method 1 to strengthen.
b. Leave 3 wires, and twist.

Pistil
Make 1 (yellow)
a. Cut a 10" piece of wire, and mark the center.

b. Put the 30 beads on the wire, push them to the center, and make three 10-bead loops.
c. Put 1 1/4" of beads on each wire.
d. Twist the entire length.

Stamens
Make 6 (black or brown)
a. Cut 5" of 34-gauge lacing wire. Put 1" of beads on the center of the wire.
b. Skipping the first bead, thread back through all of the remaining beads.
c. Twist them together in groups of 2.

Assembly

1. Lace all of the petals.

2. Lightly tape the stem wire.

3. Using assembly wire, attach the pistil and stamens to the top of the stem. Add 3 petals, and wire them in place. Add the other 3 petals below the spaces of the first set. Tape down the entire stem.

4. Position both leaves about 4" from the bottom. Wire them in place. Tape down the stem. You may also bead this stem.

Lily-Flowering Tulip

This striking tulip is so large that it only takes 3 or 4 flowers to make an impressive display. However, it's a little too large for most bouquets.

Materials Needed

1 1/2 hanks of red beads

3/4 hank of yellow beads

1 hank of green beads

20 black beads

26-gauge beading wire

30- to 34-gauge wire (for lacing)

Six 8" pieces of 28-gauge wire (to stiffen petals)

Two 9" pieces of 18- or 20-gauge stem wire (to stiffen leaves)

16" of 16-gauge (or heavier) stem wire

1/2" green floral tape

Petals (pointed top, round bottom)
Make 6 (red and yellow)
3" basic, 15 rows

   a. After completing row 9, leave 1 1/2" of red beads close to the petal.
   b. Measure about 3 feet of bare wire, and cut the petal from the spool.
   c. Add enough yellow beads to complete row 10. Add enough yellow beads to come 1 1/2" from the bottom.
   d. Add 1 1/2" of red beads, and complete row 11. Do the same thing for the next 4 rows, but use 1" of red beads for rows 12 and 13, and use 1/2" of red beads for rows 14 and 15.
   e. Leave 3 wires.
   f. Use a 6" piece of 28-gauge wire to stiffen the stem. Use Stem Stiffening Method 2.

Leaves (pointed top, round bottom)
Make 2 (green)
4" basic, 19 rows

   a. Leave 3 wires.
   b. Stiffen the leaves using Stem Stiffening Method 1.

Pistil
Make 1 (black and green)

   a. Cut a 10" piece of wire, and mark the center.
   b. Put the 20 black beads on the wire, push them to the center, and make two 10-bead loops.
   c. Put 3" of green beads on each wire.
   d. Twist the entire length.

Assembly

1. Lightly tape the stem wire.

2. Using assembly wire, attach the pistil to the top of the stem.

3. Add 3 petals, and wire them in place. Attach the second 3 petals below the spaces of the first 3.

4. Position both leaves about 4" from the bottom. Wire the leaves in place. Tape the entire stem.

Daffodil & Narcissus

It seems like all daffodils used to be yellow. Now any combination of yellow and white, pink and white, or pale green can be found. This allows you to make a bright and colorful spring bouquet using just this flower.

Materials Needed

1 hank of yellow beads
1/2 hank of green beads
1 strand of matte yellow beads
26-gauge beading wire
30- to 34-gauge wire (for lacing and assembly)
18" of 16-gauge stem wire*
1/2" green floral tape

*If you plan to use the flowers in a bouquet, use longer stem wires and attach 1 or 2 leaves to each.

Petals (pointed top, round bottom)
>**Make 12 (yellow)**
>1" basic, 9 rows (Leave 3 wires, and twist.)

Center Cups
>**Make 2 (yellow)**
>>a. Leave 2" of bare wire. Make 12 Continuous Loops using 3 1/2" of beads per loop (1" per loop for narcissus). Leave 2" of bare wire, and cut from spool. Pinch loops closed.
>>b. Lace the loops together 1/2" from the tips of the loops (lace across the center for narcissus) (fig. 31).
>>c. When you get to the edge, bring the sides together, and lace them in place. Just above the lacing, bend the tips outward.

Pistil
>**Make 2 (matte yellow)**
>>a. Using 2" of beads for the first loop, make a single Crossover Loop, and twist wires.
>>b. Make 3 Continuous Loops for the narcissus, 1/2" of beads each.

Leaves (pointed top, round bottom)
>**Make 3 (green)**
>6" basic, 5 rows
>>a. Leave 3 wires, and twist.
>>b. Lace each leaf twice.

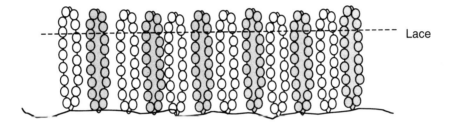

Lace

Once laced, bring the ends of the lacing wire together and twist.
Bring bottom wires together and twist them also.

Figure 31

Assembly

1. Lightly tape the stem wires.

2. Put a pistil into the center of a laced cup. Twist all the wires together.

3. Using assembly wire, attach the center assembly to the top of the stem wire.

4. Still using assembly wire, attach 6 of the petals (3 at a time). Tape down the entire stem. Repeat for the second flower.

5. Two inches from their bottoms, wire the two flowers together.

6. Position all 3 leaves. Wire them in place, and tape.

7. About 1/2" from the flower, bend the flower stems downward.

Pansy

This is such a pretty and cheerful little flower. Choose almost any color you want. You can even leave out the petal shading, if you choose.

Materials Needed

1/2 hank of petal-color beads
1 hank of green beads
1 strand of black beads
12 yellow beads
26-gauge gold or colored beading wire
30- to 34-gauge assembly wire
6" of 16-gauge stem wire
1/2" green floral tape

Petals (round top, round bottom)

Make 2 (petal color)

1-bead basic, 19 rows (Reduce to 2 wires, and twist.)

Add beads, as you need them, according to shading charts.

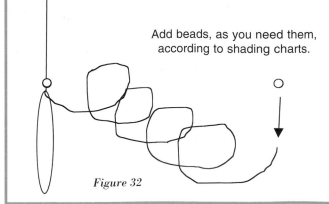

Figure 32

Make 3

1-bead basic, 17 rows

   a. Cut at least 3 feet of bare wire. Use it to form your basic wire and basic loop.

   b. Feed the beads that you need onto the cut end of the wire (fig. 32). For two of the petals, use Shading Chart #1. For the third petal, use Shading Chart #2.

   c. On the even numbered rows, add your shading beads at the beginning of the row. On the odd numbered rows, add the shading beads at the end of the rows.

   d. Complete each row with the petal-color beads.

   e. Reduce to 2 wires, and twist.

Pansy Shading Chart#1	
Row #	
1 -	1 black (basic)
2 -	2 black
3 -	2 black
4 -	3 black
5 -	3 black
6 -	5 black
7 -	5 black
8 -	6 black
9 -	6 black
10 -	7 black
11 -	7 black
12 -	7 black
13 -	7 black
14 -	7 black
15 -	7 black
16 -	6 black
17 -	6 black

Pansy Shading Chart#2	
Row #	
1 -	petal color (basic)
2 -	petal color
3 -	petal color
4 -	petal color
5 -	petal color
6 -	5 black
7 -	5 black
8 -	6 black
9 -	6 black
10 -	6 black
11 -	6 black + 1 yellow
12 -	1 yellow + 6 black
13 -	6 black + 2 yellow
14 -	2 yellow + 6 black
15 -	5 black + 2 yellow
16 -	2 yellow + 5 black
17 -	4 black + 2 yellow

Buds

Make 1 (petal color)

a. Leave 8" of bare wire. Make 2 Continuous Loops, using 1" of beads for each loop.

b. Leave 8" of bare wire, and cut. Don't twist.

c. Twist the beaded loops into a spiral.

Make 1 (petal color)

a. Leave 8" of bare wire. Make 2 Continuous Loops, using 1 1/2" of beads for each loop.

b. Leave 8" of bare wire, and cut. Don't twist.

c. Twist the beaded loops into a spiral.

Make 1 (petal color)

a. Leave 8" of bare wire. Make 3 Continuous Loops using 2" of beads for each loop.

b. Leave 8" of bare wire, and cut. Don't twist.

c. Twist the beaded loops into a spiral.

Sepals

Make 1 (green)

a. Leave 8" of bare wire. Make 4 Continuous Loops, using 3/4" of beads per loop.

b. Leave 8" of bare wire, and cut.

Make 3 (green)

a. Leave 8" of bare wire. Make 4 Continuous Loops, using 1" of beads per loop.

b. Leave 8" of bare wire, and cut.

Leaves

Make 10 (green)

1 1/2" basic, 3 rows

a. Use 3" of beads to make a loop on both the right and left side of the stem, repeat the procedure using 2 1/2" of beads for each loop (fig. 27, see page 449).

b. Leave 3 wires, and twist.

c. Flatten the loops tight against either side of the 3-row leaf.

d. Lace once across the leaf, making sure to catch 1/4" below the tips of the shortest loops in the lacing.

e. Twist wires, and tape.

Assembly

1. Slip the smallest bud into the smallest sepal. Twist the wires, and tape. Tape a leaf about 2" to 3" from the bud. Assemble the other 2 buds in the same manner. Bend the stems at an angle, about 1/2" from the buds.

2. Hold the 3 shaded petals together with their bases even. Wrap the stems twice with assembly wire.

3. Position the two large petals behind the black shaded petals. Wrap them again with assembly wire.

4. Position the last sepal tight against the back of the flower, and twist all of the wires together.

5. Wire this to the 6" stem wire. Add 2 leaves, one 3" down the stem, the second 1" below the first. Tape the stem.

6. Hold the bloom and buds together in a nosegay. Wrap the bottoms with assembly wire.

7. Add 3 leaves, at the same level, to the wired stem.

8. Drop down 1/2", and add the other 3 leaves. Tape the assembly area.

Hydrangea

Large and lovely! This flower looks great in large, tall bouquets. Choose any shade of pink or blue, as well as light green or white.

Materials Needed

2 hanks of petal-color beads

1 hank of green beads

1/2 strand of yellow beads

26-gauge beading wire

30- to 34-gauge assembly wire

18" of 1/8" rod for the stem (or 4 to 5 16-gauge stems taped together)

1/2" green floral tape

Flowerets
Make 30 (petal color)
a. Leave 5" of bare wire.

b. Using 7 beads for the first loops, make four Continuous Triple Loops (six rows across). Simply go around the Continuous Double Loop one more time.

c. Bring the wire up between the first two petals that you made, and then bring it back down between the last two petals constructed.

d. Measure 5" of bare wire, and cut the wire from the spool.

e. Intending to form an "X" in the flower's center with the wire you previously drew across the top, bring the other cut wire back up between the second and third petals. Put 2 yellow beads on the wire.

f. Bring the wire across the top, centering the yellow beads on the top of the flower. Pull the wire down the other side, completing the "X."

g. Pull the wires together, and twist.

Leaves (pointed top, round bottom)
Make 2 (green)
4-bead basic, 37 rows

a. Leave 3 wires, twist, tape, and lace.

b. Make a slight crease down the center of the leaf, and then bend the tip down slightly.

Assembly

1. Lightly tape the stem rod.

2. Make 5 groups of 4 flowerets each. About 1 1/4" from the flowerets, twist the wires and tape lightly.

3. An inch from the top of the taped area, bend the stems 90°. Use assembly wire to connect all five groups to the top of the stem rod. (This should look like a wheel with 5 spokes.)

4. Use the remaining 10 flowerets to form a nosegay. Twist and tape the stems, as in the 4 floweret groups. Drop the nosegay down into the center of the "hub" just constructed. Position the nosegay at an attractive level. Wire it in place. Tape the assembly area.

5. Wire and tape the first leaf 4" from the flower. Drop down 3" to 4", and attach the second leaf. Tape the stem again. Tug the flowerets lightly into position, filling in the empty spaces. (If there are any large gaps that cannot be filled by repositioning, make 1 or 2 more flowerets, drop them into the holes, and tape them in place.)

Gladiola

Tall and graceful, this majestic flower is a must in any large bouquet. Please excuse my fantasy color of navy blue. I needed it to go with my hydrangeas.

Materials Needed

3 hanks of petal-color beads
2 strands of contrasting-color
    beads (for the stamens)
1/2 hank of green beads
26-gauge beading wire
34-gauge wire (for the pistil
    and stamens)
18" of 20-gauge stem wire (to
    stiffen leaf)
30- to 34-gauge assembly wire
24" of 1/8" stem rod
1/2" green floral tape

Petals (round top, pointed bottom)
(Lace all of the petals.)

Make 3 (petal color)
6-bead basic, 21 rows
(Reduce to 2 wires, and twist.)

Make 6 (petal color)
6-bead basic, 19 rows
(Reduce to 2 wires, and twist.)

Make 6 (petal color)
6-bead basic, 17 rows
(Reduce to 2 wires, and twist.)

Make 6 (petal color)
6-bead basic, 15 rows
(Reduce to 2 wires, and twist.)

Make 6 (petal color)
6-bead basic, 13 rows
(Reduce to 2 wires, and twist.)

Make 3 (petal color)
6-bead basic, 11 rows
(Reduce to 2 wires, and twist.)

Buds (pointed tops, round bottoms)

Make 2 (petal color)

6-bead basic, 11 rows (Leave 3 wires, and twist.)

Make 2 (petal color)

6-bead basic, 9 rows (Leave 3 wires, and twist.)

Make 2 (green)

1" basic, 9 rows (Leave 3 wires, and twist.)

Make 1 (green)

3/4" basic, 7 rows (Leave 3 wires, and twist.)

Pistil

Make 5 (petal color and contrasting color)

a. Cut 8" of 34-gauge wire. Thread 6 beads (petal color) onto the wire, and center them.

b. Thread one end of the wire back through 5 beads, skipping the one closest to the end of the wire that you are using.

c. Add 6 beads to the wire, and thread back through the 5 beads furthest from the tip.

d. Do this once more. Bring the 2 wires together. Slide 1" of beads (contrasting color) onto the two combined wires (fig. 33).

Stamens

Make 15 (contrasting color)

a. Cut 6" of 34-gauge wire. String 1 1/4" beads onto the wire.

b. Thread back through all but 1 bead.

c. Twist the stamens together in groups of 3.

Sepals (pointed top, round bottom)

Make 20 (green)

6-bead basic, 7 rows (Leave 3 wires, and twist.)

Leaf (pointed top, round bottom)

Make 1 (green)

14" basic, 9 rows

a. After measuring the basic row, stiffen the leaf with Stem Stiffening Method 1.

b. Leave 3 wires, and twist.

Make stamens by threading back through

Figure 33

Finish by bringing the bottom wires together and threading both through the desired number of beads.

Assembly

1. Lightly tape the stem rod.

2. 3 green buds—Lightly fold each green bud petal in half, lengthwise. Add 2 sepals, twist the wires, and tape.

3. 2 petal-color buds—Lightly fold the colored bud petals in half, lengthwise. Matching the sizes, put 2 bud petals together with edges interlocking, add 2 sepals, twist the wires, and tape.

4. Flowers—Put 1 pistil and 3 stamens together, and twist the wires. Position the 3 smallest petals around the pistil-stamen group, and wrap twice with assembly wire. Add 3 of the next largest petals, and wrap again with assembly wire. Twist all of the wires together, trim them to 2 1/2", and tape. Repeat this process until all 5 flowers are completed.

5. Without cutting the assembly wire between items, use it to attach the smallest green bud to the tip of the stem. Drop down 1 1/2" and (directly below the first) add another green bud, leaving 1" of taped bud stem free.

6. Continue by adding the last green bud, the last 2 colored buds (smallest first), the flowers (smallest to largest), and the leaf in the same manner.

7. Tape the entire stem. Slightly adjust the flowers and buds (one right, one left) down the entire length.

Sansevieria
(Mother-in-Law's Tongue)

Not my mother-in-law's, of course.

Materials Needed

2 hanks of medium green beads

3/4 hank of pale yellow beads

26-gauge wire

30- to 34-gauge assembly wire

1/2" green floral tape

Leaves (pointed tops, round bottom)
Make 2 of each size

1/2" basic, 9 rows
- a. First use 7 green, measure 4" of bare wire, and cut.
- b. Make the last 2 rows yellow.
- c. Leave 3 wires, and twist.

3/4" basic, 11 rows
- a. First use 7 green, measure 9" of bare wire, and cut.
- b. Make the last 4 rows yellow.
- c. Leave 3 wires, and twist.

3/4" basic, 13 rows
- a. First use 9 green, measure 10" of bare wire, and cut.
- b. Make the last 4 rows yellow.
- c. Leave 3 wires, and twist.

3/4" basic, 15 rows
- a. First use 11 green, measure 11" of bare wire, and cut.
- b. Make the last 4 rows yellow.
- c. Leave 3 wires, and twist.

1" basic, 17 rows
- a. First use 13 green, measure 12" of bare wire, and cut.
- b. Make the last 4 rows yellow.
- c. Leave 3 wires, and twist.

1" basic, 19 rows
- a. First use 15 green, measure 13" of bare wire, and cut.
- b. Make the last 4 rows yellow.
- c. Leave 3 wires, and twist.

1" basic, 21 rows
- a. First use 17 green, measure 14" of bare wire, and cut.
- b. Make the last 4 rows yellow.
- c. Leave 3 wires, and twist.

Assembly

1. Lace all of the leaves once, one third of the way from the tips.

2. Use assembly wire to bind the two smallest leaves together. Continue to add the leaves, smallest to largest.

3. Once you have them all connected, twist all of the stem wires together tightly. Trim the stem to 2" or 3", and tape.

*I*ris

*T*all, straight, and majestic, the iris always turns heads with its striking beauty. Purples, blues, lavenders, yellows, and white give you a large choice when choosing the ideal iris for your display.

Materials Needed

1 1/4 hanks of petal-color beads
1/2 strand of yellow beads
1/2 hank of green beads
26-gauge beading wire
22-gauge green floral wire (for the leaves)*
30- to 34-gauge assembly wire
18" of 1/8" metal rod (or 4 16-gauge wires wired together)
1/2" green floral tape

*10/0 beads will usually slide on the 22-gauge wire. If you are using smaller beads or the holes are too small, use a finer gauge wire, and stiffen the leaf using Stem Stiffening Method 1.

Petals (round top, pointed bottom) (Lace all of the petals.)

> **Make 3 (petal color)**
> 1/2" basic, 21 rows (Leave 3 wires, and twist.)
>
> **Make 3 (petal color)**
> 3/4" basic, 19 rows (When completed, use Stem Stiffening Method 2.)
>
> **Make 3 (petal color)**
> 1 1/2" basic, 7 rows (Leave 3 wires, and twist.)

Beard

> **Make 3 (yellow)**
> a. Leave 3" of bare wire. Make a single loop of 3" of yellow beads.
> b. Leave 3" of bare wire, cut, and twist.
> c. Pinch the loop closed, and twist into a spiral.

Leaf (pointed top, round bottom)

> **Make 1 (green)**
> 8" basic, 9 rows on 22-gauge floral wire (Leave 3 wires, and twist.)

Assembly

1. Lightly tape the stem wire.

2. Wrinkle the edges of the 3 large and 3 small petals by bending the outer rows (similar to crimping the edges of a pie crust).

3. Using assembly wire, attach all 3 of the medium petals (the ones that have stiffened stems) to the top of the stem wire, making sure that the back sides are facing inward. Cup them top to bottom, and side to side. Leave the petals pointed upward. Set aside.

4. Matching the bottoms, lay a beard along the center of the right side of a large petal. Lightly twist the wires. Use a short piece of wire to tack the beard in place. (Push the wire up from the underside of the petal, go through just the lower side of the beard loop, about 1/4" from the tip. Thread the wire back through to the underside of the petal. Twist the 2 ends together, trim to 1/8", and tuck the wire out of sight.)

5. Place one of the small petals over the top of the beard, front side down. Match the bottoms, and twist the three wires. Mold the sides of the small petal around the beard, cocoon fashion. Bend the tip of the small petal up and back to reveal about 1/2 of the beard. Repeat with the other 2 sets.

6. Positioning the large petal assemblies below the spaces between the medium petals, use assembly wire to attach all 3 large petal assemblies to the stem. Cut the exposed petal wires to different lengths so that they feather down the stem and don't create a lump. Tape down the stem.

7. Use assembly wire to attach the leaf at an attractive position, about 7" below the bloom.

8. Tape the stem again. Rub and smooth the tape to seal the wax.

Hibiscus

This flower grows on a shrub that brings an air of elegance to any patio. Choose red, pink, orange, or yellow for a realistic effect.

Materials Needed

1 hank of pink beads
1/2 hank of dark green beads
10 yellow beads
26-gauge beading wire
30- to 34-gauge assembly wire
18" of 16-gauge stem wire
1/2" green floral tape
1/2" brown floral tape

Petals (flat top, pointed bottom) (Lace all of the petals.)

Make 5 (petal color)

1-bead basic, 23 rows

    a. Use 8 beads each for rows 2 and 3.

    b. Push the top down tight against the center bead, forming a short, flat, sideways oval.

    c. After row 3, begin forming the pointed bottom. Keep the top flat by continuously pushing the top beads down tight against the previous row (fig. 34).

    d. Leave 3 wires, and twist.

Figure 34

Stamens

Make 10 (yellow)

    a. Cut 6" of wire

    b. Fold it in half, and add 1 yellow bead to the center.

    c. Twist the entire length.

Leaves (pointed top, pointed bottom) (Lace all of the leaves.)

Make 4 (green)

8-bead basic, 15 rows

    a. Leave 3 wires, and twist.

    b. After the leaves are completed, tape the leaf stems with 1/2" green floral tape.

Assembly

1. Lightly tape the stem wire with brown floral tape.

2. Gather all of the stamens together with the top beads even. Pinch tightly 1/2" from the beads. Twist all of the bottom wires together. Use assembly wire to attach this group to the end of the brown stem, leaving 1 3/4" of the stamen assembly above the stem.

3. Attach all 5 of the petals, one at a time, making sure to overlap slightly on one side only. Trim the exposed wires to different lengths, and tape down the stem.

4. Make a circle with your thumb and forefinger. Push the flower down into the circle to form a trumpet shape. Push the centers of the petals outward to widen the center of the trumpet. Flare the petal tips outward. Spread the top 1/2" of the stamen assembly into a starburst.

5. Wrinkle the edges of the leaves slightly. Use assembly wire to attach the leaves to the stem at 1 1/4" intervals on alternate sides of the stem. Be sure to leave about 1/2" of the green, taped wire showing.

6. Re-tape the entire main stem with brown tape. Rub the stem to seal the wax.

African Violet

This is described as everyone's favorite houseplant. However, once you've killed as many as I have, this beaded beauty comes as a welcome addition to the windowsill.

Materials Needed

1/2 hank of petal-color beads
2 hanks of green beads
1/2 strand of yellow beads
26-gauge beading wire
30- to 34-gauge wire (for lacing)
1/2" green floral tape

Flowers
Make 17 (petal color)
   a. Leave 5" of bare wire. Use 3/4" of beads for each inner loop.
   b. Make 4 Double Continuous Loops, or use 4-row Crossover Loops for a more compact look. Leave 5" of bare wire, and cut.
   c. Bring one of the bottom wires up between the first two petals made.
   d. Pull the wire back down between the last two petals made.
   e. Intending to form an "X" in the center of the flower, bring the other wire up between the two side petals.
   f. Put 2 yellow beads on the wire, and center them on top of the flower.
   g. Pull the wire back down on the opposite side.
   h. Pull the two wires together, and twist lightly.

Buds
Make 4 (petal color)
   a. Leave 5" of bare wire. Use 3/4" of beads for each loop.
   b. Make 4 Continuous Loops. Leave 5" of bare wire, and cut.
   c. Pull the two wires together, and twist lightly.
   d. Pinch the loops closed, and cup them toward the center.

Leaves (pointed top, round bottom) (Lace all of the leaves.)
Make 3 (green)
1/2" basic, 25 rows (Leave 3 wires, and twist.)
Make 3 (green)
1/2" basic, 27 rows (Leave 3 wires, and twist.)

Assembly

1. Position the flowers in groups of 4. About 1" from the blooms, twist the wires lightly. The last group will have 1 bloom and 4 buds. Position all of the groups together to form a nosegay. Twist the lower 3" together.

2. Use assembly wire to attach 3 leaves to the lower 3" of the flowers. Drop down 1/4" and attach the last 3 leaves. Trim the wires to the same length, and cover the assembly area with green floral tape.

Oriental Poppy

Materials Needed

(1 flower, 1 bud, 2 leaves)

1 hank of petal-color beads

3 strands of navy or black beads

1 hank of light green beads

26-gauge beading wire

22-gauge (for 10/0 beads) or
24-gauge (for 11/0 beads) wire
(for leaves)

Four 16" pieces of 16-gauge stem
wires, or two 16" pieces of
1/8" stem wires

1/2" green floral tape

What a wonderful flower! You can make this one in red, orange, pink, white, or pale yellow. You can also omit the dark area on the petal for some varieties.

Petals (flat top, pointed bottom) (See fig. 34, page 475)

Make 6 (petal color)

1-bead basic, 23 rows

    a. Cut 6 feet of bare wire. Make a basic wire and loop as you normally would, but without the beads. You will be adding the beads, as needed, from the opposite end of the wire. (If you have trouble with the added beads sliding off the cut end of the wire, clip your hemostats on the end of the wire.)

    b. Put 1 bead on the basic wire and 16 on the cut wire.

    c. Use 8 beads for row 2, and use 8 beads for row 3. Push the rows down tight against the center bead, forming a very short, wide petal. As you work, keep the top of the petal flat and gradually work the bottom to a point.

    d. For the next 10 rows, begin each even-numbered row with 4 navy beads, and end each odd-numbered row with 4 navy beads. (Use the petal-color beads to complete the rows.)

    e. Finish the rest of the petals with the petal-color beads.

    f. Leave 3 wires, and twist.

Stamens

Make 1 (navy)

Using 2" of beads per loop, make 20 Continuous Loops.

Center Pod (String the beads on green wire.)

Make 1 (petal color, green, or navy)

Combination of beehive and basket bottom.

Note: Since you want the wires to show on the top of the pod, you will be displaying what is normally the back side of this piece.

    a. Cut three 6" pieces of green wire. Hold them together and, leaving 3" of bare wire overlapping the center, wrap the beaded spool wire twice around the center of the cut pieces.

    b. Spread the wires open like the spokes of a wheel. You will now bead around this by placing the required number of beads between the spokes and wrapping the wire around each spoke (fig. 35).

    c. Since this is "back side up," bring your wire under and around the spoke each time you wrap it.

    d. Place beads as follows (When the number of beads decreases, bend wires backwards to accommodate the shorter distances):

Round #1—Put 1 bead between each spoke.
Round #2—Put 2 beads between each spoke.
Round #3—Put 3 beads between each spoke.
Round #4—Put 5 beads between each spoke.
Round #5—Put 6 beads between each spoke.
Round #6—Put 6 beads between each spoke.
Round #7—Put 5 beads between each spoke.
Round #8—Put 5 beads between each spoke.
Round #9—Put 5 beads between each spoke.
Round #10—Put 4 beads between each spoke.

    e. Straighten the wires. Shape them into a smooth, round pod.

    f. Bring the wires together under the center, and twist (fig. 35).

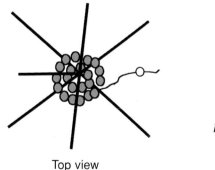

Figure 35

Top view

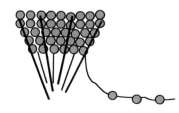

Side view

Sepals and Bud
Make 6 (green)
1/2" basic, 11 rows
- a. After completing row 5, bend the top basic wire backwards 90°.
- b. Once complete, DON'T cut the top basic wire on 3 of these.
- c. Leave 3 wires, and twist.

Leaves
Make 2 (green)
- a. Use 22- or 24-gauge wire to make these as stiff as possible. Leave 3" of bare wire.

- b. Make the following series of loops (leaving 1/2" of beads between each of the loops):

Make 3 loops using 2" of beads per loop.
Make 3 loops using 1 1/2" of beads per loop.
Make 7 loops using 1" of beads per loop.
Make 3 loops using 1 1/2" of beads per loop.
Make 3 loops using 2" of beads per loop.

- c. Leave 1" of beads and 2" of bare wire, and cut.
- d. Put 1" of beads on the beginning bare wire. Put the wires together, and twist.
- e. Fold the circle closed, and twist the entire length.
- f. Give the large individual loops a half twist.

Assembly

Using either one heavy or two light stem wires, wired together, lightly tape the stems.

Bud
1. Using the 3 bud/sepal pieces that still have the long basic wires intact, hold the tips together, and twist the top wires.

2. Trim the wires to 1/2", and tuck them inside the bud.

3. Bring the bottom wires together, and twist.

4. Use assembly wire to attach this to the top of one of the stems. Drop down about 4", and wire a leaf in place. Lightly tape down the stem.

Flower
1. Allowing 1/2" of the stem to go up inside, use assembly wire to attach the pod to the top of the second stem wire. Keep the assembly wire attached.

2. Directly below the pod, wrap the 20-loop stamen wire around the stem. Keep it as close to the pod as possible. Wrap any trailing ends with the assembly wire.

3. Add the 6 petals, 3 at a time, with the second row directly under the spaces of the first row. Center a sepal under each of the lower petals, and again use the assembly wire to secure these.

4. Drop down about 4", and wire the other leaf in place.

5. Hold the bud and flower stems together, and decide where they should be joined, if at all. If you are joining them, mark each stem where they will be coming together. DON'T join at this time.

Bead the Stems
1. String about 5 feet of green beads.

2. Do the bud FIRST. Wrap the beads down to your mark. End here by wrapping the bare wire several times around the stem, as close to the beads as possible.

3. Then spiral the wire down a few inches before cutting.

4. Do the same thing to the flower stem. DON'T cut the wire when you reach the mark. Once you reach the mark, use another piece of wire to tightly attach the two stems together.

5. Continue beading down the stem (now going around both stem wires). Stop at least 1" to 3" from the bottom. End as before.

6. Cut the wire, and cover all exposed wire with floral tape.

Tiger Lily

Change the colors and mix them up to make all sorts of garden lilies. This same pattern, completed in white, is the perfect Easter lily. Bend the petals to produce your favorite lily shape. Even change the leaves to a pair of iris leaves to produce other varieties.

Materials Needed

3 hanks of petal-color beads
1 hank of brown beads
3 1/2 hanks of medium green beads
1/2 strand of yellow beads
26-gauge beading wire
30- to 34-gauge assembly wire
Four 18" pieces of 16-gauge, or
     heavier, stem wire
1/2" green floral tape

Bud (pointed top, round bottom)
Make 4 (solid petal color)
3" basic, 5 rows (Leave 3 wires, and twist.)

Petals (pointed top, round bottom) (Lace all of the petals.)
Make 18 (For spots, mix 3 parts petal color with 1 part brown before stringing.)
2 1/2" basic, 13 rows (Leave 3 wires, and twist.)

Stamens

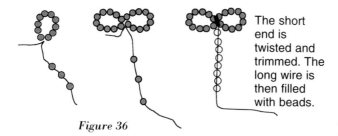

Figure 36

The short end is twisted and trimmed. The long wire is then filled with beads.

Make 18 (petal color and brown)
a. Place 24 brown beads on wire strung with petal-color beads. Leave 1" of bare wire.
b. Make two 12-bead loops.
c. Thread the 1" of bare wire down through one of the loops, and pull it tight. Trim it off close to the underside of the loops.

d. Slide 2" of petal-color beads close to the loops. Leave 2" of bare wire, and cut.
e. Twist the stamens together in groups of 2 (fig. 36).
f. Shape into a "T."

Pistil
Make 3 (yellow and petal color)
a. Cut 12" of bare wire. Put 24 yellow beads on the wire. Leave 4 1/2" of bare wire.
b. Make three 8-bead loops. Put 2 1/2" of petal-color beads on each of the wires. Twist the entire length of both wires.
c. Bend all 3 loops down to form a yellow knob on the tip.
d. Twist each pistil together with 6 stamens (three 2-stamen groups).

Leaves (pointed top, round bottom) (Lace all of the leaves.)
Make 12 (green)
4" basic, 9 rows (Leave 3 wires, and twist.)
Make 4 (green)
2" basic, 7 rows (Leave 3 wires, and twist.)

Assembly

1. Lightly tape the top 4" of the stem wires.
2. Hold all of the buds tightly together. Twist them into a spiral. Use assembly wire to attach the bud to the end of one of the stem wires.
3. Use assembly wire to attach a stamen-pistil group to the end of another wire. Add 3 petals, and wire in place. Place the next 3 petals below the spaces of the first 3, and wire in place. Tape over the assembly area. Repeat for the other 2 flowers.
4. Beginning tight against the base of the flower, bead 3" of the stem with medium green.

Beginning where the beading ends, wire all of the stems together.
5. Use assembly wire to attach the 4 small leaves where the stems meet. Attach the rest of the leaves, 2 leaves at a time, opposite each other, every 1 1/4" down the stem.
6. Finish beading the stem. Tape over any exposed wires.

Liatris
(Gayfeather)

This eye catcher makes a great focal point or filler. A full bouquet of these, in purple and white, makes a stunning upright display.

Materials Needed

1 hank of petal-color beads
1/2 hank of green beads
26- or 28-gauge beading wire
26- or 28-gauge colored beading wire
16" of 16-gauge or heavier stem wire
1/2" green floral tape

Petals

a. Begin by stringing the entire hank of petal-color beads onto the colored beading wire. Leave 3" of bare wire.

b. Using 1" of beads for each loop, make 14" of Continuous Loops, leaving 3 beads between each loop.

c. Continue by making another 14" of Continuous Loops, using 3/4" of beads per loop, with 3 beads between loops.

d. Finish with 7" of 1/2" Continuous Loops, again with 3 beads between the loops. Leave 3" of bare wire.

Leaves

a. String the entire 1/2 hank of green beads onto the green wire. Leave 3" of bare wire.

b. Make 6" of Continuous Loops, using 2" of beads per loop and 3 beads between loops.

c. Make another 6" of loops, using 3" of beads per loop and the 3 bead spacers.

Assembly

1. Lightly tape the stem wire.

Join the strands of petal loops and leaf loops so that they overlap.

Figure 38

2. Halfway along the area of the smallest petal loops (about 3 1/2" from the bottom), connect the length of leaf loops by twisting the bare green wire, closest to the shortest leaf loops, around the beaded wire (fig. 38).

3. Hold the large petal's end loop, so that the base is even with the top of the stem wire. Wrap the unbeaded wire around and down the stem.

4. Begin wrapping the petal loops (with connected leaf loops) around and down the stem by twirling the stem wire. Keep the rows tight against each other so none of the taped stem shows through. Go all the way down, until you run out of loops. Then wrap the bare wire around the stem. Cover the bare wire with floral tape.

Calla Lily

As much as I love the calla, you would think I would be able to grow one. Unfortunately, I think one of the critters in my yard also enjoys these delicate beauties. So, for now, I'll have to keep to the beaded variety. For a realistic plant, choose white, pink, lavender, red, orange, or yellow for your petal.

Materials Needed

1 hank of petal-color beads

1 1/4 hank of green beads

3 strands of yellow beads

24-gauge beading wire

30- to 34-gauge wire (for lacing and assembly)

Two 16" pieces of 16-gauge or heavier stem wire

1/2" green floral tape

Petal (pointed top, round bottom)
Make 1 (petal color)
2-bead basic, 59 rows

    a. String the entire hank of petal-color beads before you begin.

    b. After row 50, begin adding an extra bead to the basic wire.

    c. Lace 3 times, once across the center and twice more in an "X" that passes through the center.

    d. Begin on the upper right side, and end on the lower left.

    e. Leave 3 wires, and twist.

Pistil
Make 1 (yellow)

    a. Lightly tape your stem wires together.

    b. Make a small disk, 1-bead basic, 3 rows.

    c. Cut the basic loop open, but DON'T cut from the spool!

    d. Position the disk on the top of the stem wire. Bend the wires down against the stem. Hold the disk tightly in place, and bead down the stem.

    e. Use the entire strand of yellow, approximately 3" of beading.

    f. Wrap 2" of bare wire down the stem. Cut the wire, and tape lightly over it.

Leaves (pointed top, round bottom)
Make 2 (green and yellow)
1" basic, 31 rows

    a. Use one of the 9" pieces of wire and Stem Stiffening Method 2 to strengthen the leaves.

    b. To get the random yellow spots, mix 2 strands of yellow beads with 1 hank of green beads before you begin stringing. If you have a bead spinner, this is a good time to use it.

    c. Add 1 extra bead to the basic wire each time you get to the top of the leaf. This will give you a nice, sharp point.

    d. Leave 3 wires, and twist.

Assembly

1. String the remaining 1/4 hank of green beads. Bead 1" of the stem wires of both leaves. Set them aside.

2. On the pistil, beginning at the bottom of the yellow beads, bead down 1/2" with green. DON'T cut the wire!

3. Gently curl the lower edges of the petal forward. Put a pencil along the center front, and tighten the curl around the pencil. Using lacing wire, tack the two edges together where the lower legs of the lacing "X" come together. Slip the petal over the top of the beaded pistil. Position it so that the base of the petal is exactly even with the bottom of the green beads. Use assembly wire to secure the petal to the stem.

4. Continue beading down the stem for another 3". DON'T cut the wire!

5. Wire the 2 leaves in place, directly below the beads. Continue beading down the stem for at least another 1/2". Wrap several inches of bare wire down the stem. Cut the wire. Tape over any exposed ends.

Hyacinth

Without a doubt, this is our most fragrant early bloomer. I love the smell so much that I add a drop of hyacinth oil to the pot of each beaded replica as the finishing touch. The colors I see most often in our local gardens are purple, pink, lavender, and white.

Materials Needed

2 hanks of petal-color beads

1 hank of green

26 yellow beads

24-gauge beading wire

30-gauge green assembly wire

Four 9" pieces of 20-gauge stem wire (for stiffening leaves)

Two 12" pieces of 16-gauge stem wire

1/2" green floral tape

Flowers
Make 26 (petal color)
a. Leave 2" of bare wire. Using 2" of beads per loop, make six 3-row Crossover Loops. Be sure to pinch the loops closed before beading up the front and down the back. (Remember, on a 3-row Crossover Loop, there is bare wire down the back of each petal.)

b. Once completed, leave 3" of bare wire, and cut. Bring the 3" end across the bottom, up between the first two petals made, and then down between the last two petals made. Pull it tight.

c. Intending to form an "X" in the center of the flower, bring the end back up between two of the side petals, add 1 yellow bead, and bring the wire back down on the opposite side.

d. Twist the wires, and tape them lightly with floral tape that has been cut to 1/4" width.

e. Halfway along the length of the petals, bend them outward. Then pull them all toward the center to form a trumpet shape.

Leaves (pointed top, round bottom)
Make 4 (green)
6" basic, 7 rows

a. Use Stem Stiffening Method 1 to stiffen each leaf.

b. Leave 3 wires, and twist.

Assembly

1. Lightly tape the stem wires together.

2. Using assembly wire, attach a single flower to the end of the stem. Make sure that the beaded portion touches the end of the stem wire. Wrap the wire down about 3/4". Trim the excess flower wire, but DON'T cut the assembly wire.

3. Bend each of the remaining flower stems about 3/8" from the blossoms. Hold the bent portion of the next flower against the stem. Wire it in place so that the edges of the petals just barely touch those of the top flower. Attach 4 more flowers at this level.

4. Wire down about 1", and trim the flower stems. Add another row of 5 flowers at this level. Continue in the same manner until all of the flowers have been used.

5. After wrapping the last row, lightly wrap the assembly wire down the stem for another 3 1/2". Wire all 4 leaves in place with their bases even.

6. Cut the leaf wires all at different lengths, and continue wrapping the assembly wire to the bottom of the stem.

7. Beginning tightly below the bottom row of flowers, use the remaining green beads to bead the stem. End 1" below the leaves. Tape over any visibly exposed assembly wire.

Dwarf Apple Blossom

Most deciduous fruit tree blooms are quite similar. However, ornamental varieties have much larger flowers. If you would rather have the larger flowers, simply double the amount of petal-color beads you need. Then make each petal a double row instead of a single.

Materials Needed

1 hank of white or pink beads (for petals)
1/2 hank of light green beads
2 strands of yellow beads
26-gauge beading wire
34-gauge gold beading wire
30-gauge assembly wire
Three 18" pieces of 16-gauge stem wires
1/2" green floral tape
1/2" brown floral tape

Flowers
Make (approximately) 60 (petal color)
  a. Leaving at least 2" of bare wire at the beginning and end, make five 3/4" Continuous Loops.
  b. Don't twist the wires.

Stamens
Make (approximately) 60
  a. String the yellow beads onto the 34-gauge gold wire.
  b. Leave 2" of bare wire at the beginning and end. Using one bead at a time, slide the bead into position, and twist it between your thumb and forefinger until you have about 1/4" of twisted wire.
  c. Move another bead forward 5/16" from the first, and repeat the procedure. Be sure to twist the second bead until the bare wire between the first two stamens is used completely.

  d. Repeat this procedure until you have 10 stamens in the group (fig. 37).

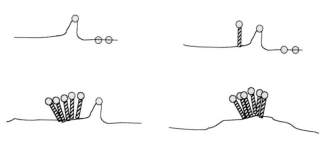

Figure 37

Leaves (pointed top, pointed bottom)
Make 8 (green)
1/2" basic, 7 rows
  a. Reduce to 2 wires, and twist.
  b. Tape the stems with 1/4" green tape.

Assembly

1. Use brown floral tape to lightly tape 1 stem wire. Set this aside.

2. Hold the other 2 stem wires tightly together, and wrap them with brown tape.

Flowers

1. Bring one of the cut end wires across the top of the flower and down between the first and second petals on the opposite side. This will close the flower.

2. Position a stamen group in the center of the flower. Bring the wires down the sides and under the bottom. Twist all 4 wires together. Leaving the bottom 3/4" bare, tape with 1/4" green tape. Repeat for all flowers.

Groups

1. Hold 5 flowers together with the bottoms of the floral-taped area even. Tightly wrap the bottoms of the taped area 2 or 3 times with assembly wire. Tape over this assembly area with brown tape.

2. In the same manner, make 4 groups of 2 leaves each.

Branches

1. Hold the first flower group so that the taped area extends beyond the tip of the thinnest stem wire. Use assembly wire to wrap it in place. DON'T cut the assembly wire. Wrap the wire down the branch at least 1", and add another flower group.

2. Wrap the wire down the branch at least 1", and add another flower group.

3. Wrap the wire down the branch at least 1", and add a leaf group.

4. Wrap the wire down the branch at least 1", and add another leaf group.

5. Wrap the wire down another 2" before cutting. Tape over the assembly area with brown tape, beginning at the tip and going down about 1 1/2" below the last leaf group.

6. Assemble the large branch in the same manner, using all the remaining flower and leaf groups. Drop down the stem about 2", and wire both stems together. Cut the bottom wires to the same length, and tape with brown tape.

Cyclamen

My book on houseplants claims that this is a favorite among blooming houseplants. Since mine is hanging over the edge of the pot, with its blooms lying on the table, I wonder if it isn't my favorite to buy and kill. Any shade of pink, red, or white can be used for this unusual plant.

Materials Needed

2/3 hank of petal-color beads

1 hank of green beads

1 to 3 strands of gray, white, or pale green beads

15 yellow beads

26-gauge beading wire

34-gauge gold wire

30-gauge assembly wire

Three 9" pieces of 20-gauge stem wire (for leaf stiffening)

16" of 16-gauge stem wire

1/2" green floral tape

Petals (pointed top, round bottom) (Lace all of the petals.)

Make 5 (petal color)
1 1/2" basic, 9 rows (Leave 3 wires, and twist.)

Stamens (yellow on 34-gauge wire)

Make 1
Use the same procedure as the Dwarf Apple Blossom stamen to create a 15-branched stamen group (See fig. 37, page 491).

Leaves (slightly pointed top, notched, round bottom) (Lace all of the leaves.)

Make 3 (green)
1/4" basic, 31 rows

  a. Begin by making your basic wire with 2 large basic loops. Do this by making the regular basic wire and loop with 1 full twist at the joint.

  b. Then form the second basic loop, and wrap the wire once around the basic wire.

  c. Use hemostats or pliers to help twist the basic loops for 1/4" to 1/2" (fig. 39). Hold a stiffening wire against the back (Stem Stiffening Method 1), and begin.

  d. Make rows 1 through 13 with a round top and round bottom.

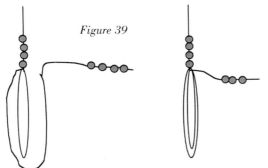

Figure 39

  e. After completing row 13, cut open the bottom of 1 of the basic loops, and spread the 2 ends slightly.

  f. For the rest of the leaf, wrap the bottom of each row around one of these cut wires, instead of the remaining basic loop (fig. 40). This will form a notch in the bottom of the leaf.

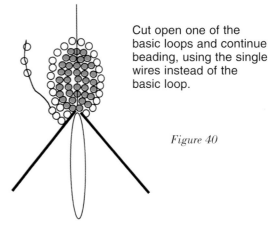

Cut open one of the basic loops and continue beading, using the single wires instead of the basic loop.

Figure 40

  g. As you work rows 14 through 25, add an extra bead to the top of the basic wire to create a slight point.

  h. After completing row 25, measure 3 feet of bare wire, and cut the petal from the spool.

  i. Shade the outside edge of the leaf by completing the next 2, 4, or all 6 of the remaining rows in gray, white, or pale green.

  j. When you are done beading, leave 5 feet of bare wire, and cut the wire from the spool.

  k. Weave the bare wire and the 2 cut, basic wires along the edges of the notch, and back up to the original basic loop. All stem wires should now be in the same place.

  l. Twist the stem wires together, and tape.

Assembly

1. Lightly tape the stem wire.

2. Position the stamen assembly against the tip of the stem, so that only 1/2 of the length of the stamens is above the stem. Wire this in place.

3. Add all 5 petals at once, with the edges overlapping. Wire these in place also, being very careful to wrap the assembly wire tightly against the bottom edge of the beads. Tape the stem.

4. Keeping in mind that you want the bend to occur in the beaded portion of the petal, not the bare wire, bend each petal down sharply. Give each petal a 1/4 twist in its center.

5. Bend the stem in the shape of a shepherd's hook, so that the stamens are pointed toward the ground.

6. Position the bloom and the leaves at attractive heights, and wire their bottoms together. Trim the stems, and tape over the assembly area.

Cactus

Materials Needed

- 1 hank of green beads
- 1/2 hank of orange beads
- 4" of yellow beads
- 26-gauge gold wire
- 26-gauge beading wire
- 30-gauge wire (for lacing and assembly)
- 1/2" green floral tape

494

Stamen-Pistil Group
Make 1 (green and yellow)
    a. String 4" of yellow beads, and add 1 1/2" of green beads. Leave 6" of bare wire.
    b. Make three 1/2" Continuous Loops of green. Pinch them together to form the pistil. Surround them with eight 1/2" Continuous Loops of yellow.
    d. Wrap the wire twice around the other wire, at the end closest to the loops.
    e. Measure 6" of bare wire, and cut. Don't twist.

Petals (round top, round bottom)
Make 1 (orange)
    a. Leave 2" of bare wire at the beginning and the end.

    b. Make nine 1" Continuous Loops.
    c. Lightly twist the wires.
Make 10
3/4" basic, 3 rows (Reduce to 1 wire.)
Make 12
1" basic, 3 rows (Reduce to 1 wire.)

Cactus (pointed top, pointed bottom)
Make 6 (green)
1" basic, 17 rows
    a. Leave 3 wires, and twist.
    b. DON'T trim the top basic wires.
Make 68
Cut sixty-eight 1 1/2" pieces of gold wire.

Assembly

Flower
1. Slip the long wires of the stamen-pistil group through the center of the orange Continuous Loops. Wrap twice with assembly wire.

2. Directly below, add the 10 small petals, and wire them in place.

3. Again, directly below, add the 12 large petals. Secure them with the assembly wire. DON'T trim the long pistil wires! They are needed to secure the flower later.

4. Twist all of the stem wires together tightly, and tape the twisted area.

5. Bead the top 1" of stem, and cover the assembly wire with tape.

Cactus
1. After lacing, fold all 6 pieces in half lengthwise, front sides inward to a 60° angle. Gather all the top basic wires together and twist tightly. Tuck the twisted wires down between 2 of the pieces.

2. To attach the thorns, begin at the very top of each of 5 of the combined petal edges. Use 2 cut wires at a time. Thread the wires through each of the outer rows of beads on two connecting pieces, center them, and give them one full twist. Continue along the petal edges, spacing the thorn groups about 1/2" apart. On the sixth edge, don't put a thorn group at the top. This will leave a small gap for the flower to be inserted.

3. Carefully slip the flower through the gap, and push it down until no tape is showing. Pull the long wires down through the bottom. Firmly twist them together with all the bottom wires. Trim the bottom, and tape.

4. Separate all the wires of the thorn groups, and trim them to 1/2" each.

Gardenia

My darling husband loves the scent of gardenias. Even though this one has no scent, he insisted that I make him one. I added scented oil to the pot. He loves it!

Materials Needed

1 hank of white beads
3 strands of medium green beads
1/2 hank of dark green beads
26-gauge beading wire
30-gauge assembly wire
One 18" piece of 16-gauge stem wire
1/2" green floral tape

Petals (round top, round bottom)

Make 2 (center petals) (white)

3-bead basic, 7 rows (Reduce to 1 wire.)

Make 6 (white)

5-bead basic, 9 rows (Reduce to 1 wire.)

Make 6 (white)

8-bead basic, 9 rows (Reduce to 1 wire.)

Make 6 (white)

12-bead basic, 11 rows (Reduce to 1 wire.)

Small Leaves with Sepals (pointed tops, round bottoms)

Make 3 (medium green)

8-bead basic, 7 rows, and 2 loops

a. After completing all 7 rows, add two 2" single loops to the base of each petal.

b. Pinch the loops closed. These will act as the sepals (see fig. 24, page 436).

c. Reduce to 2 wires, and twist.

Leaves (pointed tops, round bottoms)

Make 3 (dark green)

12-bead basic, 9 rows (Leave 3 wires, and twist.)

Make 3 (dark green)

16-bead basic, 11 rows (Leave 3 wires, and twist.)

Assembly

1. Lightly tape the stem wire.

2. Begin with the 2 center petals. Fold each sharply backwards, lengthwise. Hold them with the folds together to form a bud, and twist the wires.

3. Use assembly wire to attach the 6 small petals directly below, letting each petal slightly overlap the previous one. Bend the tips back, but leave the petals upright.

4. Add the 6 medium petals, and then add the 6 large petals in the same manner. Bend the tips back, but bend all of these down into a more "open" position.

5. Directly below the bloom, add the three leaf-sepal pieces. Position them so that a sepal is centered under each petal.

6. Drop down the stem 1", and add the 3 small leaves, all at the same level.

7. Drop down another inch, and add the 3 large leaves.

8. Tape over all exposed wires.

Note: If you use this as a shrub, add 1" and 2" 4-row Crossover Loops, twisted into spirals, as buds. Make both in medium green.

The plant on page 419 is constructed from 13 separate stems. Three are flowers, five are large buds, and five are small buds. Each stem has sepals and nine leaves.

Trillium

The perfect first flower for any beginner! In white or dark pink, this is just a beautiful little wildflower.

Materials Needed

4 strands of white or pink beads

8 strands of green beads

18 yellow beads

26-gauge beading wire

30- to 34-gauge assembly wire

12" of 16-gauge stem wire

1/2" green floral tape

Petals (pointed top, round bottom)
Make 3 (white or pink)
3/4" basic, 11 rows (Reduce to 2 wires.)

Sepals (pointed top, round bottom)
Make 3 (green)
1/2" basic, 9 rows (Reduce to 2 wires.)

Stamen
Make 1 (yellow)
  a. Put all 18 yellow beads on the assembly wire. Leave 2" of bare wire.
  b. Make 6 continuous 1/2" loops with only 3 beads on each.
  c. Twist the loops, leave 2" of bare wire, and cut. Twist the wires.
  d. Reduce to 2 wires.

Leaves (pointed top, round bottom)
Make 3 (green)
1/2" basic, 21 rows
  a. Add an extra bead to the basic wire on each row, after row 10.
  b. Reduce to 2 wires.

Assembly

1. Lightly tape the stem wire.

2. Center the stamen assembly among the 3 petals. Twist all the wires. Use assembly wire to attach this to the stem.

3. Position the sepals below and between the petals. Secure with wire and tape the assembly area. Drop down 2", wire, and tape all 3 leaves at the same level. Tape down the stem.

This slender lily will add a touch of drama to any bouquet. The natural colors are white, red, yellow, gold, orange, pink, and deep red. The plant has strap-like leaves, but they are usually gone by the time the blooms appear.

Although the flower grows in clusters, imagine how wonderful single blooms would look in a bouquet

Materials Needed

2 hanks of petal-color beads
2 strands of yellow beads
26-gauge beading wire
30- to 34-gauge assembly wire
Six 18" pieces of 16-gauge stem wires
1/2" green floral tape

Spider Lily

Petals (pointed tops, round bottoms)
(Lace all of the petals.)

Make 36 (petal color)
2" basic, 5 rows
   a. Leave 3 wires, and twist.
   b. When you have completed 3, twist the wires together (12 groups of 3 petals).

Stamens

Make 36 (yellow and petal color)
   a. Add 12 yellow beads to the wire that's holding the petal beads.
   b. Close to the tip, make two 6-bead loops.
   c. Twist well, and wrap the bare wire around the space between the loops.
   d. Measure 3" of the petal-color beads and 2" of bare wire. Then cut.
   e. Once you have completed 3 stamens, twist their wires together. Make 12 groups of 3 stamens.

Assembly

1. Lightly tape the 18" stem wires.

2. Use assembly wire to attach 2 stamen groups to a stem wire. Then attach 2 petal groups in the same manner. Tape over the assembly area.

3. Curl all of the petals back, and curl all of the stamens upwards. Assemble the other 5 flowers in the same manner.

4. If you are displaying the flowers in a cluster, group all of the stems together. Two inches from the blooms, wire the stems together, and tape.

$\mathcal{H}$ypoestes

$\mathcal{M}$y oldest brother, Mike, is a landscaper who specializes in shrub propagation. I am dedicating this plant to him. It has NO flowers.

$\underline{\mathcal{M}aterials}$ $\underline{\mathcal{N}eeded}$

1 1/2 hanks each of light green and white beads (mix evenly before stringing)
26-gauge beading wire
30- to 34-gauge assembly wire
18" of 16-gauge stem wire, cut in 3 pieces (5", 6", and 7")
1/2" green floral tape

$\mathcal{A}ssembly$

1. Lightly tape all 3 stems.

2. Use assembly wire to attach the leaves to the stems. Attach the smallest leaves on the tip. Attach the remaining leaves in order of size, using the list below.

3. Assemble 2 leaves at a time, on opposite sides. Turn 90°, drop down about 1/4", and attach the next 2 leaves. Tape over assembly wire. Join the three stems together, wire, and tape.

Leaves per stem:
    Small Stem—4 small, 4 medium
    Medium Stem—2 small, 2 medium, 6 large
    Large stem—2 small, 2 medium, 2 large, 12 extra large

Leaves (pointed top, round bottom)
    Make 8
    1/2" basic, 7 rows (Leave 3 wires, and twist.)
    Make 8
    3/4" basic, 9 rows (Leave 3 wires, and twist.)
    Make 8
    1" basic, 11 rows (Leave 3 wires, and twist.)
    Make 12
    1" basic, 13 rows (Leave 3 wires, and twist.)

Sweet Violet

This little woodland favorite can be used to decorate almost anything. You can make it purple, pink, white, or yellow.

Materials Needed

4 strands of petal-color beads
4 strands of green beads
24 yellow beads
26-gauge beading wire
1/2" green floral tape

Flowers

Make 8 (petal color)

a. Leave 5" of bare wire. Using 1" of beads for the loops, make four 3-row Continuous Crossover Loops.

b. On the fifth loop, use 3/4" of beads for the inside loop, and make a Double Continuous Crossover Loop (5 rows).

c. Cut the wire to 6". Wrap the wire across the center of the flower to tighten the blossom.

d. Intending to form an "X" in the center of the flower, bring the wire back to the top between the first two petals made.

e. Add 3 yellow beads to the wire.

f. Pull the wire back down on the opposite side to complete the "X."

g. Pull the wires tight, and twist.

h. Tape the stem with 1/4" tape.

i. Repeat until you have completed all the flowers.

Leaves (pointed top, round bottom)

Make 3 (green)

1/2" basic, 21 rows (Leave 3 wires, and twist.)

Assembly

1. Twist all of the flower stems together.

2. Position the 3 leaves. Wire and tape them in place.

Crocus

In my hometown, these flowers are not only the first signs of spring, but they often have to pop their blooms up through the melting snow. What a welcome sight! These are usually found in white, yellow, blue, or purple, as well as variegated purple and white.

Materials Needed

1/2 hank of petal-color beads
1/2 hank of dark green beads
18 yellow beads
26-gauge beading wire
28-gauge gold wire (for the stamens)
30- to 34-gauge assembly wire
6" of 16-gauge stem wire
1/2" green floral tape

Assembly

1. Lightly tape the stem wire.

2. Use assembly wire to attach the stamen to the end of the wire.

3. Add 3 petals, and wire in place. Add the last 3 petals, and secure.

4. Cut all the secured wires at different lengths to taper. Tape over the construction area and down the stem.

5. Attach all 6 leaves at the same level, 2" down from the blooms.

6. Finish by taping over the construction area.

Petals (round top, pointed bottom)
Make 6 (petal color)
1/4" basic, 13 rows (Leave 3 wires, and twist.)

Stamens
Make 1 (yellow)
  a. Put the beads on the gold wire.
  b. Position 3 beads 2" from the end of the wire. Hold the beads, and twist for 3/4".
  c. Position the next 3 beads 3/4" from the first, and twist.
  d. Continue until you have 6 stamens (see fig. 37, page 491). Leave 1" of bare wire, and cut.
  e. Bring the bottom wires together and twist.

Leaves (pointed top, pointed bottom)
Make 6 (green)
3" basic, 5 rows (Leave 3 wires, and twist.)

Shamrocks

*I don't think Daddy
has a favorite flower.
However, since he
came from Ireland to
America as a young
adult, we all supply
him with a vast
assortment of sham-
rocks. It's just a small
thank you for being
such a wonderful
father.*

Materials Needed

3 strands of green beads
3 strands of white beads
26-gauge green wire
1/2" green floral tape
(optional)

Leaves
Make 15

   a. Leave 4" of bare wire. Using 8 beads
      for the inner loop, make 3 Continuous
      Double Loops of beads.
   b. Leave 4" of bare wire, and cut from
      the spool.
   c. Twist the wires together.

Flowers
Make 8

   a. Leave 4 1/2" of bare wire. Make 8
      Continuous Loops of 12 beads each.
   b. Leave 4 1/2" of bare wire, and cut.
   c. Pinch all of the loops closed. Pinch
      them into a tight bunch.
   d. Twist the wires together.

Assembly

Twist the bottom inch of each flower stem
with the bottom inch of a leaf stem. If you choose,
you may gather them all together, twist the bottoms, and tape them. Otherwise, they can simply
be inserted as singles into a pot of moss-covered
clay.

Cymbidium Corsage

With this, you can wear flowers anytime you wish! It's a little too heavy for lightweight blouses, but looks great on most dresses and jackets.

Materials Needed

1 Cymbidium blossom
 (DON'T trim the stem wires!)
Several violets or single-loop
 flowers (optional)
8 feet of 2" petal-color, wire-
 edged, ribbon
8 feet of 1" contrasting-colored,
 wire edged, ribbon
Clear craft cement (Liquid Nails
 Clear®, or E6000®)

Assembly

1. If you're using small flowers also, position them around the cymbidium. Twist all of the wires together.

2. Cut the wires to a 3" length. Wrap them with floral tape.

3. Fan-fold the 1" ribbon at 5 1/2" intervals.

4. Mark the center, and poke a hole through all of the layers. Slide this over the flower stem. Repeat the same procedure with the 2" ribbon, folding it at 6" intervals.

5. Push both ribbons tightly against the flower(s). Place a small amount of glue around the stem to hold the flower(s) in place.

6. Once the glue dries, bend the stem at a 90° angle. Turn the corsage over to fluff and arrange the ribbon.

7. Use a hatpin or large safety pin to attach the corsage to your lapel.

Rose Hair Barrette

Although this is a simple process with any flower, I just happened to have a rose handy.

Assembly

1. Position your leaves and flower(s) along the barrette to check the fit. Add more if necessary to make sure that the beads will extend beyond the metal on all sides.

2. Place your flower upside down on the table. Place several drops of Krazy Glue on the twisted stem wires where they meet the petals. Set this aside to dry.

3. Open the barrette. Position a leaf (or group of leaves) so that the tips extend at least 1/4" beyond the end of the barrette. Make sure that no metal is showing. Cut a 2" piece of wire, and fold it in half. From the bottom, position the wire so one end goes through a hole in the end of the barrette and the other goes around the side. Push the wire through the leaf. Bring the wires together, and twist. Trim the wires to 1/8", and tuck them down between the rows of beads. Repeat this procedure on the other end of the barrette.

4. Bring the leaf stem wires (from both ends) to the center of the barrette, and twist them together. Trim the twisted wire to 1/4". Flatten it against the back of the barrette.

5. Using a scrap piece of wire, dab a small amount of the clear craft cement to the tip of each of the bent basic wires on the back of each of the flower and leaf petals. Make sure that the glue touches both the wire and the beads. This will keep the flower from becoming entangled in the wearer's hair.

6. Place a nice sized blob of clear cement on the center of the barrette. Make sure that it also covers the trimmed leaf wires. Turn the flower(s) over and carefully cut off the stem. Immediately, position the bloom on the cement-covered barrette.

7. Allow the glue to dry overnight. In the morning, if you find that you have too much cement, use nail clippers to remove the excess.

Shasta Daisy Napkin Ring

Although I chose the daisy, you can use this same method with different flowers to create a whole host of napkin rings to honor each particular season.

Materials Needed

4 strands of white beads

1 strand of yellow beads

3 strands of green beads

One 6" piece of paper-covered stem wire

26-gauge beading wire

30-gauge assembly wire

1/2" green floral tape

Petals
Make 2 (white)

   a. Leaving 3" of bare wire at the beginning and end, make twelve 3-row Crossover Loops. Use 2" of beads for each main loop.

   b. When completed, give the end wires a couple of twists.

Centers
Make 2 (yellow)

1-bead basic, 10 rows

   a. Bend the basic wire and loop backwards after row 3 to create a raised button effect.

   b. Since this has an even number of rows, you will end at the top. Leave 3" of wire, and cut it from the spool.

   c. Cut open the basic loop at the bottom.

Sepals
Make 2 (green)

   Leaving 2" of wire at the beginning and end, make six 3/4" Continuous Loops.

Assembly

1. Position the centerpiece over the petals. Bring the 4 wires down underneath to the center bottom. Push the wires up, flat against the bottom of the flower.

2. Twist the wires together with the end wires from the petal group.

3. Use assembly wire to attach the daisy to the end of the 6" stem (fig. 41).

Figure 41

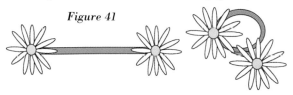

4. Place an upward bend in the center of each sepal loop. Place the sepals tight against the bottom of the petals. Twist the end wires together. Use assembly wire to secure them in place.

5. Follow the same procedure to attach the second daisy to the other end of the same stem wire.

6. Use the rest of the green beads to bead the entire stem, from daisy to daisy. To end, wrap the wire several times, directly below the bottom daisy, and cut. Put 1 drop of Krazy Glue on the tip of the cut wire.

7. Using a wire spool as a guide, gently bend the stem into a circle until the flowers overlap.

Rose Bud Bridal Veil

If you decide to make a bridal veil, be prepared to make more. Although I made this one just for the pattern, it was claimed the day after it was completed. What a simple and elegant way to add love to the bride's trousseau.

Petals (round top, round bottom)
> **Make 10 (white)**
> 4-bead basic, 7 rows (Reduce to 1 wire.)
> **Make 20 (white)**
> 4-bead basic, 11 rows (Reduce to 1 wire.)

Leaves (pointed top, round bottom)
> **Make 15 (silver)**
> 12-bead basic, 9 rows (Reduce to 1 wire.)

Assembly

Flower

1. To form the bud, fold 2 small petals in half lengthwise. Make sure that the petal backs are facing inward. Interlock the folds, and twist the 2 wires lightly.

2. Hold 2 petals, opposite each other, directly below the bud. Add 2 more petals at right angles to the first 2. Twist all of the wires together, just until firm.

3. Form a triangle of 3 leaves tight against the flower, and tightly twist all of the wires.

4. Turn the bloom upside down, and add 2 or 3 drops of Krazy Glue to the twisted stem wires where they meet the flower. Set aside to dry.

5. Cut the twisted flower stem to 1/2". Dip the entire 1/2" stem in clear craft glue, and allow it to dry overnight. Complete the other 4 flowers in the same manner.

Veil

1. Wash your hands thoroughly before beginning.

2. Measure 3" up from the tip of each leg of the headband. Make a small pencil mark on the top back edge. Measure the distance between the marks, and divide it by 4. This is the distance between flowers. Measure each one and make a small pencil mark. You now should have 5 marks and 5 flowers.

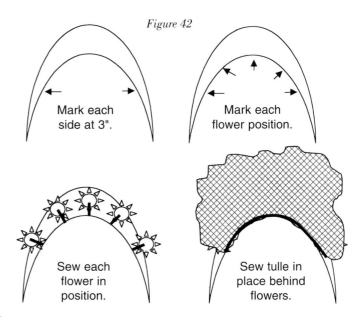

Figure 42

Mark each side at 3".

Mark each flower position.

Sew each flower in position.

Sew tulle in place behind flowers.

3. Align the end of a coated flower stem with the back top edge of the headband. Make sure to hold it on a pencil mark, and sew it securely in place. Add each flower in the same manner (fig. 42).

4. Gently lay the tulle over the rose buds (right side down). Match the sewing edge of the veil to the top, back edge of the headband. Adjust it so that the side edges extend 1" past each of the lower flowers.

5. Carefully sew the tulle to the headband, as close to the flowers as possible. Make all of the stitches small, tight, and even. Pull the tulle back over the sewn area, and fluff.

The material in this compilation appeared in the following previously published Krause Publications and appears here by permission of the authors. (The initial page numbers given refer to pages in the original work; page numbers in parentheses refer to pages in this book.)

Gourley, Elizabeth and Talbott, Ellen.	Quick & Easy Beaded Jewelry © 2002.	Pages 1, 3-127 (5-131)
Shanigan, Jeanette.	Beaded Adornment © 1998.	Pages 2-127 (132-257)
Davis, Jane.	The Complete Guide to Beading Techniques © 2001.	Pages 1, 3-156 (258-415)
Kelly, Dalene.	French-Beaded Flowers: New Millennium Collection © 2001.	Pages 1, 3-93 (416-509)

 Published by Krause Publications, an imprint of F & W Publications, Inc., 700 East State Street, Iola WI 54990. (800) 289-0963. First edition.

Other fine Krause Publications Books are available from your local bookstore, art supply store or direct from the publisher.

07 06 05 04 03 5 4 3 2 1

Library of Congress Cataloging in Publication Data

Big Book of Beautiful Beads / edited by editors of Krause Publications-1st ed.

p. cm.

ISBN 0-87349-762-7 (hc. : alk. paper)

Cover Designer: Marissa Bowers

Production Coordinator: Kristen Heller

Explore the exciting world of crafts!

CREATIVE WEDDING KEEPSAKES

Make your wedding elegant and unforgettable with these beautiful keepsake ideas. From the bridal veil to the guest book, this book provides you with 21 step-by-step projects that are fun, affordable and surprisingly easy to make. Best of all, you can complete each project using non-perishable materials, so everything can be finished well in advance of the big day.

1-55870-559-7, paperback, 128 pages, #70487-K

HOW TO BE CREATIVE IF YOU NEVER THOUGHT YOU COULD

Let Tera Leigh act as your personal craft guide and motivator. She'll help you discover just how creative you really are. You'll explore eight exciting crafts through 16 fun, fabulous projects, including rubber stamping, bookmaking, papermaking, collage, decorative painting and more. Tera prefaces each new activity with insightful essays and encouraging advice.

ISBN 1-58180-293-5, paperback, 128 pages, #32170-K

MAKING GREETING CARDS WITH CREATIVE MATERIALS

You can learn to make beautiful greeting cards and gift tags all with handy, eye-catching materials used in clever ways. Blending fun and user-friendliness with variety and creativity, this book encourages crafters to go beyond basic greeting cards to design unique projects. Techniques are easy and illustrated—from basic folds and simple cuts to extravagant embellishment with silk threads, glass beads, rubber stamps, charms, watercolor washes and other creative but readily available materials.

ISBN 1-58180-126-2, paperback, 128 pages, #31818-K

CRAFTS FROM THE HEART

Inside are easy-to-follow instructions and advice for creating thoughtful, inspiring projects using simple brush lettering and decorative painting techniques. Find 10 lovely projects, each one is embellished with an uplifting saying—perfect for lifting spirits and warming hearts!

ISBN 1-58180-464-4, paperback, 48 pages, #32721-K

FABRIC CRAFTS

Create unique, colorful crafts, including greeting cards, journal covers, picture frames, wall hangings and more with a world of exciting fabrics. All you need to get started are some old clothes, buttons, coins, cording, faux jewelry and other embellishments. Simple decorative techniques, such as fabric stamping, collage and basic stitching, are clearly explained inside, requiring no prior knowledge of sewing or quilting.

ISBN 1-58180-153-X, paperback, 128 pages, #31902-K

CREATIVE CORRESPONDENCE

Discover 16 fun, easy-to-follow projects, ranging from clever self-mailers and postcards to letters and envelopes with photo inserts, stapled booklets, special pockets and see-through address windows. You'll find techniques, which show you how each letter or self-mailer can be embellished with colored pencils, rubber stamps, custom, address labels and colorful flaps and stickers.

ISBN 1-58180-317-6, paperback, 96 pages, #32277-K

WREATHS FOR EVERY SEASON

Here are 20 beautiful wreath projects, perfect for brightening up a doorway or celebrating a special time of year. You'll find a range of sizes and styles, utilizing a variety of creative materials, including dried herbs, sea shells, cinnamon sticks, silk flowers, Autumn leaves, Christmas candy and more. Clear, step-by-step instructions ensure beautiful, long lasting results every time!

ISBN 1-58180-239-0, paperback, 144 pages, #32015-K

WILD WITH A GLUE GUN

Break out the glue gun and create with abandon! You can make each of these 65 projects regardless of your skill level and in a short amount of time. With easy-to-find materials, you can make unique gifts for friends and family working with beads, baubles, fabric, paper & paint, photos, tile & glass and more!

ISBN 1-58180-472-5, paperback, 144 pages, #32740-K

HOME & GARDEN METALCRAFTS

Discover how easy it is to create gorgeous home decor and garden art using today's new, craft-friendly metals, meshes and wire. You'll find 15 unique projects inside, ranging from clean and contemporary to wild and whimsical—perfect for adding sparkle and style to every corner of your home. You'll learn how to texture, antique and emboss your work, then embellish it with glass beads, scented candles, colorful ribbons and more.

ISBN 1-58180-330-3, paperback, 96 pages, #32296-K

PET CRAFTS

Find 28 fun projects that you can make to celebrate and pamper your beloved pet! Using simple techniques and readily available materials, there are even projects designed especially for kids, from adorable kitten and puppy slippers and stuffed animals to clever costumes and pet photo frames. Plus you'll find projects that celebrate special occasions like Halloween, Christmas and your pet's birthday!

ISBN 1-58180-503-9, paperback, 96 pages, #32847-K

These books and other fine titles are available from your local art & craft retailer, bookstore, online supplier or by calling 1-800-448-0915.